pauline frommer's

NEW YORK CITY

spend less see more

2nd Edition

by Pauline Frommer

WILEY

Wiley Publishing, Inc.

Published by:

Wiley Publishing, Inc.

111 River St.
Hoboken, NJ 07030-5774

ISBN: 978-0-470-24763-1

Editor: Marc Nadeau
Production Editor: Lindsay Conner
Cartographer: Guy Ruggiero
Photo Editor: Richard Fox
Interior Design: Lissa Auciello-Brogan
Production by Wiley Indianapolis Composition Services
Front and back cover photo © Bertrand Rieger/AGE Fotostock, Inc.
Cover photo of Pauline Frommer by Janette Beckmann

For information on our other products and services or to obtain technical support,
please contact our Customer Care Department within the U.S. at 800/762-2974,
outside the U.S. at 317/572-3993 or fax 317/572-4002.

Wiley also publishes its books in a variety of electronic formats. Some content that
appears in print may not be available in electronic formats.

Manufactured in the United States of America

5   4   3   2   1

Contents

List of Maps

About the Author

Pauline Frommer is the creator of the award-winning Pauline Frommer's Guides. *Pauline Frommer's New York City* and *Pauline Frommer's London* were named "Best Guidebook of the Year" (in 2006 and 2007, respectively) by the North American Travel Journalists Association. She is also a recipient of a Lowell Thomas Medal from the Society of American Travel Writers for her magazine work and a Webby People's Voice award for her work as the first editor of Frommers.com. Every Sunday, she cohosts "The Travel Show" with her father, Arthur Frommer, now heard on more than 100 radio stations across the United States. On Wednesdays, she appears on CNN Online to discuss the latest travel trends; you may also have seen her discussing travel on the *Today Show, Good Morning America, The Early Show, Live with Regis and Kelly, The O'Reilly Factor,* the CBS Evening News, CNN, FOX, and MSNBC. Pauline pens a biweekly column for MSN.com and contributed a chapter to the book *The Expert's Guide to Babies* on traveling with children. She is married to physical therapist Mahlon Stewart and the proud mother of two very well traveled daughters, Veronica (age 9) and Beatrix (age 5).

For my father, without whose love, support, and unsparing red pen this book would never have seen the light of day.

Acknowledgments

I am humbled and grateful for all the help I received in researching this book and bringing it to life. To Joel Fram, Martin Lowe, Kara Flannery, Rob Tate, Jennifer Bush, Elizabeth Shepherd, Susie Dempsey, Reva Rudman, Theresa DiMasi, and Rachel Richardson—clubbing, bar hopping, and gaining the 10 pounds I did reviewing restaurants wouldn't have been nearly as fun without your company. To all the people at Wiley, but most particularly my visionary publisher Mike Spring and my insightful editors Naomi Kraus and Marc Nadeau: I thank you from the bottom of my heart for the care, imagination, and wit you've lavished on this book and the other Pauline Frommer guides. Last but not least, I owe a debt of gratitude to my patient and wonderful family—husband Lonnie and daughters Veronica and Beatrix—who have had to practice violin, deal with spelling tests, and often eat dinner without me for the last 6 months.

—Pauline Frommer

An Invitation to the Reader

In researching this book, we discovered many wonderful places—hotels, restaurants, shops, and more. We're sure you'll find others. Please tell us about them, so we can share the information with your fellow travelers in upcoming editions. If you were disappointed with a recommendation, we'd love to know that, too. Please write to:

Pauline Frommer's New York City, 2nd Edition
Wiley Publishing, Inc. • 111 River St. • Hoboken, NJ 07030-5774

An Additional Note

Please be advised that travel information is subject to change at any time—and this is especially true of prices. We therefore suggest that you write or call ahead for confirmation when making your travel plans. The authors, editors, and publisher cannot be held responsible for the experiences of readers while traveling. Your safety is important to us, however, so we encourage you to stay alert and be aware of your surroundings. Keep a close eye on cameras, purses, and wallets, all favorite targets of thieves and pickpockets.

Star Ratings, Icons & Abbreviations

Every restaurant, hotel, and attraction is rated with stars ★, indicating our opinion of that facility's desirability; this relates not to price, but to the value you receive for the price you pay. The stars mean:

No stars: Good
★ Very good
★★ Great
★★★ Outstanding! A must!

Accommodations within each neighborhood are listed in ascending order of cost, starting with the cheapest and increasing to the occasional "splurge." Each hotel review is preceded by one, two, three, or four dollar signs, indicating the price range per double room. Restaurants work on a similar system, with dollar signs indicating the price range per three-course meal.

Accommodations		Dining	
$	Up to $100 per night	$	Meals for $7 or less
$$	$101–$135	$$	$8–$12
$$$	$136–$175	$$$	$13–$17
$$$$	Over $175 per night	$$$$	$18 and up

In addition, we've included a kids icon (kids) to denote attractions, restaurants, and lodgings that are particularly child friendly.

Frommers.com

Now that you have this guidebook to help you plan a great trip, visit our website at **www.frommers.com** for additional travel information on more than 4,000 destinations. We update features regularly to give you instant access to the most current trip-planning information available. At Frommers.com, you'll find scoops on the best airfares, lodging rates, and car rental bargains. You can even book your travel online through our reliable travel booking partners. Other popular features include:

- ◆ Online updates of our most popular guidebooks
- ◆ Vacation sweepstakes and contest giveaways
- ◆ Newsletters highlighting the hottest travel trends
- ◆ Podcasts, interactive maps, and up-to-the-minute events listings
- ◆ Opinionated blog entries by Arthur Frommer himself
- ◆ Online travel message boards with featured travel discussions

I started traveling with my guidebook-writing parents, arthur Frommer and Hope Arthur, when I was just four months old. To avoid lugging around a crib, they would simply swaddle me and stick me in an open drawer for the night. For half of my childhood, my home was a succession of hotels and B&B's throughout Europe, as we dashed around every year to update *Europe on $5 a Day* (and then $10 a day, and then $20 . . .).

We always traveled on a budget, staying at the Mom-and-Pop joints Dad featured in the guide, getting around by public transportation, eating where the locals ate. And that's still the way I travel today, because I learned—from the master—that these types of vacations not only save you money, but give you a richer, deeper experience of the culture. You spend time in local neighborhoods, and you meet and talk with the people who live there. For me, making friends and having meaningful exchanges is always the highlight of my trip—and the main reason I decided to become a travel writer and editor as well.

I've conceived these books as budget guides for a new generation. They have all the outspoken commentary and detailed pricing information that you've come to expect from the Frommer's guides, but they take bargain hunting into the 21st century, with more information on how you can effectively use the Internet and air/hotel packages to save money. Most important, we stress the availability of "alternative accommodations"—apartment rentals, private B&B's, religious retreat houses and more—not simply to save you money, but to give you a more authentic experience in the places you visit.

A highlight of each guide is the chapter that deals with "The Other" side of the destinations, the one visitors rarely see. These sections will actively immerse you in the life that residents enjoy. The result, I hope, is a valuable new addition to the world of guidebooks. Please let us know how we've done! E-mail me at editor@frommers.com.

Happy traveling!

Pauline Frommer

Pauline Frommer

1 My Love Letter to New York

The best the city has to offer

IN THE ANXIOUS DAYS FOLLOWING 9/11, I KNEW A LOT OF PEOPLE—parents of small children, in particular—who considered moving out of the city. We all wondered if we could continue living in a place that was so obviously a target. And as we began drawing up emergency plans, plotting escapes across bridges, telling family members under which tree in Central Park we'd meet them should another attack occur, I wondered if I was a fool for wanting to stay. There was a feeling that life would never return to normal, that we were a broken city, and that something fundamental had been lost.

Something fundamental was lost, of course—our innocence, our sense of security, and some 3,000 of our friends, neighbors, and family members. But the city and its residents have rebounded with a steely nerve and sense of exuberance that I wouldn't have thought possible in 2001. New York is thriving. Crime is at its lowest rate in decades, visitor numbers have reached historic levels, and the preschools here are turning away dozens of children because so many families are staying in the city that there just aren't enough of these facilities anymore. Though I'm too superstitious to say it out loud, there's a feeling that New York won its skirmish with the dark side—at least for now.

The main reason we stayed? There's simply no other place in the United States so brimming with opportunities. Those of us who live here open our doors to incredible options each and every day: The chance to experience the best and newest in the worlds of art, theater, dance, and music. The ability to feast on expertly prepared foods from all over the world. The belief that we can make our voices heard on political issues, in this news media capital of the nation. The opportunity to meet today's movers and shakers, the ambitious who come here because they know that if they want to achieve a certain level of prominence in their careers, or in the eyes of the world, New York is the place to do it (are you humming, "If I can make it there, I'll make it anywhere" right now?).

There's another factual reason for a New Yorker's pride. Because of the density and diversity of our population; our long history as a center of commerce and ideas; our access to the United Nations, Wall Street, and the opinion makers of Madison Avenue; and endless other resources, there's simply *more* here than in most other places. And if that claim seems extreme, well, you'll just have to regard boastfulness as another unavoidable characteristic of "the Big Apple." What would New Yorkers be without our big mouths?

In visiting New York, you, too, are opening yourself up to a world of wonderful opportunities. In fact, that's what can make New York so intimidating to visitors—there are just so many darn choices. In this chapter, I've sorted through a book's worth of options, selecting my favorites.

Impressions

"New York is an ugly city, a dirty city. Its climate is a scandal, its politics are used to frighten children, its traffic madness, its competition murderous, but once you have lived in New York and it has become your home, no place else is good enough."
—John Steinbeck, *The Making of New York*

SIGHTS YOU'VE GOTTA SEE, THINGS YOU'VE GOTTA DO

When something is the best in the hemisphere, it must be visited, and so when you come to New York, you have no choice but to visit the **Metropolitan Museum of Art** (p. 135). I think it's one of the great wonders of the U.S., right up there with the Grand Canyon, a place so stuffed with eye-popping treasures that you could spend your entire vacation here and see only a small fraction of its highlights.

But you can't stay mired in the past. New York has a trifecta of American modern art museums in the **Museum of Modern Art** (best collection, p. 139), the **Guggenheim** (best fun-house architecture, p. 141), and the **Whitney Museum** (best for cutting-edge contemporary art, p. 146); you should visit at least one of the three.

For those who care more about science than art, and require that science be artfully presented, **The American Museum of Natural History** (p. 137) is a hall of marvels. With one of the finest and most intelligently presented dinosaur collections in the world, and a state-of-the-art planetarium, it's a winner with people of all ages.

Of course, New York includes much more than museums in its cultural scene. Its **theaters** (p. 291) and **jazz clubs** (p. 271) are the best in the nation, and one night of your New York vacation must be dedicated to being an audience member. Those with more high-falutin' tastes flock to the **Lincoln Center** (p. 266) for world-class opera, ballet, and classical music.

THE FINEST HISTORICAL SIGHTS

You'll want to spend some of your vacation simply walking the city's teeming streets, staring up at skyscrapers, and visiting the areas where history was (and continues to be) made—it's an essential NYC experience.

Though New York City was captured early on in the American Revolution, much of the planning for the war took place here, as did many of the most important events in the early life of the Republic. And you'll come face-to-face with all this history in the **Lower Manhattan Historical and Financial districts** (p. 211). This area is also the site of one of the defining events of modern history: the attack on the **World Trade Center** (p. 129), and hundreds of people come here daily to pay their respects.

In New York harbor, reached by ferry, the **Statue of Liberty** (p. 127) and **Ellis Island** (p. 128) are two definitive sights that speak eloquently to the great contributions, yesterday and today, that immigrants make to the United States. Just around the river bend is New York's famous **Brooklyn Bridge** (p. 134), one of the great engineering feats of the 19th century and still the best stroll in the city. You can easily see all these sights in a very full day.

Uptown are the skyscrapers that defined Depression-era New York (and are now competing for tourist dollars with their observation decks): **Rockefeller Center** (p. 133) and the **Empire State Building** (p. 119). These are the city's goosebump-makers; both are thrilling to visit, as much for their views as for the buildings themselves.

Flanking the East River, the **United Nations** (p. 126) is the final must-see. Though visitors can no longer sit in on debates (too many disruptive protesters), touring the grounds and learning its history is a fascinating exercise.

UNCOMMON LODGINGS

Where you stay will obviously color your experience. Although most travelers simply pick a standard hotel in Times Square, you'll get a more accurate (and I think pleasant) picture of life here if you choose to stay . . . well, anywhere else.

You'll also have a more exciting visit by picking non-traditional lodgings. Why not stay in a room off a working art gallery in SoHo? Or in a spare bedroom in the home of a chef who will cook a gourmet breakfast for you in the morning? Or have an entire apartment to yourself in prized SoHo, Greenwich Village, or near Museum Row on the Upper East Side—areas where hotels are scarce, but rental apartments are abundant? In chapter 3 I give you the tools for finding these and dozens of other unusual lodgings.

If a hotel is more your speed, look into the less standard ones, those that reflect both the personality of their owners and of the city itself. At **Carlton Arms** (p. 46), or the **Gershwin Hotel** (p. 47), your room is a one-of-a-kind creation, painted (and sometimes sculpted) by a visionary artist who's been given carte blanche to create an unusual environment (the rooms range from Jackson Pollock-esque creations, in which every surface is splattered with paint; to Mexican casitas, strung with colorful cut paper; to rooms that look like they're at the bottom of the ocean, with colorful fish murals). Or choose a gracious inn, such as **Incentra Village House** (p. 48) or **Gracie Inn** (p. 56), where the decor will be quaint (floral wallpaper, antique furniture) and the service oh, so personal.

Or simply get the most for your money in a clean, comfortable room that will serve as an affordable sleeping place (so you can spend your money on great meals, or theater tickets). Some of the best value sleeps in New York include **The Chelsea Lodge** (p. 43), **Chelsea Pines Inn** (p. 44), **The Pod Hotel** (p. 41), **Second Home on Second Avenue** (p. 50), **Amsterdam Inn** (p. 54), and **Larchmont Hotel** (p. 47). All are exceedingly pleasant places to stay, where you give up an amenity (at some you may have to climb a flight of stairs or perhaps share a bathroom) for a terrific price.

DINING FOR ALL TASTES

Though you'll have traveled only to NYC, your tongue can travel the world, odd as that may sound, at the many excellent ethnic restaurants that dot the city. In **Chinatown,** you can visit veritable palaces of **dim sum** for brunch (p. 84), choosing your meal from carts that career through these vast banquet halls, laden with dumplings, noodles, and other starchy delights. Or head to the East Village's **Little Japan** (p. 92) to try foods usually found only in Japan, from *shabu tatsu* meals (you cook your own steak in a vat of boiling water) to teahouses to fast-food stands selling *okonoyake* (a sort of Japanese pizza, made with squid). Uptown in the area near the Theater District, your choice ranges from **Uzbekistani kebabs** (p. 76) to **Ethiopian stews** (p. 74). And in Harlem, you get the finest in **Southern-style soul food** at a bevy of friendly, dinerlike places.

And then there are those New York classics: deli sandwiches, bagels, hot dogs, and pizza. Don't try to eat all four in one day—the damage to your digestive system could end your vacation right there—but you should try at least one during the course of your stay. For pizza, I like **John's** (p. 70) in the Theater District and Greenwich Village; for hot dogs dash into a **Gray's Papaya** (you'll find them at Sixth Ave. at 8th St., Broadway at 72nd St., and Eighth Ave. at 37th St.), or simply pick one up at a sidewalk stand; for deli food, go with the classic **Katz's Delicatessen** (p. 94); and for bagels, the choices are many (see p. 114 for a full list of options).

Gourmet fare is an obsession in Manhattan, so you're going to want to have at least one hoity-toity meal. And it might well be affordable: in 2007 the James Beard Foundation named David Chang "Rising Star Chef of the Year," yet you can have a satisfying meal at his pork-obsessed **Momofuku Ssam Bar** (p. 91) for as little as $9. Celeb chef David Bouley also throws a bone to us budget eaters with his **Upstairs at Bouley** (p. 107), where you can dine on a strange but tasty mix of Italian food, salads, and Japanese fare, quite reasonably. And if you just love desserts—who doesn't?—make a pilgrimage to **ChikaLicious** (p. 90), where $12 will get you an imaginative, ultra-gourmet dessert tasting menu.

THE FINEST "OTHER" EXPERIENCES

Get off the tourist treadmill and take part in one of the dozens of activities performed by actual New Yorkers each day. Attend a **lecture at the 92nd Street Y** (p. 177) or a **cooking class at the Institute of Culinary Education** (p. 178); take a free lunchtime **tango class at the Argentine consulate** (p. 179); pray at a **gospel service in Harlem** (p. 191); or spend an afternoon **steaming at the Russian and Turkish Baths** (p. 187) of the East Village. Really adventurous travelers can venture out to Brooklyn to the artists' studios and galleries of **Williamsburg** (p. 194) or the vodka-soaked **Russian nightclubs of Brighton Beach** (p. 190). Or see how the lucky among us work by taking a **backstage tour of the Metropolitan Opera** (p. 184), of the Broadway show *Wicked* (p. 184), or by being part of an **audience at a TV taping** (p. 180). These and many more activities covered in chapter 6 allow visitors to see sides of the city that outsiders rarely know about and, most importantly, to meet actual New Yorkers.

2 Lay of the Land

The geography of New York: The city's top neighborhoods and the best ways to get around

LOTS OF PEOPLE TRAVEL TO NEW YORK, PLOP THEMSELVES DOWN INTO Times Square, and never go anywhere else. They live in fear of venturing into the neighborhoods that exist for purposes other than tourism.

You don't have to be among them. By devoting just a few minutes to the basic geography of New York and its distinctive neighborhoods, you can immensely enhance your enjoyment of this multifaceted city. And once you absorb the highly logical organization of New York's transportation system, you'll find that you can zip from place to place with minimal fuss and expense.

THE GRID PLAN OF MANHATTAN

Finding your way around Manhattan is easier than in almost any other city because of the careful plan that was adopted for laying out the city's avenues and streets. In the areas above 14th Street, the city fathers imposed a strict and unnatural grid upon Manhattan, leveling hills and tearing down existing homes to create straight, evenly spaced thoroughfares in all but a few places. The grid consists of numbered streets and avenues that cross each other at right angles. If you can count up to 100, you can get around this surprisingly compact island.

Streets in Manhattan are numbered and run from east to west. So if you're on 23rd Street and wish to get to 42nd Street, you simply go 19 blocks north. To get from 80th Street to 75th Street, you walk 5 blocks south.

The avenues of Manhattan run north to south, with some bearing numbers and others names (which does complicate the picture, but only a bit). Those that are numbered ascend from east to west, with First Avenue being close to the East River, and Twelfth Avenue on the far west side of the island. Interspersed between these numbered avenues are several named avenues, including (among others) Park, Lexington, and Madison. The named avenues live primarily on the East Side, between Fifth and Third avenues in Midtown and Uptown; on the West Side, Seventh, Eighth, and Ninth avenues turn into Columbus Avenue, Central Park West, and Amsterdam Avenue above 59th Street.

The exceptions to the grid rule (all found below 14th St.) are the Financial District, Chinatown, the Lower East Side, Greenwich Village, SoHo, and TriBeCa. These southern parts of Manhattan were the first to be settled, and therefore follow a haphazard non-system of streets and alleys that curve and twist, sometimes doubling back on themselves (most famously in Greenwich Village, where 4th St. collides with . . . 4th St.). Because most of these southern-section streets bear names rather than numbers (Delancey St., Wall St., Church St.), orienting yourself can be

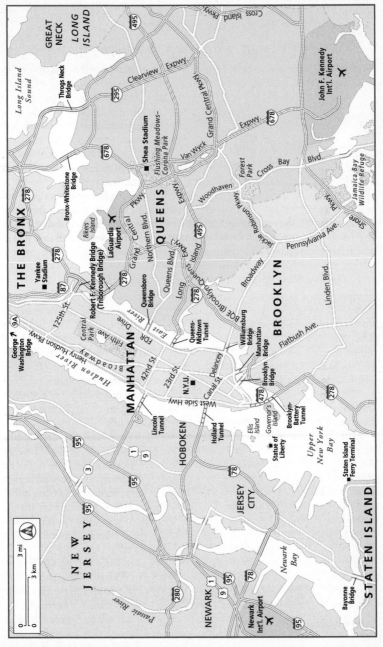

tricky, so it's important to carry a good map and to ask for directions when necessary—even native New Yorkers get lost down here.

GETTING AROUND MANHATTAN

Because most travelers confine themselves to Manhattan, I will as well in this section. Those traveling to the outer boroughs can be confident, however, that public transportation—subways, buses, ferries, or some combination of the three—can get you anywhere you wish to go in the city proper, whether it be the sandy shores of Brighton Beach, Brooklyn, or Yankee Stadium in the Bronx. The city's transportation network is run by the Metropolitan Transportation Authority (aka the MTA); maps and schedules for NYC's myriad transportation options can be found at **www.mta.nyc.ny.us**. You can also key in your itinerary at **www.hopstop.com**, a "Mapquest" for the subway set, which will give you complete directions, including how far you'll walk to get to the station and whether you'll also need to take a bus. Hopstop will also estimate taxi fares, a handy trick.

> **"**A car is useless in New York, essential everywhere else. The same with good manners. **"**
>
> —Mignon McLaughlin

SUBWAY

I wish I could confine my transportation advice to just two words—"**the subway**"—and be done with it. To my mind, the New York City subways, 100 years young in 2004, are the single most efficient, rapid, easy, and affordable way to get about anywhere you'd want to go in Manhattan, with the exception of some far eastern sections of the Upper East Side (First Ave., York Ave., and so on) and of those times you have to cross town while north of 59th Street. But because of the starring role the subways have played in action films set in New York over the years, with squinty-eyed thugs menacing timid grandmothers as lights flicker on and off in graffiti-riddled trains, many visitors are scared to go underground.

That fear is unwarranted. Not only is the graffiti gone, but a refurbishing of the system has eliminated the "haunted house" quality of the lighting. The trains are now kept surprisingly clean, and thanks to the persistent efforts of those invisible transit cops (you rarely see a transit police officer, but there are 3,000 of them keeping order underground and on buses), the subways are safer than ever.

Of course, that doesn't make them Disneyland. Though the cars are heated in the winter and air-conditioned in the summer, the platforms are not, and they often feel 10 degrees colder in winter than the city streets and 10 degrees hotter in summer. Pickpockets remain a problem, as they are in London, Rome, and every other city where large numbers of people jam together in small spaces. So remember to move your wallet to a place where you can keep track of it before boarding the trains (if you're wearing pants, the front pocket is usually best).

The subway trains

Until you get the system under your belt, the trains can be confusing to navigate. Briefly, here are the major lines and where they generally go within Manhattan (once they reach other boroughs, all bets are off):

Your New Best Friend: The MetroCard

In order to use the subways, you'll have to purchase a MetroCard—a thin, bendable plastic "credit card" that you can fill up with money at subway stations or buy pre-filled at some neighborhood stores (most stores that sell MetroCards will post a sign). MetroCards are swiped for entry at subway turnstiles and can also be used on buses.

Ostensibly, each subway ride costs $2, but because there are a number of fare card options, the amount is actually slightly flexible. An **unlimited MetroCard** allows you to board as many subways and trains as you like within a set period of time for one low cost. A 1-day unlimited card is $7; a weeklong pass is $25. To make this unlimited card pay for itself, you'll need to ride four times in 1 day for the daily pass, or at least twice a day on the weeklong pass. Only one person can use this type of card at a time; once swiped, it becomes inoperable for 20 minutes.

If you'd prefer a **pay-per-ride MetroCard**, the minimum amount you can put on it is $4 (or 2 rides); and if you have to change from subway to bus, you'll automatically get a transfer on your card at no extra charge, so long as you board your second trip within 2 hours of the first. There is no limit on how many people can share this card.

A word on swiping: Look at your card closely and follow where the arrow points as you're dipping or swiping, so that the magnetic strip lines up correctly with the electronic card reader. It sounds silly but you don't want to swipe too slow or too fast, or the card may not work. Also, never try a different turnstile if you've swiped unsuccessfully, as you may end up being charged for an extra ride. (Sometimes dust stops the magnetic strip from working, so wipe the card on a tissue or your shirt and try again if you're having problems.)

♦ The **④**, **⑤**, and **⑥** (each number appearing in a green circle) run the length of Manhattan (mostly along Lexington Ave.) on the East Side. You can remember that these are East Side trains by the fact that they're the color of money (and so is the Upper East Side). The **⑥** is a local train; the other two skip stops.

♦ The **①**, **②**, and **③** lines are red (a comment on the formerly radical nature of the Upper West Side?), and run roughly parallel to the **④**, **⑤**, and **⑥** but on the West Side of Manhattan (along Seventh Ave.). The **①** is the local.

♦ The yellow **Ⓝ**, **Ⓡ**, and **Ⓠ**, **Ⓦ** trains follow the twisting path taken by Broadway, up to Central Park (57th St.) and then, perhaps to satisfy a yen for great Greek food, veer off at that point towards Queens.

♦ The orange line (**Ⓥ**, **Ⓕ**, **Ⓑ**, and **Ⓓ**) is a wild card, splitting into two branches at 53rd Street (it runs along Sixth Ave. in Midtown) and confusing even native New Yorkers. The **Ⓓ** should stand for "dangerous" because if you don't hop off at 59th Street, you'll be riding it for 66 blocks without an "off" (which is lovely if you want to go to Harlem, and a real time-waster if you don't).

- The blue line (**A**, **C**, and **E**) restricts itself primarily to the West Side, going the farthest west of any of the subways as it runs along 8th Avenue from 50th to 14th streets. If you're taking it to get to the Museum of Natural History, remember the Duke Ellington tune *Take the A Train,* which advises that if you don't get off at 59th Street, you'll be going straight up to Harlem (the C is the one you want for this route).

- Lastly, the small but mighty shuttle train **S** simply trudges back and forth between Grand Central Station and Times Square. It serves a vital function, though, as the lack of other cross-town trains connecting the different lines in Midtown is one of the major flaws in the system. The **L** at 14th Street serves much the same function, traveling from Eighth Avenue on the West Side, to First Avenue on the East Side, before heading onward to Williamsburg, Brooklyn, and beyond.

BUS

I recommend using buses to head east or west, and then switching to the subway as quickly as possible; a MetroCard will get you an automatic and free transfer from one to the other. Although buses can give you a nice view of the city, they are subject to the whims of traffic and can be extremely slow, especially between the hours of 7:30 and 9:30am, and 4 and 7pm. The one zone where buses are handy is the Upper East Side, especially along First Avenue, Second Avenue, and York Avenue—areas far from the subway. As these are primarily residential neighborhoods with few restaurants or sights of note, most visitors never venture this far east.

To ride the bus, you must use a MetroCard (you can purchase this fare card in subway stations) or have exact change of $2. Drivers do not provide change, though if you're stuck, other passengers will usually exchange coins for bills if you ask plaintively enough.

During the daytime, buses stop only at marked junctures along their route. You'll know that you're at a bus stop if there's a sidewalk shelter or a short pole on which a map is posted giving bus routes. Generally, the buses that run from Uptown to Downtown or vice versa stop every 2 to 3 blocks; "limited" buses are express runs that stop every 8 to 10 blocks—or whatever the distance is between

---

Why Yellow?

When John Hertz, the founder of the Yellow Cab Company, was trying to decide on a color for his vehicles in 1907, he commissioned the University of Chicago to conduct a scientific study of which colors stand out best at a distance. Yellow won and became so associated with taxis that, in 1969, the city decided to make all medallion cabs yellow to distinguish them from "gypsy" or non-licensed cabs.

Renting a Car and Driving around the City

In three words: Don't do it.

Rental-car rates in the New York City area are among the highest in the nation. Parking on the streets can be a full-time job, and parking in lots will drain your vacation budget. Driving in the city is an exercise in frustration, battling traffic jams, errant pedestrians, and streets that never seem to go in the direction that you want.

I'll repeat: Don't even think about it.

---

the major east-to-west streets (14th St., 23rd St., 34th St., 42nd St., and so on). Crosstown buses that run east to west (or vice versa) stop at every avenue. At night, buses still stick to their routes in terms of pickups, but they will often drop off passengers between stops, so be sure to ask.

TAXI

The starting price for just getting into a taxi is $2.50. Then every fifth of a mile (which roughly translates to 4 street blocks or 1 avenue block), the meter ticks off another 40¢; if you're stuck in traffic for 2 minutes, standing still, the meter will tick off yet another 40¢. There are also surcharges for certain busy times of day: You'll pay $1 more between 4 and 8pm; and 50¢ more for a night ride between the hours of 8pm and 6am. It's appropriate (and expected) that you tip 15% to 20% of the meter's total.

Before the 2004 price hike, sharing a cab was sometimes cost-effective for couples. It doesn't usually work out that way anymore. On a trip between, say, the Metropolitan Museum of Art and the TKTS booth in Times Square, a cab will cost approximately $8.50 ($9.50, with tip) if you're traveling during the afternoon rush hour, which is more than double what you'd pay on public transportation. The expenses all add up, so take the subway or a bus when you can (unless you're traveling with 3 or 4 people). By law, taxis cannot accommodate more than four people, so don't even try it.

Because of heavy traffic, subways are also often two to three times as fast as taxis, even with the wait time factored in. If you're in a rush, dash to the nearest subway and avoid cabs.

THE NEIGHBORHOODS OF NEW YORK

It never fails to amaze. I'm strolling along a pleasant street of small brownstones, I come to the corner, and suddenly, the landscape morphs and I'm a small ant in a canyon of skyscrapers, or else I'm a visitor to India, surrounded by cumin-scented restaurants and men with strong accents beckoning me into their curry joints. New York is a city of multiple personalities, and like Sybil they can shift on a dime, within the space of one block going from elegant to seedy, from industrial to chic, from ethnic to all-American.

It's this quicksilver quality, this constant metamorphosis, that endows even a simple stroll in New York with real excitement. I urge you to spend at least part of your vacation simply ambling around, window-shopping, eavesdropping on passing conversations, or exploring places beyond the most heavily touristed areas.

Here's what you'll find in the various—and strikingly different—neighborhoods of New York City.

LOWER MANHATTAN—THE FINANCIAL DISTRICT

Best for: Museums, historic sights, architecture, access to Ellis Island and the Statue of Liberty

What you won't find: Great dining, evening entertainment

This is, quite simply, where New York City—then New Amsterdam—was born. The area packs the same historical wallop as do the colonial sections of Boston and Philadelphia. It was on Wall Street that George Washington took the oath of office as the nation's first president. It was here, at Fraunces Tavern, that the brave Sons of Liberty gathered to plot the overthrow of the British. It was at Castle Clinton and then Ellis Island that millions of immigrants flooded the city in the 19th and early 20th centuries to get their first glimpse of a "promised land." The great financial movers and shakers also stalked the area (and continue to do so today), and a visit to these "canyons of greed" at the beginning of the day or at 5pm, when those men and women in suits and trader's smocks pour onto the streets, still buzzing with adrenaline, is an exciting sight.

Recent history, of course, has overshadowed these sights for many visitors, and the area has been inundated with visitors wishing to pay their respects at the World Trade Center. You should visit the center, especially if it's your first time in New York City. But do try to be respectful, as many who live in the area lost loved ones on September 11, and they find the sight of tourists smiling for photos in front of the site a disturbing one.

CHINATOWN (AND LITTLE ITALY)

Best for: Affordable gourmet dining and shopping

What you won't find: Top museums, streets without gridlock

At points, Chinatown takes on the aspects of Shanghai or Beijing: the dense crowds on the streets, the awnings with Chinese characters, the pinging sound of Chinese conversation everywhere. It's a fun, truly transporting area to visit and one that has been voraciously swallowing up other neighborhoods—Little Italy, the Jewish Lower East Side—for the past few decades. In fact, except for 2 blocks of Mulberry Street (from Canal to Broome), strung with colored lights, Little Italy has ceased to exist (because of the ever-expanding growth of Chinatown) and is really only a tourist-trapping shadow of its former self. There are a handful of interesting shops and some worthwhile cafes for gelato and cappuccino, but no noteworthy restaurants and very few real Italian-Americans around anymore.

No, if you're going into this area, what you really want to see is Chinatown. To do this, you want to bury your inhibitions, if you can, and wander in and out of the fish markets; the herbal pharmacies; and the fruit stands with the odd, spiky produce. Talk to the shopkeepers, bargain for goods, and ask questions (don't be shy!). You should also taste everything you can because this is one of the cheapest and best neighborhoods for chowing down.

Go to p. 83 for a full description of all your options, including a list of places where you can simply nosh as you sightsee.

Manhattan Neighborhoods

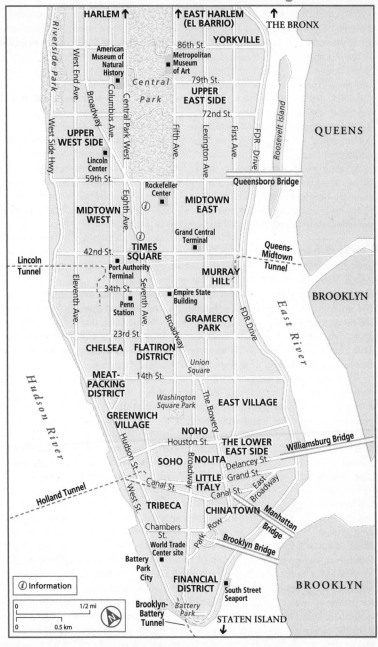

TRIBECA, NOLITA, AND SOHO

Best for: Dining, bars, star-sightings, great architecture, shopping
What you won't find: Top-rated art galleries (they're now in Chelsea) and museums
What is it about former factories and tenements that the ultra-rich find so appealing? Though they certainly wouldn't want to work in them, these formerly industrial areas have been drawing a lot of bolded names lately: media whizzes, movie stars, financial aces, and other proud members of the *nouveau riche* (the old money is still firmly entrenched uptown). And with these *arrivistes* has come a welcome wagon of hot new restaurants, boutiques, spas, and *boites,* making the entire section a great place for average folks to window-shop and dine (primarily on splurge meals).

These areas, especially SoHo and TriBeCa, also have a grand look about them thanks to their cobblestone streets, old-fashioned streetlights, and profusion of cast-iron buildings (SoHo has the most of any area in the world), with their proud columns, porticos, and other frills. For my walking tour of SoHo, which will give you a bit more of the history of the area, go to p. 233.

LOWER EAST SIDE AND EAST VILLAGE

Best for: Dining, bars, dance and music clubs, innovative theater, and local designer-clothing shops
What you won't find: Museums (there's only one of significance here)
For millions, this area was once the portal to America. In fact, the buildings you see on the Lower East Side were built expressly to house the millions of immigrants who flooded into New York between roughly 1840 and 1930. At the turn of the last century, this was the most densely populated area in the world, with a dozen to an apartment, and pushcarts jamming the streets.

Nowadays, this is where crowds flock in the after-hours for some of the city's most happening bars, lounges, and music clubs. It's here that you'll find new designers opening up their own tiny stores for cutting-edge fashion; where food prótegés of the great chefs come to start their first restaurants; where "poetry slams" thrive and indie bands wail in dank basement clubs; and where recent college grads bunk eight to a two-bedroom apartment. I may be prejudiced because I live in the East Village, but I find it the most vibrant area of Manhattan, though many blocks have lost their gritty edges thanks to rising real estate prices.

GREENWICH VILLAGE

Best for: Strolling, dining, historic sights, lovely architecture, specialty food shopping, theater, live music clubs, star sightings
What you won't find: Museums, many hotels
Greenwich Village has always been the area where the city's outsiders and oddballs have found a haven. In Dutch Colonial times, it was farmland set outside the walls of the city, and a number of slaves were given conditional freedom in return for providing the burghers with food (and fighting off Native Americans). At the turn of the 20th century, the area became known as a bohemian enclave, where artists of all sorts could find cheap lodging and companionship. In the 1950s it was at the center of the Beat movement; in the 1960s and '70s the area around Christopher Street became the center of a burgeoning gay rights movement (in the '80s it was a hotbed for AIDS-related activism).

Today, high real-estate prices have dulled the Village's edge and you're more likely to see moms with strollers than long-haired poets walking the pavement near Sheridan Square. And that mom might be Sarah Jessica Parker or Uma Thurman, two of the many celebrities who now call the tree-shaded brownstones of the Village home sweet home. But the charm of the area is still intact, as is the illusion that you've entered another city altogether. Very few buildings in the neighborhood reach over 10 stories (most are lower than that), and small shops elbow out chain stores. It's a wonderful place to simply come and get lost in.

GRAMERCY SQUARE, UNION SQUARE, AND THE FLATIRON DISTRICT

Best for: Dining, historic sights, nice architecture, and Off-Broadway theater
What you won't find: Museums, top shopping (with a few exceptions)
If you look up as you meander through these three bustling areas, you're likely to see brown street signs proclaiming LADIES MILE. It was on this stretch, mostly on Broadway and Park Avenue South, that the first wave of department stores transformed the lives of New Yorkers in the 1850s. Instead of hopping from the dry goods shop for fabrics to the milliner's for hats to the cobbler for shoes, women from all over the city came here to outfit themselves and their homes in stores that, wonder of wonders, had everything they needed under one roof. Notice the large plate glass windows on many of the facades, another department-store innovation. Above, the windows are much smaller and point to the second meaning of "Ladies Mile": brothels. When the stores closed for the day, the establishments upstairs opened and ladies of the evening took over the mile. And where there's prostitution, theater often follows: The area around Union Square was New York's first show district.

Interestingly, this same area has become another important theater district for New York's thriving Off-Broadway scene in recent years. In fact, around half of the Pulitzer Prize–winning plays of the past decade made their debut in the theaters located off Union Square and downtown. The dining scene is also especially hot here, with hugely popular restaurants such as Gramercy Tavern, the Union Square Café, Craft, Fleur de Sel, and Café Mono all in residence.

For the best strolling, head directly for Gramercy Park, the only privately owned park in the city (the keys go to those apartment owners whose windows overlook the park). Around the park are a number of beautifully preserved historic homes and clubs, including the wisteria-clad home of former Mayor James Harper (4 Gramercy Park S.), the Players Club (at 16 Gramercy Park S., whose members included Edwin Booth, Mark Twain, and Thomas Nast), and the National Arts Club (15 Gramercy Park S., a hangout of Woodrow Wilson and Theodore Dreiser).

CHELSEA AND THE MEAT-PACKING DISTRICT

Best for: Art galleries, nightlife, gay bars and clubs
What you won't find: Theater, museums
Manhattan's Chelsea neighborhood is today what SoHo was 10 years ago, and what Greenwich Village was 15 years ago. The major SoHo galleries (and a host of newcomers) have moved to Chelsea, as has Greenwich Village's large gay population. This makes for a lively cultural scene with many bars and clubs. To read

about these many galleries, go to p. 152. The so-called Meat-Packing District, named for the slaughterhouses in the area (though the name is a double entendre, as this formerly unpopulated area was, in the 1980s, a place where many gay men came to have trysts), has also become an extremely popular nightlife destination. An offshoot of Chelsea, it's New York's adult Disneyland, filled with late-night clubs, bars, and restaurants that are unhindered by the city's zoning laws (as there are no schools or churches in this part of town).

MIDTOWN WEST, INCLUDING TIMES SQUARE

Best for: Theater (of course) and entertainment of all kinds, shopping (in the Garment District and at Macy's), catching a train
What you won't find: Top-notch dining (with a few exceptions), museums (with the exception of the museums of 53rd St.), serenity

Midtown is what most people think of when they think of New York, and the reason that so many visitors say with a smirk, "Well, it's a nice place to visit but I couldn't ever live there." And because they're basing their judgments on crowded, loud, pushy Midtown, they're absolutely right—it is unlivable . . . which is why so few *New Yorkers* actually live in this area. In certain areas of Midtown, there is no residential housing whatsoever, and it's only the tourists who even attempt to get a good night's sleep in this bustling neighborhood.

So what is Midtown West? I'm defining it roughly as the area from 30th Street—where Pennsylvania Station and the subway stations beneath it disgorge a full one million people each day—up to Columbus Circle, with its chichi Time Warner Center mall and the start of the Upper West Side. In between, you'll find Broadway theaters, the shopping wonderland of Macy's and the Manhattan Mall, the Garment District (located primarily in the 30s, the area where designers have their offices), sun-blocking office towers, the mini-museum mile of West 53rd Street, and the ethnic restaurant strip that is Ninth Avenue from 42nd Street to 57th Street. As you can see, it's an eclectic area with much to recommend it but also much to avoid. I make this plea in the hotel chapter, and I'll make it again here: If you can lodge in another area of the city, do so. You'll have a much more manageable, pleasant, and authentic New York experience if you do.

MIDTOWN EAST

Best for: Christmas displays and window shopping (along Fifth Ave.), historic sights, great architecture
What you won't find: Museums, interesting nightlife (with a handful of exceptions)

In the 1950s, Madison, Park, and Lexington avenues started to sprout with sky-scrapers and soon were rivaling the Wall Street area for office space. Moving east from Fifth Avenue to Third Avenue, north from 42nd Street to 57th, that's primarily what you'll find here: people in suits, looming glass towers, and lots of traffic. Among the great architectural sights are Grand Central Terminal (p. 168), the Chrysler Building (p. 167), and the Seagram Building (p. 169). Go closer toward the East River, and the area becomes largely residential, with little to recommend it to the visitor beyond Bloomingdale's department store and the United Nations (p. 126).

A tremendously popular part of Midtown East is Fifth Avenue as it runs from 57th Street down to the Empire State Building at 34th Street, a delightful street to stroll on a sunny afternoon for the superb window-shopping (at Tiffany & Co., Bergdorf Goodman, Saks Fifth Avenue, and the many tony boutiques that line both sides of the avenue). This stretch is also home to the largest Catholic cathedral in the United States, St. Patrick's, and (right across the street) the grand urban masterwork that is Rockefeller Center.

UPPER WEST SIDE

Best for: Museums, Central Park, bars, kid-friendly restaurants, classical music and dance
What you won't find: Top-notch dining (with a few exceptions), great shopping (again with a few exceptions)

In some ways, the Upper West Side has the most suburban vibe of any of Manhattan's neighborhoods. National chain stores line the major thoroughfares, and the sidewalks swarm with strollers. This is arguably the most popular area in the city for middle-class families, thanks to its proximity to both Central Park and Riverside Park, and to such kid-friendly attractions as the Children's Museum of Manhattan and the American Museum of Natural History.

It wasn't always this way. When I was growing up on the Upper West Side, and even before that, the neighborhood had a reputation for being an intellectual hotbed, a place where highly political New Yorkers planned protests, burned bras, and held potluck fundraisers. No more. But it's still an extremely pleasant place to visit, with good if unoriginal shopping; a handful of top-notch museums; New York's famous art hub, Lincoln Center; and, of course, access to the glories of Central Park. The recent addition of the Time Warner Center, on Columbus Circle, gives the neighborhood the dubious distinction of having the priciest food court in the world; at Masa, the Japanese restaurant on-site, diners pay $300 for an *omakase* (a tasting lunch or dinner). And that's before drinks!

UPPER EAST SIDE

Best for: Museums, fine dining, architecture, window-shopping, Central Park
What you won't find: Affordable restaurants (with some exceptions), theater, clubs

10021 is the richest zip code in the world and it belongs to the Upper East Side, in particular that swank swatch of pavement that runs from 61st to 80th streets. Also known as the "Gold Coast" and "Millionaires' Mile"—don't be surprised if you see Robin Leach lurking about—this is the stomping ground for New York's high society: the Prada-clad women (thin until they die) and bowtie-wearing gents who sit on the boards of the neighborhood museums, go to a lot of cocktail parties, and endow scholarships for kicks. Their mansions and marble-faced town houses make for nifty sightseeing among those interested in architecture; and the shops along Madison Avenue are a nose-at-the-window paradise, a peek into the extravagant and sometimes slightly oddball fashions adopted by the ultra-rich and the top designers who serve them.

Museums also play a key role on the Upper East Side, and there's a greater concentration of top-flight museums here than there is anywhere else in the country, with the exception of The Mall in Washington, D.C. You'll want to spend at least one day of your stay exploring "Museum Mile"—the Metropolitan, the

Guggenheim, the Whitney, the Cooper-Hewitt, and more—though if you're watching your pocketbook, you should probably dine and shop elsewhere.

Interestingly enough, once you cross Third Avenue, prices drop precipitously both for restaurants and shops. That's because the lack of good public transportation in this part of town has made it one of the least desirable areas in Manhattan in which to live, so rents and general cost-of-living are lower here than on other parts of the island.

HARLEM

Best for: Dining, clubs, historic sights

What you won't find: Theater, worthwhile shopping, museums (with the exception of the Studio Museum)

Perhaps the most rapidly transforming neighborhood in the city, Harlem is safer and cleaner than it's been in decades . . . and may be losing some of its intrinsic character as a result. A largely African-American neighborhood since the 1920s—and home to some of the greatest black writers, politicians, and artists of the 20th century—the neighborhood is now drawing an increasing number of Caucasian residents, lured here by lower real-estate prices and the beauty of a brownstone-lined community. My recommendation: Visit here soon before the authentic soul and Caribbean food joints disappear, the gospel churches lose their swing, and the rhythm of the streets changes its beat. There's much to see, including Hamilton Grange (the home of Alexander Hamilton; p. 225), the Studio Museum (p. 158), dozens of well-preserved Beaux Arts brownstones, and hopping clubs.

AWAY FROM MANHATTAN: THE BOROUGH OF BROOKLYN

Best for: Museums, parks, lovely architecture, ethnic dining, great views of Manhattan, innovative galleries

What you won't find here: Notable theater (with the exception of the Brooklyn Academy of Music and St. Anne's Warehouse)

If Brooklyn had not traded its sovereignty to become a borough of New York City in 1898, it would be the fourth largest city in the United States today, just after New York, Los Angeles, and Chicago. With 2,465,326 citizens (according to the latest census), it certainly is the most populous borough in the city, and at 71 square miles it's also the largest. Which is all a long way of saying that it's very difficult to pin down the nature of Brooklyn, as it's just too darn big to be summarized in a nutshell.

The two most affluent neighborhoods are Brooklyn Heights, which is right off the Brooklyn Bridge, boasting spectacular views of Manhattan; and Park Slope, the area surrounding Frederick Law Olmstead's *other* great work of landscape architecture (after Central Park), Prospect Park. Both are stellar strolling areas, filled with lovely Beaux Arts brownstone buildings (Brooklyn Heights was the first neighborhood in the city to be landmarked).

The borough's artists tend to live in Williamsburg, with a few holdouts still in DUMBO (the area "Down Under the Manhattan Bridge Overpass") and, to a lesser extent, in the Italian-American stronghold of Red Hook. You can pop by all three for afternoons of gallery-hopping. Williamsburg also has one of the largest

---

Funfact

The ❼ subway line that spans Queens was declared a "Millennium Heritage Trail" by the White House in 1999, placing it in the same category as the Lewis and Clark Trail in terms of importance to the nation. It earned that honor by vividly reflecting the immigrant experience in the U.S. People from over 150 different nations use the train on a daily basis and peacefully live side-by-side with neighbors from around the globe.

Hasidic Jewish communities in the world. Walk the streets peopled by this sect and you may feel as if you've stepped back into an old country Shtetl (an illusion only somewhat ruined by the incongruous but ever-present cellphones).

Eastern Europe also makes an appearance in Brighton Beach, which has the largest ex-pat Russian community in the world. It's not the friendliest place to visit, but it's fascinating nonetheless, with stores selling endless rows of nesting dolls and Lenin T-shirts, and small-scale nightclubs that outglitz and outcrass Las Vegas (see p. 190). Just up the shore from Brighton Beach is famed Coney Island, still an amusement park, but with less panache than in its earliest days. Though much of it is closed and some of it is falling apart, it's still worth a visit, if only for the legendary Cyclone (one of the scariest, shakiest roller coasters in the world) and for the yearly Freak Show, one of the last of its kind in the United States. Visiting the beach here or in Brighton Beach is another highlight.

THE BOROUGH OF QUEENS

Best for: Museums, ethnic dining
What you won't find: Theater, great shopping, top architecture (with a few exceptions), top non-ethnic restaurants

Archie Bunker no longer lives in Queens. In fact, the grouchy, bigoted xenophobe at the center of the famed 1970s sitcom *All in the Family* probably wouldn't recognize the borough today. In just the past 50 years it has gone from being a somewhat insulated, working-class community of Irish- and Italian-Americans to the most international community in the States.

It's this ability to globe-trot in an afternoon that makes Queens appealing, despite the dreary, industrial look of so much of it. Whether you're downing samosas and shopping for saris in very Indian Jackson Heights; breaking plates at the late-night clubs of Greek Astoria; or buying miracle water and tacos at a Mexican *botanica* in Corona, there's much to taste, smell, and experience.

Museums are another big draw, and the borough now tops Brooklyn for its cultural attractions, boasting four great ones—The Museum of the Moving Image, PS 1 Museum of Contemporary Art, Isamu Noguchi Galleries, and the Louis Armstrong House. Combining a visit to one of these outstanding institutions with a meal at a local ethnic restaurant is a recommended outer borough adventure.

THE BOROUGH OF THE BRONX

Best for: Baseball, Italian restaurants, zoos, and gardens

What you won't find: Museums, nightlife, other types of worthy restaurants, hotels, theater

I may be condemned for this assessment, but to my mind there are only four reasons a tourist should even think of going to the Bronx: Yankee Stadium; the Bronx Zoo; the New York Botanical Gardens; and the Italian restaurants and stores of Arthur Avenue. If you have no interest in any of these sights, you can skip this giant borough without too much regret.

THE BOROUGH OF STATEN ISLAND

Best for: Views of Manhattan from the ferry

What you won't find: Notable museums, nightlife, hotels, theaters, truly great restaurants, top architecture

And I'll again be blunt: Except for the fun and free ferry ride you can take here (which will get you a terrific view of the Manhattan skyline) and possibly historic Richmond Town (a living-history museum), there's no reason a tourist should visit this highly residential borough. Yes, there are a handful of cultural and historic sights here, but none that justify the hour-long commute.

3 Accommodations, Both Standard and Not

In which you'll discover all the options, from spare cots in private apartments to comfy digs in boutique hotels

TIME NOW FOR A CHANGE OF MOOD. IN A BOOK THAT CELEBRATES THE fun and attractions of New York, it's necessary for just a short while—the length of this chapter—to deal with a far less pleasant topic: the high-priced, over-priced accommodations of New York. By and large, hotels in Gotham charge more than hotels anywhere else in America (an average of $325 per night) for rooms that aren't nearly as spacious or full of amenities. Why? Over 43 million people visited NYC in 2007, keeping occupancy rates at over 85% for much of the year. Hotels could charge pretty much whatever they darn pleased . . . and most of them did.

Though I admit this unpleasant fact, I'm not discouraged by it. Bargains can be found. Values exist. If you carefully and patiently review all your options, you will eventually and invariably find a decently priced place to lay your head. To aid in that task, I discuss in this chapter no fewer than **(a)** 64 individual hotels, **(b)** 7 organizations for apartment rentals and private B&B stays, and **(c)** 9 hostels, specialty hotels, and retreat houses.

And to spotlight the city's very best values, I'll start with the city's many private apartments, whose owners rent their spare rooms (sometimes their entire apartment) for far less than a hotel would charge for similar space and comfort. These are fascinating possibilities that justify—in my view—placing our hotel discussion in the second half of this chapter.

RENTING A PRIVATE APARTMENT

In New York, a whole world of alternative lodgings is based upon what one critic called "the dirty little secret of American life, that no one has enough money." More supposedly well-off New Yorkers than you'd ever imagine are supplementing their incomes and balancing their budgets by inviting visitors into their well-appointed apartments, converting their homes into mini-hotels. My stepsister is one of them, actually. When she is short on cash, she simply arranges to stay at a friend's house for the weekend or for a week, and then rents out her spacious, Upper West Side doorman apartment. Her temporary guests get lodgings twice as big as any hotel room, in a wonderful neighborhood, for three-quarters the cost, and with a kitchen to boot. It's a win-win situation for both she and her guests.

Don't Dismiss Brooklyn and Queens

By choosing a hosted stay in Brooklyn or Queens, guests can sometimes pay hostel-level prices for a private room with private bathroom in some of the loveliest areas of the city. NY Habitat, for example, represents hosts in Astoria, Queens (approximately a 20-min. subway ride from Manhattan) who rent spacious double rooms for as little as $62 a night. The same prices can sometimes be found in the area near Prospect Park and right across the river in Williamsburg, Brooklyn.

There are also those New Yorkers who aren't as "nomadic" as my stepsister, who simply rent out a room within their apartments, often with a private bathroom attached. Though the privacy for the visitor isn't as complete, the prices are even lower.

And in that kind of "hosted" situation, visitors get a rare glimpse of actual life in Manhattan. They set up house in a real neighborhood, get to know the deli guy, the locals-only restaurant, and the bar around the corner.

What kinds of apartments are available to the visitor?

◆ *A tidy room off an artist's gallery in SoHo. In the mornings, you breakfast surrounded by elongated Plexiglass nude sculptures; at night, the French expat artist who is your host invites you to dine with his family in the apartment downstairs.*

◆ *A town house in Greenwich Village with a decor Martha Stewart would applaud, where you sleep in an antique mahogany four-poster bed and awake in the morning not to traffic noises but to the calls of birds chirping in the backyard garden.*

◆ *The first-floor apartment of a historic Victorian Harlem town house, where the walls sport African art, with African baskets in the corner for decoration. For breakfast, your hostess gives you coupons to the excellent French patisserie down the block.*

As you can see, each of these New York B&Bs is radically different from the next, bearing little resemblance to the doily-and-dried-flower inns of New England and the Midwest.

And unlike many B&B inns in the rest of America, where a quaint decor translates into a huge upswing in price, these B&Bs are significantly less expensive than hotel stays. At the Harlem apartment, for example, a large, comfortable space with a full kitchen, a washer/dryer, and an in-room bathroom, is just $75–$100 a night for one person, $100–$150 for two, and $175 for three (there's a second brass bed in one of the two apartments). At the artist's loft, prices start at $130 at night. And while the Greenwich Village apartments are more expensive at $190 to $250 a night, a Gotham hotel room this luxurious and well-located would cost at minimum of $300 a night.

I drew the above examples from **BedandBreakfast.com**, a 14-year-old online registry service—just one of the many resources travelers can use to book this kind of stay.

YOU HAVE TWO BASIC CHOICES

In the world of New York apartment rentals there are basically two types of accommodations:

- **Unhosted apartments:** Full apartments that the renters have entirely to themselves for the course of their stay. (Many agencies will not allow visitors to rent an apartment for fewer than 5 nights, though with certain units and at slower times of the year, a 3-night minimum might apply.)
- **Hosted apartments:** Apartments that the guest shares with a New Yorker who lives on premises. Usually the host rents just one room and sleeps in another bedroom. Only a 3-night minimum stay is required for a hosted arrangement.

There are pluses and minuses to each type of lodging. At **unhosted apartments,** guests have total privacy. You can come and go at will without worrying about disturbing anyone, buy your own food, cook meals, and live essentially as you would in your own home. The downside can be the lack of any kind of guidance: If you need advice, there's no one on premises that you can turn to, and you're also alone if the toilet won't flush or the key jams in the lock (the rental agency or owner will fix the problem, but it will probably take a bit of time). Also, these types of rentals are usually a good 25% to 50% more expensive than hosted rentals.

At **hosted rentals,** you may feel constrained by the presence of the host and in some, but not all cases, may have to share a bathroom. That's usually the worst it gets. In the best-case scenarios, your host will act as an affable advisor, helping to pave your way in the big city, and perhaps forming a friendship that lasts beyond the visit. In fact, one unsung perk of doing a hosted rental is that you meet unusually gracious, resourceful, quirky New Yorkers. "Most hosts are off the corporate grid," explains Margaret Borden of City Sonnet. "We get a lot of artists, actors, musicians, chefs, and other creative types because these sorts of people have the time to do a second job and often need the extra income. Most are extremely well traveled and all really enjoy meeting travelers." In hosted situations, breakfast is usually included in the cost of the stay and, as I said before, guests typically pay less for this type of lodging.

Two very nice standard perks offered in both hosted and unhosted rentals are free local calls and Internet access. As with hotels, 99% of all B&Bs, of both types, provide cable TV in the bedrooms.

What B&Bs don't offer are the services and amenities that you'll find at hotels—there's no concierge on-site to help you book theater tickets or make restaurant reservations. And you can forget about daily maid service. Most hosts clean the apartment only between guest stays, and rely on you to make your own bed and sometimes even take out the garbage. The only room service will be from the pizzeria down the street, and your business center will probably be the local Kinko's, so think long and hard about whether or not this type of stay, and the independence it entails, is for you.

If you do decide to go the B&B route, the most logical way of finding lodgings is through a rental company. I've vetted all of the major agencies in New York, visiting dozens of the properties they represent, and have pared the firms down to four recommendations. I also include a short section at the end of this

B&B Stays: Questions to Ask Your Potential Host

Though most in-apartment B&B stays are fun, carefree holidays, some-times . . . well, things can go mighty wrong. It's extremely important to find out what sort of person you may be sharing your vacation with and what the apartment's like before you put down a deposit. Call your poten-tial host or the agency to go over any concerns you may have before com-mitting to any hosted stay.

Some questions you may want to ask:

1. What is the host's schedule?

   Some hosts will be in their apartment for most of the day, while oth-ers work outside the home, meaning that you'll have the apartment to yourself for large chunks of time. Find out before you leave.

2. Where does the host sleep in relation to the room you'll be using?

   Another privacy issue: Will your host be in the room right next door, eavesdropping, intentionally or not, on your every sigh or snore? Or will there be a room or two between your two bedrooms? In some extremely rare cases, cash-crunched hosts have been known to rent out their own bedrooms and take the living room couch for a week. If the listing is for a one-bedroom, you may want to find out if this is the case, as that can be an uncomfortable situation, especially if you have to walk through the living room to get to the bedroom or bathroom. (From what I understand, this is not a common scenario, but hey, it's better to ask.)

3. Is the bathroom shared or private?

4. Are there pets in the house?

5. Are there any rules the host has for his or her guests?

   Whether or not guests can smoke in an apartment is obviously an important issue, as is a guest's use of the shared space (I once met a host who only allowed the guests she liked to venture into the liv-ing room). Most hosts do not allow guests to cook, except to reheat prepared foods, so if this is an issue for you, discuss it before you book. And sometimes the rules can be even more unusual—I know of a hostess who keeps kosher and requires guests to separate the plates used for dairy products and meat products (not an easy task).

6. What does the bedroom face?

   Does the room get a lot of sun in the morning? Does it face a busy street, or a quiet back courtyard? These questions may be key if you're a light sleeper.

discussion on "registries" that will guide you to B&Bs, but I have not inspected nor do I guarantee any of the lodgings they list.

Here are four companies that have vetted the apartments they represent:

Affordable New York City

Contact Info: ☎ 212/533-4001; www.AffordableNewYorkCity.com.

Prices: Hosted stays: $95–$120 single or double with shared bathroom, $130–$150 single or double with private bathroom. Unhosted stays: $150–$250 per night in a studio apartment, $185–$250 in a one-bedroom, $300–$500 per night in a larger apartment.

Examples of available rentals: With deep-red walls, beautiful antiques, and oil paintings galore, one Midtown share looks very much like a set from a Merchant-Ivory film (not surprising, as the hostess is a set decorator). As the bathroom is shared, these elegant digs go for about $120 per night. Or rent a landmark building in Chelsea, with full kitchen, 14-foot ceilings in the bedroom, and a large living room lit by a room-wide skylight. Or bunk down in a duplex apartment, considered a one-bedroom but large and private enough for four. Its massive windows and terrace bring the outdoors in.

Pluses: Large selection; expert staff.

Negatives: Will not accept children under 10; does not handle properties outside of Manhattan.

Tip: When she can, owner Freschel will accept last-minute bookings, and during slow periods she is open to bargaining (just don't try it in May, June, Oct, Nov or Dec).

The largest of the services that handle both hosted and unhosted stays, Affordable New York City represents approximately 120 apartments, which is more than double the number of the closest runner-up. According to owner Susan Freschel, wider coverage means greater numbers of options for the renter: "I like to give potential clients four or five choices each time someone writes me," she says. "I give my clients more options than other B&B services." She also has an odd habit of underselling apartments; her website gives cursory descriptions of some truly fabulous apartments. So the home of an antiques dealer on the Upper West Side, where you sleep in an ancient Chinese wedding bed (don't worry, it's quite comfortable) surrounded by exquisite antiques, is described simply by the size of the room and its amenities. So if you have additional questions, either call and ask, or study the many photos up on her site (they aren't doctored). In business for 8 years, Freschel has a terrific reputation and a loyal following among both hosts and guests (about 40% of her bookings are either repeat customers or referrals).

City Sonnet

Contact Info: ☎ 212/614-3034; www.citysonnet.com.

Prices: Hosted stays: $110 to $125 single in Brooklyn, $140 to $175 single in Manhattan; $125 to $145 double in Brooklyn, $150 to $175 double in Manhattan. Unhosted apartments: $175 to $300 for doubles and triples, $350 to $700 for rentals that can sleep up to eight.

Examples of available rentals: An artsy studio with full kitchen right on Fifth Avenue in Greenwich Village, available for unhosted stays. Or a screenwriter's antiques-filled guest room (there's even a four-poster bed) near the Theater District.

Pluses: Excellent customer service; well-located, personality-filled apartments.

Negatives: No last-minute bookings; probably won't bargain on prices.

City Sonnet places guests into some of the most exclusive and sought-after areas and buildings in the city. Lower Manhattan—Greenwich Village, the East Village,

SoHo and TriBeCa—is their forte, and they offer hosted and unhosted apartments in the very centers of these neighborhoods. Only about 10% of City Sonnet's apartment owners work with other agencies, so you'll find apartments here that are unique to this broker, such as a lovely chinoiserie-laden B&B on the Upper East Side, run by a globe-trotting Guatemalan expat; or a light-drenched SoHo loft of a professional chef who sometimes prepares a gourmet breakfast of roasted pineapple with raspberry sauce and fresh scones for her guests.

A smaller agency with just two full-time employees, one part-timer, and a stable of approximately 50 apartments, City Sonnet picks its hosts with care, and checks up on them at least once a year. "We don't take on a place unless we'd like to stay there ourselves," says owner Margaret Borden. "If the apartment is ugly or the host seems weird or unfriendly, we simply don't work with them." As City Sonnet works with a small number of apartments, it's necessary to call at least a month to a month and a half in advance to reserve a place. Then it can take several days of phone calls and e-mails to complete the booking, as the staff here sees the process as one of "matchmaking." "There are bookings we won't make," says Borden. "If we feel that the guest really needs the services of a hotel or a facility that we don't have, we'll refer them elsewhere. We want to make sure that each guest has a quality experience."

At Home in New York
Contact Info: ☎ 800/692-4262 or 212/956-3125; www.athomeny.com.
Prices: Hosted stays: $100 to $135 single, $135 to $175 double, $200 to $225 triple. Unhosted apartments: $180 to $250 studio, $225 to $280 for one or two-bedrooms.
Examples of available rentals: A very private room in a two-floor apartment in the Union Square area, filled with art objects from all over the world, collected by the owners, who are professional photographers. Elsewhere, "Mi casa es su casa" is the motto at a high-rise in the East 60s, where the gracious host even allows guests to throw parties on her oversized terrace. Across town, on the West Side, views of Lincoln Center and the river add to the luster of an oversized one-bedroom unhosted rental in a doorman building.
Pluses: Prime locations; personality-filled apartments; highly personal service.
Negatives: Not as many options as larger agencies.
Tip: There is some wiggle room on prices here, so don't be shy about bargaining. For an apartment on the Upper East Side or West Side, turn to At Home in New York, which specializes in those areas and offers a total of 30 hosted and unhosted units. Lois Rooks, the owner, has to be the most hands-on of all of the agents, checking in guests herself at the apartments, supervising the cleaning staff, even buying new sheets and pull-out couches for owners who are out of town. When I asked her how often she inspects apartments, she laughed and said, "Oh, I'm over at the apartments all the time; I can't count how many times in a year I'll see them." A former actress, Ms. Rooks has been in the business for 22 years and knows her territory (and hosts) backwards and forwards. My only complaint would be with the At Home in New York website, which doesn't show enough pictures of the properties. Rooks, however, will send additional large pictures by e-mail to anyone who is interested in a particular apartment.

For unhosted stays mainly

NY Habitat

Contact Info: ☎ 212/255-8018; www.nyhabitat.com.

Prices: Hosted stays: May go for as little as $62/night in Brooklyn, but generally range from $90 to $160 single occupancy, $100 to $200 double. Unhosted stays: Studios average $138, one-bedrooms average $150 to $165, two-bedrooms average $280 to $350, 3-bedrooms or larger average $400.

Tip: Like the other agencies, the staff here is sometimes willing to bargain, so give it a try (they have a lot of apartments to move).

Examples of available rentals: A high-rise two-bedroom with river views and polished wood floors in the West 30's, corporate decor, sleeps up to six. Or a Theater District two-bedroom that sleeps up to eight people, four on fold-out couches located in the dining room and living room. Clean and roomy with a large balcony; bland-looking furnishings. Or an East Village one-bedroom walk-up, home of a stylish "performance artist" with silver taffeta drapes, quirky antiques, and a bathtub in the kitchen.

Pluses: Excellent customer service; large number of units available at any one time; a higher-than-average percentage of family-size apartments and uncluttered corporate-style apartments.

Negatives: Steeper-than-normal fees (35% commission); many apartments in the somewhat bleak midtown West and far Chelsea area.

NY Habitat is one of the oldest and largest of the vacation rental companies—so big, in fact, that it's branched out to cover stays in Paris, London, and the French Riviera. For New York alone, it lists approximately 350 apartments at any one time (out of the 1,200 it has in its database); there are seven full-time staffers who inspect these apartments (generally once every 2 years) and follow up on complaints. These busy folks also take the pictures and write the dry but accurate descriptions you'll find on the NY Habitat website.

Approximately 85% of NY Habitat's listings are for unhosted stays. Half of these come from huge companies that rent out dozens of furnished apartments at a time. As you might expect, these are not stylish, unique digs—some of these big companies even rent the furniture they use, adding just one more layer of corporate blandness to the enterprise. That being said, the apartments are clean and utterly uncluttered. Unlike other agencies, NY Habitat offers a large number of oversized one- and two-bedroom apartments, perfect for families. Many of these can house four, six, or eight people quite comfortably (though Junior may have to sleep on a fold-out couch).

NY Habitat also works with individual owners who may rent their apartments for a few weeks when they leave town. This doesn't, however, seem to be the primary focus of their business, especially since NY Habitat has now instituted a policy of only working with hosts who can be upfront with their landlords or co-op boards about accepting short-term "boarders." It's a controversial issue (and I'll note at this point that NY Habitat is the only company in town with this policy). While hosting guests is not illegal (owners pay taxes on these stays, after all), it is frowned upon in some buildings, which is why other agencies will ask guests to be discreet when first checking into the B&B. The folks at New York Habitat refuse to do that. "I'm not going to ask someone to lie and say they're visiting a friend," says Nick Borg, manager. In practical terms, this policy relegates NY

Habitat to apartments that may be in the less attractive, less residential neighborhoods, primarily in the West 20's, 30's, 40's and 50's as these areas are less likely to be dominated by co-ops (many of which have house rules forbidding boarders).

Directory Services (with no guarantee of quality)

♦ **BedandBreakfast.com:** There are also those online services which leave "due diligence" to the vacationer and simply provide a forum for guests and would-be hosts to "hook up" with each other. One of the largest and oldest of these (founded in 1994) is BedandBreakfast.com, a global Yellow Pages for inns around the world. It primarily lists traditional, multi-room inns—places that offer four, five, six, or more rooms to the public (in fact, it represents some of the larger inns that I have profiled later in this chapter, such as Chelsea Lodge and Gracie Inn). Unlike some services, the inns must pay a fee to list here, which eliminates fly-by-night operations from the mix. The lodgings that I've obtained from BedandBreakfast.com, which I have visited and then profiled, have been consistently professional, clean, and darn nice in all instances.

(Two other websites, **BnBfinder.com** and **ILoveInns.com**, are organized in a similar fashion to BedandBreakfast.com, but they offer far fewer listings, and repeat what you'll find on BedandBreakfast.com [40 choices]).

♦ **Craigslist (www.craigslist.org)** is a massive website offering nearly unlimited listings with absolutely no filter at all (for all the good and bad that implies). It receives over 10 million visitors a month. Folks with apartments or rooms to rent can post here at absolutely no cost, and dozens do so every month, so you'll have a tremendous number of options in all price ranges. I periodically check this site and have found Village studio apartments renting for as little as $85 a night, and a large three-bedroom apartment with full kitchen, living room, and dining room going for $300, so there are real steals to be found. But Craigslist comes with some risks. Obviously, none of the rentals have been inspected, and many of the owners will be renting for the first time, meaning that you could end up in a remote neighborhood, sleeping on a futon on the floor, or bathing in a shower that hasn't been scrubbed since the Clinton administration. I've also heard charges that some of the listings are scams, so be very careful if you go this route. I'd avoid those posting e-mail addresses from free services such as Yahoo! and hotmail. And be wary of someone who wants a money order or cash, and demands full payment upfront many months in advance. One address—148 West 58th St—has come up regularly in these scams, I've been told (there is no building at that address). That warning aside, you could score a gem. It's a gamble, and I do have to say that the vast majority of listings are for apartments in the same price ranges of the agencies I list above. In such cases I would think the logic is clear—go with the known quantity over the unknown.

AND NOW, THE HOTELS OF MANHATTAN

Maybe out of sheer inertia or habit, maybe out of prior bad experience with a room in someone's apartment, most visitors to New York will choose to stay in a standard hotel. I profile 62 of these properties in the remainder of this chapter, grouped according to the geographical area of New York in which each is found.

A Tale of Three Seasons

Conventions affect hotel prices (see p. 304 for those), as do holidays, but in general, three seasons dictate how much you'll spend on a Manhattan bed.

January 10 through the end of February is the cheapest time to visit New York City by far, when rates (and temperatures) hit bottom.

September, October, November, and December, when the city is swarming with shoppers and businesspeople, is the peak season, with rates reaching their pinnacle the week the "Big Ball" drops.

The rest of the year comprises a hazy "middle season" with summer rates sometimes dropping near deep-winter prices, though that practice may be disappearing thanks to the increasing popularity of New York in June, July, and even sweltering August.

Hotels within each area are set forth in ascending order of cost, starting with the cheapest and moving upward to end with an occasional "big splurge." Each hotel listing is preceded by one, two, three, or four dollar signs, indicating its price range per room, as follows:

$: Up to $125 a night
$$: $126 to $175
$$$: $176 to $225
$$$$: Over $226 per night

In addition, many hotel listings carry a cluster of stars ★, indicating our opinion of the hotel's desirability (this does not have anything to do with price, but with the value you receive for the price you pay). The stars mean:

No star: Good
★ Very good
★★ Great
★★★ Outstanding! A must!

As you begin your quest, let me suggest that you don't call just the hotels in this chapter. To get the best rate, shop around first, surf the Internet and, in some cases, wheedle and bargain (I'll include some tips below on how to do just that). Hotel rooms are a time-sensitive product and if they go empty, hoteliers lose money, so you do have *some* muscle (not much in NYC, but a bit) when it comes to getting a good price.

TIMES SQUARE

In other world cities, hotels tend to cluster around train stations, but in New York, the largest concentration of hotels is in the Theater District which, while not the geographic heart of Manhattan, is considered by many to be the de facto center of the city. It's also the most crowded, cacophonous neighborhood in

Midtown, Chelsea, Union Square & Flatiron District Accommodations

Americana Inn **34**
Big Apple Hostel **37**
Barclay Intercontinental **40**
Benjamin Hotel **41**
Carlton Arms **21**
Chelsea Inn **18**
Chelsea Lodge **16**
Chelsea Pines Inn **17**
Chelsea Savoy Hotel **14**
Colonial House Inn **15**
Da Vinci Hotel **3**
Edison Hotel **10**
Gershwin Hotel **22**
Gracie Inn **43**
Grand Hyatt **35**
Herald Square Hotel **31**
Holiday Inn Express
  Fifth Avenue **39**
Hotel 17 **20**
Hotel 31 **26**
Hotel 414 **7**
Hotel Deauville **23**
Hotel Grand Union **27**
Hotel Stanford **30**
Hotel St. James **34**
Hotel Woolcott **32**
Hotel Wellington **4**
House of the Redeemer **44**
Hudson Hotel **1**
La Quinta **29**
Leo House **9**
Mayfair Hotel **6**
Milford Plaza **8**
Millennium Broadway **11**
Paramount Hotel **9**
Park Savoy **2**
The Pod Hotel **42**
Ramada Inn Eastside **25**
Red Roof Inn **28**
Skyline Hotel **5**
Soldiers', Sailors', Marines',
  and Airmans' Club **33**
Super 8 Times Square **38**
Travel Inn **12**
Union Square Inn **19**

Manhattan, with few grocery stores, drugstores, good restaurants, or other amenities that help make a visit pleasant. Staying in this often ugly neighborhood and
fighting the crowds on a daily basis is not my idea of a relaxing vacation, but
because so many travelers insist on being close to the theaters (and as there are so
many options in this part of town), I'll start with it, and list those Times Square
digs that offer the best value for money spent. Be sure to check the box on
Priceline, for more on money-saving ways to stay in midtown Manhattan.

$–$$ And as budget digs go, the **Hotel St. James** (109 W. 45th St., btwn Sixth
Ave. and Broadway; ☎ 212/221-3600; ❶, ❷, ❸, Ⓝ, Ⓞ, Ⓡ, Ⓢ, Ⓦ, ❼ to Times
Sq.; AE, DC, MC, V) may be the least expensive hotel choice in this area (at least of
the hotels that aren't scary—you won't find any of those in this book). It's come
up quite a bit in the last two years, both in terms of decor and unfortunately, in
pricing. The double rate now swings from $125 to $175 ($145–$195 for rooms
with two double beds, big enough for four). You still ain't getting the Taj Mahal
here; the rooms look a bit like they were designed by someone wearing a blind-
fold, with a famed print hung too high and askew on a wall here, odd color
choices there. But rooms are larger than usual and quite clean, with good beds,
cable TV, and full bathrooms. Some are recently renovated, others will be a bit
older, so ask to move if you're not happy with the one you're assigned (especially
if it's in the front of the hotel which can get noisy). And try to score a room on a
lower floor as the elevator is painfully slow. (When I asked if they have a gym yet,
the desk clerk laughed and said: "Our guests don't need one, they get enough exercise on the stairs!")

$–$$$ Just west of Times Square, on a block that also houses the Majestic
Theater and Eugene O'Neill Theater (and the crowds that descend on them 8
times a week), the **Mayfair Hotel** ★ (242 W. 49th St., btwn Broadway and Eighth
Ave.; ☎ 800/556-2932 or 212/586-0300; www.mayfairnewyork.com; Ⓝ, Ⓡ, Ⓦ to
49th St.; AE, MC, V) bills itself a "European-style, boutique hotel," which I've
found to be the code phrase for "Our rooms are very, very small, but they sure do
look pretty." That's certainly the case here, with rooms that are oddly shaped, usu-
ally opening onto a tiny alcove area with a doorway to the bathroom, behind
which is wedged a full, queen, or king-size bed and a small desk. Pretty comes into
the equation with the Wedgwood china–like bedspreads and curtains, white with
either baby blue or pink scenes of peasants at play. As with many Theater District
hotels, rates rise sharply on the weekends, bringing the cost of a single room up
from $100–$130 to $145 in the summer and deep winter. A double can increase

Staying Connected to the Internet

High-speed Internet access either through cables or via Wi-Fi is now a given at
every non-hostel-type hotel in Manhattan. I only mention this amenity at the
hotels that offer the service for free; all the rest charge a standard $9.95 per day
for Internet access.

from $130 to $210 during those same periods. During the popular fall and spring periods and at holiday times, single rooms can start at $145, with doubles going for $250, but usually even during these pricey periods you'll pay less than that (the desk clerk is almost always willing to play "let's make a deal," so do your best to bargain). Penny-pinching couples can rent single rooms to share but this is only recommended for very loving twosomes (it's a tight fit). There's free Internet access and computers in some rooms.

$–$$$ Despite what you may have heard—and for many years, the **Milford Plaza** ★ (700 Eighth Ave. at 45th St.; ☎ 800/221-2690 or 212/869-3600; www. milfordplaza.com; **A**,**C**, **E** to 42nd St.; AE, DC, MC, V) had one of the worst reputations in the city—this old-timer is now on the up and up. New management has raised the level of professionalism and given the hotel a complete makeover. Some hints of the bad old Milford do remain—the overhead lights still buzz with the telltale sound of fluorescent tubes; windows are not double-paned so traffic noise can be a problem (ask for a room OFF noisy Eighth Ave.); you'll encounter an errant scuff mark here and there along the walls; and with 1,300 rooms, there are going to be times it's difficult to get a quick response from the front desk. But for the most part, digs are spiffy if dated-looking and about a fifth larger than you'll encounter elsewhere. The Milford also has a lot of amenities you don't usually get in this price range including: a terrific gym, a gift shop, and bellhop service. There are even plans afoot to add room service. The Milford's a player on every discounter in town's roster, so it's difficult to get a bead on pricing (be sure to do a thorough search before booking); I've seen rooms here start at just $109 during quiet times, and scrape $215 when the town's partying. Usually you'll pay somewhere in between.

$$–$$$ Like the Milford Plaza, the **Edison Hotel** ★ (228 W. 47th St. off Times Square; ☎ 212/840-5000; www.edisonhotelnyc.com; **1**, **2**, **3**, **N**, **Q**, **R**, **S**, **W**, **7** to Times Sq.; AE, DC, MC, V) is a constant presence on the hotel discounters' websites. Here's why: It has 800 rooms to fill, it's an older property so it has some structural no-no's that turn off modern travelers (like Lilliputian bathrooms and uneven floors in places), and though it's just steps from the bright lights of the Square, it has no views to speak of. The Edison also tends to book large groups, which can be a hassle for independent travelers (overheard in the elevator: "Did you see all those European teens!! It's like a small country's here.") Beyond those qualms, I'd say it's a step above "just fine." The rooms themselves are immaculate and comfortably sized (in general), there's a large gym on the top floor, and the staff seems to genuinely enjoy helping travelers. So if you get a deal—$149 to $179 seem to be the discounts usually offered here on doubles (though of course, prices can go higher)—I'd say go for it.

$$–$$$ Charm is a pricey amenity in the world of NYC hotels, which is why I was so pleased to stumble upon **Hotel 414** ★★ (414 W. 46th St. btwn Ninth and Tenth aves.; ☎ 866/414-HOTEL or 212/399-0006; www.hotel414.com; **N**, **R**, **W** to 49th St. or **1**, **9** to 50th St.; AE, DC, MC, V). Set in two small apartment buildings connected by a lovely little courtyard, it's decorated with what can only be called "élan"—the walls are bathed in chic colors, furnishings are cheeky (a chest of drawers that looks like a wooden file cabinet, suede checkerboard headboards, elongated vases with flowers) and rooms, while on the small side, never feel cramped. Breakfast is included in the daily rate, which starts at $159/night, but tends to settle closer to $209 most of the year. Guests have access to a shared kitchen (with fridge, microwave, and two burners). To top it all off, the staff is genuinely gracious. Free Wi-Fi, too.

$$–$$$$ Super 8 Times Sq. ★ (59 W. 46th St., near Sixth Ave.; ☎ 212/719-2300; www.super8.com; **N**, **R**, **W** to 49th St.; AE, DC, MC, V), part of the Apple Core group, prides itself on providing luxe amenities at proletarian prices. Problem is, sometimes its rates are good, and sometimes they're pretty, well, luxe—with certain dates in the summer, fall, and early winter rising to a hefty $300 for a very simple though well-proportioned motel-like room that's clean and faceless but with a firm bed, a roomy closet, and a bathroom. The amenities they like to tout include an exercise room on property (good only for cardio as there are no weights), a concierge desk, and a downright opulent continental breakfast served each morning, with such goodies as doughnuts, bagels, cereals, fresh fruits, and pastries. If you hit it right, it can be a terrific deal at just $129 per night. If not . . . well, you get the picture.

HELL'S KITCHEN—AN OUTER PART OF TIMES SQUARE

$$–$$$ In an area of Manhattan that could be best described as "Siberia," the **Skyline Hotel** ★ (kids) (725 Tenth Ave. at 49th St.; ☎ 800/433-1982 or 212/586-3400; www.skylinehotelny.com; **C**, **E** to 50th St.; AE, DC, MC, V) does its best to offset its dreary, far west location with a cluster of amenities that can only be replicated at one other hotel in the city (see the Travel Inn, below). First off, the Skyline has that rarest of all luxuries: an indoor swimming pool, and a nice one at that, on the roof. The lobby, a tony space, boasts a large on-site restaurant, a cocktail bar, and a gift shop. Guests can store cars or vans for a mere $10 per day in the hotel's basement parking lot. And the rooms, enormous by New York standards, are bright and comfortable, and come with such nice extras as Nintendo games and Wi-Fi. In the front wing (slightly smaller rooms), rates start at $139 a night but can soar to $400 (usually they hover in the mid-200s, and I wouldn't pay more than that). Rooms in the back are even pricier and not worth the extra money.

$$–$$$ Travel Inn ★★ (kids) (515 W. 42nd St., near Tenth Ave.; ☎ 800/869-4630 or 212/695-7171; www.newyorkhotel.com; **A**, **E**, **C**, **7** to 42nd St.; AE, DC, MC, V) is a dead ringer for the Skyline (see above), but with a few important differences. Like the Skyline, it has a pool, a gym, and parking facilities, but it one-ups its rival with the size of its pool (a summer-only facility about twice as large as its rival's), its gym (also a hair bigger), and the fact that it gives guests free parking—a very, very rare perk in this parking-poor city. Rooms are renovated each year and

Bringing the Kids

Children are welcomed at hotels across the city. Those under the age of 12 rarely incur a charge when sharing a room with their parents.

Turning to the Web for a Hotel Discount

Before going to the Web, it's important that you know what "flavor" of discount you're seeking. Currently, there are three types of online reductions

1. Extreme discounts on sites where you bid for lodgings without knowing which hotel you'll get. This type of discounting is so terrific, I've devoted an entire box to it on page 38.
2. Discounts on the hotel's website itself.
3. Discounts on outside sites such as **hotels.com**, **quikbook.com**, **Expedia.com**, and the like.

The second type of discount is most common at the large "chain" hotels such as Best Western, Holiday Inn, and the W Hotels. About 7 years ago, these chains (and others) pledged to the public that they would not be undercut by outside agencies such as Orbitz, Expedia, and Travelocity, and for once, corporate America was true to its word. Within months these companies started offering better or equal prices on their own websites. So if you have a particular hotel in mind that's a member of a national chain, it's always best to simply go to that chain's website to book (or try a blind bidding site; see p. 38).

If you don't know which chain hotel you prefer, you can turn to an "aggregator" site such as **Sidestep.com**, **Kayak.com**, or **Mobissimo.com**. These three sites perform a "spider search" of all of the big chains' websites (and some independent hotels as well) and will return a list of options, from cheapest to most expensive, of rates that you may not find on Expedia, Orbitz, Travelocity, and the other online travel agencies. These aggregators also have the ability to "winnow" your search by the type of amenities you want (free breakfast, pool, Internet access) as well as location. **Travelaxe.com**, another top site, works in a similar way, searching not only the hotel chains but the discounters' sites as well. The only drawback to this online tool is that you must download it to your hard drive. If you're a frequent traveler, I'd recommend you use it; no spyware will be installed, Travelaxe is ethical about privacy issues, and its side-by-side searches can be a savings boon.

So you can stop surfing there, right? I wish. It's now the better part of wisdom to check a couple of online discounters as well. Companies such as **Hotels.com**, **Quikbook**, and **Last Minute Travel** have taken to buying New York hotel rooms in bulk and then reselling them at a discount. You won't find these discounts through an aggregator site; instead, you'll need to search the sites individually.

It's a lot of surfing, I know, but in the hothouse world of Big Apple hotel pricing, this sort of diligence can pay off.

are therefore immaculate, with good firm mattresses and a standard motel look, but they're markedly smaller than Skyline's though the prices are similar. Here a room with a queen-size bed or two doubles will start at $125, going up to as much as $300 during the peak fall and winter season (at most times of the year they cost $225–$250). Rooms with king beds are about $25 more but come with fridges and microwaves. In an unusually generous gesture, the hotel allows kids up to the age of 16 (rather than the usual 12) to stay free when sharing rooms with their parents. Locale? Though it's as far west as the Skyline, in this area of town the Off-Broadway theaters crawl down 42nd Street all the way to Tenth Avenue, so it feels less remote.

MIDTOWN WEST: NEAR HERALD SQUARE

Just south of Times Square, but still in the middle swath of Manhattan known as "Midtown," is the heavily commercial district whose prime draws are the Empire State Building and Macy's department store—the latter is on Herald Square. Just as crowded and manic as the Theater District during the day, the area tends to empty out at night when the office workers and shoppers go home, affording visitors some much-needed quiet. Of the many budget choices in this area I've narrowed the field to those that give the best value.

$–$$$ Hard-core budgeteers—but those who value their sleep—would do well to consider the **Americana Inn** (69 W. 38th St., just off Sixth Ave.; ☎ 212/840-6700; www.theamericanainn.com; **N**, **R**, **Q**, **W**, **B**, **D**, **V**, **F** to 34th St.; AE, DC, MC, V). This is another bathless wonder: Here three to four rooms share a bathroom with shower (rooms do come with sinks), and though the rates are no longer the lowest in the city, they're reasonable for singles at $75 to $145. Those needing rooms with double beds or two twins pay significantly more at $90 to $175 a night; at the upper end of that scale, this place ain't worth it as rooms are miniscule with little decoration beyond a TV set (basic, no cable), a direct-dial phone, and standard, motel-like furniture. Mattresses though are top quality. To ensure that you make the most of your stay, ask for a room in the back, away from the street noise. One handy perk here is the kitchenette on each floor available for guest use (along with coffeemakers).

$–$$$$ I also very much like the **Herald Square Hotel** ★★ (19 W. 31st St. btwn Fifth Ave. and Broadway; ☎ 800/727-1888 or 212/279-4017; www.herald squarehotel.com; **N**, **R**, **Q**, **W**, **B**, **D**, **V**, **F** to Herald Sq./34th St.; AE, DC, MC, V), but what an emotional roller-coaster it puts its guests on! The outside is promising, a lovely Beaux Arts facade complete with gold-leaf cherub, but once you enter you're confronted with that most ominous of hotel sights: a bullet-proof, glass-encased check-in desk. It turns out that's merely a holdover from the bad old days when this was a welfare hotel, but what a terrible first impression it makes! Of course, first impressions aren't everything, and the solicitous staff and tremendously spiffy rooms should soon dispel any lingering worries. In the most expensive rooms (at published rates between $249 and $269 a night, but sometimes dropping as low as $189), the mattresses have comfy pillowtops, the lighting is via crystal-laden chandelier, you watch flatscreen TVs, and a fancy dream-maker clock radio/iPod station wakes you in the mornings. Although the smaller, cheaper rooms are nowhere near as *au courant* in their appearance or amenities (bye bye flatscreens, though the mattresses are fine), they're white-glove clean and pleasantly decorated with brass beds, white duvets, and framed *Life* magazine covers (the building was erected in 1894 to house the magazine's offices and staff). Small standard rooms with a private bathroom start for as little as $149; singles with private facilities cost just $109; and for a mere $99 a night, year-round, you can score one of the shared bath singles (ask for one with a sink; some have them, some don't). Free Wi-Fi.

$–$$ One short block away, **The Hotel Stanford** ★ (43 W. 32nd St. btwn Fifth Ave. and Broadway; ☎ 800/365-1114 or 212/563-1500; www.hotelstanford.com; **N**, **R**, **Q**, **W**, **B**, **D**, **V**, **F** to 34th St.) attracts a mostly Korean clientele (the hotel's on a block known as "Little Korea" for its abundance of grill-your-own-dinner spots, nail salons, and other Korean businesses). They get a hotel that's a bit plusher than the Red Roof and La Quinta (see below) down the street. The ample rooms here have been fully remodeled in the last two years here to give what I'd consider an Asian view of Colonial elegance—sniffy Ethan Allen–like furnishings but in stronger color schemes than most New Englanders would tolerate. What can be tricky here is dealing with the staff (many of whom speak only minimal English), and finding the right rate. I've seen it vary by as much as $100 for the same night depending on where you book. Sometimes the rates are best direct with the hotel, sometimes not, so do shop around. If you hit it right, you can get this one for between $149 and $249 a night ($189 pops up a lot). Good luck!

$–$$$ Of slightly lower quality, in my view, are the two Apple Core Hotels that sit opposite one another on West 32nd Street. **La Quinta Inn** ★★ (17 W. 32nd St., Fifth Ave. and Broadway; ☎ 800/567-7720 or 212/736-1600; www.applecore hotels.com; **N**, **R**, **Q**, **W**, **B**, **D**, **V**, **F** to 34th St.; AE, DC, MC, V) and **Red Roof Inn** ★★ (6 W. 32nd St.; ☎ 800/755-3194 or 212/643-7100; subway, credit card info, and website same as La Quinta Inn's), though nominally members of different chains, are twins in the quality of their rooms (just fine) and pricing (which, like the other Apple Cores, ping-pongs more than I'd like). Though both have pleasant lobbies with Art Deco touches (La Quinta's may have the edge as it offers a handy gift shop and bar), the rooms turn neo-Georgian in their design, and are capacious, with floral bedspreads, and curtains and chairs covered with heavy woven fabric of a quality you'd expect to find at a more expensive hotel. Both hotels have free Wi-Fi, Nintendo, and cable; crisp white private bathrooms with full tubs; decent closet space; complimentary breakfast; and good-size cardio workout rooms with TVs. And the prices? Well, if you hit it right you could be paying just $129 a night for your digs, but those same rooms can cost $300 when the city's busy. On average, you'll pay about $209, it seems.

$$–$$$ The neighborhood is also home to that old budget standby, **Hotel Wolcott** (4 W. 31st St., just steps from Fifth Ave.; ☎ 212/268-2900; www. wolcott.com; **N**, **R**, **Q**, **W**, **B**, **D**, **V**, **F** to 34th St.; AE, MC, V), where they're discounting majorly, but won't admit it (according to the front desk, double rooms start at $180/night). But I've discovered that the hotel works with such extreme discounters as **Hostelworld.com** (used primarily by backpackers) and through that site you can often get a room with two twin beds for as little as $90–$140 a night, even during busy periods. Here, even more so than usual, it's

Bidding Blind for Big Savings

It's not necessary to give up entirely on hotels with high-thread-count sheets and legions of uniformed attendants at your beck and call, just because you're a budget traveler. Those who "bid" for travel on such sites as Priceline.com and Hotwire.com are often rewarded with some of the swankest digs in town, for prices that are 50% to 70% below the published rates. How do I know? Because I periodically troll Biddingfortravel.com, a site where ordinary travelers spill the beans about what they bid on Priceline and which hotels they got. And the same hotels do tend to come up over and over. I created a spreadsheet of bids for the last 12 months and found that the following hotels come up most often, with prices ranging from just $100 a night up to $250 at the busiest times of the year. **Please note:** Star ratings and locations listed are Priceline's designation and not mine:

- **The Hotel Wellington** (871 Seventh Ave.; ☎ 212/347-3900; www. wellingtonhotel.com). A 2.5-star choice under "Midtown West" it's located near Carnegie Hall. Rooms are dated in looks and can occasionally be noisy. But the location's nice and the rooms tidy.
- **Holiday Inn Express Fifth Avenue** (15 West 45th St.; ☎ 800/465-4329; www.ichotelsgroup.com). The second-most likely 2.5-star bid in the Midtown West area, it has rooms that are compact but cute, with LCD TVs and soft beds. Free breakfast included in the rate.
- **The Paramount Hotel** (235 W. 46th St.; ☎ 212/764-5500; www.nyc paramount.com). The usual 3-star win in the Times Square/Midtown West ain't much of a win, as the rooms are painfully small. To avoid it, go either 2.5-star or 4-star when making your bids in this area.
- **The Benjamin Hotel** (125 E. 50th St.; ☎ 212/715-2500; www.the benjamin.com). Its claim to fame is its pillow menu, which allows sleepers to choose from about a dozen different varieties before bedtime. The dull cream-on-cream color scheme and the size of the rooms puts the lie to its status as a deluxe hotel (I think). However, all rooms do have fridges and microwaves, which come in handy. This will go as a 4-star choice in Midtown East.
- **The Hudson Hotel** (356 W. 58th St.; ☎ 212/554-6000; www.hudson hotel.com). Trendy decor and a happening lobby bar don't quite make up for the fact that rooms here are miniscule. I'm assuming that's

imperative that you shop around and play all the angles. As for the rooms, they're a bit Dickensian in looks, for all the good and bad that implies. Some rooms have nice period touches such as high ceilings with intricate plaster designs (the building was erected in 1904); others are swathed in dreary, mud-colored wallpaper, made even more dingy looking by light-trapping, wall-facing windows. Other disappointments: Beds are a bit hard for my taste, and though the rooms vary wildly why it ain't filling up and is going frequently as the 3-star get on the Upper West Side and Upper Midtown West/Central Park South areas.

* **Grand Hyatt** (109 E. 42nd St.; ☎ 212/883-1234; www.grandnewyork. hyatt.com). Rooms are very, very nice here, decorated in rich colors with fab beds and lots of space. My only guess as to why this is going so often on the bidding sites (as a 4-star pick for Midtown East) is the massive number of rooms here and the crazy-making location right next to crowded Grand Central Station.

* **Millennium Broadway** (145 W. 44th St.; ☎ 212/768-0064; www. millenniumhotels.com). I can only assume that the huge number of rooms here is why this Midtown West 4-star choice (Priceline's designation) is on the chopping block because the digs here are drop-dead gorgeous, with a decor that recalls the hotel's Singaporean roots and great views from the upper floors.

* **Barclay Intercontinental** (111 E. 48th. St.; ☎ 212/755-5900; www. ichotelgroup.com). Built by the Vanderbilts as a mixed-use facility— some apartments for their execs, some clubs, some businesses—you never know quite what size or shape room you're going to get, which may be why the business set may be avoiding it. The gym's miniscule, too, though the lobby is one of the grandest spaces in Manhattan.

Strategy is extremely important when bidding on Priceline.com. My advice would be to get reservations at a non-Priceline or Hotwire hotel you can stomach (a backup meant to be cancelled if one of the opaque services obtains a better hotel). Then start your bidding about 2 to 3 weeks before arrival (as that's when most hotels cave in and give their unsold rooms to Priceline and Hotwire). Get the lay of the land on what the going prices are, at a site such as Kayak.com, and then bid a good 50%–70% less than that, including only one area in your initial bid. If you're rejected, add another area and go up a bit in price.

Important note: If your bid is accepted, your credit card will be charged and you will not be able to cancel the hotel for which you've bid. So this is not a method for those given to second guessing themselves. As well, you'll usually only get standard rooms (though at chichi hotels), so if you're looking for an upgrade, these ain't the sites for you.

in size, those in the same category are priced identically, so you could end up paying a premium for a closet-sized room. I do have to say, though, that the lobby is one of the most impressively bizarre of any budget hotel, with its giant columns, fake Louis XIV plasterwork, and bilious green and pink walls, all installed by the architect who designed Grant's tomb.

MIDTOWN WEST: NEAR COLUMBUS CIRCLE

This section of Midtown, close to Carnegie Hall and the Time Warner Center, is a short walk north of Times Square. Its proximity to Central Park makes this a pleasant area to lodge, though it's primarily a business district, meaning many local stores are shuttered over the weekend and restaurants can get mighty crowded at lunchtime. Drawbacks aside, a number of subway lines service the area, and Fifth Avenue's best window-shopping is just a stroll away.

$–$$ When I was making my first visit to the **Park Savoy** ★★ (158 W. 58th St., btwn Sixth and Seventh aves.; ☎ 212/245-5755; www.parksavoyhotel.com; Ⓝ, Ⓡ, Ⓠ to 57th St.; AE, MC, V) for this guidebook, I met another guest who figured out what I was doing there (I guess not that many guests wander around taking notes). He told me, with a disconcerting grin, that he was in town because his sister had died, but that he "couldn't be happier with the hotel." It seemed an odd time to be happy about anything, but I could see why he was pleased: The location is prime, just 1 block off the Park behind the much pricier hotels that line Central Park South. And the rooms, while unpretentious and small—in a room with just one double bed, I measured a mere 1½ feet between the bed and the wall—were neat and well-tended, some offering desk, dresser, cable TV, and fridge. The staff is gracious and the price *so* right at just $145 to $155 for a room with one double bed and private bathroom (depending on season), and between $115 and $155 for much larger digs with two beds and a private bathroom. My only quibbles with the place are the beds, which were overly firm for my taste (though not lumpy), and the color scheme which involves a lot of orange and dyed green wood furniture, kind of like what you'd see in a teenage boy's room, or a diner.

$–$$$$ Speaking of diners, the **Da Vinci Hotel** (244 W. 56th St., btwn Broadway and Eighth Ave.; ☎ 212/489-4100; www.davincihotel.com; Ⓝ, Ⓡ, Ⓠ to 57th St., or Ⓘ, Ⓐ, Ⓒ, Ⓑ, Ⓓ to Columbus Circle; AE, MC, V) shares its awning and building with a bustling Italian one (same owners) which can make it hard to spot. And in some ways, the hotel feels like an afterthought to the restaurant: Some rooms are renovated in soothing tans, with upgraded TVs and beds, while others look a bit "Bates Motel"-ish with grungy carpeting, ugly hunter green bedspreads, and rock-hard beds. And prices change more often than the daily pasta special at the eatery below. In the months of January and February, for example, a room with one queen-size bed ranges anywhere from $99 to $149 a night, sometimes surging up for one night within the week before dropping down again the next night. Rooms with two doubles during this period go from $139 to $169. In more popular months, like October a one-bed room could cost anywhere between $169 and $269, with two-bed digs going for between $199 and $319 (ouch). My advice: Get a guarantee that you're going to be in a newly renovated room before you book, and only accept that room if the price is right. If not, there are better values elsewhere in the city.

MIDTOWN EAST

For a quieter but still central location, the area east of Fifth Avenue (but not too far east, as you want to be near a subway) may be a good alternative to the bustle and buzz that is the West 30s, 40s, and 50s. The downside to this elegant district is that it can be a bit dull, but good transportation options can whisk you away in an instant.

$–$$$$ Visiting **Hotel 31** (120 E. 31st St., off Lexington Ave.; ☎ 212/685-3060; www.hotel31.com; ❻ to 33rd St.; AE, DC, MC, V) is déjà vu all over again for me (to quote Yogi Berra), as it's a near replica of its sister hotel, from the unimaginative name (that one's the Hotel 17, because it's on, you guessed it, 17th St.) to the winding, dimly lit hallways and cramped lobby. As at the "17," "31" has a somewhat Victorian look and rooms that are all shapes and sizes (so ask to move if you're not happy with the first choice). Rooms with a shared bath start at $89 per night in January and February, but the desk clerk once let me in on a little secret: At that time of year, such companies as Expedia and Hotels.com get these same rooms for just $70 and mark them up to $80. If you offer $70 during a slow period, your "bid" just may be accepted. But don't try that during September or October when the United Nations rents out almost the entire hotel; rooms are at a premium then and through the Christmas holidays, with these very basic lodgings going for as much as $150; rooms with private bath range from $140 to $200.

$–$$$ Right around the corner from Hotel 31 is the **Ramada Inn Eastside** ★ (161 Lexington Ave., btwn 31st and 30th sts.; ☎ 800/567-7720 or 212/545-1800; www.ramada.com; ❻ to 33rd St.; AE, DC, MC, V), the least expensive of the Apple Core chain hotels. Although its rates won't drop below $89 a night—the lowest deep-winter rate for a standard double—they usually go for about $10 less than the Super 8 Times Square, La Quinta, Red Roof, or Days Inn (see earlier in this chapter) because of the Ramada's less-popular location and lack of a concierge. Expect to pay an average of $169 per night here, though prices can drop and rise further. Like the other Apple Core hotels, room rates include a hearty continental breakfast and use of an on-site gym (this one's particularly small, with just a treadmill, a step-machine, and a stationary bike). Rooms are simple and clean, but of a good size, with such nice extras as two phones in some rooms, state-of-the-art mattresses ($2,000 "spa" mattresses from Posturepedic) and Nintendo games on the TVs. The bathrooms, like the guest rooms, are mid-size and spotless.

$–$$$$ **The Pod Hotel** ★★ 🧒 (230 E. 51st St., off Third Ave.; ☎ 800/742-5945 or 212/355-0300; www.thepodhotel.com; ❻ to 50th St.; AE, DC, MC, V) is one of the most unusual of New York's affordable hotels, a shotgun wedding of high style with low prices. The rooms have a very Scandinavian look, with clean-lined light wood and brushed metal furnishings, fine modern prints on the walls, and such non-budget touches as flatscreen TVs, free Wi-Fi, CD players, and iPod recharging stations in each room. Most of the rooms are pretty small—combining and enlarging them would have forced the owners to raise prices—and some still do share a bathroom, but even these negatives don't detract too much. The designer has done a bang-up job of making smart use of the space, building dressers into the bases of the beds, for example, or attaching small TVs at each level of the bunk beds. Beds are swathed in brightly-colored, sofalike covers so that they can be used as couches during the day. Single rooms with shared bath range from $99 to $129 per night, doubles with shared facilities are $129 to

$169; small double rooms with shower and toilet (and you can't be shy in these rooms, as the shower is behind a glass wall that looks directly into the bedroom) go for between $179 and $229 a night, and larger queen-bed rooms with more private facilities are $229 to $279 a night.

$–$$$ Murray Hill Inn ★ (143 E. 30th St. btwn Lexington and Third aves.; ☎ 212/683-6900; www.nyinns.com; ❻ to 33rd St.; AE, MC, V) is not nearly as stylish as the Pod, but it's comfortable, well-maintained, and affordable. Here most of the rooms have sleek hardwood floors, snazzy newly tiled bathrooms, and satellite TVs that get about 60 different stations. The simplest of rooms, with somewhat old-fashioned furnishings, are the wee doubles with full-size beds that go for between $99 and $159 per night; slightly larger doubles are $10 more. There are also chic new "superior" rooms with flatscreen TVs, neo-Shaker dark wood furniture, swirling gold bedspreads and again, brand-new bathrooms. These go for between $139 and $149 in January and February (the higher prices are for weekend stays), and $179 and $189 in the popular fall months. Two small doubles on the property that share a bathroom go for just $79 to $89 year-round. Prices include a coupon for a continental breakfast at a nearby deli. Sometimes such sites as Hotels.com and Expedia offer the best rates, so surf the Web first. **One warning:** There are steps up into the main lobby and more steps leading to many of the guest rooms, so if you have limited mobility, this probably is not a good choice.

CHELSEA

One of the most sought-after residential areas in the city, Chelsea has an unusually large number of friendly small guesthouses, places that go out of their way to create a homey atmosphere for visitors. It's also a good choice for art lovers who wish to be near the gallery scene, and people who want to go to the all-out parties in the clubs and bars of this area or its offshoot, the trendy Meat-Packing District.

$$–$$$ The cheapest lodging option in this area is a gay guesthouse (that's open to and welcoming of all), called the **Colonial House Inn** ★ (318 W. 22nd St., btwn Eighth and Ninth aves.; ☎ 800/689-3779 or 212/243-9669; www. colonialhouseinn.com; ❹, ❺, ❻ to 14th St.; MC, V). It boasts an ideal location along a lovely and quiet tree-lined street. Although the rooms are teeny-tiny, even for NYC, they are tidy and snug, decorated entirely in white, and filled with late owner Mel Cheren's colorful, sometimes commanding, sometimes simply quirky paintings (look for pieces in the hallway that are lit by black lights). Economy and standard rooms ($110 and $130 a night) share a shower and toilet (only a few steps away) but have their own sinks. The larger deluxe rooms have private loos, and some even have a fireplace (Duraflame logs only); they cost $160 a night. Rates cover an expanded continental breakfast that includes freshly baked muffins served between 7am and noon in the pleasant lobby-cum-art gallery-cum Internet cafe (there's a high-speed Internet kiosk in one corner). There's also a nice roof deck with a clothing-optional section for those who take their tanning seriously.

$–$$$$ A similar alternative, without the gay roots, is the **Chelsea Inn** ★ (46 W. 17th St., near Fifth Ave.; ☎ 800/640-6469 or 212/645-8989; www.chelseainn.com;

Ⓞ, Ⓝ, Ⓡ, Ⓛ, ④, ⑤, ⑥, Ⓛ to Union Sq.; AE, DC, MC, V), which straddles the border between two great neighborhoods, the Flatiron District and Chelsea. Like the Chelsea Lodge (see below), many rooms have shared bathrooms (though at the Chelsea Inn, no more than two rooms share a toilet); and also like it, this one has a homey, friendly ambience, thanks to a decor of mismatched antique bedsteads, old wooden armoires, gracefully swooping curtains, and patchwork quilts on the firm beds—kind of like what you'd find in the home of an elderly aunt. Rates, which include continental breakfast at the small deli in the basement, start at just $89 a night in July, January, and February, peaking at $149, for the bathless rooms. Studio rooms with private facilities range from $129 to $179 during these periods, whereas a lovely two-room suite, big enough for a family and including a kitchenette, goes for between $189 and $259. Another nice touch: All rooms have small fridges and coffeemakers.

$–$$$$ What do you get when you cross a traditional Greek Revival town house with a Midwestern hunting and fishing cabin? The result might be very close to what you find at the refreshingly original **Chelsea Lodge** ★★★ (318 W. 20th St., near Eighth Ave.; ☎ 800/373-1116 or 212/243-4499; www.chelsea lodge.com; Ⓔ, Ⓒ to 23rd St; AE, DC, MC, V): an exceptionally well-kept and whimsical guesthouse in the heart of the neighborhood whose name it bears. The only downside here is that, with the exception of four suite/apartments, guest rooms have only showers and sinks, with guests sharing toilets, one for every four rooms. But that seems like a small inconvenience for lodgings this charming and friendly. There's a down-home feel here, to be sure, with mounted swordfish and goose decoys overhanging the check-in desk, and brightly colored busts of Native Americans presiding over the stairs. Looking down from the walls are original hand-colored portraits of heaven-knows-who, giving that instant feeling of a family home, which is continued in the guest rooms with their gingham wallpaper, and Hershey kisses on each pillow. Rooms come equipped with free Wi-Fi, usable desks, and flatscreen cable TVs. Nightly cost is $119 for single travelers, $129 for two—year-round. Deluxe suites, some in the building, others down the block, come with their own bathrooms, kitchenette, and TV with DVD, and are $229 single or double.

$–$$$ A few doorways down from the artsy if pricey Chelsea Hotel is a hotel that is its opposite in every way imaginable, **Chelsea Savoy Hotel** ★ (204 W. 23rd St., off Seventh Ave; ☎ 866/929-9353 or 212/929-9353; www.chelseasavoynyc. com; Ⓐ, Ⓔ, Ⓒ to 23rd St.; AE, DC, MC, V). Where the Chelsea Hotel is quirky and art-filled, the Savoy is bland and standard (the decor is so unimaginative, you'll forget what your room looks like the moment you walk out the door). Its beds are a bit hard, its staff even harder (they're not unpleasant, just exceptionally brusque). But unlike its neighbor, the Savoy's prices are down to earth, with coffin-size single rooms (yes, they're mighty small, but serviceable with private bathrooms) starting at just $99 during slow times, and peaking at $145; and well-proportioned doubles, again with private bathrooms, going from $125 to about $185 during really busy times (up to $295 over holiday periods). There are also quads from $145. A fridge and safe are in each room. My advice: Stay at the Savoy, but go hang out in the lobby of the Chelsea Hotel to take in the hipster vibe.

$$–$$$ The most welcoming hotel in the Chelsea area (and one of the friend-liest in Manhattan), **Chelsea Pines Inn** ★★★ (317 W. 14th St. near Eighth Ave.; ☎ 212/929-1023; www.chelseapinesinn.org; Ⓐ, Ⓔ, Ⓒ to 14th St.; AE, DC, MC, V) is owned and run by Jay Lesiger, a native Brooklynite who seems bent on dis-pelling the myth that New Yorkers are cold and unfriendly. Jay bends over back-wards to make sure guests enjoy their visit; along with personally baking a different loaf of bread for each morning's breakfast (it's served amidst an ample spread of bagels, fruits, and cereals), he and his staff publish a daily newsletter for guests covering walking tours, concerts, and other events happening that day. Jay also serves as concierge and is happy to make dinner reservations (he's worked out a 10% discount at some of the best local restaurants), book limousines, and get theater tickets, for which he takes no commission whatsoever (in fact, he scours the Web for cheaper seats for his guests). He and his partner opened the guest-house in 1985 when it was a run-down boarding house. To hide the scarred walls (since renovated), Jay covered them with his large collection of movie posters, and the tradition stuck: Now each room is named after a different star and filled with movie memorabilia. Rooms are painted in soothing beiges and are larger than most NYC hotel digs, each with a small fridge, TV, safe, and phone. Beds are firm, comfortable, and topped with 300-thread-count sheets; and each front-fac-ing room comes with a white-noise machine to block out street sounds. Deluxe rooms have queen-size beds (and sometimes daybeds), as well as their own bath-rooms, and cost between $169 and $279 depending on the season (deep winter is cheapest). Each economy room has its own shower and sink but shares a toilet (one for every two rooms); they cost between $129 and $179. I'd recommend a room on the second or third floor, where the ceilings are higher. *One final note:* Though 70% of the guests at Chelsea Pines are gay, everyone is made to feel com-fortable here, and I highly recommend this hotel for people of all orientations. It's a genuinely special place.

UNION SQUARE, THE FLATIRON DISTRICT & GRAMERCY PARK

While not as picturesque as the Village (except for the streets directly abutting Gramercy Park), this is an exciting area for visitors, filled with top-notch restau-rants and lively bars and clubs. Despite the bustle, the side streets where most of the hotels are tend to be quiet and calm.

$–$$ Here is what has to be one of the simplest, plainest hotels in Manhattan (and proof positive that having a Madison Avenue address is no guarantee of posh digs). The **Madison Hotel** (62 Madison Ave., corner of 27th St.; ☎ 800/9-MADISON or 212/532-7373; www.madison-hotel.com; Ⓖ to 28th St.; AE, DC, MC, V) is bare-bones to the extreme, with thin sheets on the beds and the cheapest types of industrial rugs and furnishings. But someone here takes pride in the place because the mattresses are good; and there's not a frayed bit of carpet to be found, nor a speck of dust, nor even a shoe mark against the bottom of a door. Prices are admirable as well at just $138 for a small double with private bathroom, $150 for larger digs, and $163 for a room with two double beds. (All of these rates include breakfast next door at the Bun Tikki Deli; January and February rates are 20% lower.) Rooms boast cable TV, phones, and air-conditioning. People with limited mobility should note that there's usually a step up into the bathroom that may make some of the rooms unusable—ask for a room that's all on one level. Though the lobby is forbidding, with the staff behind a wall of bullet-proof glass, the clientele on my visit seemed utterly respectable—mostly European tourists for whom "simple" doesn't translate as "scary."

$–$$ My award for most improved hotel goes to the **Union Square Inn** ★ (209 E. 14th St. just off Third Ave.; ☎ 212/614-0500; www.unionsquareinn.com; ❶ to Third Ave. or ❹, ❺, ❻, ❼, ❽, ❾ to Union Sq; AE, MC, V). In fact, I didn't even include it in the first edition of this guide because the idea of getting my bare feet anywhere near the mildewed tiles in the bathrooms or the grungy guest room carpets made my skin crawl. A thorough renovation, however, has removed the rugs (replacing them with shiny red wood floors), retiled the bathrooms, and added natty new furniture throughout, including much better quality mattresses. There's not much they could do about the room size, which still tends to be tight (though I've seen much smaller); and unfortunately they haven't replaced the staff (who tend to be a bit gruff). But at these prices ($99–$159 for rooms with one queen bed, $159–$189 for rooms with two double beds) in this terrific location, near some of the best restaurants and nightlife in the city, the improvements earn them placement in this guide and one star. All rooms have private bathrooms here.

$ Though its location is quite posh, right down the block from the only private park in Manhattan and the multi-million-dollar apartments and town houses that surround it, the **Hotel 17** ★ (255 E. 17th St., near Third Ave.; ☎ 212/475-2845; www.hotel17ny.com; ❶ to 3rd Ave., or ❹, ❺, ❻, ❼, ❽, ❾ to Union Sq.; MC, V) has a hostel-like vibe, attracting an ever-changing cast of European and Australian backpackers (though there are no dorm rooms here). What attracts these budgeteers are dignified, Victorian-looking lodgings (but with modern mattresses, safes, and clock radios) and reasonable prices: Rooms with shared bath go for between $99 and $150, those with private start at $140 and go to $190. It's also a good pick for claustrophobics—the ceilings are higher than the norm; many of the guest rooms feature bay windows; and the triple rooms are positively huge, with room for two king-size beds, though currently they only house a double and a twin-size bed. For a preview of the hotel, rent Woody Allen's *Manhattan Murder Mystery* (Allen gets caught in the hotel's elevator in that flick).

$$–$$$ The **Hotel Grand Union** (34 E. 32nd St., btwn Madison and Park aves.; ☎ 212/683-5890; www.hotelgrandunion.com; ❻ to 33rd St.; AE, DC, MC, V) is an older property that's nonetheless well preserved, each medium-size room done up in dignified blues, grays, and plums, with a fridge, desk, small closet area, and tidy bathroom. Though the rooms don't get much sunlight and the beds don't have much give, they'll be fine for those who like to sleep late on extra-firm mattresses. My only complaint would be the fluorescent lighting, but at just $110 a night (in Jan and Feb) for a room with a private bathroom, who am I to complain (prices go to $155 in Mar, $165 Apr-Sept, and $175 the rest of the year)? The published rates for twin bed and triple rooms range from $135 to $215 and quads from $160 to $255, but you can usually bargain the manager down $20 to $30 or so (give it a try).

A Surreal Stay in the Artful Apple

"I always tell the guests that if you ask us a question that starts with the words 'Do you have . . . ' the answer is always 'No,'" grins John Ogren, the droll, friendly manager of the **Carlton Arms Hotel** (160 E. 25th St. off Third Ave.; ☎ 212/679-0680; www.carltonarms.com; ❻ to 23rd St.; MC, V). "Because, let's face it, our rooms don't have phones or TVs, nor do we have room service, an elevator, Wi-Fi, or any of that other stuff."

Doesn't sound like much of an endorsement, right? Well, I'll start off by saying that this is not a place for everyone. If you get worried when you notice that your room is listing a bit to the right, if you expect a maid to change your sheets daily, if you prefer a hotel with more than two phone lines (yes, you'll sometimes get a busy signal when you call), then this is not the hotel for you. But if you're the type who wants to try something really new, or who finds the idea of being cocooned in art interesting, then choose this 160-year-old hotel with the soul of William Blake in all of its wacky, joyous excess.

Over the years, the Carlton has invited artists to paint murals and create unusual environments in their guest rooms, which many have done with wild glee. There's the Egyptian Hallway, with mummy portraits of each of the staff members; the Japanese Room, with its elaborate dragons and Buddhas; and the Goth Room, where "she-male" portraits leer down at the occupants. While other hotels have taken the same tack—using art to try and camouflage a small or older room—none have done so with this level of abandon and success. It's a real looker, and some of the artfully painted rooms reach museum level in their artistry.

The Carlton Arms is also now the cheapest in this 'hood, with double rooms with private facilities going for a low $130 year-round and singles for $110. There are also triple rooms at $155 and quads for $180. Those on very tight budgets can choose a room with shared bathroom and pay just $80 for a single, $110 double, $130 triple.

One final note: Like many hotels in NYC, the Carlton has upgraded some of its amenities in the last year, and now boasts all new bathrooms in many of the rooms, as well as darn good mattresses throughout (a welcome change!). So take any reviews you read on user-generated sites with a grain of salt.

$–$$$ Hotel Deauville ★★ (103 E. 29th St., just off Park Ave.; ☎ 800/333-8843 or 212/683-0990; www.hoteldeauville.com; ❻ to 33rd St.; AE, DC, MC, V), another tidy tourist-class property, has really turned around since 2002, when current owner Mel Frielich took over. Before then, the elderly owners had let a number of problems fester (worn carpeting, hot water problems, a faulty reservations service), but Frielich has been slowly but surely working through these issues and now the property boasts cushy new carpeting throughout, steady water pressure, and humble but extremely clean rooms with good-quality mattresses (not too hard, not too soft). The building was erected around 1912 as a luxury apartment building; consequently, rooms are of all different sizes, but most have a tad more space than their competitors do, with gloriously high ceilings to boot. Furnishings tend to be mismatched but serviceable; each room has a fridge and microwave. I'm giving the Deauville two stars for its solicitous staff, who really go beyond the call of duty to make their guests comfortable (when I first visited, one of the front desk clerks was sewing a button onto a guest's jacket for him). Interestingly enough, the hotel has become a favorite of jazz musicians and it's not unusual to get a little concert in the afternoon when guests are practicing for an evening's performance. Rates vary widely by room type; small doubles with private bathrooms go for $139 to $169 a night in winter and spring, up to $189 September through December. Larger, queen-bed rooms go for $20 to $30 more. Two-room suites are also available and boast kitchenettes ($189–$289). Rooms with numbers ending in "03" have large windows and lovely views of the street, but no private facilities. These bathless doubles can range from $89 a night up to $119. (Ask to be housed on the third floor, which is where the facilities are; guests on other floors must use the stairs or elevators to get to the loo.) Free Wi-Fi.

$–$$$$ From the outside, the **Gershwin Hotel** ★ (7 E. 27th St., btwn Madison and Fifth aves.; ☎ 212/545-8000; www.gershwinhotel.com; **N**, **R** to 28th St.; AE, DC, MC, V) looks like an extension of the Museum of Sex next door, with huge Plexiglas and metal appendages thrusting upward in a most provocative manner from this 100-year-old Beaux Arts building. They are just the first trumpetings of a hotel infatuated with pop art; not only are many walls covered with silk screens and paintings, but many of the guests are artists and musicians (everyone who plays at Joe's Pub stays here), and there's even a resident artist program to help struggling would-be-Warhols. What the Carlton (see above) is to Dalí-esque experiential art, the Gershwin is to those who find beauty in a can of Campbell's Soup. The hotel has a number of different types of guest rooms, from dorm rooms ($34 for a stay in a 10-bed room, $44 per person in a 6-bed) to small, colorful doubles with private facilities ($109–$129, year-round with the higher rates for weekend stays) to larger doubles ($155–$300) and pricey suites. In all the rooms with private facilities, the mattresses are firm, the walls thick, and the housekeeping top-notch. The dorm rooms are also clean, though reports have it that they can get a bit rowdy—a carryover from the raucous on-site bar.

GREENWICH VILLAGE

The legendary haunt of artists and writers, full of history, quaint town houses, and tree-lined streets, "the Village" is another of those New York neighborhoods I can heartily recommend, one that can guarantee your enjoyment of a New York stay. Very few New Yorkers can afford an apartment in Greenwich Village, so if you get a chance to stay here, jump at it. This is simply a lovely, lovely neighborhood of period homes, wonderful restaurants, and neighborly residents.

$–$$ Location, location, location. Those are the key elements that **The Larchmont Hotel** ★★ (27 W. 11th St., btwn Fifth and Sixth aves; ☎ 212/989-9333; www.larchmonthotel.com; **A**, **E**, **C**, **B**, **D**, **F** to W. 4th St.; AE, MC, V) offers in spades, as it's situated on one of the prettiest tree-lined streets in the

Village, a block of historic brownstones just a short stroll from top dining, shopping, and the subway. What the Larchmont doesn't have (because the hotel is housed in a Beaux Arts–era brownstone without the plumbing or structure to support it) are private bathrooms and showers for the guest rooms. Instead, travelers share two toilets and two showers per floor (with either 6 or 7 rooms per floor). Should this keep you from choosing this hotel for your stay? I hope not because other than the fact that you have to pad down the hallway to use the facilities, this is a charming, extremely well-maintained hotel in which the owners have striven to keep the period feel throughout, filling the rooms with rattan furniture, bookshelves brimming with hardcover books, and good firm beds. There are also some very high-class amenities here, such as portable sacks of really nice soaps and shampoos, cotton robes and slippers, and high-speed Internet access. Room rates are $89 to $115 for admittedly small single rooms, $109 to $135 for double-bed digs, and $129 to $145 for a lovely and spacious queen-bed room with a view of the street (the higher rates are on weekends). In winter, the hotel often offers a fourth-night free promotion; always check the website before booking, as it sometimes offers $10- to $20-a-night discounts. Rates include a quality continental breakfast.

$ In 1912 when the survivors of the Titanic landed in New York, many stayed at the hotel that is now **The Jane** ✦ (114 Jane Street at the West Side Highway; ☎ 212/924-6700; www.thejanenyc.com; AE, DC, MC, V). It seems appropriate therefore that most of The Jane's rooms don't resemble hotel rooms at all, but highly compact ships' cabin. How small? When I was standing in one, I spread out my arms and came within about 5 inches of touching both walls at once. They're shareable, but just barely. Another oddity here: Half of the hotel's 200 rooms are occupied by long-term tenants, some of whom have been here for a good 30 years and therefore pay just $5 a night for the privilege of sharing bathrooms with hotel guests. (The $99 rooms all share bathrooms; larger rooms will have private ones. They were still being renovated when I visited and prices weren't yet set). To take off the sting, The Jane's partners (who are also behind such trendy, ultra-pricey hotels as The Maritime and the Bowery) are giving these doll-house-size rooms every luxury they can cram in: The walls are paneled with burnished anigre wood, a marble counter at the window doubles as a tiny desk with an iPod docking station, and a flat screen TV is attached to the wall. Two bars—one on the roof and one in a massive, first floor lounge area—promise to become real scenester haunts. Eventually, the basement will have a working pool and saunas, a rare treat in NYC. The final perk: free Wi-Fi.

TWO REASONABLE SPLURGES

$$$–$$$$ Another Village beauty, this time with private facilities, **Incentra Village House** ✦✦✦ (32 Eighth Ave. near Jane St.; ☎ 212/206-0007; www. incentravillage.com; Ⓐ, Ⓔ, Ⓒ to 14th St.; AE, MC, V) is actually three small former one-family homes that have been divided up into guest apartments. Each guest room has its own doorbell from the street, and all but two have working fireplaces and full kitchens (I know of no other hotel in New York with both of these amenities). Rates favor single travelers, with all of the rooms but two starting at $169 per night for solos. When two vacationers inhabit that same room, the rate leaps to $219; triple occupancy is $249; and four people are charged

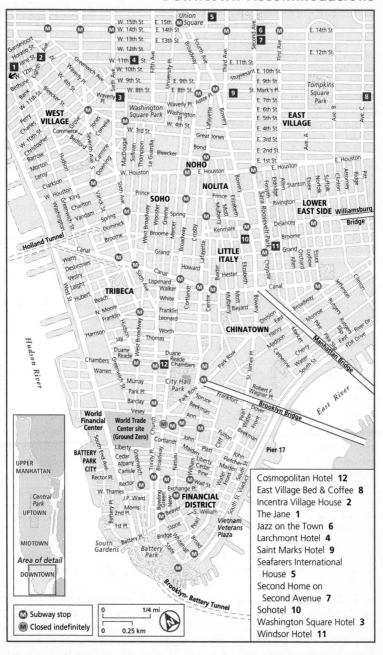

Cosmopolitan Hotel **12**
East Village Bed & Coffee **8**
Incentra Village House **2**
The Jane **1**
Jazz on the Town **6**
Larchmont Hotel **4**
Saint Marks Hotel **9**
Seafarers International House **5**
Second Home on Second Avenue **7**
Sohotel **10**
Washington Square Hotel **3**
Windsor Hotel **11**

Ⓜ Subway stop
Ⓜ Closed indefinitely

0   1/4 mi
0   0.25 km

$279. The larger rooms—one of which is a split-level suite, the other has the only access in the house to the willow-tree shaded garden out back—cost about $30 more. I wish the prices didn't increase so sharply, but I have to say, since these digs have full kitchens, savings can be made on meals. And they're very nice: All are large and sunny, filled with period furniture (brass beds in some, four-posters in others) and caring touches such as rocking chairs, cable TV, free Wi-Fi, and a grand piano for the guests' use in the communal and very Victorian parlor. Two of the rooms are on the ground level, good for travelers with disabilities; the others require that you climb some steps (there's no elevator). You're also doing a lot of good by staying here: Founder Gaylord J. Hoftieser died of AIDS in 1994; his trust runs the place and donates the proceeds to AIDS research.

$$$–$$$$ The **Washington Square Hotel** ✦✦ (103 Waverly Place at MacDougal St.; ☎ 800/222-0418 or 212/777-9515; www.washingtonsquarehotel. com; Ⓐ, Ⓒ, Ⓔ, Ⓑ, Ⓓ, Ⓕ to W. 4th St.; AE, DC, MC, V), has always had a top location, right off graceful Washington Square Park, but today has a decor to match, filled with Art Deco touches and paintings, murals, and photos that pay homage to the many stars who stayed in this historic hotel. Built in 1904, it served as a second home for many top vaudeville and Broadway performers until the '50s, when it devolved into a rather seedy apartment hotel housing a number of struggling artists, actors, and musicians including Joan Baez, Bob Dylan, Barbara Streisand, Bill Cosby, and Phyllis Diller. Legend has it that the Mamas and the Papas wrote "California Dreamin" on a gray winter day at the Washington Square. Nightly rates don't seem to change much by season (unusual), with air-shaft facing singles going for $205, and slightly larger doubles for $235. The rooms, though small, are well-designed with cushy duvets, richly jeweled colored walls, and space-saving features (such as the wall-mounted TV) that make the rooms appear slightly bigger than they actually are.

EAST VILLAGE & LOWER EAST SIDE

Welcome now to Bohemia, where the median age on the street (if not in the apartments) is 27; where a new music club or lounge/restaurant seems to sprout each week; and where works of art constantly appear on street corners and lampposts. The hotels of this area are just as quirky; you won't find any Marriotts or Westins! With rare exceptions, the lodgings are small and possess an "attitude," lacking such amenities as room service and gyms; they make up for those missing features with odd, whimsical murals on staircases or owners who will chat with you for 20 minutes about local restaurants.

$–$$ And that advice-giving hotelier, in case you were wondering, is Carlos Delfin, the dashing Peruvian émigré who owns **Second Home on Second Avenue** ✦✦ (221 Second Ave., btwn 13th and 14th sts.; ☎ 212/677-3161; www. secondhomesecondavenue.com; Ⓞ, Ⓖ, Ⓒ, Ⓝ, Ⓡ to Union Sq., or Ⓛ to Third Ave.; AE, MC, V). He's the heart and soul of this place and has taste that I envy (though I'm proud to say that he picked the same shower curtains I did for his bathrooms). Each room has a theme—either modern, Peruvian, Caribbean, or tribal—but these are subtly carried out. Guest rooms are not only well-sized and comfortable but are also filled with bold and interesting pieces of art—many created by his father—and well-made and unusual furniture (such as a bed with plumbing joints artfully incorporated into the frame). There are two classes of rooms. Those that share a bathroom are, of course, cheaper at $105 to $125 per night, depending on how many share the room. Two suites, which go for $190 to $210 a night, can sleep up to six and do have private facilities. ***Note:*** As the guesthouse is part of a 19th-century home, it's a two-story-climb to get to the first floor of rooms. Delfin also rents out a nearby apartment; ask.

$–$$ Ann Erdris, ex-wife of East Village hotelier Carlos Delfin (see above), runs the area's second top bargain, **East Village Bed & Coffee** ✮ (110 Ave. C, off 9th St.; ☎ 212/533-4175; www.bedandcoffee.com; no nearby subway stop; AE, DC, MC, V), which was actually the former couple's first hotel and has many of the same touches as Delfin's more expensive Second Home (again, see above): It's a walk-up, guest rooms share a bathroom, and rooms are "themed," though the decor is even more whimsical here. Pick the "French Room," for example, and you'll be sleeping on Eiffel Tower sheets and surrounded by walls speckled with Impressionist prints. The "Mexico room" contains all the colors of a Frida Kahlo painting; the "flying" room has model airplanes floating from the sky-blue and fluffy white-clouded ceiling. Each of the two floors has four bedrooms, which share a bathroom, a kitchen (stocked with coffee, tea, and condiments), and a small living room, which has a phone, a computer, and a TV (with DVD). There's also a small garden in back and four bikes that Anne lends to guests, free of charge. Rooms range from $105 to $120 for a single, $120 to $140 for a double, more for triples and quads. Like Carlos, Anne is an attentive, knowledgeable, and interesting host (you can see how they'd be a couple). The only downside to staying here is the lack of a nearby subway stop; still, the walk to transportation is an interesting one, past community gardens just bursting with wildflowers, and bustling, chic restaurants and bars. Free Wi-Fi.

$$ In the very heart of the East Village, **Saint Mark's Hotel** ✮ (2 St. Mark's Place, right off Third Ave.; ☎ 212/674-0100; www.stmarkshotel.net; ❻ to Astor Place, or ❶, ❷, ❸, ❹ to 8th St; cash only.) used to be a well-known "hot sheets" operation. It has since cleaned up its act and decor, offering tasteful double rooms with private bathroom with shower (no tub) for $140 a night year-round; rooms with two twins are $160 and two double beds (sleeping up to four) go for $170. Rooms have a streamlined, modern beige on white look, but beds can alternately be too hard or too soft (like the princess and the pea, you may have to try a few mattresses before finding one that suits your sensibilities). Ask for a room in the back, as St. Mark's Place is the East Village's premier party place, with bars, tattoo parlors, street vendors, and T-shirt shops; it can get quite loud.

CHINATOWN

New York's Chinatown is the real thing, not a set piece for visitors. It's long been a vibrant immigrant neighborhood and you're as likely to hear Cantonese on the streets here as English. Along with the many grungy hotels geared towards new arrivals from Asia are two more pleasant options:

$–$$$$ One of the oldest hotels in the city (built in 1822), **Sohotel** ✮ (341 Broome St. near Bowery; ☎ 800/737-0702 or 212/226-1482; www.thesohotel. com; ❸, ❹ to Grand St; AE, DC, MC, V) housed Union soldiers during the Civil

War. They probably wouldn't recognize it today—in fact, people who visited just two years ago wouldn't recognize it, as the hotel's been inputting some major improvements. Flatscreen TVs and handsome bureaus now grace rooms; walls are chic exposed brick or painted a handsome shade of green. There are some lapses still, especially in the mattress department: If you get a stony one, ask to be moved (they vary by room). Also ask for another room if you're placed in one ending in the numbers 21, 23 or 25 as these overlook a popular bar and can be noisy. But in general, the standard of service and comfort has changed for the better. Unusually, the hotel charges by the room, not by the number of people occupying it, so if you really need to save money, know that you can pack these rooms (all of which have private bath) for not a penny extra. Rooms with one double bed go for $119 to $179 (depending on season), those with two double beds are $129 to $209, and quite large three-bed rooms are $139 to $219. *Warning:* This is not the place for people with mobility impairments as there are steps to the lobby and many of the rooms.

$$–$$$$ Deeper into Chinatown, the **Windsor Hotel** ✸ (198 Forsythe St. btwn Grand and Broome Sts; ☎ 212/226-3009; www.windsorhotelinc.com; ❶, ❷ to Grand St.; AE, DC, MC, V) is as generic as they come, surprising for such an exotic neighborhood (around the corner are two incense-scented Buddhist Temples). I'm not saying it's not pleasant. In fact, the hotel has a few touches, like free Wi-Fi and slippers, that put it a notch above most budget lodgings. I just wish there was something, well, a bit more Chinese about the place. Standard doubles start at $155 but can jump to $198 pretty easily and up to $208 during peak times. Rooms with two double beds go for $10 more, and deluxe doubles are an additional $20 to $30 over the base rate. But the Windsor often discounts quite deeply with Quikbook.com, so check there first before booking.

TRIBECA

In TriBeCa rates drop rather than rise over the weekends, as the hotels in these quarters tend to host businesspeople almost exclusively; they're working in the nearby Financial District. TriBeCa is more of a residential neighborhood and quite appealing, with dramatic cast-iron buildings, top restaurants, and many posh stores.

$$ George Washington never slept here, but the staff at **Hotel Cosmopolitan** ✸✸ (95 W. Broadway, at the corner of Chambers St.; ☎ 888/895-9400 or 212/566-1900; www.cosmohotel.com; ❶ to Chambers St.; AE, MC, V) swear that Abraham Lincoln did, back when the building was Hotel Girard. Built in the 1840s, it's always been a hotel of some sort or another, and the Lilliputian dimensions of some of the cheaper rooms reflect how much smaller people were back then. Despite the cramped quarters, the Cosmopolitan is a value, on the northern edge of exclusive TriBeCa on a corner that's lively during the day but fairly quiet at night (important, as all rooms face one of two major thoroughfares). A crack housekeeping staff keeps the place extremely tidy; no frayed carpets, no telltale signs of the last guest; you won't even see scuff marks on the walls. The cheapest choices, at $135 to $210 a night, are odd "duplexes," minuscule rooms that place the beds up near the ceiling in a loft to better utilize the space. For $10 more, you

Upper West Side & Harlem Accommodations

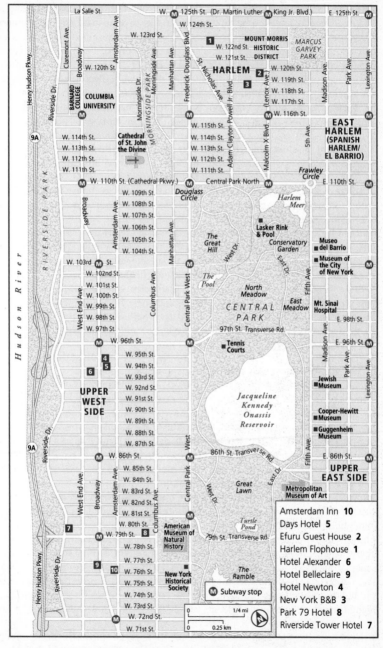

Amsterdam Inn **10**
Days Hotel **5**
Efuru Guest House **2**
Harlem Flophouse **1**
Hotel Alexander **6**
Hotel Belleclaire **9**
Hotel Newton **4**
New York B&B **3**
Park 79 Hotel **8**
Riverside Tower Hotel **7**

can sleep on the same level as the cable TV set. There are other configurations as well, at different price levels; happily they charge by the room, not by the number of people, so groups can score.

SEINFELD TERRITORY: THE UPPER WEST SIDE

Family-oriented, near Central Park, and highly residential, this is another top area for visitors. The Upper West Side is well served by seven subway lines (❶, ❷, ❸, Ⓐ, Ⓒ, Ⓑ, Ⓓ), making it a snap to get from here to any other area of the city (though you'll have to take a crosstown bus to get to the Upper East Side).

$ Looking very much like the Columbia University dorm building it was not so long ago the **Riverside Tower Hotel** ✰ (80 Riverside Dr. at 80th St.; ☎ 800/724-3136 or 212/877-5200; www.riversidetowerhotel.com; ❶ to 79th St.; AE, DC, MC, V) offers very basic accommodations . . . but with a smile and a dust mop held high (rooms are quite clean and the staff kindly). Each guest room comes equipped with a small fridge and microwave oven; those on the higher floors have panoramic Hudson River views. But I don't want to whitewash the place as it won't suit everyone: Rooms are miniscule, their private bathrooms even more so, and the carpeting is a tad grungy. But if you're just looking for an affordable place to sleep between the theater and museum visits the next morn, it's hard to do better especially because this hotel—Hallelujah!—doesn't play poker with its room rates. Singles cost $114 year round, doubles are $119, and there are "suites" (really just two small rooms, each with a bed, connected by a bathroom), that go for $129 to $149, depending on how many guests they'll be housing. All rooms have private bathrooms with showers, no tubs.

$–$$ **Amsterdam Inn** ✰ (340 Amsterdam Ave. at 76th St.; ☎ 212/579-7500; www.nyinns.com; ❶, ❷, ❸ to 72nd St; AE, DC, MC, V) is the third of the NY Hotel Group's properties, and its spotless rooms are the equivalent of what you'd find at its sister properties, the Murray Hill Inn (p. 42) and the Union Square Inn (p. 45). Most of the rooms feature smooth-to-the-touch polished wood floors, neo-Shaker furniture, and newly tiled bathrooms. Deluxe queen-bed rooms, which contain microwave and fridge, range from $139 to $169 a night year-round; without the cooking corner, these rooms go for $109 to $139. There are also smaller, less stylish rooms (older furniture and mattresses) with shared bathrooms at $89 to $99. As with the other inns in this group, the rate includes a coupon for breakfast (at neighborhood fave, the Bagel Café). Interestingly enough, the Amsterdam Inn has worked out a $10-a-day workout deal with the plush Equinox gym nearby; at the fancier hotels in the 'hood, the daily Equinox charge is $25. *Two warnings:* The lobby is up a flight of very steep stairs, and many of the rooms include additional stairs (so those with mobility issues should stay elsewhere). This also isn't the one to pick if you're a late sleeper: adjacent to the building is a massive construction site, and I very much doubt the building being erected will be finished before mid-2009.

$–$$$$ As plain as a monk's robe but not quite as stylish, the **Hotel Alexander** (309 W. 94th St.; ☎ 212/665-0003; www.hotelalexandernyc.com; ❶, ❷, ❸ to 96th St.; AE, MC, V) is where you stay when you want to be in this neighborhood, and the other choices in this chapter are booked. I'm not saying it's bad—the beds are serviceable (though covered with plastic, which I hate) and rooms are clean, if worn. But it's far from a first choice. Rates range from $79 per night double with shared bath in low season (up to $179 in high season); to $129 to $149 for a room with a private bath and either one or two beds ($234 in high).

$–$$$$ Somehow, in its changeover from a Quality Inn to the **Days Hotel Broadway** ⋆ (215 W. 94th St., right off Broadway; ☎ 800/DAYS-INN or 212/866-6400; www.daysinn.com; **❶**, **❷**, **❸** to 96th St.; AE, DC, MC, V), it got Edwardian pretensions, filling its lobby with fake leather books and nailed-down, faux Grecian busts. You see a tiny hint of this mind-set in the guest rooms as well, with their brightly patterned bedspreads and elegantly shaded (though still nailed-down) lamps. They're a good size as are their closets and bathrooms. As at so many places, prices vary wildly, sometimes starting as low as $89 even during high season. On weekends during holiday times, the rate for a standard room can peak at $249, but in general you won't pay more than $190 for a night here. The key is to hit the hotel when it doesn't have a massive group of Europeans in residence (it works with the tour company "Explore America" to fill many of its rooms).

$–$$$$ Just around the corner, directly on Broadway, **Hotel Newton** ⋆⋆ (2528 Broadway; ☎ 800/643-5553 or 212/678-6500; www.newyorkhotel.com; **❶**, **❷**, **❸** to 96th St. AE, DC, MC, V), is literally "coming up roses," thanks to a peachy new color scheme, flatscreen TVs, and handsome red wood furnishings that have given guests rooms a much posher look than they used to have. Rooms with one queen-size bed can drop as low as $95 a night (an excellent value for lodgings with private facilities), but you're more likely to pay between $150 and $180, depending on the season, with rates peaking at $250 during holiday periods. Single rooms are about 20% cheaper. Along with more expensive "superior" rooms and suites, two rooms per floor share a bathroom; these go for $85 to $160 depending on the date. (*Hint:* Ask for a 3rd-floor shared bathroom as there's only one room on that floor without private bath, meaning you get de facto private facilities, though they're down the hall.)

$–$$$$ Budget-conscious travelers who enjoy a dash of style with their savings can't do better than **Hotel Belleclaire** ⋆⋆ 🄺🄸🄳🅂 (250 W. 77th St., on the corner of Broadway; ☎ 877/HOTELBC or 212/362-7700; www.hotelbelleclaire.com; **❶**, **❷**, **❸** to 72nd St.; AE, MC, V) in this area, though for truly budget digs, they'll have to accept a room without private facilities ($129–$200, ask for an 07 line room as these are larger). Still, these are among the loveliest rooms I've seen anywhere, averaging a generous 350 square feet with excellent quality mattresses, fluffy duvets, chic ultra-suede backboards, CD players, tidy little sinks, bureaus, and usable closets. There are three of these rooms per floor, and they're set off in their own little section, sharing one bathroom, with another door closing them off from the hallway (and thus making them perfect for large families or groups of five or six). The rate for rooms with private bathrooms increases sharply to between $169 to $399 for a queen-bed room, about $10 more for rooms with two double beds, and even more for two-room suites. Ask for a room in the back of the hotel and on a higher floor for great views of the Hudson River. The hotel also has a well-equipped gym and 24-hour room service.

$$–$$$$ Location is the big lure at **Park 79** (117 W. 79th St. off Columbus Ave.; ☎ 866/3-PARK-79 or 212/787-3300; www.park79hotel.com; ❸,❻ to 81st St.; AE, DC, MC, V), which literally sits in the shadow of the Museum of Natural History, a 5-minute walk from Central Park. I also like the comfy touches here like cushy duvet covers for the beds, 25-inch flatscreen, satellite TVs, and fridges in each room. And the staff is just as sweet as pecan pie. The negatives? The building was once an SRO—a single room occupancy hotel for homeless people—so rooms can be tiny. Doubles with shared bath (and they only share with one other room) go for between $85 and $129 a night. Doubles with private facilities can hop from $115 to $229 all the way up to $319 (go for those ending in number 11 or 12 as these are twice the size of the regular doubles at the same rate). But the manager may play ball especially if you tell her you're visiting someone who lives in the 'hood (they give a 10% discount to local guests), so do try and bargain.

UPPER EAST SIDE

You'll pay more to stay in this area of town, and if your hotel's near the park, you'll shell out more not only for your room, but at local diners, drugstores, and grocery stores. Still, the Upper East Side has its allure, with its trim, effortlessly chic Madison Avenue moms; its soldierlike doormen along Park Avenue, each charged with guarding the homes of the wealthiest families in the U.S.; and, of course, its museums, which are the finest in this hemisphere. Because affordable lodgings are so few and far between, I've found only one hotel that I can recommend in good conscience (look into apartment and private B&Bs at the beginning of this chapter for more options in this area).

$$$$ **Gracie Inn** ✪ (502 E. 81st St. just off York Ave.; ☎ 800/101-2252 or 212/628-1700; www.thegracieinn.com; ❻ to 79th St.; AE, DC, MC, V), takes its name from the mayor's official residence (Gracie Mansion) nearby. It has the look of a New England country inn, all lace curtains and flowered wallpapers. It's a bit of a splurge, but some factors keep the costs here within the budget ballpark. First off, each room comes equipped with a fully serviceable kitchen, though if you don't feel like cooking, a deluxe continental breakfast of fruits, muffins, pastries, and croissants is provided. And in a very guest-friendly move, the hotel charges by the room, not by the number of guests, so a one-bedroom unit, which actually holds two beds (one queen and one double) costs no more for four people than it does for two, and could comfortably hold the four, with closets and flatscreen TVs in each room. Other room amenities include free Wi-Fi and a CD player. One-bedroom units start at $199 in low season, but usually go for $235; studios $149 to $189.

HARLEM

No neighborhood in New York has made such a complete turnaround in the last 3 decades as Harlem. Where there once were abandoned buildings, there are now million-dollar brownstones; where crack dealers and their customers once haggled, there are Starbucks and Mac cosmetic stores; and where gangs once terrorized the populace, Bill Clinton looks down benignly from his top-floor office on 125th Street. Yes, there still are certain areas of Harlem that can be a bit dodgy (particularly East Harlem), but for the most part this friendly, historic area—especially the section where the hotels below are located—is as safe and as welcoming as any other area of Manhattan.

$ The oldest guesthouse in Harlem, **New York B&B** (134, 140, and 239 W. 119th St., near Malcolm X Blvd.; ☎ 212/666-0559; ❷, ❸ to 116th St.; AE, DC, MC, V) is also the cheapest. Chatty, helpful owner Giselle Allard has a mini-empire going with five separate brownstones catering to travelers on extremely low budgets (private rooms with shared bathrooms cost $100 double, $90 single year-round; dorm accommodations run $25 a night). The Lenox property has a fully equipped kitchen for guests to use; they also have access to the laundry facilities at the Malcolm X Boulevard building. That being said, these guesthouses are showing their age. The buildings, all turn-of-the-20th-century family homes, have lovely period details—molding, elaborate stair rails, high ceilings, and windows—but are about 5 years overdue for a paint job, and each room is filled with a chaotic assortment of thrift-store furniture. I will give Ms. Allard credit for investing in the most important object in any hotel: the mattresses. These are all good quality, ensuring that those who do stay here will get a solid night's sleep. Her next outlay needs to be for air conditioners: Currently they can only be found on the top floors (so ask for one of those rooms if you plan to visit in summer). *One final note:* No breakfast served, despite the name.

$–$$ For a classier introduction to the neighborhood, choose **Harlem Flop House** ✪✪ (242 W. 123rd St., btwn Frederick Douglass and Adam Clayton Powell blvds.; ☎ 212/662-0678; www.harlemflophouse.com; ❷, ❸ to 125th St.; MC, V), an 1870s row house that was a famous flophouse in the 1920s, patronized by numerous top musicians and artists of that era. With that history in mind, owner Renée Calvo has restored the house to what it might have looked like before the stock market crashed, dotting the rooms with found objects such as antique radios, lamps shaped like penguins, and Victorian furnishings and wallpapers, which are often artfully ripped in spots so that visitors can see the old wallpaper or wooden details underneath. The four rooms are tremendously comfy, over-sized, and airy, with large, lace-curtained windows, bureaus, desks, flatscreen cable TVs, free Wi-Fi, and sinks. Each pair shares an artistically tiled bathroom (one with skylight) as well as a verdant, overgrown garden out back where Renee often invites guests in summer to an impromptu barbecue. There's a precinct at the end of the block, to assuage the fears of visitors who still might be wary of lodging this far uptown. The only negative to staying here, that I can detect, is the lack of air-conditioning; other than that, this is a terrific year-round deal at about $125 most of the year (prices drop to $100 in the deep winter and summer months, and hit $140 in Sept, Oct, Nov, and Dec). Preference is given to guests staying a week or more, though it is possible to book 3- or 4-night stays as well.

$–$$ Though not nearly as charming, **Efuru Guesthouse** ✪ (106 W. 120th St. btwn Malcolm X and Adam Clayton Powell boulevards.; ☎ 212/961-9855; www. efuruguesthouse.com; ❷, ❸ to 125th St; MC, V) makes up for its somewhat generic though brightly colored medium-size rooms with its excellent pricing: A double room with private bathroom and kitchenette goes for between $105 and $150 a night (June–Dec for the priciest rates); those that share a bathroom are a reasonable $85 to $105 a night. There are other nice extras here as well, including a lovely private garden off one of the guest rooms; use of the large, fully equipped kitchen; a private entrance for guests (everyone gets his or her own set of keys); and high-grade beds, cable TV, and free Wi-Fi. Because there are only five guest rooms, call at least 2 months ahead, 6 months for holiday periods.

BROOKLYN & QUEENS

In the first edition of this book, I was able to confine my recommendations for lodgings to the borough of Manhattan. That policy seemed (back then) to make sense, as Manhattan is where the majority of visitor attractions are. With the steep increase in prices in the last 2 years, I've been forced widen my net. I did, however, decide to limit my additional choices to Brooklyn and Queens, as these boroughs boast important museums and historical sights in their own rights, as well as terrific restaurants, bars, and other neighborhood attractions that should make them appealing to visitors. Though low-cost lodgings also exist in nearby New Jersey, as well as in the Bronx and Staten Island, these latter areas simply don't have enough attractions, good eats, and well, oomph, to make them lodging-worthy (I think; so sue me!).

Because I realize that most readers will still likely be spending the majority of their time in Manhattan, I've only covered lodgings that are near subway lines, so that visitors won't have to add the unnecessary expense of a rental car. At the end of each listing is the estimated time from the hotel into Manhattan via subway, so you can best weigh convenience against cost.

BROOKLYN

$–$$ What a difference a borough makes! Had the **Sofia Inn** ✪✪✪ (288 Park Place; ☎ 917/865-7428; www.brooklynbedandbreakfast.net; ❷, ❸ to Grand Army Plaza or ❸, ❹ to Seventh Ave.; MC, V) been located in Manhattan, it would be one of the most celebrated and exclusive little inns on the island, and its asking price would top $300 a night, I have little doubt. But since it's in Brooklyn, this charmer comes in at just $115 to $125 for a room with shared bath, and $165 to $175 for a massive suite with kitchen and lovely balcony overlooking a garden (there's a table there for al fresco dining). Owner Billy Tashman was a public school math teacher (he's a very sweet guy) and managed to salvage massive posters from the 1950s of such topics as "Symbiosis" and "Evolution"; these give each room a quirky beauty, which is further enhanced by the antique chandeliers, carved wooden bedframes, and lovely armchairs he and his designer bought mostly from Craigslist (they truly are bargain shoppers par extraordinaire). Those rooms that don't get a full kitchen have microwaves and small fridges. And here's the clincher: The fridges are filled upon arrival with sodas and beers, all free for the taking. Now that's hospitality! The Sofia's set in a 1901 brownstone on a leafy street near Prospect Park and has free Wi-Fi throughout. 25 minutes to Times Square.

$–$$ Ten years ago, the neighborhood of **Spencer Place B&B** ✪ (15 Spencer Place; ☎ 718/360-9227; www.spencerplacebedandbreakfast.com; ❸, ❺ to Franklin Ave. or ❹ to Nostrand Ave.; AE, DC, MC, V) defined the word "iffy." But with the arrival of hundreds of Senegalese and Sudanese immigrants, the drug dealers have

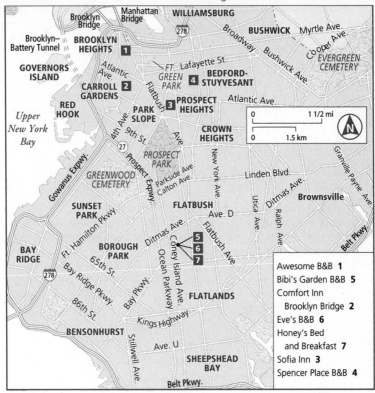

been pushed out and the streets have become calm. So I have no worries about sending you to this gracious, welcoming B&B today, which is run by two really cool TV producers. They live in the basement with their young son; guests have the run of the main 1870s house, which is filled with lovely moldings, 10-foot ceilings, and original gas light fixtures (electrified now, of course). Three of the four rooms here are quite small, but guests don't have to spend all of their time in them: A tiny living room with computer and TV is open to all, as is a kitchen. Teeny weeniest of the rooms go for $75 to $85 a night; the larger ones are $125 to $140, with a 10% discount for stays of a week or more. All have Internet access and share bathrooms. An organic breakfast is included in the rate. 45 minutes to Times Square.

$$–$$$ "This B&B is a mistake I made that's lasted 10 years," laughed Carl Wilson of **Awesome B&B** (136 Lawrence St.; ☎ 718/858-4859; www.awesome-bed-and-breakfast.com; **A**, **C**, **F**, **M**, **N**, **R**, **W**, **2**, **3**, **4**, **5** to Borough Hall; AE, MC, V), when we last met. He was joking of course; he and his wife LeAnne Iverson, a jewelry designer, have lovingly labored over the place, giving each room a signature look, which can range from Madagascar-esque to cozy beach house. It all has a creatively homespun quality to it, a bit hippieish, a bit jazzy (in fact, there's always jazz playing in the hallway). Guests here are mostly European.

Brooklyn's B&B Street: Westminster Avenue

Around 1905, a speculator named John Corbin bought up a vast tract of farmland in Brooklyn. Convinced that the nearby Park Slope area was becoming overcrowded, he contracted with a local firm to premake dozens of wood frame houses in the Queen Anne and Colonial Revival–styles. Parts for these homes were shipped to the former farm fields of Midwood, Brooklyn and almost overnight, a new, middle-class neighborhood was born.

It still exists today, its gracious wooden homes a surprising contrast to the apartment buildings and brownstones that dominate the rest of the city. And because these homes are so spacious, a cottage B&B industry has sprung up. Of the many in the 'hood, I have three favorites, all on the same street:

$ Eve's Bed and Breakfast ✶ (751 Westminster Rd.; ☎ 347/256-2577; ⓞ, Ⓑ to Newkirk; AE, MC, V). Chandeliers, Wedgewood china blue–walls, framed Renior prints: You know from the moment you walk in that Eve has a regal sensibility. It's sometimes a bit oddball (some of the chandeliers are of the blocky '60s variety, a CD rack is in the shape of a guitar), but that doesn't detract from the fact that a stay here is a terrific bargain: $90 to $120 covers an entire apartment (there are four on offer here), so no sharing bathrooms, there's a kitchen to use, and an extended continental breakfast is included in the cost. The only downside—some find the service here to be a bit indifferent. 38 minutes to Times Square.

$ Opposite in every way (it's even on the opposite side of the street), Honey's Bed and Breakfast ✶✶✶ (770 Westminster Rd.; ☎ 917/873-9493; www.honeysbedandbreakfast.com; ⓞ, Ⓑ to Newkirk; MC, V accepted,

"They get our vibe," says Carl. The house is set on a bustling commercial block in Brooklyn Heights, just one subway stop from Manhattan. The convenient location may be why it's more expensive than the other two B&Bs I've mentioned; though all its rooms share bathrooms, they go for $140 and $165, up to $200 in high season for the one with kitchenette. However, Carl will give a 6% discount to those who pay in advance and advises that others who book direct through the B&B itself tend to pay between 10% and 20% less than they would through hotel bookers. Children stay free, Wi-Fi is complimentary, and rooms have no TV or phone. 20 minutes to Times Square.

$$ Okay, let's get this out of the way first: Despite its name, our last choice in fair Brooklyn, the Comfort Inn Brooklyn Bridge (279 Butler St. near Third Ave.; ☎ 866/427-6108 or 718/855-9600; www.comfortinnbrooklyn.com; ⓞ, Ⓜ, Ⓝ, Ⓡ, ②, ③, ④, ⑤, Ⓑ, ⓞ to Atlantic Ave; AE, DC, MC, V) is nowhere near the Brooklyn Bridge. In fact, it's smack dab in the center of a neighborhood of graffiti-laden warehouses. This less-than-ideal location (though it's near a great subway stop and a short walk from hopping Park Slope), plus the fact that it's so new (it opened in May of 2007), is keeping the lid on prices. I've seen it go for as little as $115 in

but cash preferred) has a minimum of froufrou and offers the warmest welcome imaginable. "I try to offer a very comfy atmosphere," says owner Laura Berger (the B&B is named for her dog Honey). "I love talking to people and giving them information." And you'll love talking to Berger, who's a dynamic and fascinating person, with a deep knowledge of Brooklyn history (as well as what's on and interesting right now throughout the city). Her home is cheerfully furnished with pretty plates from around the world gracing the walls and a large living room and porch for guests to lounge in. Rooms ($105–$125) are medium-sized, each sharing a bathroom, with pillowtop mattresses and such niceties as bay window, original wood paneling, and stained-glass windows (in places). Every two rooms share one bathroom and a usable kitchen. She has one other tiny room that she rents only occasionally ($95). Free Wi-Fi. 38 minutes to Times Square.

$–$$$ Priciest of the three, but still worth recommending, **Bibi's Garden B&B** (762 Westminster Rd.; ☎ 718/434-3119; www.bibisgarden. net; ❷, ❸ to Newkirk; MC, V) takes its cues from the quaint B&Bs of New England. So you're going to find a lot of lace scattered here and there (at the top of dressers, as curtains), as well as antique furnishings and flatscreen TVs. One room has an in-room private bath ($165-$185), another a private bath across the hall ($135–$150), and three with shared bathroom ($120–$130). All have access to two kitchens and living rooms that the guests can use; a full breakfast of eggs or pancakes is included in the cost. 38 minutes to Times Square.

March, about $170 during busier seasons, only occasionally hopping up to $219 when the big ball in Times Square drops (for the most part it seems to stay in the $149–$189 range; check discounters' websites and use your AAA memberships). For those sums you get small but pristine rooms, with comfy decor (think moss green and tan everything) and some nice amenities (sleep-encouraging mattresses, cushion-bottomed trays so that you can peck at your laptop in bed, desks in case you prefer to sit up, and a 24-hour business center if you want to work outside your room). The Inn was custom built, so you don't encounter any of the problems with noise or poor plumbing that you sometimes experience in re-purposed motels. Rooms with two double beds are just large enough for a family of four; there are also king-bed digs. And though the direct area around the Inn is industrial, it's as safe as any of the others mentioned in this chapter. Breakfast included, free Wi-Fi. 25 minutes to Times Square.

QUEENS

$–$$ Because Long Island City is right across the bridge and just one to three subway stops from Manhattan (depending on the address), it's seen an explosion of

Queens Accommodations

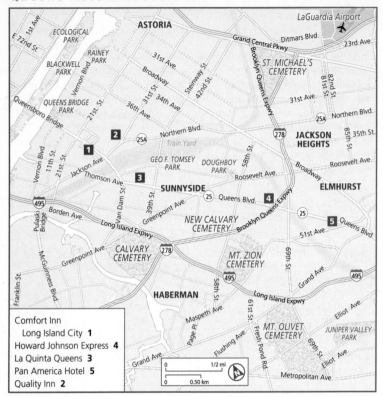

Comfort Inn
  Long Island City **1**
Howard Johnson Express **4**
La Quinta Queens **3**
Pan America Hotel **5**
Quality Inn **2**

motel building just in the last 3 years. Those that are up now are all members of well-respected national chains (Days Inn, Quality Inn, and the like) and have the sleek, uncluttered look that purpose-built corporate properties tend to have, plus such nice amenities as flatscreen TVs, quality mattresses, and usable coffeemakers. Of the three I'm going to recommend in this area, the best is surprisingly also the cheapest, maybe because it's three subway stops from Manhattan, rather than two. But for that extra 7 minutes on the subway—yes, I timed it—you get truly roomy rooms at **La Quinta Queens** ★ (37-18 Queens Blvd.; ☎ 800/531-5900 or 718/729-8775; www.lq.com; ❼ to 33rd St.; AE, DC, MC, V), a good one-third larger than most you'll find in Manhattan or the other Long Island City properties, for that matter. They're given a cheery, warm decorating scheme of yellows and florals, and each room even has an easy chair with a foot rest that pulls out. Prices go from $99 to about $139 for a room with one king-size bed, and about $149 to $169 for a room large enough to house four, with two queen-size beds. Gym, business center, free local phone calls, and Wi-Fi. 18 minutes to Times Square.

$–$$$ The other two Long Island City properties I'll recommend—though not as highly—are the **Comfort Inn Long Island City** (42–24 Crescent St.; ☎ 877/424-6423 or 718/303-3700; www.comfortinn.com; ❿, ⓦ, ❼ to Queensboro Plaza;

AE, DC, MC, V) and the **Quality Inn** (30–03 40th Ave.; ☎ 718/391-0202; www. qualityinn.com; **N**, **W** to 39th Ave.; AE, DC, MC, V). Rooms at both of these are clean but tiny and decorated in unfortunate mudtones. At the Quality Inn, there's no fitness center; at the Comfort Inn, the business center shares its space with the tiny gym, oddly enough (so your e-mails may stink of sweat). Expect prices a good $20 to $40 more per night than at the La Quinta (though occasionally all three will have the same pricing). 14 minutes to Times Square.

One word about Long Island City: It ain't the prettiest place. Given over to industry, it's got the grimy, graffitied look of New York City in the 1970s. The subway is above ground here, too, and all three hotels are quite near it (convenient, but noisy; ask for a room away from the tracks).

$ Farther into Queens, in residential Flushing, you'll get a better picture of the multicultural lifestyle of the borough. That's especially true of the **Howard Johnson Express Inn** (65–09 Queens Blvd.; ☎ 718/426-6200; www.hojo.com; **R**, **V** to 65th St.; AE, DC, MC, V), which serves as an extra bedroom for the Indian ex-pats of this neighborhood. It's here they house their cousins and parents when they come for a visit, and the atmosphere is consequently low-key and friendly. Rooms are a bit older than in the Long Island City motels but are spotless and comfortable. Those with two beds ($109–$119) face the avenue which can get loud (bring earplugs); rooms with one queen bed are in the back ($89–$109) and quite quiet. Each has a fridge and coffeemaker; a bus outside zips to the Queens Center Mall. It's about an 8-minute walk to the subway. 30 minutes to Times Square.

$–$$ My final Queens pick has to have the oddest motto in the boroughs: "New York's Most Convenient Hotel!" trumpets the sign outside the **Pan America Hotel** ✯ (79–00 Queens Blvd., Elmhurst; ☎ 718/466-7676; www.panamhotel newyork.com; **G**, **R**, **V** to Grand Ave.; AE, DC, MC, V). Huh? Convenient to what? The lube shop next door, or the Great Wall Asian grocery store down the street? Yes, the free airport shuttle makes the Pan American convenient for those with early flights, but other than that . . . well, they've got me stumped. So, its location may not be the best for Manhattan touring—it's a good 10-minute walk to the subway, though past interesting ethnic restaurants and shops—but it does have a number of amenities that make it seem less like a budget property than a full-service hotel. I'm talking about room service, bellmen, concierge desk, gift shop, in-hotel restaurant, free use of a fab gym 2 blocks away, and that aforementioned shuttle. Rooms, too, are dignified and spacious with Ethan Allen–esque furnishings. Yet prices start at a reasonable $112 a night in deep winter, rarely nudging past $149 even in high season ($136 seems to be the average here). Free parking. 33 minutes to Times Square.

HOSTELS & LOW-COST SPECIALTY HOTELS
SPECIALTY HOTELS
A number of New York hotels simply aren't for everyone—either because they require a certain mind-set or because they are clubs, meant only to admit certain types of individuals. Because these lodgings have raisons d'être that have

absolutely nothing to do with making money, they can be wonderfully affordable and interesting places to stay.

$ This is particularly true of the **Soldiers', Sailors', Marines' & Airmens' Club** ✦ (283 Lexington Ave., btwn 36th and 37th sts.; ☎ 800/678-8443 or 212/683-4353; www.ssmaclub.org; ❻ to 33rd St.; AE, DC, MC, V), which has a much broader admission policy than you would expect. Not only does it admit veterans and active military (including soldiers and sailors from Allied nations), beginning in 2004 it opened its doors to America's so-called "first responders": firefighters, police officers, and EMS workers. The prices are laughably low; in fact, Executive Director Peter J. Le Beau told me with a resigned smile, "Our costs are always escalating, but we don't raise the prices, so the more people we accommodate, the more we lose." (As you might imagine, much of his time is spent fund-raising. If you'd like to donate to this noble enterprise, go to the website for information.) Enlisted troops in categories E1 to E4 and cadets pay just $30 a night; enlisted men and women E5 and above pay $40 a night; officers and retired military (including widows and widowers) pay between $50 and $60, depending on rank, with children between the ages of 3 and 14 paying $10 per night. For these sums, each person gets one bed, usually in narrow two-, three-, or four-bed rooms (couples and families obviously are housed together) that are simple but pleasant, with framed prints on the walls, pretty curtains, and reasonably comfortable twin-size beds. The only real military touch in the rooms is the use of lockers rather than closets for personal belongings. Rooms do not have private facilities; instead, the men share one bathroom per floor, the women the other. Also shared are the flag-laden lounges (which look like they could have been lifted from the private quarters of the White House), where guests hang out to watch TV or use the Internet.

$–$$ Even more inclusive, **The Seafarers and International House** ✦✦ (123 E. 15th St., just off Irving Place; ☎ 212/677-4800; www.sihnyc.org; ❹, ❺, ❻, ❷, ❽, ❻, ❾, ❶ to Union Sq.; DC, MC, V) has admitted members of the general public since the 1970s. Today about 40% of its guests are merchant marines and other sailors, while 60% of the guests are . . . well, anyone and everyone. There seem to be no real requirements for admission to this Lutheran mission, though you do have to plan ahead, as rooms can sell out up to a year in advance. Why is it so popular? Though the rooms are plainly furnished, they have more of those all-important little touches than you'll find at most budget properties: The linens on the beds are soft; there are extra rolls of toilet paper in the bathrooms; the furniture looks brand new and matches; and each room has a remote control, not only for the TV but also for the air-conditioning—telling, small details that say much about the quality of the upkeep and service here. These extras are all the more remarkable considering that double rooms with private bathrooms go for just $131 and singles with private bathrooms are just $111 year-round. Also offered are shared bathroom singles ($82) and doubles ($102). Though the building is run by the Lutherans and there is a weekly service on premises, there's no real spiritual component to a stay here.

$–$$$ The Village People had it right: Not only is staying at the YMCA not painful, it can be downright fun. That's particularly true if you choose the **West**

Side YMCA (5 West 63rd St. right off Central Park West; ☎ 917/441-8800; www. ymcanyc.org; **Ⓐ**, **Ⓑ**, **Ⓒ**, **Ⓓ**, **❶** to Columbus Circle; AE, MC, V), which is considered a "model" Y and therefore has cushier digs than its brethren. Its renovated rooms (on the 12th and 13th floors) have furnishings as nice, if not nicer, than many of the city's budget hotels—framed prints of classic NY scenes, solid wood furnishings, even almost-stylish comforters and carpets. These go for $161 to $181 a night with private bath, $115 to $120 with shared bath. But even the older rooms, which have more of a hospital-room ambience, are well-maintained and comfortable ($157 with private bath, $92–$120 without). There are no dorm rooms here, though there are larger family rooms available ($147–$180). Million-dollar views of Central Park from many of the rooms make this Y a find, as does the fact that guests have free use of the center's huge pool and marvelous gym facilities (including the various yoga, Pilates, and other workout classes). Along with this Y are two others in Manhattan, two in Brooklyn, and two in Queens.

RELIGIOUS RETREATS

For a religious setting, you'll need turn to one of the numerous retreat houses and church-run guesthouses in New York that offer affordable and dignified accommodations, sometimes only for members of one faith, in other cases for almost anyone who requests shelter.

$–$$ One of the foremost such retreats is **The House of the Redeemer** ★★★ (7 E. 95th St. off Fifth Ave.; ☎ 212/289-0339; www.houseoftheredeemer.org; **❻** to 96th St.; cash only), which was deeded by Edith Shepard Fabbri—a great-granddaughter of Cornelius Vanderbilt—to a board of trustees to create "a place apart" for spiritual contemplation by people of all faiths. This was Fabbri's own house, a palatial Italian-Renaissance mansion with grand stone staircases, coffered ceilings, and entire rooms brought over intact from Italy (the library is one of the great treasures of the city, built in the 1400s for the Ducal Palace of Urbino and shipped through submarine-infested waters to the U.S. during World War I). Guests needing doubles stay in one of the family's five rooms, surrounded by the exquisite artwork and furniture left in the house by the Fabbris. These rooms go for either $110 (with shared bathroom) or $140 (with private facilities). The other eight single rooms ($90 each) are on the servant floors—there were three times as many servants as there were family members—and are simpler and without private bathrooms, but are still quite lovely with lace curtains in the windows, wooden furnishings, and comfortable new beds. In each room are crosses and other pieces of religious art—a purposeful touch, as spirituality plays a key role here. There are morning and afternoon prayer services in the chapel, weekly Bible study sessions and evening meditation classes and, though not mandatory, the retreats for which most guests come here specifically, sometimes in groups that book the entire house (so call well in advance if you're interested in staying here).

$–$$ Although not nearly as posh, **The Leo House** (332 W. 23rd St., btwn Eighth and Ninth aves.; ☎ 800/732-2438 or 212/929-1010; **Ⓔ**, **Ⓒ** to 23rd St.; MC, V) is a decent second choice, operated by the Catholic Church, but with less of an overtly spiritual mission. The house was founded in 1889 by German Catholics to help their countrymen (and co-religionists) find their footing upon arrival in the "New World." Today it accepts travelers of all nationalities and religions—Baptist, Jewish, Animist, you name it—though there are limits to tolerance here. Administered by nuns, the rooms can only be shared by guests with their spouses or children (no "living in sin" or bringing back someone you met in a bar). In a particularly ironic, if not surprising policy, gay couples are not welcome to this, the only retreat center in New York's most flamboyantly gay neighborhood, Chelsea. What does the place look like? Well, to be honest, it looks like it was decorated by nuns, both homey and homely at the same time, with rather hard beds and crosses on every other wall. Still, this 64-room facility is quite affordable, with singles that have toilet and sink but no private shower going for $70 a night, and the same types of doubles for $90. The vast majority of rooms have private facilities, and go for $80 (single), $100 (double), and $160 (family rooms holding four to six single beds). (Rooms numbered 10, 12, or 14 face the back and are quietest.) Rates don't include breakfast, though there's a cafeteria onsite featuring pastries and breads the sisters bake.

HOSTEL OPTIONS

The Upper West Side is chockablock with hostels, most of them above 96th street. That makes them a bit remote from Midtown, though if you walk to 96th and Broadway, the express train can get you to Times Square in 10 minutes flat.

$ Hosteling International New York ★ 🧒 (891 Amsterdam Ave., at the corner of 103rd St.; ☎ 212/932-2300; www.hinewyork.org; ❶ to 103rd St., or ❶, ❷, ❸ to 96th St; AE, DC, MC, V) is a mammoth, bustling operation—the largest hostel in the United States and third largest in the world, with a staggering 624 beds. It's more like a little city than a lodging, albeit a city in which most of the citizens are under 30 and speak 40 different languages. Along with guest rooms it offers an abundance of extras, including a tour desk, a gift shop, a cafe, two game rooms (one with video games, the other with pool tables), a highly usable shared kitchen, laundry facilities, two peaceful outdoor lounging areas, and a large TV lounge and volleyball court (where there are weekly tournaments in summer). For those planning to spend only their sleeping hours here, there are perks as well in the forms of large free lockers in each room, and immoveable, unshakeable, mightily solid bunks with decent mattresses that go for $32 to $40 a night, depending on the time of year. Some dorm rooms are co-ed; others are divided by gender. There are also "family" rooms that are monastery-like in their utter lack of any decoration whatsoever (there's not even a print on the wall) but they are really large and clean as a whistle, with a queen-size bed and a bunk bed for $135 a night (with shared bathroom); $150 with private toilet, sink, and shower.

$ Jazz on the Park (W. 106th St. btwn Manhattan Ave. and Central Park West; ☎ 212/932-1600; www.jazzonthepark.com; ❸, ❹ to 103rd St.; AE, MC, V) is the hipster's hostel, with house music blaring in the art-filled lobby, weekly barbecues in summer ($5), movie and poker nights when the weather's colder, photos of great jazz musicians in the hallways, and a color scheme in the rooms that is taken straight out of the *Wizard of Oz*. Dorm rooms come with two, three, four, five, or six bunk beds, and the numbers on the beds aren't as prominent as they should be (which can lead to some awkward situations come bedtime). Another problem here are the mattresses, which are so thin in many cases that you can feel every ridge and spring; they do vary by bed, so test-drive a couple when you check in. Those reserving private rooms (with shared bathroom only) may go 1 block uptown to the hostel's second building, again a mural-laden, vibrantly colorful place that is generally clean. The cheapest dorm beds are the 10- or 12-bedders for $30 a night, 6- to 8-bed rooms for $32, and 4-bed rooms for $34 (in Jan and Feb, these prices drop by $10). If you're traveling with a friend, it might make the most sense to share a private room at $65 to $90 a night for two twin beds (without private facilities). Rates cover a bagel and a cup of tea or coffee in the morning.

Note: Jazz on the Park has a second and more cramped hostel in the East Village called **Jazz on the Town** (307 E. 14th St. at Second Ave.; ☎ 212/228-2780; **L** to Third Ave.; **4**, **5**, **6**, **N**, **Q**, **R**, **L** to Union Sq.; MC, V), which is a decent choice for those who prefer staying downtown. Prices and amenities are the same, though there are no private rooms.

$ The third choice in the neighborhood, the **Central Park Hostel** (19 W. 103rd St., off Central Park West; ☎ 212/678-0491; www.centralparkhostel.com; **B**, **C** to 103rd St.; MC, V), falls squarely between the first two in terms of upkeep (better than Jazz on the Park, not as good as H.I.) and cool ambience (where it's one up on H.I. thanks to brightly colored walls and a funky lounge area, but well below Jazz's non-stop party). In rooms that house 10, beds go for $28 a night; there are also 8-bedders ($30), 6-bed digs ($32), and 4-bed units ($36). But the best value here may well be the private rooms, which feature good quality beds (actually, mattresses are good throughout), cable TVs, microwaves, and private bathrooms; they start at $119 per night.

A Times Square Hostel

$ The **Big Apple Hostel** ★★ (119 W. 45th St., btwn Broadway and Sixth Ave.; ☎ 212/302-2603; www.bigapplehostel.com; **1**, **2**, **3**, **N**, **Q**, **R**, **S**, **W**, **7** to Times Square; MC, V), a backpacker magnet right in the heart of the Theater District, is the best you'll do in this neighborhood. It's spotless, it's extremely friendly, and it offers guests a number of nice extras, including on-site laundry; a fully-usable kitchen; free Wi-Fi in the lobby (and locked cabinets where you can store your laptop and other valuables); an outdoor deck; and an indoor lounge with PlayStation 2 (at a charge), a TV, and two computers. Rooms hold two bunk beds apiece (so there's less chance of getting a snorer); one bed costs $39 (including tax) except between March 1 and July 31 when it rises to $45. There are also double rooms for $125 to $150, each with its own sink but no shower or toilet; a rack for clothes; and a desk and chairs—the rooms are clean and midsize, if a bit bedraggled (you can find better shared-bathroom accommodations elsewhere).

4

Dining Choices

For all tastes and pocketbooks

ITS COMPETITORS ARE HONG KONG AND PARIS, BRUSSELS AND SAN Francisco, Rome and New Orleans. But I'll argue hard that none of these other great restaurant cities has quite the same number of serious, satisfying eateries as New York, nor its amazing variety of cuisines in every price range . . . and quirk. Would you believe that restaurants serve only mac 'n' cheese or peanut butter concoctions—and flourish doing so?

How did the surprising volume and variety of NY restaurants come about?

- New York has a larger and more varied immigrant population than any of the other foremost restaurant cities—and that means ethnic specialties of every sort;
- New York has an unprecedented number of top-notch cooking schools, the offices of international magazines devoted to the art of cooking, and the headquarters of the Food Channel;
- The pace of life here is more hectic and pressured than in other famous restaurant cities, creating a vast population with "no time to cook."

Mix all these reasons together, sauté them over the bright flame of the city's celebrity, and you have a mecca for foodies, a place where people obsess over the gratification of their taste buds without anyone thinking it odd. In China, one way of saying "hello" is to ask, "Have you eaten?" In Gotham, we say, "Where have you eaten—and do you need a reservation?"

VALUE FOR MONEY SPENT: And it isn't only the costly places that produce expert, inventive cooking. For every renowned New York chef (think Daniel Boulud, Jean George Vorgerichten), there's a young sous-chef furiously chopping shallots while lining up investors to help him open his own little restaurant. And it's at these tiny start-ups—which have been sprouting like morels all over the East Village, the Flatiron District, and the Lower East Side of Manhattan—that you get gourmet fare (sometimes "borrowed" from the recipes of former bosses) at a third to a half less than the price of the snooty, old-guard establishments.

The bargains are even greater at the ethnic restaurants, which are the most vivid outlet for the incredible diversity of cultures and nationalities that make up this city. For nearly a century and a half, New York has been the staging point for gustatory invasions, if you will, of new foods, new techniques of cooking, and new recipes.

Between 1899 and 1910, a vast influx of Italian immigrants brought the first platters of spaghetti to the city (and thus created a staple of the American cuisine ever since). In 1910, Eastern European Jews began arriving in droves with the food most associated with New York City: the humble but proud bagel. (Though, to be fair, a chewier, sweeter version arrived in Montreal at about the same time.) The Greek Civil War in the late 1940s brought waves of Greeks to the city, and they established the first diners, where typical American dishes would eventually be offered side by side with souvlaki, gyros, and spanakopita.

Then, as now, the "ethnics" offered locals a chance to try new foods at prices lower than the conventional American restaurants charged. Today hundreds and hundreds of ethnic restaurants are found in all parts of Manhattan. I know one 5-block area in Midtown where there's a taste-boggling choice of Malaysian food, Greek food, Brazilian empanadas, Peruvian tamales, German sausages, pizza, Thai food, and that Esperanto of cuisine, "fusion." Each restaurant was founded and is currently staffed by immigrants from the country represented (with the exception of the fusion places, because, well . . . where would those people come from?). Best of all, patrons get complete meals, and good ones at that, for less than $15.

> *Small, inexpensive restaurants are the home fires of New York City.*
>
> —Maeve Brennan, *The Long Winded Lady: Notes from the New Yorker*

That said, not all areas of the city are equal when it comes to dining well, and the neighborhoods that attract the most tourists tend to have the highest percentage of bland national chains and the lowest of decent food. So if you accidentally leave this book in your hotel (or, heaven forbid, at home), use the Manhattan equivalent of the "truck-stop rule": Go to the neighborhoods where the locals live, and look for the restaurants with lines out the door. In this way, you'll be doing just what New Yorkers do: Though we hate lines, we rarely patronize restaurants that don't have them.

THE QUEST FOR GOOD MEALS: As elsewhere in this book, I've grouped my selections geographically, starting with the most popular tourist areas (which aren't, I need to repeat, the best areas for tasty cuisine or low prices) and proceeding to the outlying Manhattan areas where, for one reason or another, you may happen to be. My discussion here is limited to the island of Manhattan, but in the index I've included restaurants from other chapters and other boroughs that you may wish to try. And helpful symbols will appear next to the names of my restaurant choices, with dollar signs indicating the general cost of the restaurant:

$: **Main courses for $8 or less**
$$: **Main courses for $9 to $14**
$$$: **Main courses for $15 to $21**
$$$$: **Main courses $22 and over**

and stars for those selections deemed to have special merit:

No stars: Good
★: **Very good**
★★: **Excellent**
★★★: **Not to be missed**

My picks are listed in ascending order of cost, starting with the cheapest, so that you can quickly choose a restaurant charging what you want to pay. If all you crave is a quick bite, start with the opening selections. When you're ripe for something more elaborate, move down the text.

TIMES SQUARE (THE THEATER DISTRICT)

You'll likely be near the Broadway theaters at some point in your stay, and in need of a meal. But this is perhaps the only Manhattan area where good restaurants of skill and dedication are greatly outnumbered by the do-it-by-rote places designed only for tourists. The top selections are pearls in a sea of mediocrity, and it's often important to know where NOT to eat.

Tops on that list are obviously the Olive Gardens, Bubba Gumps, Mickey D's, and Red Lobsters that add to the neon in Times Square. Every time I walk by and see the masses crowding in to one of these places, I have the urge to physically yank these tourists (no actual New Yorker would be caught dead in one of these places) by the elbow, pull them out into the street, and walk them calmly to one of the restaurants below. In a city with multitudes of unique local restaurants, run by the most ambitious and talented chefs in the nation, it absolutely floors me that visitors would even consider eating at a chain they can visit in their own hometown.

Not only do these corporate chains serve mediocre, pre-frozen, highly processed food, they're often more expensive for what you get than at the local eateries. And yet they dominate the major avenues directly facing the alluring neon signs and big screens of the Square itself. If you can drag yourself away from the lights, however, you'll find four really good picks on the side streets right off the square (and a larger number of choices just one and two avenues east and west of the "Great White Way").

$ For a quick but filling bite, the cheapest, well-prepared burger ($3.75) in the Times Square area is had at the **Edison Café** (228 W. 47th St., right off Times Sq.; ☎ 212/840-5000; closes Mon–Sat at 9:30pm, and 6:30pm on Sun; ❶, ❷, ❸, ⓝ, ⓡ, ⓞ, ⓢ to Times Sq.; AE, DC, MC, V), the place that was immortalized in 2001 in "45 Seconds from Broadway," the worst comedy Neil Simon ever wrote (trust me, I suffered through the first act). It's a genuinely weird place—a scruffy diner, complete with fake wood Formica-paneled booths, plopped down in the midst of a grand hall, its vaulted ceilings covered with bas-relief putti and painted bright pink and baby blue. It's also probably the only diner in the city that has a section roped off for VIPs—the Broadway producers, directors, and actors who make this an unofficial clubhouse. Though you can get all the diner standards here, including that perfectly serviceable burger, you may want to stick with the central European specials—luscious blintzes ($7.20) and matzo Brie ($7, a comforting scramble of eggs, onions, and matzo meal)—that give this place its nickname, the "Polish Tearoom."

$–$$ **John's Times Square** ★ kids (260 W. 44th St., btwn Broadway and Eighth Ave.; ☎ 212/391-7560; www.johnspizzerianyc.com; reservations recommended; daily 11:30am–10pm; ❶, ❷, ❸, ⓝ, ⓡ, ⓞ, ⓢ to Times Sq.; AE, DC, MC, V), about a half-block west of Broadway, has the best pizza in the area, served in a soaring, elegant space that was once a church (you can still see the lovely stained-glass windows in places). Like its downtown and uptown cousins (at 278 Bleecker St., in Greenwich Village and 408 E. 64th St.), John's serves only large full pies big enough for two—no slices—so bring an appetite, because these are potently tomatoey, charred, thin-crusted circles of delight (and reasonable at $10 to $14 per pie, more if you want extra toppings). You can also order salads and pastas, but it's the pizza that's exceptional.

$–$$ Ever see that Japanese film, *Tampopo?* The one about the couple who spent their time tramping from one ramen place to another searching for the perfect noodle? I've always fantasized that the hunters in the film might one day leave Japan and end their search just 7 short blocks up from 42nd Street at **Sapporo** ★★ kids (152 W. 49th St., off Seventh Ave.; ☎ 212/869-8972; daily 11am–11pm; ®, ® to 49th St., ❶ to 50th St.; cash only), which certainly has the best Japanese noodles I've ever had (and looks a bit like the ramen shops in the film, crowded with legions of office workers earnestly slurping their soups while chefs manically shout to one another in Japanese behind the wood counter). Portions are sumo-sized: huge, steaming bowls of broth with a tangle of noodles, corn, scallions, and (in the non-vegetarian versions) slices of pork (from $7). Sapporo is a good choice for kids as they'll love slurping the long noodles (just don't order them the *tantan-men,* which is a scrumptious but somewhat spicy sesame soup, $8.60).

$$–$$$ Close to a number of theaters, on the east side of Times Square, **Virgil's Real Barbecue** kids (152 W. 44th St., right off Seventh Ave.; ☎ 212/941-9494; www.virgilsbbq.com; reservations recommended; Mon 11:30am–11pm, Tues–Sat 11:30am–midnight, Sun 11am–11pm; ❶, ❷, ❸, ®, ®, ® to Times Sq.; AE, MC, V) serves up bona fide, South-of-the-Mason-Dixon-Line barbecue smoked for up to 12 hours in a "Southern Pride" smoker. Platters, which come with two side dishes, can easily serve two hungry people (I've never been able to finish one on my own). Ranging from $15 up to $21, they cover all of the classics of 'cue, from Carolina-pulled pork ($17) to sliced Texas beef brisket ($19), and use recipes the owners discovered during a pilgrimage they took across the South before opening up in 1994. You wash it all down with brew from one of the most extensive beer and ale menus in the city, in a checked-oilcloth, bi-level setting that is pure Tennessee. The noise level (high) makes this an ideal place to take the kids, as there's no chance they could disturb anyone here.

WEST OF TIMES SQUARE, ON NINTH AND TENTH AVENUES

$–$$ Having exhausted the possibilities a half-block or less from Times Square, we turn our attention to nearby Ninth and Tenth avenues (a short walk away from the theaters), where dozens of small local eateries offer tasty cuisine from all corners of the globe. One of the best is **Pam Real Thai** ★ (404 W. 49th St., right off Ninth Ave.; ☎ 212/333-7500; Sun–Wed noon–midnight, Thurs–Sat noon–1am; ®, ® to 50th St.; cash only), which supplies—splendidly—what the name of the restaurant promises: real Thai food (a rarity in New York, where sugar too often substitutes for spice). Be careful with your reply when they ask if you want your dinner spicy, because they mean business: The fiery fare will drain your sinuses (in

Midtown, Chelsea, Union Square & Flatiron District Dining

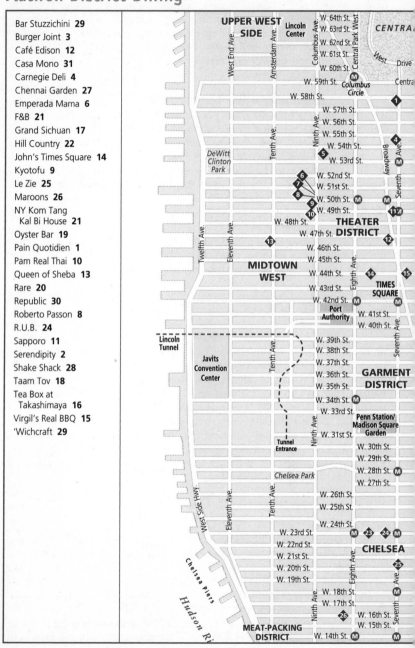

Bar Stuzzichini **29**
Burger Joint **3**
Café Edison **12**
Casa Mono **31**
Carnegie Deli **4**
Chennai Garden **27**
Emperada Mama **6**
F&B **21**
Grand Sichuan **17**
Hill Country **22**
John's Times Square **14**
Kyotofu **9**
Le Zie **25**
Maroons **26**
NY Kom Tang
  Kal Bi House **21**
Oyster Bar **19**
Pain Quotidien **1**
Pam Real Thai **10**
Queen of Sheba **13**
Rare **20**
Republic **30**
Roberto Passon **8**
R.U.B. **24**
Sapporo **11**
Serendipity **2**
Shake Shack **28**
Taam Tov **18**
Tea Box at
  Takashimaya **16**
Virgil's Real BBQ **15**
'Wichcraft **29**

fact, there's a constant symphony of patrons blowing their noses and clearing their throats). But even the most combustible dishes are tremendously flavorful, loaded with fresh vegetables, sweet coconut milk, and complex spices. I usually make a meal of the appetizers, soups, and salads, which are more successful than the curries. Particularly good is the *som tum* ($4.95), a green papaya salad that's big enough for a main dish, and sweet, sour, spicy, and everything in between. Or try the *tom kha gai* soup ($3.75), a creamy lime-and-coconut delight; or the *yums* (meat and seafood salads for $6–$10), which are truly . . . well, yummy. While this isn't a place for a special occasion dinner—the decor's too plain for that—the service is speedy enough for you to eat here before the theater, and get to your seats in time.

$–$$ Not willing to stick with just one national cuisine (as Pam Real has), **Empanada Mama** ✪ (763 Ninth Ave. btwn 51st and 52nd St.; ☎ 212/698-9008; ⦿, ⓔ to 50th St.; daily 11am–midnight; AE, DC, MC, V) takes on the cuisines of all the Latin American nations, and creates some new variations on the theme, as well. A cheeky railroad car–sized place, with pea soup green banquettes, brick walls, and a dance club soundtrack, it attracts a 20- and young 30-something crowd primarily (penny-pinching age groups, certainly). They tend to make a meal of the empanadas ($2–$2.75 each; two will fill you up) and so should you, mixing and matching at will. Standouts among these are the Cuban *pernil* (slow roasted pork), the Brazilian beef (spiced to a T and studded with olives and potatoes), the Greek spinach pie, and believe it or not, the Cheeseburger empanada (with Latin spices that marry well with the gooey American cheese). If you want to go a bit healthier, handsome large salads ($6.95–$7.95) are on offer; if you're ready to party, order up a pitcher of sangria.

$–$$ While its food is too light for a full meal, **Kyotofu** ✪✪ (705 Ninth Ave. btwn 48th and 49th sts.; ☎ 212/974-6012; www.kyotofu-nyc.com; ⦿, ⓔ to 50th St.; Sun and Tues–Wed noon–12:30am, Thurs–Sat noon–1:30am; AE, DC, MC, V) is a swell, and very chic, place to head for a before- or after-theater snack or dessert (it calls itself a "dessert bar"). Almost all the preparations here use tofu in some form (hence the name) and the flexibility of the stuff is pretty astonishing. On the savory side of the menu, you can choose warm simmered tofu ($10), a science experiment of a dish. You're brought a vat of liquid tofu that you add another liquid to and simmer for 10 minutes above a flame. It solidifies and the result is a soothing, delicate stew, with side dishes of wasabi salt and pickles to pep it up. Satisfying too, are the tofu sliders with teriyaki chicken ($8). And unlike many Japanese desserts, those served here aren't too sweet. Dishes like the sweet tofu with black sesame tuile ($7) and chestnut and fig mochi chocolate cake ($10) are instead elegantly composed and quite satisfying. Along with the food, you can indulge in a wide selection of rare sakes (there's even a sparkling one) and an atmosphere that's more trendy lounge than restaurant.

$$ A longish walk west of the Square, on the corner of Tenth Avenue and 46th Street, **Queen of Sheba** ✪ (650 Tenth Ave.; ☎ 212/397-0610; daily 11:30am–11:30pm; ⦿, ⓔ to 50th St.; MC, V) serves up bona fide Ethiopian food. If you've never had that cuisine before, let me tell you it's a real experience. The waiter arrives with a large round platter of *injera* (a spongy, bubbly bread made from fermented

When the Discount's Not Worth It

You gotta know who to trust. NYC & Company, the official tourist board of the city, has a lot of great advice for travelers—but when it comes to restaurants, plug your ears. Among the reams of info they pass out is a "savings guide" listing restaurants that give discounts to tourists. Every one of these establishments is either past its prime . . . or never had one. Use the list to figure out which eateries to avoid; the small savings offered simply won't be worth it. Also ignore any restaurant that hands out fliers in Times Square: There's a reason they have to go to such desperate lengths to advertise.

teff, which is a ryelike grain) upon which are mounded piles of stew. No silverware is supplied; instead, you scoop up the various stews with pieces of the bread, savoring the alternately spicy, sour, and garlicky flavors. Couples or even threesomes can easily share a "Taste of Sheba" combo platter ($17, or $12 vegetarian), which will allow them to sample several beef and ground beef stews, two lamb dishes, and both a spicy and a mild lentil stew. The delicately sweet *gomen wat* ($9.50, collard greens) is a good addition to the plate should you have a larger group (or you could simply do one veggie combo and one meat combo). Be aware that dishes that come with *berbere* sauce have a slow rising heat that will catch up with you.

$$–$$$ For that big night out, the one you get dressed up for and go to the theater, you want a restaurant with seriously gourmet food in an elegant atmosphere near the Great White Way. I'd recommend **Roberto Passon** ★★ (741 Ninth Ave. at 50th St.; ☎ 212/582-5599; www.nycrg.com; reservations recommended; Mon–Fri noon–11:30pm, Sat–Sun 11am–11:30pm; ◉, ◉, ◉, ◉ to 50th St.; AE, DC, MC, V), which is named for the well-known New York restaurateur who has nine other popular, Italian joints in his stable. But none of the rest come close to touching the mastery and warmth of this eponymous eatery. It features the cuisine of Friuli, the area of Italy closest to and most influenced by Austria; thus, the food has a pleasant heaviness that is unusual for Italian food (Friuli is not a region of olive groves, so lard is often used in the cooking instead of olive oil). The massive white asparagus appetizer ($11, share it), for example, comes not only with prosciutto, but with a poached egg perched in the middle of the plate. It's then sprinkled with Parmesan cheese and doused with brown butter, and the richness of the dish is extraordinary. The monkfish is also wrapped in prosciutto ($17), a seductive mix of surf and turf, swimming atop a piquant white wine sauce. The pastas are especially good—and happily cost $2 to $3 less than at other neighborhood restaurants; they range from a simple but perfect spaghetti alla carbonara ($11) to the delightful flat tortellis (a type of pasta) stuffed with herbed goat cheese in a creamy tomato sauce ($12). Even the look of this restaurant is just right, with its floor-to-ceiling windows, its candlelit tables, and its racks and racks of wine bottles giving the whole enterprise the air of abundance and comfort. Try it also for lunch: a 3-course prix fixe here is just $13.

EAST OF TIMES SQUARE, FROM BROADWAY TO FIFTH AVENUE

$ In New York's famed "Diamond District" (the countless diamond merchants on 47th St., between Fifth and Sixth aves.), a number of kosher eateries serve a large population of Hasidic Jewish jewelers who staff and often own the stores here. The best of these is also the most hidden, **Taam Tov** (41 W. 47th St., btwn Fifth and Sixth aves., on the third floor; ☎ 212/768-8001; www.nytaamtov.com; Mon–Fri 10am–5pm; ❸, ❹, ❻ to Rockefeller Center), which you enter through an unmarked door, and up two flights of stairs. The cuisine here is Uzbekistani—bet you never thought you'd be trying *that* when you came to the Big Apple—and it's very simple, flavorful fare, reminiscent of what you'd find at a Middle Eastern restaurant, with a dash of deli thrown in for good measure. There are heaping fresh salads ($3); skewers of well-spiced lamb, chicken, or beef kebabs ($2.99 including a side dish); stuffed cabbage ($6.99); meat- and carrot-laden rice pilafs ($5.99); and soups like Grandma used to make, with as much chunky veggies and meats as broth ($3.99). On each table is a homemade hot sauce which is more tomatoey than spicy and should be used generously. Taam Tov itself is a plain-looking place, with plastic tablecloths, framed prints on the wall, and a small balcony for outdoor dining (it's heated in winter), but it may well have the highest table occupancy in New York at lunchtime. It's an adventure to eat here among all the wigged women and cellphone-toting jewelry dealers, who never stop doing business, even at lunch.

$–$$ Right in the heart of lovely Bryant Park, '**wichcraft** ✸ (11 W. 40th St. at Sixth Ave.; no phone; www.wichcraftnyc.com; Mon–Fri 7am–7pm, Sat 9am–7pm, Sun 9am–5pm; ❸, ❹, ❻, ❼, ❼, to 42nd St.; AE, DC, MC, V) serves as the outdoor canteen for all the fashionistas and media types who slave in the area (and many bring their laptops as the park has free Wi-Fi). Created by TV show *Top Chef's* Tom Collicchio, 'wichcraft consists of two sandwich kiosks where that knotty problem of how to keep food between wedges of bread from tasting dry has happily been solved. They do it by using only artisan, solid, sometimes nutty breads from fine bakeries around the city; and layering sandwiches with such soft, moist spreads as goat cheese, soft-boiled eggs, and pesto. In the middle is a range of meats and vegetables, from slow-roasted pork and meatloaf to marinated white anchovies or black trumpet mushrooms and white truffle fondue. Sandwiches range in price from $7 to $9.50, breakfast items from $2. A number of outposts have opened all over the city, but the most convenient for visitors will be the ones right near Macy's (34th St. at Broadway), in Rockefeller Center (1 Rockefeller Plaza at 50th St.), and on Fifth Avenue (at 46th St.).

NORTH OF TIMES SQUARE, NEAR CARNEGIE HALL

$$$ If you don't make it down to Katz's Delicatessen on the Lower East Side, but are determined to have authentic deli food while in New York, your only real choice is the **Carnegie Deli** (854 Seventh Ave., at 55th St.; ☎ 800/334-3606 or 212/757-2245; www.carnegiedeli.com; ❶, ❷, ❸ to 57th St.; daily 6:30am–4am; cash only). At Katz's, as I've pointed out below, the dish to order is corned beef. Here you want to go for the pastrami, preferably in a Reuben ($21). You'll notice that the price is pretty hefty for a sandwich, but that's because no one can ever

The Burger Wars

In Gotham, the question of which pizza is best can lead to fist fights, but there's a more interesting competition among burgers, which can range from haute to healthy, greasy to great. Here are my nominees for the best between two buns:

- **Shake Shack** ★★ (outdoors in Madison Sq. Park, off 23rd St. btwn Broadway and Madison Ave.; daily 11am–11pm, Apr–Nov, rain or shine; AE, MC, V). At near-McDonald's prices—just $3.25 for a single—you get a just-big-enough patty, loosely knit of sirloin and brisket ground across the street at owner Danny Myer's much snootier restaurant, 11 Madison Park. The resulting burger is juicy and tasty and perfectly sided with crisp fries and a "concrete" shake of custard that's made fresh throughout the day. One tip: There's no need to pony up an extra dollar for a "shack burger," as the special sauce adds nothing. Here's a perfect "picnic in the park" burger.

- **Corner Bistro** (331 W. 4th St., near Eighth Ave.; ☎ 212/242-9402; Ⓐ, Ⓑ, Ⓒ, to 14th St., Ⓛ to Eighth Ave.; Mon–Sat 11:30am–3:30am, Sun noon–3:30am; cash only). The common consensus among New Yorkers is that the Corner Bistro has the best burgers in the city, and their "bistro burger" is a Goliath: an inch-and-a-half thick, dripping with juice, and topped with quality cheese, pickles, raw onion, a full lettuce leaf, and a tomato slice. I personally prefer a more even ratio of bun to burger, but for those who think bigger is better, this Village bar is the place to go.

- **Burger Joint** (118 W. 57th St., btwn Sixth and Seventh aves.; ☎ 212/245-5000; Sun–Thurs 11am–11:30pm, Fri–Sat 11am–midnight; Ⓝ, Ⓠ, Ⓡ to 57th St.; cash only). A greasy spoon among silver spoons, the Burger Joint is hidden behind a curtain in the lobby of the ultra-swank Parker Meridien Hotel. Pull back that curtain and you enter a hidden diner that looks like it was yanked off some side street in Detroit. But it serves up the juiciest, most perfectly charred burgers ($5.50) in the western half of Midtown. Order them with "the works" (red onions, lettuce, tomato, pickles, mustard, and mayo) for not a cent extra.

- **Rare** (303 Lexington Ave. at 37th St.; ☎ 212/481-1999; www.rare barandgrill.com; Ⓖ to 33rd St.; Mon–Thurs 7am–11pm, Fri 7am–midnight, Sat 8am–midnight, Sun 8am–11pm; AE, DC, MC, V). Longing for some truffle butter or a hunk of foie gras between your burger and bun? Rare has it. At this Midtown pub, the burger goes gourmet with all kinds of fancy-pants dressings, condiments, and recipes (including a Kobe beef "burger" encased in puff pastry for $21). If you don't want to get carried away with all of that, you could just go for a perfectly cooked, freshly ground patty between two solid but soft buns (the classic at $8.50)—down-home and haute are done equally well here.

finish one of these pound-and-a-half meat Cadillacs on their own; order one and share it with Mom, Pop, and the kids. Be sure to try an old-fashioned egg cream (a classic mix of seltzer, milk, and chocolate syrup).

VICINITY OF THE EMPIRE STATE BUILDING

$$$ It's endlessly fascinating to watch different ethnic groups adopt areas of the city as their own, re-creating the look and feel of their homelands in just 1 or 2 short blocks. In the area of that most American of icons, the Empire State Building, a small replica of Seoul has popped up on 32nd Street between Broadway and Fifth, and it has that "vertical" look so typical of Asian cities, with stores and restaurants housed not only on the ground floors but on upper stories as well, trumpeting their existence with huge window signs that grow bigger the higher in the building they are. This is where you should come and eat if you're in this part of town (there really are few other choices) and my favorite among the Korean restaurants—though they're all good—is also the oldest, **New York Kom Tang Kal Bi House** ★ (32 W. 32nd St., btwn Broadway and Fifth Ave.; ☎ 212/947-8482; ❶, ❷, ❸, ❹, ❺, ❻ to 34th St.; Mon–Sat 24 hr.; AE, MC, V); it occupies three stories on what was once the spot where Bergdorf and Goodman tailors plied their trade (before they opened the department store). Unlike other Korean barbecue places, here you grill your meal over real coals (rather than gas jets), brought to the table on a tray along with eight small side dishes. The waiter will lay out your meat for you on the grill and even flip it over when it's time, giving you advice on which condiments to use when you wrap your meats in the large lettuce leaves provided. It's best to eat here with a group because two orders of barbecue (the minimum allowed for this dish) will cost $20 each and can easily feed four people, especially if you dig into the accompanying (no extra charge) side dishes. There's no need to order appetizers, as the entrees are more than filling.

MIDTOWN EAST

$–$$ In the area of Murray Hill known as (chuckle, chuckle) "Curry Hill," the finest South Indian restaurant is also the most inclusive. Jains and hard-core Buddhists savor its offerings as do Orthodox Jews because **Chennai Garden** ★★ (129 East 27th St. off Lexington Ave.; ☎ 212/689-1999; daily 11:30am–3pm and 5pm–10pm; AE, DC, MC, V) is both vegetarian and kosher. But even meat lovers will enjoy the place as the curries, dosais, idlis, and other dishes engage all parts of the palate—the stews are savory, the breads crisp and airy, and the multi-hued chutneys alternately sour, citrusy sweet, fiery hot or cooling. Best deal is the $6.95 lunch buffet which avoids "tired hot plate syndrome" by only offering four dishes, which are so frequently replenished they always taste fresh. And Chennai is so popular you may be sent by the maitre d' up to the buffet even before you've been assigned a table—one will usually have emptied by the time you finish heaping your plate.

$–$$ Though it's mainly for ice cream and not for a meal, I can't help adding this New York institution. If you plan to shop at Bloomingdales, allot a good 30 to 45 minutes to brave the line and eat at **Serendipity 3** ★★ 🅺🅸🅳🆂 (225 E. 60th St., off Third Ave.; ☎ 212/838-3531; www.serendipity3.com; ❹, ❺, ❻, ❼, ❶, ❷, ❸ to 59th St.; AE, DC, MC, V), a good ol'-fashioned ice cream parlor complete with Tiffany-style lamps and a toy shop that you have to pass to get in and out (quite a feat when you have sugar-crazed kids in tow). The dish to order here (one tureen of it will easily satisfy two or three) is the deservedly famous Frozen Hot Chocolate ($9.50), a slushy, utterly satisfying chocolate soup. You can get an idea of the magical effects of that treat if you rent the slightly treacly John Cusack comedy *Serendipity*, which was filmed here.

$–$$ The other place to nosh near Bloomies is **Grand Sichuan Eastern** ★ (1049 Second Ave. at 55th St.; ☎ 212/268-5028; **N**, **R**, **W**, **4**, **5**, **6** to 59th St.; AE, DC, MC, V). Just know that there are no concessions to American taste-buds here; the flavors served are extreme, at times almost violently spicy, deeply sour, or emphatically citrusy. This is where "Mao's home cooking" (as the menu puts it) is served up, and the results are exciting. Start with an order of "green parrot with a red mouth," actually a vegetarian sauté of pea shoots in a tart lemon sauce that's bracing and refreshing at the same time ($5). Follow it, if you dare, with sour string beans with minced pork ($8.95, but the serving is big enough for three to share), a platter of scorchingly hot but piquant chopped string beans with little bits of meat. Also recommended is the delicately sweet sautéed pumpkin served family-style (another huge dish for $7.95; order it mild). You eat all of this in a dignified if uninspired Chinese restaurant, surrounded (usually) by Chinese ex-pats. Grand Sichuan now has other outlets at, 19–23 St. Mark's Place (off Third Ave.), 229 Ninth Ave. (at 24th St.), but its restaurant in the Times Square area has closed.

$$ The great Broadway composer Stephen Sondheim wrote a song called "The Ladies Who Lunch" that begins with a boozy toast to the wealthy women who spend their days doing little more than shopping for hats and "planning a brunch." Though the song was penned in 1975, those ladies still exist. Their natural habitat, at lunch and teatime at least, is the **Tea Box at Takashimaya** ★★ (693 Fifth Ave., near 54th St.; ☎ 212/350-5179; **4**, **5**, **6**, **S** to Grand Central; Mon–Sat 11:45am–5:30pm; AE, MC, V), set in the basement of one of the most expensive department stores on the planet, in a room with burnished silver walls and a linen-draped ceiling that just screams "money." Despite the surrounding excess, meals here are affordable, starting at just $9.75 for a chichi sandwich or salad plate. The cuisine is a subtle and refined fusion of Japanese and Continental fare with such delicacies as shrimp marinated in tea ($13), smoked salmon "sandwiches" on beds of pressed rice ($9.75), and a trio of lightly spiced, gem-colored soups in tiny shot glasses ($5.75). At teatime, a small pot of unusual tea and a plate of buttery cookies will run you $8.50.

$$–$$$ If you come into the city by train or just happen to be in the vicinity of Grand Central, consider the famed **Oyster Bar** ★ (Dining Concourse of Grand Central Station, 42nd St., btwn Lexington Ave. and Vanderbilt; ☎ 212/490-6650; www.oysterbarny.com; **4**, **5**, **6**, **S** to Grand Central; Mon–Fri 11:30am–9:30pm, Sat noon–9:30pm; AE, DC, MC, V). Opened in 1913, this Gilded Age holdover has changed very little in nearly a century, and the architecture—a series of swooping, tiled vaults that always remind me of the grand crypts of some European cathedrals—still impresses. Don't bother going to the restaurant side; you want to be able to see the handwritten menu above the shelling station (on the right as you enter), where the best choices will be laid out. There will be fresh oysters and clams, flown in from all parts of North America ($1.35–$4 each); shellfish pan-roasts and stews (from $9.45); and, of course, chowders of all kinds (from $4.75). Ignore the paper menu entirely (for some reason, everything that comes out of the kitchen is overcooked and tepidly sauced); confine yourself to the list of foods that is prepared right at the bar and you'll have a real, old-fashioned feast.

UNION SQUARE & THE FLATIRON DISTRICT

It's just in the last decade or so that these two areas have really become destina-tions for dining. Today there are scores of chic little places to choose from, many housed in what had been the first department stores of the U.S. way back in the 1840s (the area was called "Ladies Mile" back then, both for the big shops—notice the large plate glass windows on many facades here—and for the houses of prostitution that were housed above the stores). For reality TV fans, this area defines the dog-eat-dog world of Manhattan restaurants, as the ill-fated Rocco's of *The Restaurant* was filmed right on 18th Street, between Broadway and Park Avenue South. Restaurateur Jeffery Chodorow, the villain or hero of that show, depending on your point of view, has since had two other mediocre restaurants right on the same spot.

$–$$$ Though Rocco di Spirito wasn't able to thrive in the area, the up-and-coming chef Paul di Bari (formerly of the celebrated Austrian restaurant Walse) has. He's the guiding force behind **Bar Stuzzichini** ★★ (928 Broadway at 22nd St.; ☎ 212/780-5100; ❶, ❷, ❸ to 23rd St.; Mon–Thurs 11:45am–11pm, Fri–Sat 11:45am–midnight, Sun 11am–10pm; AE, DC, MC, V)—the name means "small bites"—which gives the tapas treatment to Italian food. Instead of heading up to a long antipasto bar, little nibbles (which sometimes can be quite substantial) parade onto your table, piping hot. A mix of five is just $24 and if you choose the larger ones, they could be a meal for two. Among the biggies are garlicky steamed clams, crisp rice balls, platters of *sopressata,* and stuffed eggplant. But if you only eat the small plates you're going to miss out on what may be one of the niftiest pasta dishes in the city: tagliolini with pistachio and lemon zest ($16, just writing about it makes me hungry). As for the ambience: It's a bit by the numbers, looking like any number of other restaurants, but still nice enough for a special occasion.

$–$$$ It's not chefs but well-known pit master Robbie Richter, who's behind the success of **Hill Country** ★ 🅺 (30 W. 26th St.; ☎ 212/255-4544; Sun–Thurs 11:30am–11pm, Fri–Sat 11:30am–midnight; ❶, ❷, ❸ to 28th St.; AE, DC, MC, V). A massive, barnlike space (down to the bales of hay as decoration), with long communal tables, it wins my award for "most likely to become a chain restau-rant." I don't mean that in a snarky way. It just seems like they've been able to cod-ify a formula for fun. Instead of waitered service, diners head up to three feeding stations (barbeque, side dishes, and dessert) and get their bills stamped—kids love that part. The food is wrapped, as it would be in a deli, with no plates given (my four-year-old thought that was pretty cool, too). And then you chow down, no waiting for the waiter to arrive, going up for more when you need it (I know par-ents will appreciate that). Because you buy the food by weight, you can spend as little or as much as you want to. On my last visit, I made a satisfying meal of a quarter pound of tender brisket ($5) with a side dish of creamed green beans ($5).

Restaurant Week(s)

For 4 weeks each year—usually the last 2 weeks in June and January—New York's finest restaurants slash the cost of a three-course meal to just $24 at lunch, $35 at dinner. Started as a means of luring Democrats out of the convention hall and into the city during the 1992 Democratic Convention, the program proved so popular that it became a yearly tradition, and many other cities now hold "restaurant weeks" of their own. To get the best quality meals, go with the eateries that offer food off their usual menu (rather than cheaper substitutes); you can ask what's for lunch when you call to make a reservation. To find out which restaurants are participating, go to **www.nycvisit.com**.

My daughters had the mac and cheese ($6) and my husband went for a big helping of ribs ($15) sided by baked beans ($4). Live country music is performed most nights of the week in the basement.

$–$$ Right on Union Square, **Republic** (37 Union Sq. West; ☎ 212/627-7172; www.thinknoodles.com; Sun–Wed 11:30am–10:30pm, Thurs–Sat 11:30am–11:30pm; Ⓝ, Ⓠ, Ⓡ, ④, ⑤, ⑥, Ⓛ to Union Sq.; AE, MC, V) boasts a menu heavy on Asian noodles. Its look is "Communist Russia—industrial space, long communal tables—meets New York fashion shoot," thanks to the oversized photos of beautiful people eating noodles that grace the walls. The best affordable eats right on Union Square, Republic's dishes are healthy (lots of salad choices and freshly squeezed juices) and its prices reasonable (all of the massive, toothsome noodle dishes cost a mere $7–$10).

$$$–$$$$ The relatively affordable "celeb chef" choice in this foodie neighborhood is Mario Batali's foray into Spanish cuisine, **Casa Mono** ★★★ (125 E. 17th St. at Irving Place; ☎ 212/253-2773; daily noon–midnight; ④, ⑤, ⑥, Ⓝ, Ⓡ, Ⓛ to Union Sq.; AE, MC, V). If you don't like sharing, you won't like this lively tapas restaurant, where the act of digging your fork into your companion's plate and stealing the best bits is raised to an art. That's because many of the dishes are so exotic that it's the worst sort of culinary faux pas not to rotate the plates around the table for everyone to try. And an adventurous palate is rewarded here—the more unusual the dish, the more delicious it tends to be. This certainly goes for the *fideos* with clams and chorizo ($15), a mix of toothpicklike pasta with seafood and sausage; the lustily sweet pumpkin croquettes ($9); and yes, the duck hearts ($13), which is a symphony of textures and flavors. Portions tend to be substantial, so you can keep the bill under control by ordering just two plates per person. Casa Mono shares the same sort of rustically elegant look that Batali's other eateries do, with dark wood paneling, rough wooden tables, and wine bottles everywhere. But it's much smaller than any of the other joints, so you'll want to make reservations well in advance. Even the 5:30 seating is jam-packed, and the host has an unfortunate habit of letting you know, as soon as you sit down, that there's a meter running on your table.

CHELSEA

With its galleries and gay bars, Chelsea is one of the best places in the city for just leaning back and taking in the view—the parade of bared bellies, tight T-shirts, and muscled men is non-stop. There are a lot of sexy-looking restaurants here, too, as well as an increasing number of good eats. Here are my picks among the well-priced options.

$ For simply a fast meal hereabouts, consider **F&B güdtfood** ★ 🧒 (269 W. 23rd St., btwn Seventh and Eighth aves.; ☎ 646/486-4441; www.gudtfood.com; also at 150 E. 52nd St., btwn Lexington and Third aves.; Mon–Fri 11:30am–11pm, Sat noon–11pm, Sun noon–10pm; ◯, ◯ to 23rd St.; AE, MC, V)—the acronym stands for frites and beignets—a bricks-and-mortar paean to European street foods. Tops on the menu are the custom-made sausages topped by squiggles of brightly flavored sauces and mounds of vegetables. One of the most bedecked and satisfying is the "Great Dane" ($3.65), a neon-red, Danish pork sausage topped with crispy fried onions, lightly pickled cucumber slices, and a sweet but not cloying apple-tomato ketchup. And there are smoked tofu dogs as well, such as the "Athenian" ($3.65), which is smothered in creamy hummus, julienned carrots, and black olives (it tastes better than it sounds). On the side, try the *haricots frites* ($2.95), a healthier take on French fries with green beans subbing for spuds. Though not fancy, the shop is quite modish with azure walls, fresh flowers on the eating counters (there are stools for diners), wine and beer service, and a pulsating Euro-pop and fusion soundtrack.

$$–$$$ Just up the block from F&B, the similarly named **RUB** ★★ (or **Righteous Urban Barbecue,** 208 W. 23rd St., near Seventh Ave; ☎ 212/524-4300; www.rubbbq.net; Mon–Thurs 11:30am–11pm, Fri–Sat 11:30am–midnight, Sun 11:30am–10pm; ◯, ◯, ◯ to 23rd St.; AE, DC, MC, V) elevates American backyard cooking to an art. Read any article about 'cue in NYC, and this place will be named as one of the top five in the city. Not a surprise as owner Paul Kirk *always* wins when it comes to barbecue: He has seven World Barbecue Championships under his belt and was inducted into the Barbecue Hall of Fame in 1990. His food here is blue-ribbon quality, swooning-off-the-bone tender, and sided by a smoky, tartly sweet barbecue sauce that has a heat that sneaks up and subsides just as you're about to take the next bite. The only quibbles I have with this joint, probably the reason I give it two stars rather than three, are the service, which is friendly but glacially slow, and the lack of atmosphere. The place is so plain it would make a Texas roadhouse look chic. But those are small complaints, and for the heaping platters of food you get, served on round aluminum trays as big as pizza tins, you certainly get good value for the dollar. You can choose a platter with two sides (pick the sassy barbecued beans and the crisp and greaseless fried onions) and one meat for $15; add another meat and it's $19; and so on. **Warning:** Because the barbecue can take up to 14 hours to cook, they don't make more when they run out for the evening. So if you want to have one of the really popular items (such as ribs), you'll have to get here early in the evening.

$$–$$$ Venturing east of Eighth Avenue, the neighborhood loses its party-hearty atmosphere and becomes a bit dour, but it has one major saving grace in

Le Zie ★ (172 Seventh Ave., on the corner of 20th St.; ☎ 212/206-8686; www. lezie.com; Mon–Fri noon–11:30pm, Sat–Sun noon–11pm; ❶ to 18th St.; AE, MC, V), a bustling, Venetian trattoria that brings to New York the fresh and slightly more exotic Italian tastes of that watery city (because Venice was a major trading route for many centuries, its cuisine incorporates a number of typically Asian spices). You'll see these many influences in the very Chinese version of red snapper (market price), cooked to silky perfection in a salt crust. Its signature dish, a sublime version of good ol' spaghetti and meatballs ($13), is chunky with bits of softened garlic and tomatoes, and I detected a hint of cinnamon and all-spice in the weightless meatballs. The Venetian-style bean soup is also unique, less chunky than the classic "pasta and fagiole" and more of a rich purée, delicately spiced, with just a few small nubs of pasta ($5.95). Though the front room is dignified and pleasant, ask if it's possible to sit in the back, in either the lushly romantic green garden or in the Galleria Room, with its high wood-beamed ceilings and dramatic works of art on the walls.

$$$ My final neighborhood fave is a little place called **Maroons** ★★★ (244 W. 16th St., off Eighth Ave.; ☎ 212/206-8640; www.maroonsnyc.com; Sun–Tues 11:30am–11pm; reservations recommended; ❶ to Eighth Ave., or ❶, ❶, ❶ to 14th St.; AE, DC, MC, V), which is slyly and quietly "desegregating" the Manhattan dining scene (in fact, until you eat here, you won't realize how homogenous most restaurants are). But Maroons, which takes its name from the bands of slaves who fought for their freedom in Jamaica, attracts a rainbow crowd: white and Asian gay men and women from the neighborhood, and young hetero couples out on dates, make up about half the clientele; the other 50% is African American. I know of no other restaurant in the city with quite this demographic, and it's a testament to just how welcoming this stylish little converted brownstone is. It also speaks to the high quality of the food (the cocktails are killer, too). As the name suggests, the menu is divided between Caribbean and Southern specialties, many of which are outstanding. It's fun to mix and match, so pair the crisp and spicily sauced fried green tomatoes with an entree of even more fiery jerk chicken ($18); or go to town with fluffy codfish fritters ($9) followed by a juicy slab of meatloaf ($15). All are delish, especially when sided by Maroons' buttery, non-bitter collard greens (how do they do that?) and slightly peppery mac and cheese.

CHINATOWN & LITTLE ITALY

For a cheap, fresh, and tasty meal, there's no better area in the city than Chinatown, and we can thank the history of Chinese immigration for that.

Let me explain. In 1882, the U.S. Congress enacted what has to be one of the most shameful and cruel laws in the history of American jurisprudence: the Chinese Exclusion Act. The first law ever to be directed solely at one ethnic group—a group that had proved invaluable in the development of the economy of the Western United States (it was Chinese labor that built the rail lines there)—the act denied the Chinese the right to apply for naturalization and denied new entry to Chinese immigrants who didn't already have family in the States.

The effect of the act was dramatic. Overnight, Chinese Americans became second-class citizens in the eyes of the law, and all of the men (95% of the Chinese Americans) who had come here hoping to eventually bring wives and family over,

Subway Directions

To get to most parts of Chinatown, you're going to have to hoof it a bit. The nearest subway stop for this neighborhood is the Canal Street Station served by the ④, ⑤, ⑥, ⑭, ⑮, ⑯, and ⑰ trains. From here it's about 3 long avenue blocks to most of the eateries listed in this section.

were in essence stranded. Chinatown became a "bachelor society," which, oddly enough, led to a boom in Chinese restaurants. You see, the Chinese immigrants had to work very hard just to survive, so there was little time for cooking. Without the support of a family, these men ended up eating all of their meals from street vendors or in small, cheap restaurants, and Chinatown became a neighborhood simply bristling with eating options. To accommodate the vast number of diners, many of whom were eating solo, the restaurants used Lilliputian tables, just big enough for one. You'll see these lonely table configurations in many of Chinatown's older restaurants even now, as restrictions on Chinese immigration continued all the way until 1965.

Today, a boom in immigration from all parts of Asia has made Chinatown one of the city's most vibrant and fast-growing neighborhoods. With the exception of some 4 short blocks, it has pretty much taken over Little Italy, and the hold is culinary as well as physical. There's but one worthwhile restaurant left in Little Italy (see below); the rest is all "tourist" food, sloppily cooked and indifferently served (though there are still some good places to get cheeses and Italian cured meats that I list in our shopping chapter). But if you like Asian food, dining here can't be beat.

DIM SUM

The classic Chinatown meal is the dim sum brunch or lunch. Dim sum, for those who've never tried it, is a meal made up of many small dishes, primarily different sorts of dumplings and buns, a tradition that started in the teahouses that lined China's Silk Road many centuries ago (scholars believe the custom began shortly after A.D. 300, when the long-held notion that tea should not be accompanied by food fell out of favor). In China, as well as in Asian communities across the world, it remains a social occasion, a chance for family and friends to gather and talk. That may be why the words "dim sum" don't actually refer to food; they can be roughly translated as "a little bit of heart." Today, when you go for a dim sum brunch, it's likely that you'll be seated at a large round table with other diners, so don't be shy; use that seating as an opportunity to meet the locals.

$ Many really good dim sum joints are scattered across Chinatown; in fact, it's hard to go wrong with this type of cuisine. For a Hong Kong–style dim sum restaurant (where the food is wheeled through the dining room in carts with patrons choosing as they go by), your best choices are **Jing Fong** (20 Elizabeth St. btwn Elizabeth and Canal sts.; ☎ 212/964-5256; daily 9:30am–11pm; AE, MC, V), **The Golden Unicorn** (18 E. Broadway, btwn Catherine and Market sts.; ☎ 212/941-0911; Mon–Fri 10am–11pm, Sat–Sun 9am–11pm; AE, DC, MC, V), **and HSF** (46

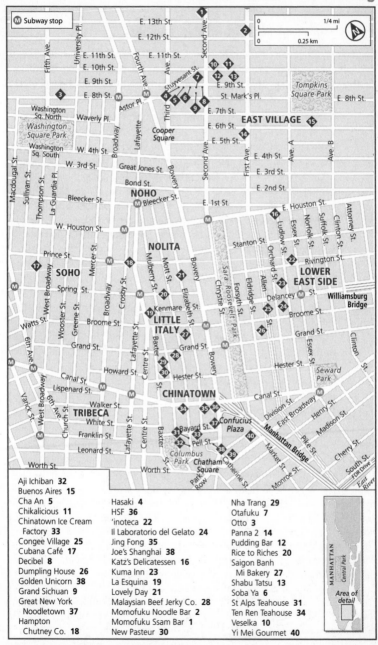

Chinatown Noshes

Though you can—and should—enjoy a sit-down meal in the neighborhood, there are few more fun (and fattening) ways to spend an afternoon than simply going store to store and grazing on little bites from around the continent of Asia. Not-to-be-missed munchies include:

◆ **Dumplings:** Head to **Dumpling House** ✦ (118A Eldridge St., off Grand St.; daily 7:30am–9:30pm; cash only), where a mere $1 buys five delectable pork and chive dumplings. Light at the top, crispy at the bottom, they're much less gummy than standard dumplings because owner Vanessa Duan—the slight lady with the big smile behind the counter—and her staff roll the dough by hand (most dumpling places use a machine) and make a thinner dough than Cantonese chefs do, reflecting the Beijing origin of the recipe used here. Be sure to eat at the back counter so you can sample the house-made vinegar sauce.

◆ **Malaysian beef jerky:** As soon as you open the door of **Malaysian Beef Jerky Inc** ✦ (95 A Elizabeth St., off Grand St.; ☎ 212/665-0796; daily 10am–8pm; cash only) the ambrosial smell hits you: a musky mix of exotic spices and bubbling honey. It sets you up for the jerky itself, which is much more pliant than Americans are used to—quarter-inch slices of beef, chicken, or pork that are slightly greasy to the touch but tremendously flavorful. A quarter pound, enough for a good-sized snack for three adults, costs between $3.75 and $4.

◆ **Dried fruits, beans, seafood, and meats:** You don't even have to pay to sample all of the unusual food at **Aji chiban** (37 Mott St.; ☎ 212/233-7650; daily 10am–6pm; **free**), a member of a Hong

Bowery, off Canal St.; ☎ 212/374-1319; Mon–Fri 11am–10pm, Sat–Sun 10am–10pm; cash only). Jing Fong is the largest of the three by a hair, an enormous room that's two football fields long. It offers, along with cart service, a nice buffet featuring such delicacies as chicken feet (which taste oddly jellied), taro cakes, and freshly cooked clams in black bean sauce. The Golden Unicorn has multiple floors in a faceless building on East Broadway, one of the less touristy areas of Chinatown. You wait in the lobby until the hostess sends you up the elevator to your assigned dining floor. It's a tad less frenetic than Jing Fong (where I'm always slightly worried that I'm going to get mowed down by a steaming cart of dumplings), though the wait for tables here can be longer. HSF is the oldest of the three, having been around for over 3 decades, and according to a Chinatown resident I met, supplies many of the surrounding restaurants with their dumplings, a claim I've never been able to substantiate—though ever since he said it, I've thought that the food here does taste the freshest. Expect to pay between $10 and $15 for a full meal for two people of dumplings, sticky rice, and more,

Kong–based chain. This dried-stuff store offers a plateful of samples atop each food-bearing bin in the hope that you'll buy if you enjoy the sample. You can graze a little meal, perhaps starting with an appetizer of barbecued shredded squid, moving on to some different sorts of beef jerky or dried fish (I like the one that's speckled with sesame), and finishing up with a desiccated fruit dessert (the "seed-less lover prune" not only has a great name, it's quite tasty).

◆ **Unusual ice cream:** There is a Häagen-Dazs in Chinatown, but I have no idea how it stays in business since it is less than a block from the never-empty **Chinatown Ice Cream Factory** (65 Bayard St., btwn Elizabeth and Mott sts.; ☎ 212/608-4170; cash only), a 23-year-old storefront that sells flavors you can't get anywhere else: spicy ginger, lychee with little chunks of the fruit, a potato-like taro, and a sur-prisingly yummy avocado ice cream. These are their "standards." The flavors they mark as "exotic"? Vanilla and chocolate, of course.

◆ **Bubble tea:** Definitely an acquired taste, this craze from Hong Kong first came to Chinatown about 8 years ago and has been slowly work-ing its way uptown (there are now tea shops as far up as the West 30s). Very simply, it's a drink that's also a dessert—cold flavored tea in a clear cup with pearls of tapioca that you sip through an extra-wide straw. I personally find the experience of sucking globs of starch through a straw a bit disturbing, but many people love it, and the drinks do give you that sugar charge. **Ten Ren Tea** (75 Mott St. or 138 Lafayette St.; ☎ 212/732-7178; Sun–Thurs 10am–11pm, Fri–Sat 10am–midnight; AE, MC, V) is a popular, buzzing spot to try it.

at any of the three places. ***Important note:*** Dim sum is a lunch and brunch spe-cialty and is cooked early. Don't try it after 3pm, or you'll be disappointed.

NEW TO NEW YORK VARIETIES OF CHINESE FOOD

$ Deep in the bowels of Chinatown, right next to the Manhattan Bridge over-pass (when this neighborhood becomes chic, some genius will undoubtedly nick-name it *MOBA*), is a tiny dynamo of a Fujian steam-table restaurant called **Yi Mei Gourmet** ✿✿ (51 Division St., off Market St.; ☎ 212/925-1921; daily 7am–9pm; cash only). Just in the last decade, some 300,000 Fujians from southeastern China have entered the U.S., many settling in the New York area. They're still the "new immigrants on the block," and a restaurant like Yi Mei illustrates that: The counter staff speak rudimentary English, you eat at folding tables on folding stools, and when you go to the front to order, you have to simply go with what looks good, as the explanations of what the 33 dishes are will be absolutely incom-prehensible. It's a real adventure but I promise the food will make up for any discomfort you feel while ordering. For a mind-boggling $2.75(!), you get rice, soup, and four different dishes. The last time I was here, I chose a handful of hard-shell crabs in a delicious gingery sauce, lightly sautéed pea shoots, and dry fried string beans with a hint of pepper; and then I asked the woman behind the counter to recommend one more. She pointed to a stew she called *"peekur."* I couldn't figure out what "pee-kur" means, but it was my favorite: tangy strips of a bumpy something with fried tomatoes and mushrooms.

$–$$ In the more central area of Chinatown, on Pell Street (which had been the street where all the bachelors got their haircuts; notice the large number of barbershops still there today), **Joe's Shanghai** ★ (9 Pell St., btwn Bowery and Mott sts.; ☎ 212/233-8888; there's also a not-quite-as-good uptown location at 24 W. 56th St., btwn Fifth and Sixth aves.; Mon–Sun 11am–11pm; AE, MC, V) is at the very center of the "soup dumpling" craze. Joe's was one of the first to bring to New York the puffy, puckered center dumplings that have swept the city (next to "bubble tea"—see box above—they are by far the most popular new Chinese food). Eating them involves a complicated ritual. You take one of those ladlelike Chinese spoons, carefully retrieve a dumpling from a bamboo steamer, leave it on your spoon, bite off the top, and then pour in a special sauce of soy, sweet vinegar, and slivered ginger. Then, even more carefully, take a delicate bite of the dumpling so its innards will squirt into your mouth (and if you're not fast enough, onto your shirt), a jet stream of lava-hot soup and sauce plus chive-laced pork and/or crab. Absolutely delicious, and worth it at $6.65. Joe's has a complete menu, of course, of other Shanghai dishes (try the slivered pork with dried bean curd and jalapeño for $9.95), but the dumplings are why you choose Joe's.

AN UNBEATABLE OLD FAVORITE

$–$$ **Great New York Noodletown** ★★★ (28 Bowery at Bayard St.; ☎ 212/349-0923; daily 9am–4am; cash only) is a giant among noodle shops. It ain't much to look at: The lighting's too bright, the seats are crowded together, and the chairs and tables are getting flimsy from overuse, but there are few finer dining experiences to be had in this restaurant-crammed city. In fact, in the years I've been coming here, I've seen chefs from Nobu (one of the city's most celebrated Japanese restaurants), still in their chef's whites, dining here after their shifts were over. I couldn't see what they ordered, but I always go for the sautéed pea shoots ($9.95), a delicate, very green taste sensation; the salt-baked squid ($8.95), the seafood equivalent of potato chips, they're that light and crunchy; some slices off one of the ducks ($3.50) that hang in macabre style in the window; and the heat-packing Singapore chow fun ($5.95), an al dente, spicy mix of thin, long pasta, diced vegetables, and pork. Come prepared for a line; Noodletown doesn't take reservations.

CHINATOWN'S VIETNAM

$ One block west of Bayard is Baxter Street, which could be called the city's "Little Vietnam," with three really good Vietnamese restaurants: **Nha Trang** (87 Baxter St.; ☎ 212/233-5948; daily 10am–10pm; AE, MC, V); **New Pasteur** (85 Baxter St., btwn Bayard and Canal sts.; ☎ 212/608-3656; daily 11am–10pm; AE, DC, MC, V); and **Thaison** (89 Baxter St.; ☎ 212/732-2822; daily 10:30am–10:30pm; AE, MC, V). I've eaten at all of them, and there's not much difference

---

Your Best Choice in Little Italy . . .

Ain't Italian (sorry!). But I'm betting that the humble Vietnamese sandwich that you'll taste here is going to be one of the highlights of your trip. I'm further predicting that the *bahn mi,* which is already nearly as popular in NYC as pizza, is going to be one of those foods that makes its first appearances in NYC and then spreads like wildfire to the rest of the country (its startling mix of flavors and textures is truly delish). If you'd like a preview of the porky goodness that may be coming to a storefront near you, head to **Saigon Banh Mi Saigon Bakery** ★★ (138 Mott St. btwn Grand and Hester; ☎ 212/941-1451; Tues–Sun 10am–7pm; ❸, ❹ to Grand, ❻, ❶, ❼, ❽, ❾, ❿ to Canal; cash only), where you'll have a choice of eight baguette sandwiches stuffed a variety of ways. The classic: freshly grilled pork, pickled carrots, cilantro, daikon, and a mayo-mustard dressing ($3.75). Vegetarians are well served, too. No seating, takeout only.

---

between them (to my palate): You get a hearty, affordable meal of deeply flavorful entree-sized noodle soups ($4–$5), crabs with a finger-licking ginger and scallion sauce (market price), cold summer rolls ($3.50, a bouquet of legumes wrapped in a white cold pasta sheet and sided by a vinegary dipping sauce), all for practically nothing (expect to pay no more than $8 per person for a filling meal). Desserts at these places can be odd, but if you're game, try the Che Ba Mau, a parfait glass filled with condensed milk and (I kid you not) multi-colored gummy worms, corn, and red beans. After the initial shock, you may just like it.

EAST VILLAGE

Ethnic eats, NYU hangouts, young chefs striking out on their own—after Chinatown, this area and the Lower East Side (see later in this chapter) are tops for budget dining (as well as fancier fare), and the East Village certainly has more than its fair share of superlative little restaurants, as well as a few classic picks that have passed the test of time.

$ The East Village is home to New York University, which has 12 official and utterly unnecessary cafeterias and cafes for students, as most of them seem to dine exclusively at **Dojo** (14 W. 4th St. at Mercer St.; ☎ 212/505-8934; Sun–Thurs 11am–12:30am, Fri–Sat 11am–1:30am; ❶, ❷, ❸ to 8th St., or ❻ to Astor Place; cash only), a mildly Japanese health food canteen, with sit-down service and some of the cheapest prices in the city. For a pita pouch overflowing with chicken *sukiyaki* (chicken stir-fried with cellophane noodles and vegetables) and sided by a large and very good salad with ginger dressing, the cost is just $3.75; order stir-fried vegetables over brown rice with salad, and you'll pay just $5.25. Also available: soy burgers ($3.25), dinner salads ($4.75–$5.50), BBQ chicken ($7.45), and much more.

$ On Sixth Street, between First and Second avenues, is one of the city's three "Little Indias," neighborhoods where cardamom and ginger scent the air, and every other restaurant you pass has either a sitar player in the window, or an Indian man outside eagerly waving you into his curry palace. Though you'll have a good, affordable meal at any of the restaurants along the block, I prefer to go around the corner to **Panna II** ✹✹ (93 First Ave., btwn 5th and 6th sts.; ☎ 212/598-4610; www.panna2.com; daily noon–midnight; ❻ to Astor Place or ❺ to Second Ave.; AE, MC, V), which the *Village Voice* once called the "best unintentional art installation" in New York. It's a wacky-looking place. Over the years the owners have covered every possible inch of this small restaurant with Christmas lights, chile lights, hanging beach balls, Hawaiian leis, and other kitsch, packing the place so tightly with decorations that anyone over 5'8" has to duck to get to a seat. Once inside, you dine on delicious and outrageously cheap Indian food, with curries starting at just $4.50 and soups for $1.25. Even if you hadn't planned on visiting this neighborhood, it's worth traveling here to dine.

$–$$ **Veselka** (144 Second Ave. at the corner of 9th St.; ☎ 212/228-9682; www.veselka.com; ❻ to Astor Place; daily 24 hr.; AE, DC, MC, V) is another NYU haunt, though it's also a popular spot for East Village hipsters, Goth guys and gals, families, businesspeople, and anybody who's ever had a deep need for cold borscht at 3 in the morning. When Veselka debuted in 1954 the area was awash in Ukrainian diners, but most have since gone belly-up (or have upgraded to the point of assimilation), leaving this crowded, tall-windowed eatery the standard-bearer for solid, cheese-laden eastern European fare. Though you can order American dishes here, it's better to stick with such old country favorites as *pierogis* ($7.95, fried meat or cheese dumplings), the sauerkraut-laced hunter's stew of kielbasa and veal ($12), or the best borscht in the city ($4.50 per bowl).

$$ Eating at my next choice is one of those "only in New York" experiences, an exercise in excess, and one of the most fun dining events in the city. The place is called **ChikaLicious** ✹✹✹ (203 E. 10th St., right off Second Ave.; ☎ 212/995-9511; www.chikalicious.com; Wed–Fri 3–5pm and 7–10:45pm, Sat–Sun 3–10:45pm; ❻ to Astor Place; MC, V), which sounds like a porn shop, I know, but is actually a dessert-only restaurant, owned by a diminutive pastry chef named Chika Tillman who presides from behind the central counter in this glossy, all-white restaurant (it reminds me a bit of the "Milk Bar" in the movie *A Clockwork Orange*). All customers get a three-course tasting menu for $12, which starts with an *amuse bouche* (literally, a small amusement for the mouth), goes on to a choice of eight main desserts, and finishes with petit fours. And what desserts they are! Ms. Tillman, who has baked at some of the top restaurants in the city (including posh Gramercy Tavern), has a rich imagination when it comes to food, and though the pairings she makes seem weird—molten chocolate tart with red peppercorn ice cream (studded with little bits of pepper) and red wine sauce; a Monet-like swirl of multi-colored, multi-flavored fruit compote; Earl Grey jelly with spicy cinnamon ice cream—they're right on. Better than that, actually; if desserts can be revelatory, these are. Spring for a dessert wine pairing ($7 more) to further enhance your visit. If you're in a rush, grab dessert to-go across the street at Chika's new **Pudding Bar** (204 E 10th St. off Second Ave; ☎ 212/475-0929; daily 1pm–midnight).

Momofuku You

Winning a James Beard award is as career-making a milestone for a chef as winning an Oscar is for an actor. And in 2007, the winner for one of the most sought-after of the Beard awards—Rising Star Chef—wasn't some stiff in a toque, dishing up $40-a-plate concoctions of foie gras and truffles, but New York's own David Chang. To use a term from academia: what a paradigm shift! You see, Chang is a culinary bad boy, who keeps his restaurants streamlined—just blond wood counters and a few tables, no tablecloths, and rock music on the CD—and serves up reasonably affordable meals, no reservations taken. As I write this he has two superb restaurants operating (and another under construction): **Momofuku Ssam Bar** ★★★ (207 Second Ave at 13th St.; ☎ 212/254-3500; www.momofuku.com; daily 11am–2am; ❶ to Third Ave.; AE, DC, MC, V) and **Momofuku Noodle Bar** ★★★ (171 First Ave; ☎ 212/777-7773; daily noon–4pm and 5:30–11pm; ❶ to First Ave; same website and credit card info). What ties them together is the creativity and exuberance of his vision. You see, Chang will try anything, but more importantly, he makes it work. I've had some of the weirdest and seemingly least gourmet meals here, and they've all been a revelation. I'm talking Asian apple tart topped with pork-infused whipped cream ($8); stellar *banh mi* sandwiches made with Berkshire pork belly ($9); and even ramen noodles that elevate the genre, topped with egg and neck of pork ($14). If you're noticing a trend here, that's because Chang is in love with the humble pig and uses parts of it to splendid effect in many of his recipes. By the way: Momofuku means "lucky peach"—and you'll feel like one after you've dined here.

$$–$$$ Though it's technically in the East Village (as it's just east of Fifth Ave.), **Otto** ★★ 🧒 (1 Fifth Ave., with the entrance actually on Eighth St.; ☎ 212/995-9559; www.ottopizzeria.com; daily 11:30am–midnight; reservations recommended; ❿, ❹ to Eighth St., or ❹, ❻, ❽, ❿ to W. 4th St.; AE, DC, MC, V), this pizza parlor–cum–wine bar has more of a Greenwich Village vibe, appealing to a well-coiffed crowd of upper-middle-class families and professional singles on the make. Designed to look somewhat like a train station, down to a fake moving sign at the front that lists Italian trains and their times of departure (if you ask, they'll make it spin for you), it's one of many in chef Mario Batali's empire—apparently, he created this slightly downscale place so that his kids would have a place to come eat. A couple of the thin-crusted pizzas ($9–$14 per pie) are named after these tykes, and children are treated like royalty here, with coloring maps of Italy and a box of crayons given to each child on arrival. That being said, this isn't just a kiddie place: Along with such child-friendly items as pizza with red sauce and cheese, the menu features a range of sophisticated, highly authentic Italian dishes such as the *penne con piselli e ricotta* ($9), a startling, minty noodle dish with flavorful al dente peas; or the *lardo* pizza, which is just what it sounds like—a pizza

Tokyo on 10th Street, Nagano on 9th

While the East Village has long been known for its Ukrainian and Indian restaurants, in the last 8 years it's also become a center for Japanese cuisine . . . and not just sushi. On 2 special blocks—9th Street, between Third and Second avenues; and 10th Street, between First and Second avenues—the restaurateurs from Japan cater to a knowledgeable expat crowd with authentic plates and drinks at unique eateries:

- **Cha-an** (230 E. 9th St.; Sun–Thurs noon–11pm, Fri–Sat noon–midnight; ☎ 212/228-8030; ❻ to Astor Place; cash only). This is the only place in the city, and possibly the U.S., that serves typical tea *kaiseki* or small plate meals. It does this in a setting that looks somewhat like the restaurants that have served monks for centuries next to the temples of Kyoto, down to the small rock gardens at the entrance and the traditional wooden teahouse in the corner. For information on the traditional Japanese tea ceremonies that take place here weekly, see my write-up on p. 187.

- **Decibel** ✸ (240 E. 9th St.; ☎ 212/979-2733; www.sakebardecibel. com; Mon–Sat 8pm–3am, Sun 8pm–12:30am; ❻ to Astor Place; cash only). Grungy, gritty, and hip, this basement sake bar is the polar opposite of Cha-an, its serene neighbor to the east. It's where punk Japanese young men and women go, their hair dyed a burnt shade of orange and often sticking straight up. Along with sake, Decibel serves the potato liquor *imo-jochu* (which a friend of mine who lived in Japan insists you can drink by the quart without paying for it the next day) and a full menu of typical Sino bar snacks, from yakitori ($6) to more exotic fare such as lotus roots ($3), pickled squid ($3), and octopus in wasabi sauce ($4).

- **Hasaki** (210 E. 9th St; ☎ 212/473-3327; Mon–Tues 5:30–11pm, Wed–Fri noon–3pm and 5:40–11pm, Sat–Sun 1pm–4pm and 5:30pm–11pm; ❻ to Astor Place; AE, MC, V). If Japanese food means sushi to you, head here for fresh and affordable slaps of fish on perfectly cooked rice. In warm weather, ask for garden seating.

- **Otafuku** (236 E. 9th St.; ☎ 212/853-3503; Mon–Fri 1pm–10pm, Sat–Sun 11am–10pm; ❻ to Astor Place; cash only). "Otafuku" is a

doused in delicious, fatty cured pork fat. There are scrumptious cheese platters ($10 for three, sided by truffled honey, black cherries, and dried peaches); a terrific wine list (with glasses served by the "quartino," so you actually get a glass-and-a-half per order); cured meat platters ($10); and what has to be some of the top gelato in the city.

$$$–$$$$ New York is famous for its steakhouses but at $35 and up on average for a hunk of meat (side dishes are extra and as exorbitant), what's a devoted, brown sauce as popular in Japan as Heinz ketchup. It's sloshed over *okonoyake* ($7), the "pizza" of Japanese fast foods—a thick pancake of cabbage, carrots, and ginger in batter stuffed with either squid and shrimp or pork bellies. It's a greasy, sweet treat, and the only place it's fried up in the city (and perhaps the country) is at this teeny storefront where that other Japanese fast food, *takoyaki* ($3–$5)—to put it bluntly, octopus balls (meat, not gonads)—are also on the menu. If you don't want to try these exotic foods (and some will find them a bit much), it's interesting just to stop at the window and watch the counterstaff preparing the foods, armed only with toothpicks and a lot of patience. (I can't explain the method fully; you'll have to see it for yourself.)

◆ **Soba Ya** ★ (229 E. 9th St.; ☎ 212/533-6966; daily noon–3:50 and 5:30–10:30pm; ❻ to Astor Place; AE, DC, MC, V). A strong atmosphere of Zen is set off here by a tinkling fountain at the entrance, and the mood continues through the meal, which for most patrons consists of bowls of house-made soba or udon noodles with finely slivered vegetables, and thin but intensely flavored soup or dipping sauce. *Warning:* The restaurant will turn away families with young children if none of the booths in the back are empty, as they want to keep the place serene.

◆ **Shabu Tatsu** ★★ 🄺🄸🄳🅂 (216 E. 10th St.; ☎ 212/477-2972; Sun–Thurs 5pm–11pm, Fri–Sat 5pm–1:30am; ❻ to Astor Place; AE, DC, MC, V). A cook-your-own-meal place, it offers one solid hour of "eatertainment" as you swish paper-thin slices of rib-eye beef, vegetables, and noodles in a vat of boiling water at the center of your table, and then dip them into two contrasting sauces—a tangy soy-vinegar mix and a lush sesame sauce. After you finish your main dish, you're given little bowls for spooning out the "soup" you've created while dipping. The food is simple yet flavorful and the cooking so much fun that even picky children will chow down (though because of the possibility of burns, I wouldn't recommend Shabu Tatsu for kids under 4). A shabu meal is $19/person (but an order for 2 is enough for 4).

but penurious, carnivore to do? Graze at **Buenos Aires** (513 E. 6th St., off Ave. A; ☎ 212/228-2775; Sun–Thurs 1pm–midnight, Fri–Sat noon–1pm, Sun noon–midnight; ❶ to First Ave.; AE, DC, MC, V), where the steaks on the menu—grass fed and imported from Uruguay and Nebraska—start at a $19 and are tender and well charred. A delightful, homemade pico de gallo sauce set on each table adds to the flavor. No, the floor isn't covered with sawdust, nor are the waiters grumpy old men in bow ties (they're actually a delightfully peppy Latin American group), but you're enjoying a juicy cut of steak and perhaps some empanadas ($4 per platter) to a tango soundtrack, so why complain?

THE LOWER EAST SIDE

$ Karaoke and comfort are on the menu at **Congee Village** (100 Allen St., btwn Delancey and Broome sts.; www.sunsungroup.com/congeevillage; daily 10:30am–2am; ❻ to Delancey St., or ❶, ❽, ❷ to Essex St.; AE, MC, V), a veritable multiplex of Chinese porridge. It's a large, three-story restaurant that houses not only two dining rooms (charmingly hokey, with lots of bamboo and fake trees), but a pastel neon bar and a basement of karaoke rooms, all of which are dedicated to the consumption of *congee,* a deceptively simple yet extremely satisfying rice gruel that comes with an assortment of add-in ingredients such as sliced pork, crab, frog meat, and duck. A bubbling ceramic pot, which the smiling waitress will spoon out for you into a smaller bowl if you're male (this courtesy doesn't seem to be extended to female guests . . . or maybe it's just me?), costs between $4 and $5. If you want to vary your meal, choose from a large selection of Cantonese dishes.

$ For dessert in this distinctive area, head 1 block west to Orchard Street and **Il Laboratorio di Gelato** ★★ (95 Orchard St., near Delancey St.; ☎ 212/343-9922; daily 10am–6pm; ❻ to Delancey St., or ❶, ❽, ❷ to Essex St.; cash only), where John F. Snyder, founder of Ciao Bella, plays the "mad scientist," whipping up new flavors in the back while his mother (often) serves customers. Double-scoop cups or cones start at $3.50, and are concocted from wacky, fun ingredients. Try the sour cream gelato, the black sesame, or the mocha (which tastes as much of coffee as of chocolate) if they're on the menu. All in all, Snyder has devised 60 flavors, but only 12 are on sale at any one time, with flavors rotating on a near-daily basis.

$$ To pair an Italian meal with your gelato, your choice should be the nearby **'inoteca** ★★ (98 Rivington St. on the corner of Ludlow St.; ☎ 212/614-0473; www.inotecanyc.com; reservations recommended; Mon–Fri noon–3am, Sat–Sun 10am–3am; ❻ to Delancey St., or ❶, ❽, ❷ to Essex St.; AE, MC, V), which was founded by Jason Denton, a protégé of Mario Batali (who's a partner in this venture). 'inoteca is actually an *enotecca,* an Italian wine bar that pairs the vino with food, as one always should—plates of cheeses, cured meats, hot-pressed sandwiches, and salads of all types. I like to come here with a big group of friends so that we can compose an entire cocktail spread for dinner and really make it a party. There are 31 Italian cheeses to choose from (a plate of three costs $11), 7 types of meat from speck to prosciutto that's been aged for 18 months ($7–$10), plus such savory large salads as baby rucola with pickled onions and Pecorino ($8), or my favorite, a chunky-sweet but citrusy beet salad with oranges, mint, and hazelnuts ($8). All of it is top quality, imported directly from "the Boot," as are many of the regional wines that you won't find anywhere else in the city. Another reason to come with a group: You can reserve a table downstairs in the curved-ceiling wine cellar, a sexy, candlelit space.

$$–$$$ Foremost among the Lower East Side perennials is **Katz's Delicatessen** ★★★ (205 E. Houston St., at Ludlow St.; ☎ 212/254-2246; www.katz deli.com; Sun–Tues 8am–10pm, Wed–Thurs 8am–11pm, Fri–Sat 8am–3am; ❻, ❻

to Second Ave.; AE, MC, V), one of the city's longest-running success stories, in business since 1888. You may feel a sense of déjà vu as you enter, as this is where Meg Ryan, ahem, made a scene in *When Harry Met Sally*, and it looks just as it did in the flick: a cavernous, loud space with linoleum-topped tables; celebrity photos and testimonials plastering the walls; and curtains of hanging salami in the window. Though its menu is varied and long, only the uninitiated bypass the corned beef sandwich ($12)—the best in the city—a towering stack of meat cured for as long as 30 days, which gives it a richness and depth that you simply don't find with commercially prepared corned beef (which is "pressure injected" to cure in a mere 36 hours). If you're feeling a bit radical, order your sandwich as a Reuben ($13), and the corned-beef flavor will be enhanced (or overwhelmed, depending on your taste) by melted Swiss and sauerkraut.

$$–$$$ The find of the neighborhood, quite literally, as it's tucked away in a hard-to-find upstairs space that was formerly an art gallery, is **Kuma Inn** ★★★ (113 Ludlow St., 2nd Floor; ☎ 212/353-8866; reservations recommended; Sun and Tues–Thurs 6pm–11pm, Fri–Sat 6pm–midnight; ❻ to Delancey St.; cash only), a stylish little place that serves Thai and Filippino tapas. Created by King Phojanakang, a former protégé of the two big "B"s of the New York cooking scene—David Bouley and Daniel Boulud—the restaurant's menu changes daily, based on what's best at the green market; it usually features the tenderest of grilled octopus, marvelous Thai sausages, and all manner of sprightly vegetable dishes. All are served on "small plates" that range in price from $5 to $10, but the actual size of the servings varies, with some plates big enough for a meal, so I'd recommend ordering conservatively at first and then adding dishes if you find you're still hungry. One of the delights of dining here is meeting Phojanakang, who serves as maitre d'. He's a charming host and endlessly patient with customers agonizing over the sake list and menu. You'll feel like you've been to the house of a good friend when you leave, albeit one who cooks like an angel.

$$$–$$$$ At some point in their lives, nearly every New Yorker makes his or her way to **Sammy's Famous Roumanian Restaurant** ★★★ (157 Chrystie St. at Delancey St.; ☎ 212/673-0330; Mon–Thurs 4pm–10pm, Fri–Sat 4pm–11pm, Sun 3pm–9pm; reservations recommended; ❻ to Delancey St., ❷, ❹, ❺ to Grand St.; AE, MC, V), a nightly bar mitzvah masquerading as a steak joint. Set in a basement on the Lower East Side, its decor is gloriously tacky: business cards stuck all over the ceiling, balloons at the tables, and photos of patrons cramming the walls. Completing the ambience is an aged fellow at an electric keyboard who regales the crowd with Yiddish songs, selections from *Fiddler on the Roof*, and the hoariest Jewish jokes you've ever heard. Diners dance in the aisle, and sometimes members of the crowd take to the microphone to sing as well (especially if they've ordered the house special drink: a bottle of Belvedere vodka encased in a block of ice). The crusty, gruff waiters will try to push you into ordering too much food: Resist them. There's no reason whatsoever to order the prix fixe menu ($40); and the steaks are a foot long and overhang the plate, so order one for every two people with just one side of fried potatoes. You have to start with a helping of the chopped liver, a heart attack in a bowl, which the waiter mixes tableside, combining the liver with fried onions, plain onions, and literally a cup and a half of schmaltz (for the uninitiated that's liquefied chicken fat). One order of the liver is enough for four people. Bring a group if you can, as there are few better places in the city for a blowout party.

GREENWICH VILLAGE

Though it's no longer the Bohemian enclave it once was, Greenwich Village is still very much a "village" apart from the rest of the city, and one that takes its rhythms and habits more from Europe than the U.S. Very few big grocery stores are found in this part of town. Instead, residents stroll from the cheese store to the butcher shop to the fresh produce vendor, sniffing, sampling, squeezing fruits, improvising that night's dinner from what's freshest at the various markets (and I'll discuss some of those markets in chapter 11).

The restaurants in the area adopt the same relaxed, sensual approach towards food, and because this is an area primarily of historic town houses and tree-lined streets, there's ambience galore. The downside to eating in the Village? The prices, which can be high—but we've found a handful of places that give good value for the money.

OFF WASHINGTON SQUARE PARK

$ **Peanut Butter & Co.** 🧒 (240 Sullivan St. at 3rd St.; ☎ 212/677-3995; www. ilovepeanutbutter.com; Sun–Thurs 11am–9pm, Fri–Sat 11am–10pm; Ⓐ, Ⓒ, Ⓔ, Ⓑ, Ⓓ to W. 4th St.; AE, DC, MC, V) is the peanut butter–centric restaurant I joked about at the opening of this chapter. Mea culpa! I shouldn't have made fun because I actually love to dine here and so do my daughters (in fact, we always make sure to pick up a jar of the house-ground peanut butter so we can try to replicate the experience at home). Looking like an 8-year-old's room turned restaurant, with sunshine-yellow walls plastered with old-fashioned ads for peanut butter (who knew that Heinz once made peanut butter?), it's a fun, friendly place with lightning-quick service. My kids go for the classic when they come here—a PB&J, with a choice of raspberry, strawberry, apricot, or grape jelly—and I tend to kick out more, choosing the "Elvis" ($6.50, the PB, banana, and honey mix that gave the King his, um, regal girth); the surprisingly right-tasting BLT with PB ($6.50); or the most exotic and satisfying choice on the menu, spicy peanut butter with pineapple jam and grilled chicken ($6.50). There's also "ants on a log" (celery sticks with PB and raisins for $5), chocolate peanut butter offerings, and peanutty desserts, all to be washed down with an icy glass of milk ($1.50).

$ One block west is MacDougal Street, and though this stretch between Washington Square Park and SoHo has to be one of the most touristy areas in the city, it contains a few genuine gems. The famed **Caffe Reggio** (119 MacDougal St.; ☎ 212/475-9557; www.caffereggio.com; Sun–Thurs 9am–2am, Fri–Sat 9am–4am; Ⓐ, Ⓒ, Ⓔ, Ⓑ, Ⓓ to W. 4th St.; cash only), for one, has been charming locals and tourists alike for decades. Opened in 1927, it's an antiques-filled haven, with carved dark wood loveseats and mottled brown walls covered with oil paintings (one from the 16th-century school of Caravaggio), carved relief sculptures, and etchings. The restaurant claims that it first introduced cappuccino to the city, and whether or not that's true, it's the thing to order ($2.75), accompanied by an Italian pastry ($2.75–$4.50). There are also main dishes, though like most everyone who frequents the cafe, it's never occurred to me to order a meal.

Greenwich Village & Meat-Packing District Dining

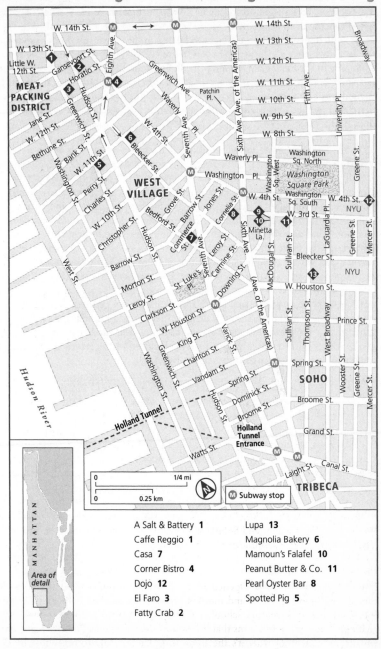

| 0 | 1/4 mi |
| 0 | 0.25 km |

Ⓜ Subway stop

A Salt & Battery **1**	Lupa **13**
Caffe Reggio **1**	Magnolia Bakery **6**
Casa **7**	Mamoun's Falafel **10**
Corner Bistro **4**	Peanut Butter & Co. **11**
Dojo **12**	Pearl Oyster Bar **8**
El Faro **3**	Spotted Pig **5**
Fatty Crab **2**	

$ For that, I'd go right next door to **Mamoun's Falafel** ⭐ (119 MacDougal St.; www.mamounsfalafel.com; daily 11am–5am; Ⓐ, Ⓒ, Ⓔ, Ⓑ, Ⓓ to W. 4th St.; cash only), which serves the best ultra-cheap falafels in the city at just $2 per sandwich (to decide whether it's the very best would involve a slugfest with fans of the eatery Alfanoose in the Financial District; p. 102). Quarters are extremely cramped, with just three booths for eating along with half-a-dozen stools, but when the weather is good, you can carry your lunch to nearby Washington Square Park for a messy, delectable picnic. This is also a good late-night snack spot, as it stays open daily until 5am.

$$$–$$$$ For a more formal meal, stroll 1 block west towards SoHo to **Lupa Osteria Romana** ⭐⭐⭐ (170 Thompson St., near Houston St.; ☎ 212/982-5089; www.luparestaurant.com; reservations recommended; Ⓥ or Ⓕ to W. Houston St.), another jewel in the crown of restaurateur/chef Mario Batali who, to my mind, can cook no wrong. At Lupa especially, the food is bold, gutsy, and exciting, a truly authentic take on the trattoria cuisine of Rome, with flavors and ingredients you won't find anywhere else in the city. The menu changes regularly, but if it's offered, try the fresh salt cod, which rides astride a sweet pile of caramelized fennel, slapped with a complementary citrus vinaigrette ($16); or a bowl of puffy ricotta gnocchi sided by chunks of hearty, spicy sausage ($15); or the sea vegetables (basically seaweed) in a rich, fiery red sauce ($6). If you want a table, you'll need to make reservations well in advance as it's always jammed, but I prefer to eat at the bar—the bartenders are a delight, friendly, and knowledgeable (if you're game, they'll walk you through a grappa tasting)—and the bar stools give you a good vantage point from which to soak in the atmosphere, which is as sophisticated and, yes, as Roman as it gets in the Big Apple.

WEST OF SIXTH AVE, SOUTH OF CHRISTOPHER STREET

$–$$ **A Salt & Battery** (112 Greenwich Ave., btwn 12th and 13th sts.; ☎ 212/691-2713; ❶ to Christopher St.; or 80 Second Ave., btwn 4th and 5th sts.; ☎ 212/254-6610; daily 11:30am–10:30pm; ❻ to Astor Place; www.asaltandbattery.com; AE, MC, V) is an authentic Brit fish-and-chips shop, from the accented blokes behind the counter, to the crusty slabs of haddock and cod ($6–$8) and veddy soggy fries, just like in London. Owners Nicky Perry and Patsy Carroll, both from across the pond, have even imported that most absurd of limey desserts, the deep-fried Mars bar. Dipped in the same batter as the fish, it tastes like hot fudge surrounded by a wedge of thinned, almond bubble gum, if that makes any sense, and it's really yummy (though you may feel a bit sick afterwards). As in England, there's counter service only, but the seating area is neat as a pin.

The downside? The restaurant is too popular for its own good. The Spotted Pig only takes reservations for parties of six and over, so the average wait time for a table is an hour to 90 minutes at dinner. Since this is a pub, nobody leaves while they're waiting for a table; instead, the sexy young things who make up the clientele here crush together at the bar, pretending to enjoy their exotic ales (Blue Point Hoptical Illusion, anyone?) as they gasp for oxygen. If you can manage to get here early or late (or better yet, for lunch), you have a chance of avoiding the mob scene. But do try and visit if you can; it's an outstanding culinary experience.

A British Invasion

"Gastropub"—sounds like some sort of intestinal illness, right? Actually, gastropubs are the latest craze in the U.K., where restaurateurs are taking over pubs and keeping the classic look—lots of dark wood, long bars, fine ales on tap—but serving up pub grub that you don't have to be drunk to enjoy. Now this same formula has hit the States, and its standard bearer is the **Spotted Pig** ★★★ (314 W. 11th St.; ☎ 212/620-0393; www.the spottedpig.com; Mon–Fri noon–1am; **Ⓐ**, **Ⓒ**, **Ⓔ**, **Ⓛ** to 14th St.; AE, MC, V), run by chef April Littlefield—she's buddies with the "Naked Chef" Jamie Oliver, and cooked previously at famed Chez Panisse—at the helm. Her food is, quite simply, wondrous. I can't remember another meal when I've emitted so many "Wows!" in the course of an evening. Whether it be the Gnudi appetizer, quite literally a "nude" ravioli, with pasta gone and only ethereally light balls of ricotta left, doused in browned butter and topped with fried sage leaves ($16); or velvety calves' liver married to caramelized onions ($15); or a creamy, nutty Jerusalem artichoke salad ($18); or any of her other innovative offerings—all are awesome.

WEST OF SIXTH AVENUE, DOWNTOWN OF CHRISTOPHER STREET

$ For dessert in this part of the Village, you need to go where the crowds are: the sublime **Magnolia Bakery** ★ (401 Bleecker St. at 11th St.; ☎ 212/462-2572; Mon noon–11:30pm, Tues–Thurs 9am–11:30pm, Fri 9am–12:30am, Sat 10am–12:30am, Sun 10am–11:30pm; **Ⓐ**, **Ⓒ**, **Ⓔ** to 14th St.; AE, DC, MC, V), which has become so popular that folks line up around the block to get in, and there's a maximum (strictly enforced) of 10 cupcakes sold to each customer. It's a tiny, sweet little shop that serves up the best old-fashioned baked goods in the city: rich, creamy icebox cakes, Snickers pie, red velvet cake, and, of course, the famous cupcakes—which have a delightful buttercream frosting, a third of an inch thick. There's no place to sit here, but you can squat on one of the nearby stoops (again, you'll be in a charming part of the Village, so this is not a disadvantage). Magnolia now has an uptown branch at 200 Columbus Avenue.

$$$–$$$$ I may be wrong, but I think that when most Americans think of Brazilian restaurants, they imagine large, bustling *churrascurias,* with waiters theatrically slashing at large slabs of meat and brandishing skewers of roast beef like culinary Zorros. **Casa** ★★ (72 Bedford St., on the corner of Commerce St.; ☎ 212/366-9410; Mon–Sat 6pm–midnight; reservations recommended; **Ⓛ** to Christopher St.; AE, DC, MC, V), which specializes in the home cooking of Brazil, is the antithesis of that. A chicly simple whitewashed room fronted with floor-to-ceiling windows, it gives just a hint of South America in its decor, with a bunch of bananas hung here, a lace place mat there, a small painting of a colonial church by the bar.

But in its food and its effusively gracious service, it's all Brazilian. The typically gorgeous waitstaff (if you've been to Brazil, you'll know how supernaturally good-looking these people can be) are a friendly lot, who will carefully walk you through the menu, leading you to the best of the Brazilian specialties: the meat, fish, and cheese pastry plate, crisp outside and oozing with flavor within, somewhat like the croquettes you get in Amsterdam ($6.95); the wonderfully creamy and chunky seafood stew called *moqueca de frutos do mar* ($19); and the classic *feijoda,* in which the meats are tenderized for a full 2 days before they hit the plate ($20). Unless you have a big appetite, the main dishes here can easily feed two. Skip dessert, but do indulge in a *caparinha* ($7), a potent sugar-cane-liqueur cocktail that will leave you feeling like you've stumbled into your own Carnaval.

$$$–$$$$ Marble counters go where plywood boards would normally be, and the crowd comes dressed to impress (not to tan), but if you close your eyes, open your mouth, and take a briny bite off the plate in front of you, you'll swear that you are at a clam shack on the coast of Maine. But no, you're at **Pearl Oyster Bar ★★** (18 Cornelia St. off Sixth Ave.; ☎ 212/691-8211; Mon–Fri noon–2:30 and 6pm–11pm, Sat 6pm–11pm; Ⓐ, Ⓔ, Ⓒ, Ⓑ, Ⓓ, Ⓕ, Ⓥ to W. 4th St.; MC, V), where seafood has that just-off-the-boat freshness, especially the famed lobster roll, an extravagant mountain of shredded meat on a buttered hot dog roll accompanied be a stack of shoestring fries at least 4 inches high. Entrees are market-priced but average $24, with appetizers priced from $6 to $10. Though the restaurant doubled in size a few years back to two rooms (one is counter-seating only), it's still pretty small and the no-reservations policy guarantees a line. Still, you'll be standing on a pretty street in the Village, among a chic, sophisticated crowd of diners—not too much of a hardship.

MEAT-PACKING DISTRICT

No, you don't go here for burgers (though there are still meat distributors in the area); this is New York's hottest dance club and bar scene, a tiny district that's become a magnet for hedonists of all types, including gourmands.

$$–$$$ Cheap classic **El Faro ★** (823 Greenwich St., at the corner of Horatio St.; Sun, Tues–Thurs noon–11pm, Fri–Sat noon–midnight; Ⓐ, Ⓒ, Ⓔ to 14th St.; AE, DC, MC, V) has been in business since 1927 (when its now-darkened murals of flamenco dancers were painted). Here you get the most copious tapas in the city, plates that aren't so much "small bites" as huge mouthfuls of garlicky, fresh Spanish fare that you must down with the house's seemingly endless sangria (even the half-pitcher will last longer than you can). The trick here is not to order too much: The paella off the tapas menu ($10) comes in a tureen that two people won't be able to polish off; nippingly tart white anchovies in vinaigrette are served eight to the plate ($8.50); and though they aren't on the menu, you can order six soft, puffy catfish croquettes for just $5. Every two tapas dishes are accompanied by either rice or potatoes: Choose the thinly sliced spuds which taste like warm, well-salted potato chips. If you order wisely, you can easily have an abundant feast here for less than $12 per person.

$$–$$$ In the first edition of this book, I included the trendy and ambitious Spice Market for it's unusual Asian fare and fabulously over-the-top bazaar decor. Alas, while it's still as good, its prices have risen precipitously. I'm dropping it in this edition in favor of nearby **Fatty Crab** (643 Hudson St. btwn Gansevoort and Horatio sts.; ☎ 212/352-3590; www.fattycrab.com; Sun–Wed noon–midnight, Thurs–Fri noon–2am, Sat 11am–2am, Sun 11am–midnight; **Ⓐ**, **Ⓒ**, **Ⓔ** to 14th St., **Ⓛ** to Eighth Ave.; AE, DC, MC, V), which has food as robust, complex, and exotic, but in a simpler (and much smaller) setting. (Arguably the crowd is just as trendy, if you care about that.) I'm always tempted to call Fatty Crab "messy" crab—its signature dish, a bowl of crabs in a pungent, spicy orange sauce may well be one of the hardest dishes in Manhattan to eat. With most of the meat hidden away in the hard to get nooks and crannies of the shell, the dish is tasty but time-consuming, and will leave your hands with an *eau de crustacean* perfume for a good two days after you dine here. Because it's also the most expensive item on the menu by far (market price, which can translate to as much as $30), I recommend some of the other dishes more highly: the Lincoln Log–like construction of papaya slices with sugar, salt, and spice ($5); fatty duck, a dish which rivals Peking duck in the crisp snap of the skin and the spice-infused tenderness of the meat ($14); or the steamed pork buns ($9) which are served with *kicap cair,* a type of gooey soy sauce that's the Malaysian equivalent of ketchup (you'll understand why its so popular there after you taste it). No reservations are taken, so be ready for a wait.

NEW YORK'S FINANCIAL DISTRICT

It's not easy to find a decent, decently priced meal in the Financial District, and I blame the stockbrokers. With shockingly large expense accounts and shockingly little time to actually eat, they have transformed the restaurant landscape here as effectively as the imported rabbits that munched the Australian outback into a desert. Nowadays, the vast majority of the eateries down here are either greasy, faceless take-out joints (for at-the-desk meals); Irish pubs; or plush, burnished temples of gastronomy more notable for their exorbitant pricing than for their food. It's gotten so bad that one rival NYC guidebook (I won't mention its name) skips the area altogether in its dining chapter.

I won't do that, as this is an important area for tourists, with its many historic sights, Ground Zero, and the ferry terminal to Ellis Island. But because so many visit here during the daylight hours, I have included one choice that's open only for lunch, but is still worth a visit.

$ That daylight-only luncherie is **Sophie's Cuban Cuisine** ✦ (73 New St., btwn Beaver St. and Exchange Place; ☎ 212/808-7755; www.sophiescuban.com; **Ⓐ**, **Ⓢ** to Battery Park), a local chain as ubiquitous in lower Manhattan as Bush-blue power ties. Founded by Peruvian immigrant Sofia Lunes (who noticed the number of Caribbean workers in the area and guessed correctly that Cuban food would be popular), these restaurants serve fresh, protein-heavy meals, prepared from scratch each morning and served to a swinging salsa beat. The menu changes daily, with all dishes but two—a shrimp in a startlingly pink garlic sauce ($11) and oxtail stew ($11)—costing $7 and accompanied by a heaping mound of rice and beans. I favor the *pernil,* a meltingly tender roasted pork accompanied by vinegared onions, though the *ropa vieja* (shredded beef) is darn tasty as well.

Huge, mayonnaisey Cuban sandwiches are also available for $6.95 from the take-out counter that occupies about a third of the space in these sparely furnished but always crowded restaurants. There are now six branches in Manhattan.

$ If you're in the vicinity of Ground Zero, the place to stop is **Alfanoose** ★ (8 Maiden Lane, near Broadway; ☎ 212/528-4669; www.alfanoose.com; closed Sun and after 9pm; ❶, ❾, ❍, ❺ to World Trade Center). The name means "magic lantern" and if you peer closely at the shelves, scattered here and there are a couple that look like they can be rubbed. They provide the only decoration in this spartan Middle Eastern restaurant, which is jam-packed with local office workers at lunchtime. Most come for the falafel, which is in an orb-to-orb competition with the balls at Mamoun's Falafel (p. 98) for the title of "Best in the City." Crispy with a supple interior, perfectly spiced and heated—in fact, each is fried to order, which can slow the service—they're lovingly rolled into tahini- and vegetable-spiked sandwiches, and doused with a just-fiery-enough homemade hot sauce ($5.75). Other Lebanese specialties are equally good, whether you choose an over-flowing platter of moist lamb *schwarma* on a bed of *mojadara* ($14, cracked wheat or rice with lentils and lots of dry-crispy fried onions); or a *shish tawook* sandwich ($7.95, charcoal grilled chicken breast). There's no waiter service, but once you get your meal there's always room at one of the long tables to hunker down and enjoy.

$ Another low-cost eating option near the World Trade Center site, about 5 blocks uptown to be specific, is **The Pakistani Tea House** (176 Church St., btwn Duane and Reade sts.; ☎ 212/240-9800; daily 10am-4am; ❶, ❷, ❍, ❍, ❺ to World Trade Center; AE, MC, V), which serves very little tea but lots of slow-burn-ing curries, freshly baked rounds of naan bread, and tandoori grilled lamb, chicken, and fish. For an overflowing plastic plate of food, consisting of a meat dish and two veggie options with either rice or bread, the price is a low $6. Speaking of veggie options, they're abundant and flavorful, making this a good choice for vegetarians (a similarly copious serving of just-vegetarian fare comes to only $4.49). It's also a good place to catch a cab, as this is where Pakistani drivers come at all hours of the night and day to get a little taste of home.

$$ With all there is to see and do in the Financial District, you may not choose to take the time for a sit-down meal. If the urge to picnic hits you, head directly to the New York Stock Exchange. No, they won't let you throw down a gingham blanket on the trading floor (though stranger things have happened there). Instead, make a beeline for **Daisy May's BBQ cart** ★ (www.daisymaysbbq.com) right outside the New York Stock Exchange (11 Wall St., though you'll find the cart on the Broad Street side of the building). Though the cart's hours are erratic, it usually lingers there for the lunch hour and a bit beyond, peddling straight-from-Carolina pulled pork ($9.50); tomato-less, heat-packing Texas chili ($8, it uses four different types of chiles in the mix); and, of course, ribs of all kinds. The carts and a mother-ship restaurant located on a barren stretch of 11th Avenue (at 46th St.; ☎ 212/977-1500; go to www.daisymaysbbq.com for more information on where the carts park) were created by Adam Perry Lang, a protégé of famed chef Daniel Boulud. You'll also find the carts trolling the Theater District and Midtown East.

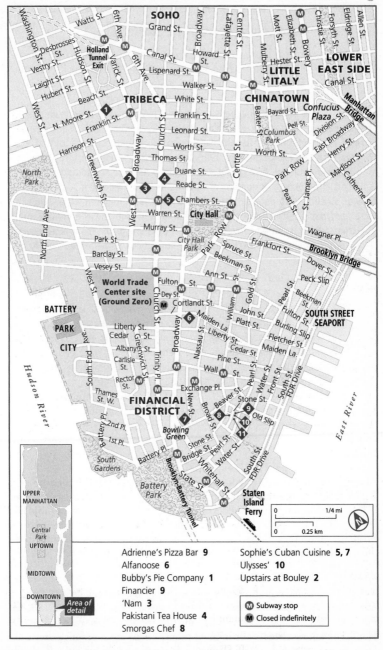

Adrienne's Pizza Bar **9**
Alfanoose **6**
Bubby's Pie Company **1**
Financier **9**
'Nam **3**
Pakistani Tea House **4**
Smorgas Chef **8**

Sophie's Cuban Cuisine **5, 7**
Ulysses' **10**
Upstairs at Bouley **2**

Ⓜ Subway stop
Ⓜ Closed indefinitely

History Written in Stone Street

Until 3 years ago, Stone Street was an interesting stop on walking tours of lower Manhattan, an abandoned alley boasting 15 decrepit if beautiful Greek Revival industrial buildings, all built right after the great fire of 1835, off Hanover Square. You went, you saw, you left.

But then, as always happens eventually on this overcrowded island, people realized that space was being wasted—a cardinal sin in Manhattan—and took action. The Landmarks Preservation Commission anointed the area with landmark status in 1995 and poured $2.5 million into repaving what had been the first paved street in New Amsterdam, adding old-fashioned streetlamps. A number of developers also stepped in, and soon it was bustling with cute-as-kittens little restaurants, each of which claimed a spot not only in these historic buildings but right on the cobblestone street, which is closed to traffic to allow for some of the most picturesque al fresco dining in Manhattan (to read more about Stone Street history go to p. 216 in chapter 8).

- **Smorgas Chef** ✸ (53 Stone St.; ☎ 212/422-3500; www.smorgas chef.com; daily 10:30am–10:30pm; ®, ⊙ to Whitehall St., or ➍, ➎ to Battery Park; AE, MC, V) is a sunny yellow and sea-blue Scandinavian restaurant that exposes its customers to all the greatest hits of the region: Norwegian smoked salmon (on top of eggs, chives, and bread, $12), salty herring from Denmark ($10), and, yes, Swedish meatballs as light as beach balls and carrying a nice smattering of lingonberry sauce ($12 sandwich, $19 as an entree).

- **Ulysses'** ✸ (58 Stone St.; ☎ 212/482-0400; www.ulyssesbarnyc. com; daily 11:30am–4am; same subways; AE, DC, MC, V), which bills

TRIBECA, SOHO & NOLITA

Though the wealthiest zip code in the United States (10021) belongs to the Upper East Side, the areas of TriBeCa (the "Triangle below Canal Street"), SoHo ("South of Houston Street"), and to a lesser extent Nolita ("North of Little Italy") are catching up quickly, as these neighborhoods draw more and more celebrities, financiers, and other filthy-rich types. Not surprisingly, the restaurants in these 'hoods can be pretty exalted, not only in decor and ambition, but in price.

SOHO

$–$$ For a quick snack in SoHo, pop by **Hampton Chutney Co.** (68 Prince St., btwn Crosby and Lafayette sts.; ☎ 212/226-9996; daily 11am–9pm; ⊙, ® to Prince St., ➏ to Spring St.; AE, MC, V), the Big Apple's version of an Indian "Dosa Hut." The quintessential subcontinent munch, *dosas* are sourdough crepes, here made from lentils and rice and folded into sandwiches as long as a 7-year-old's arm. Fillings range from classical Indian *masala* (a curried potato stew for $7.45) itself as a Greco-Gaelic pub, if you can imagine that, anchors the street on its north end. More Irish than Greek (though there are tributes to the Greek hero on some of the walls), it's huge but divided adroitly into intimate "snugs" and furnished with several tons of County Clare shale (forming oh-so-Irish country walls). What's not-so-Irish about this place is the food, which is much better than I've had in the pubs of Eire, especially the lunchtime carvery, where you can get a heaping plateful of meat and veggies (terrific barbecued spare ribs, juicy roast beef, crispy fries, braised escarole, and more), starting at a reasonable $10. Monday is Lobster Night, featuring $15 dinners and, of course, the Guinness is foamy, icy, and well pulled.

♦ Also on Stone is a très Parisian dessert place, the patisserie **Financier** ★ (62 Stone St.; ☎ 212/344-5600; Mon–Fri 7am–8pm, Sat 8:30am–6:30am; ®, ◎ to Whitehall St., ❹, ❺ to Battery Park; AE, MC, V), which has so-so sandwiches, soups, and salads but turns out exquisitely creamy, puffy, sweet pastries; and **Adrienne's Pizza Bar** (54 Stone St.; ☎ 212/248-3838; Mon–Sat 10:30am–midnight, Sun 10:30am–10pm; same subways; AE, DC, MC, V), a reasonably priced and stylishly appointed parlor where the pies are square, thin-crusted, and well spiced (one can easily feed three people at a cost of $7). The salads tower over the plates ($7 for an entree-sized heap), and such Italian classics as eggplant parmigiana ($7) and lasagna ($8) round out the menu, along with beer and wine. Though eight restaurants are found on the street, the above four offer the best value and food.

to Mediterranean-inspired Kalamata olives cushioned in goat cheese and topped with arugula, diced tomatoes, and roasted onion ($8.95). One dosa should be big enough for all but the hungriest of couples to share. A second branch is at 464 Amsterdam Ave., near 82nd St.

$–$$ Cuban food lends itself to many moods. At the Sophie's Cuban Cuisine chain (p. 101), the tasty but unfussy grub is meant to sate the legions of office workers who flock there on their lunch hours. At **Cubana Café** ★★ (110 Thompson St., btwn Prince and Spring; ☎ 212/966-5366; www.cubanacafeel chulo.com; daily noon–11pm; ◎, ® to Prince St.; cash only) it's food to party with. Set in a chicly disheveled basement, with Caribbean yellow walls and tiny tables jammed one up against the next, the restaurant attracts an attractive, 20- to 30-something crowd, fueling up before hitting the dance clubs. But like its more straight-laced competitor, the food is delicious and cheap, with piping hot Cuban sandwiches costing just $7.50, a perfect *picadillo* (beef or turkey stew, laced with

The Lowdown on Tipping

You must tip in every restaurant you visit, no ifs, ands, or buts about it. Waiters in New York make less than minimum wage, just $5.41 per hour, because the government assumes that their income will be supplemented by tips. In fact, it taxes them on the tips they assume they're making, so if you're stingy, they pay for it. It's customary to tip about 15% to 20%, which can be easily calculated by simply doubling the amount of tax on the meal (meal tax in NYC is 8.65%). If your waiter has been particularly attentive, go a bit higher; who knows, you could be helping the next Jennifer Aniston or Kelsey Grammar, both of whom waited tables before they hit it big.

raisins, olives and nuts) for $8, unctuous pulled pork with whipped plantains for $9, and rum (or cachaça)-laden cocktails for $6 to $8. Don't skip the homemade salsas.

NOLITA

$ A speedy but top-quality lunch or dinner can be had at **La Esquina** ★★ (106 Kenmare St., at the corner of Cleveland Place; ☎ 646/613-1333; daily 8am–5am; ⑥ to Spring St., or ⓝ, ⓡ, ⓦ to Prince; AE, MC, V), a brushed-steel diner turned taqueria, with a more chic (and expensive) restaurant below, as well as a cafe around the corner. All three serve the complex, vivid food of Mexico City, but you'll spend the least at the taqueria, where the tacos cost just $3 to $4 each (though you'll have to down two if you're really hungry). And this ain't Taco Bell! The tacos themselves are floury, soft, and freshly baked; the fillings go beyond the norm, whether you get one with a piquant pineapple *habanero* salsa, the *chiote* rubbed pork, or shredded cabbage with a flaming chipotle salsa.

$$ New York is such an international city that favorite neighborhood hangouts are as likely to feature squid and lemongrass as they are burgers and fries, and such is the case in chic Nolita, where **Lovely Day** ★ (196 Elizabeth St., btwn Spring and Prince sts.; ☎ 212/925-3310; Mon–Thurs noon–10:30pm, Fri–Sun 11am–11:30pm; ⓝ, ⓡ, ⓦ to Prince St.; AE) dishes out Thai and Vietnamese food to a crowd of regulars, who squat at the rough wooden tables outside, dangling babies and calling to tattooed friends as they stroll by. Inside, it's as much of a clubhouse, but a friendly one, with cute little red booths and walls stenciled with cheery flowers. The menu runs the gamut from Asian standards such as summer rolls ($4.80) and pad Thai ($8.50), to more inventive fare, such as the seared tuna wrapped in crepes and balanced atop a plate of deeply green lettuces and puddles of peanut and wasabi sauces ($13). Accompany your meal with one of the fruity cocktails that fuel the friendly scene here.

$ You'll be tempted to stay for dessert at Lovely Day, but instead take a short walk down Spring Street to **Rice to Riches** ★★ 🄺 (37 Spring St., btwn Mott and Mulberry sts.; ☎ 212/274-0008; www.ricetoriches.com; Sun–Thurs 11am–11pm,

Fri and Sat 11am–1am; **N**, **R** to Prince St.), a delightful one-trick pony that serves only rice pudding. This isn't the rice pudding your mom made, however; it's tarted up with all sorts of exotic flavorings and unfortunately cutesy names such as "Sex, drugs and rocky road" and "Surrender to Mango." I have yet to discover a flavor that wasn't absolutely ambrosial. The shop is self-consciously chic and usually overcrowded, so I'd suggest taking your puddings to the playground across the street (an especially good idea if you have kids with you—they'll need to run off the overload of sugar these puddings pack). A bowl costs $6, but it should be shared, and if you ask, the staff will put two flavors into one bowl.

TRIBECA

$–$$ The quintessential TriBeCa restaurant, a place where celebs go for their mac-and-cheese fix, is **Bubby's** ★ 🄺 (120 Hudson St.; ☎ 212/219-0666; **1**, **9** to Franklin; hours below; DC, MC, V), a temple of "down-home cookin'," though the menu does career from jerk chicken wings to quesadillas to matzo ball soup. My advice? Stick with the homey American classics: the crunchy buttermilk fried chicken ($16), the slow-cooked pulled pork ($13), gooey mac and cheese ($11), fluffy sour cream pancakes ($5.95), perfect omelets ($11), and all of the other breakfast goodies they have on order (weekend brunch is the most popular meal here, and the line for tables can snake down the block). All of these items are top-notch and more in keeping with the space, which looks like a cross between your grandmother's parlor and a roadside diner. Kids will love this place too, not only for the child-friendly menu, but for the endless supply of crayons and paper doled out by the staff, and the bookshelf in the back, brimming with children's books. (Bubby's hours are complicated: it's open 8am–4pm and 6–11pm Mon–Fri, 9am–4pm and 6pm–midnight Sat–Sun.)

$$–$$$ Chic and "Vietnamese restaurant" don't usually appear in the same sentence, except when you're discussing TriBeCa's own 'Nam (110 Reade St., btwn Church St. and W. Broadway; ☎ 212/267-1777; Mon–Thurs noon–2pm and 5:30–10pm, Fri noon–2pm and 5:30–11pm, Sat 5:30–11pm, Sun 5:30pm–10pm; **A**, **C** to Church St.; AE, MC, V), an elegant, bamboo-laden eatery with imaginative cocktails and mighty fine rice-paper rolls, noodle dishes, and stews. The one item on the menu that should not be skipped is the *bo luc lac* ($8), a beef-and-watercress salad in a perky tamarind vinaigrette. If you go with an entree-sized noodle soup always bobbing with roasted peanuts and an assortment of seafood, expect to pay $8 to $11; other entrees range from $12 to $18, making this one of TriBeCa's more affordable eating options.

$$–$$$$ When the World Trade Center was attacked in 2001, downtown chef David Bouley was one of the many New Yorkers who stepped up to the plate—in his case, literally. He supplied plates, and food, and chefs to the site, working in tandem with the Red Cross to feed over one million meals to recovery workers at Ground Zero in the crucial first weeks after the attacks. His damaged restaurants, Bouley Bakery and Danube, closed and in rebuilding (and reopening), he created a second-floor eatery above a more expensive one, called appropriately **Upstairs at Bouley** ★★ (130 W. Broadway at Duane St.; ☎ 212/219-1011; Mon–Fri 5:30pm–11:30pm, Sat 11am–4pm and 5:30pm–11:30pm, Sun 11am–4pm;

Eating Out with Children in Gotham

Take it from this Mom, you don't have to go to stupid theme restaurants (where the tabs will be high and the food execrable) or confine yourself to Mickey D's, just to keep the kids happy. Average New Yorkers take their kids out to dine all the time, and most restaurants will have high chairs, kid-friendly grub, and tolerant waitstaffs. Here are a few that I've found to be extremely easy with babies, toddlers, and tykes:

- **Bubby's:** Gourmet comfort food that everyone will enjoy, plus huge racks of children's books to borrow in the rear. (p. 107)
- **Celeste:** Excellent pizza and pasta in a setting so rambunctious, even the loudest baby's wails will simply melt into the general din. Many of the waiters are actually from Italy, and they have a delightful way with kids, even the cranky ones. (p. 109)
- **Hill Country:** Serve-yourself southern food means no wait for grub and a quick in and out. Top quality barbeque, tasty cocktails, and rollicking country music may convince you (and the kids) to linger longer. (p. 80)
- **Otto:** An upscale pizzeria with a top-flight wine list, it's loud enough to bring small babies to, and the friendly waitstaff will bend over backwards to keep the older kids amused (a fistful of crayons and a place mat with puzzles on it will also be offered as soon as you sit down). (p. 91)
- **Peanut Butter & Co.:** Peanut butter and jelly sandwiches with three choices of jelly, right near some nice Village playgrounds. Need I say more? (p. 96)
- **Sapporo:** Japanese food that's unthreatening (even to picky kids), healthy, fast, and right in the Theater District. (p. 71)
- **Serendipity:** An old-fashioned ice cream parlor and toy store right near Bloomingdales. The "frozen hot chocolate" is legendary. (p. 78)
- **Shabu Tatsu:** Older children will love cooking their own food at this authentic Japanese barbecue and soup joint, where beef is king and the food tasty but simple enough even for kids who usually won't stray beyond hot dogs and grilled cheese. (p. 93)
- **Virgil's Real Barbecue:** Where else in town will your kids be encouraged to eat with their hands? Another excellent Times Square option. (p. 71)

AE, DC, MC, V). I like to think "Upstairs" was influenced by his democratizing food experience at the WTC site. It's an open-kitchened space (during the daytime he often holds cooking classes there) with wraparound windows for an action-packed view of the street below, and tables so tightly crammed together your meal will be scented with the smells of those of your neighbors. But it's also much cheaper than this celeb chef's other places, and it's where he comes to experiment; the menu, a gastronomic playground really, ranges from sushi to Italian pasta to market fresh salads. Anything with mushrooms is terrific (especially the wild mushroom salad with truffle dressing, $8.25) and the pastas hit the spot (and don't hit the wallet too hard either at $13–$14 for a big bowl). The Japanese food is less successful (I think).

UPPER WEST SIDE

Our award for "most improved" food neighborhood goes, without the slightest hesitation, to the Upper West Side.

A mere 8 years ago residents had to cross the park or hop a subway downtown to get the authentic ethnic eats and high-quality gourmet fare that folks in other parts of the city take for granted. But with the opening in 2004 of the United State's first "gourmet food court," the Time Warner Center (including the NY version of Napa Valley's French Laundry, here called Per Se and an impossible reservation to snag) and the similar opening in the 5 or so years prior to that of a handful of excellent Mediterranean, Latin, and French restaurants, the Upper West Side can finally hold its head up in foodie circles. Though it doesn't have the number of really terrific restaurants that, say, the East Village does, it's on its way.

$–$$ Starting with the epicenter of UWS dining, the Time Warner Center's **Bouchon Bakery** ✦ (10 Columbus Circle; ☎ 212/823-9366; Mon–Fri 8am–9pm, Sat 10am–9pm, Sun 10am–7pm; ❶, Ⓐ, Ⓑ, Ⓒ, Ⓓ to Columbus Circle; AE, MC, V) is a surprisingly affordable spot to grab a quick meal. Surprising because the founding chef is none other than that Hercules of gourmet dining, Thomas Keller himself (his much pricier restaurant Per Se is just upstairs). Now, I'm not saying you're going to get cut-price versions of the caviar-, tapioca pearl– and foie gras– laden fare he's serving at Per Se. But you will get upgraded *boulangerie* fare: lovely large salads, sandwiches with a twist (like the CB&J: cashew butter with apricot jam, $9.75) and the most gratifying tomato soup and grilled cheese sandwich I've ever had ($13, and if you don't dip the sandwich, the concerned waitress will come over to recommend it). As you might expect from an eatery with the words "bakery" in its name, the pastries are mighty fine, too. Bouchon is on the third floor, right in the middle of the floor (no walls).

$–$$ Though it looks like a Chinese restaurant, **Flor de Mayo** (484 Amsterdam Ave. btwn 83rd and 84th sts.; ☎ 212/787-3388; daily noon–midnight; ❶ to 86th St.; AE, MC, V) is actually the city's most outstanding hybrid "Chino-Latino" restaurant. What this means really is a mixed Hispanic and Chinese staff cooking up terrific south-of-the-border fare, and mediocre Chinese food (I don't know why, but that's always the way it is with Chino-Latino). As long as you order off the Latin side of the menu—be it the chopped beef with yellow rice ($8.50), the excellent avocado salad ($3.95), or Dominican chicken with rice ($7.50)—you can't go wrong. Lunch specials lower the cost of a plate with an entree, salad, and rice to just $5.55.

$$ Nearby, the spirit of the city of Naples is being channeled at quirky **Celeste** ✦✦ 🦐 (502 Amsterdam Ave. near 84th St.; ☎ 212/874-4550; Mon– Thurs 5pm–11pm, Fri 5pm–11:30pm, Sat noon–3pm and 5pm–11:30pm, Sun

Upper West Side, Upper East Side & Harlem Dining

Amy Ruth's **15**
Bouchon Bakery **6**
Café Sbarsky **11**
Celeste **2**
EJ's Luncheonette **8**
Flor de Mayo **4**
Kefi **3**
Lexington Candy Shop **10**
Miss Mamie's
  Spoonbread Too **14**
Miss Maude's
  Spoonbread Too **16**
Pain Quotidien **7, 9**
Pio Pio **12**
Shackshack **5**
Table d'Hote **13**
Turkuaz **1**

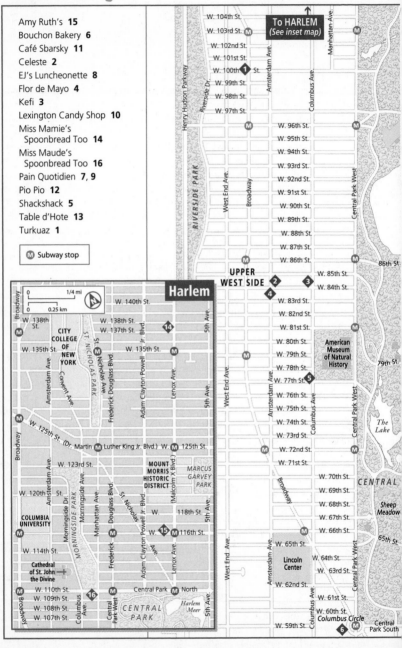

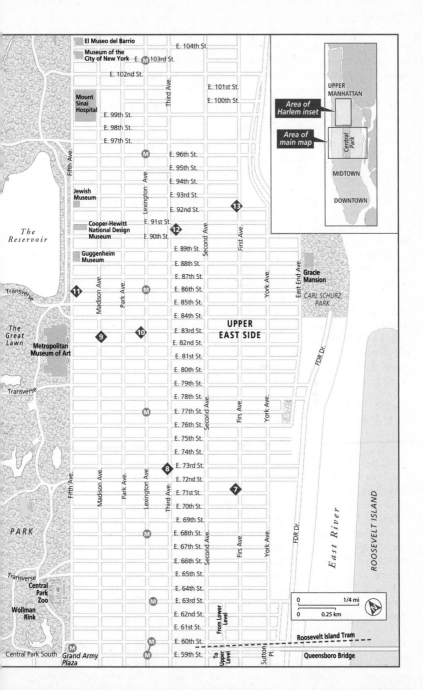

El Museo del Barrio
Museum of the City of New York
E. 104th St.
E. 103rd St.
E. 102nd St.
E. 101st St.
E. 100th St.
Mount Sinai Hospital
E. 99th St.
E. 98th St.
E. 97th St.
E. 96th St.
E. 95th St.
E. 94th St.
Jewish Museum
E. 93rd St.
E. 92nd St.
Cooper-Hewitt National Design Museum
E. 91st St.
E. 90th St.
Guggenheim Museum
E. 89th St.
E. 88th St.
E. 87th St.
E. 86th St.
E. 85th St.
E. 84th St.
E. 83rd St.
E. 82nd St.
Metropolitan Museum of Art
E. 81st St.
E. 80th St.
E. 79th St.
E. 78th St.
E. 77th St.
E. 76th St.
E. 75th St.
E. 74th St.
E. 73rd St.
E. 72nd St.
E. 71st St.
E. 70th St.
E. 69th St.
E. 68th St.
E. 67th St.
E. 66th St.
E. 65th St.
E. 64th St.
E. 63rd St.
E. 62nd St.
E. 61st St.
E. 60th St.
E. 59th St.

The Reservoir

The Great Lawn

PARK

Transverse
Transverse
Transverse

Central Park Zoo
Wollman Rink

Central Park South
Grand Army Plaza

Fifth Ave.
Madison Ave.
Park Ave.
Lexington Ave.
Third Ave.
Second Ave.
First Ave.
York Ave.
East End Ave.
Firs Ave.
Sutton Pl.

UPPER EAST SIDE

Gracie Mansion
CARL SCHURZ PARK

FDR Dr.

East River

ROOSEVELT ISLAND

From Lower Level
To Upper Level

Roosevelt Island Tram
Queensboro Bridge

UPPER MANHATTAN
Area of Harlem inset
Area of main map
Central Park
MIDTOWN
DOWNTOWN

0   1/4 mi
0   0.25 km

noon–3pm and 5–10:30pm; ❶ to 86th St.; cash only), for all the good and the bad that implies. Starting with the possible negatives (and some may well enjoy this), it's a cacophonous little place, made even louder by the cheerful insults the waiters sling at one another as they rush around the room. Reservations aren't accepted so there's always a wait. Tables are so close together you're going to feel as if you need elbow pads to dine safely. But all that may well recede into the background when you get your first taste of the food, so authentic, so fresh, and so darn toothsome it's almost as if they teleported it direct from the Boot. Delicate and grease-free fried artichokes ($7.50); free-form, thin, smoky wood-fired pizzas ($10); gnocchi ($9) that is cotton ball light and draped in a tomato sauce that tastes like sunshine—you get all this and more at prices a good $4 to $5 lower than other less accomplished Italian restaurants in the neighborhood.

$$–$$$ When it came time to make my first research visit to the Greek restaurant **Kefi** ✮✮✮ (505 Columbus Ave. at 85th St.; ☎ 212/873-0200; Sun–Thurs 5pm–10pm, Fri–Sat 5pm–11pm; ❶ to 79th St.; AE, DC, MC, V), I brought along two foodie friends, Jeff and Elizabeth. It took some convincing. They seemed oddly reluctant to try the place. But they liked the decor, which seems lifted directly from Greece. And once the platters of food arrived, they tucked in. On that first visit, we tried a number of dishes that were to become my favorites here, unchewy grilled octopus salad ($8.95), roasted garlic-infused meatballs ($5.95), and shrimp with orzo, spinach, and feta ($14). And with each new platter, the chorus of oohs and aahs and "this is *absolutely sublime*" (well, they are real food lovers) grew louder and louder until they finally admitted to me that neither usually liked Greek food—an animus against feta cheese—but that Kefi had converted them. It really is that good, and don't skip the desserts which, like the rest of the menu, go far beyond the same-old-same-old Greek grub.

$$–$$$ My vote for best "date place" in this part of town goes to **Turkuaz** ✮✮✮ (2637 Broadway at 100th St.; ☎ 212/655-9541; www.turkuazrestaurant.com; Mon–Thurs 11:30am–11pm, Fri–Sat 11:30am–1am, Sun 11am–11pm; ❶, ❷, ❸ to 96th St., or ❶ to 103rd St.; AE, MC, V), a happily exotic Turkish restaurant, with a look that's pure Arabian Nights. The main dining room is outfitted like a large tent with billowing drapes of fabric all around, twinkling cut-metal lanterns, richly embroidered pillows, and a staff that stands at stiff attention near your table while dressed in traditional Turkish costumes. The food continues the happy mirage with a combination of the well-known Middle Eastern spreads—hummus, puréed smoked eggplant, or red caviar spread (about $5.50 each and top-notch)—and lesser-known delights such as intricate fingers of salmon wrapped in grape leaves ($17), a sensuously moist lamb kebab slathered in rich yogurt and tomato sauce ($16), or simple but succulent chicken kebabs ($13). Try to dine here on a Thursday, Friday, or Saturday, and start your meal no earlier than 8:30pm so that you'll be in your seat when the free belly-dancing show starts at 10pm. It's a perfect end—or beginning?—to a sensual evening on the town.

THE UPPER EAST SIDE

The Upper East Side has a split personality. Near Central Park it's all old money, high rents, and overpriced restaurants (even the diners in this area cost 20% more than in other parts of the city). Go towards the river, though, and prices drop dramatically as this neighborhood, because it is not well served by subways, has some of the cheaper housing in Manhattan and attracts a number of recent college graduates. The restaurants on York, First, Second, and Third avenues tailor their offerings to meet these penny-pinchers' needs; dine instead on Fifth, Madison, Lexington, or the numbered streets that connect these avenues together, and you'll pay painfully for doing so. Problem is, most of the museums that you'll want to visit are on the more pricey thoroughfares. But I've found two options within a short hop of Museum Mile and a few more that will require a bit more of a hike.

$–$$ For a quick, simple meal, I have two diners to recommend. For heavy nostalgia points, there's the **Lexington Candy Shop** ★ 🌟 kids (1226 Lexington Ave at 83rd St.; ☎ 212/288-0057; Mon–Sat 7am–7pm, Sun 9am–6pm; ❹, ❺, ❻ to 86th St.; AE, DC, MC, V), which has been filling its lunch counter with burgers ($7) and malts ($5) since 1925. You'll truly feel like you've stepped into an Edward Hopper painting when you open the door. **EJ's Luncheonette** (1271 Third Ave. at 73rd St.; ☎ 212/472-0600; Mon–Sat 8am–11pm, Sun 8am–7pm; ❻ to 77th St.; cash only) is a retro-'50s diner, and it stays open well into the night to serve such American classics as grilled cheddar sandwiches ($5.75), burgers ($7.50), and club sandwiches ($7.50). It also has a good collection of tasty oversized salads ($9.50–$12), breakfast items, and soups ($3.95 a bowl). Also at 447 Amsterdam Ave.

$–$$ Also inexpensive, healthy, and pleasant is **Le Pain Quotidien** (1131 Madison Ave. at 82nd St.; ☎ 212/327-4900; www.lepainquotidien.com; Mon–Fri 7am–7:30pm, Sat–Sun 8am–7:30pm; ❹, ❺, ❻ to 86th St.; AE, DC, MC, V), an international chain of Belgian bakeries that devote a large part of their spaces to rough-hewn wooden tables where full breakfasts, lunches, and early dinners are served. The menu is appropriately bread-centered, with the best of the offerings—sandwiches—served on solid nutty brown breads or baguettes, topped with lots of vegetables and sided by salads. Full salads are also available, as are breakfast plates, tarts, and pies galore, and big bowls of café au lait. An average meal here will cost less than $12. Along with the Madison Avenue location, Le Pain Quotidien has about a dozen other branches scattered throughout the city. This one is a find as it's one of the few really good budget places near the Metropolitan Museum.

$–$$ Julia Child once said that her favorite meal was a simple but perfectly roast chicken. I'm sure she had in mind a French technique for the roasting, but I think she might have become a convert had she ever tried the Peruvian birds at **Pio Pio** (1746 First Ave btwn 90th and 91st St; ☎ 212/426-5800; daily 11am–11pm; ❹,❺,❻ to 86th St.; AE). Spear one of them with a fork, and clear juice just gushes forth—they're that tender. And the crackling skin is covered with a blend of spices I can't name (but are delish) which are further enhanced by the garlic sauce you smear on. One bird costs $12 and can easily feed a family of four; go easy on the side dishes and a group can dine for $6 or $7 per person here, including a pisco-based cocktail. As for the look of the place, it's small and cute with colorful paintings on the wall. If you have a really large group, head to larger Pio Pio Salon on the West Side (702 Amsterdam Ave.).

The Great New York Bagel Debate

A handful of glutinous wheat mixed with a bit of malt and rolled into a circle that is boiled and then baked—that's the simple recipe behind New York's edible mascot, the bagel. You wouldn't think something as basic, as simple as this little bit of circular bread would inspire so many heated debates, such rapturous praise, but in Empire City, the bagel is king. So you should try one sometime during your visit (just don't ask to have it "scooped out," the sacrilegious craze among carb-phobics today). The best places to try them (all of them modest in price) and where you're likely to get them fresh out of the oven, are:

- **Absolute Bagels** (2788 Broadway at 107th St.; ☎ 212/932-2052; ❶ to 110th St.)
- **Bagel Bob's** (51 University Place btwn 10th and 11th sts.; ☎ 212/533-2627; ❻ to Astor, ❽, ❾ to 8th St.)
- **H&H Bagels** (2239 Broadway btwn 80th St.; ☎ 212/595-8000; ❶ to 79th St.; or 1551 Second Ave. btwn 81st and 82nd sts.; ❻ to 86th St.)
- **Murray's Bagels** (500 Sixth Ave. at 13th St.; ☎ 212/462-2830; ❸, ❻ to 14th St.; or 242 Eighth Ave. btwn 22nd and 23rd sts.; ❸, ❹ to 23rd St.)
- **Kosar's** (367 Grand St. btwn Essex and Norfolk sts.; ☎ 877/4-BIALYS; ❻ to Delancey St.)

$$–$$$$ Right on Museum Mile is **Café Sabarsky** ✫ (1048 Fifth Ave., entrance on 86th St.; ☎ 212/628-6200; www.neuegallery.org; Mon and Wed 9am–6pm, Thurs–Sun 9am–9pm; ❹, ❺, ❻ to 86th St.; AE, MC, V), which in any other part of town would not be considered reasonably priced in the slightest. But for a seat in a wood-paneled mansion designed by Carrere and Hastings (architects of the New York Public Library at 42nd St.), overlooking Central Park, paying $12 for a sandwich can't be matched. Part of the Neue Gallery, a museum of Austrian and German art (p. 158), the transplanted Viennese cafe serves all the heavy Teutonic specialties of that city: bratwurst ($14), liverwurst sandwiches ($12), and spatzle with a bouquet of vegetables ($15), along with an assortment of lighter salads and sandwiches. These are all fine, but you really come here for the delicious pastries and Viennese coffee so strong it will grow hair on your tongue. The cafe hosts classical performances on Wednesday and Thursday afternoons and Friday evenings, which you can attend for the cost of a strudel ($7).

$$$–$$$$ Not far from the Cooper Hewitt museum, **Table d'Hôte** ✫ (44 E. 92nd St. off Madison Ave.; ☎ 212/348-8125; reservations recommended; Mon–Fri noon–10:30pm, Sat 11:30am–10:30pm, Sun 10:30am–9pm, ❹, ❺, ❻ to 86th St.; AE, MC, V) has a full range of "tasting" options and early evening prix fixes that keep the prices within the realm of reason. The prix fixe is $20 before 7pm and includes three courses. And for almost every entree on the menu, there are half-portions, which I find to be quite filling, the meat a little larger than the size of a pack of cards (which is, after all, the size recommended by most nutritionists), and the rest of the plate is as well-stocked with veggies as the full portion. The cuisine here is sophisticated French and quite well done, with such options as a rich roasted quail with rosemary stuffing ($17 half-portion), hangar steak sided by Stilton potatoes ($17 half-portion), and a lovely salad of goat cheese fritters and beets ($12). *Note:* The place is tiny; in fact it looks a bit like a little cottage in Provence, with all-white wooden walls and flowered banquettes, so you should make reservations, as it does fill up fast.

HARLEM

$$–$$$ For dining up in Harlem, Sylvia's is an institution. Problem is, it's been around so long that the food has become rather institutional, and today it's tourists on escorted tours (in my experience) that primarily go there. Instead you'll want to visit some of the new ladies of Harlem: **Miss Maude's Spoonbread Too** ★★ (547 Lenox Ave., near 137th St.; ☎ 212/690-3100; Mon–Sat noon– 10pm, Sun 11am–9:30pm; AE, MC, V), **Miss Mamie's Spoonbread Too** ★★ (366 W. 110th St., btwn Columbus and Manhattan aves.; ☎ 212/865-6744; hours same as above; AE, MC, V), and **Amy Ruth's** ★★ (113 W. 116th St.; ☎ 212/280-8779; www.amyruthsharlem.com; Sun–Thurs 7:30–11pm, Fri–Sat 24 hr.; ❷, ❸, Ⓑ, Ⓒ to 116th St.; AE, DC, MC, V). The first two, as you might have guessed, are sister restaurants, actually named for owner Norma Jean Darden's mother and aunt, who passed down to Darden the recipes featured on the menu. They feel like family affairs as well, with old black-and-white photographs of relatives staring down at you from the walls, and homey touches, such as paper butterflies hanging from the lights at Miss Maude's and yellow wainscoting at Miss Mamie's. The food continues the theme, with many recipes that could be served up at a family reunion: exceedingly tender BBQ ribs ($14), big slabs of slightly spicy corn bread, greaseless fried chicken and shrimp ($12 and $15), and delectable smothered pork chops ($15). The only missteps here occur when you leave the South—the jerk chicken is numbingly spicy. Other than that, the food is first rate. By the way, if Darden's name sounds familiar, it's because she penned, along with her sister, the best-selling cookbook *Spoonbread and Strawberry Wine.*

Amy Ruth's was named for the grandmother of owner Carl Redding, and he'll readily admit that it's her recipes that he uses in the dining room. But part of what makes the food so good here is the freshness of the ingredients: very green veggies, perfect sweet potatoes, and the honey for the honey-fried chicken that comes from beehives on the roof. You'll also enjoy dining here if you know anything about New York politics, as this is the unofficial clubhouse, along with the Abyssinian Baptist Church, for Harlem's political elite, many of whom have dishes named for them on the menu. It's not unusual to see Congressman Charles Rangel when you're eating the tasty meatloaf platter named for him, or Al Sharpton when you're munching on "his" waffles and chicken platter ($9.50, the best in the city). Prices are equivalent to what you'd find at Miss Mamie's.

$$–$$$ Of course Harlem isn't just about soul food. Along a stretch of 116th street known as *Le Petit Senegal,* West African fare takes center stage, and it's a lipsmacking, terrifically satisfying cuisine, even for those who've never tried it before.

Interestingly, the food served varies depending on time of day. At lunch, the menu is centered around a number of savory stews: *Thibeu Djen,* Senegal's national dish, a blend of fish, casava, eggplant, carrots, and tomatoes made succulent by palm oil; tender *yassa* chicken or fish smothered in sauteed onions, which have themselves been smothered in a tangy lemon sauce; lamb *mafe* in which the meat is braised in a creamy peanut sauce; and more. In the evenings, grilled meats and fish prevail, often saturated with the flavors of garlic, lemon, or palm oil. You can try these dishes at a number of the restaurants along the strip between Adam Clayton Powell Boulevard and Frederick Douglas (along with shopping for West African clothes, CD's, DVD's and more—it's a pretty fascinating area) but the classy atmosphere, and high-quality ingredients bring me back, time and again, to **Africa Restaurant** ✪ (256 W. 116th St. near Frederick Douglas Blvd.; ☎ 212/666-9400; www.africakine.com; daily noon–1am; ❸, ❹, ❷, ❸ to 116th St.; AE, DC, MC, V). Yes, there's TV's silently playing in the background (that's de rigeur in West African restaurants), but here the windows are shaded by swooping curtains, the floor is a shiny wood, and in the evenings, there's often live *akonting* music (a stringed instrument with a gourd as a body). And there always seems to be a party going on when I come here, with family members heartily greeting one another in French, and little girls in frilly dresses giggling in the corners. You really feel like you've jumped continents when you dine here (it's an experience). As for the prices, they're quite reasonable: Most entrees range from $9–$12 and can easily serve two, with a few jumping up to $14 or $15. *One note*: The restaurant is on the second floor. The movie theater–like counter as you enter is for take-out food only. Head up to the hostess to be seated.

5

Remarkable Sights & Attractions

Let's rank the ones you definitely must see

ASK NEW YORKERS ABOUT THEIR FEELINGS FOR THEIR CITY, AND THEY WILL often respond, "There's just one New York." By that they mean: one city so full of museums (more than 40 major ones); historical sights; world-famous institutions; parks; zoos; universities; lectures; concerts and recitals; theaters for opera, musicals, drama, and dance; architectural highlights; presidents' homes; and kooky galleries, that its diversions are limitless and you can never be bored. If you had the speed and stamina of a Lance Armstrong, you would still be hard put to cover all of the attractions in several months of touring.

Because your own time is more limited than that, I'm confining my coverage to two categories of sights in this chapter:

First up are the city's "iconic" attractions, the places universally associated with Gotham—the headliners that make the city so massively popular. These include the major museums (the Metropolitan Museum of Art and the Guggenheim, just to name two); the great historical and architectural sites (including Ellis Island and the Brooklyn Bridge); and, in a category all its own, New York's most sobering site: the vast graveyard that was once the World Trade Center.

Next are the less famous, secondary attractions that, if they were magically transported to almost any other city in America, would instantly become that city's top cultural draw and bring it acclaim, prestige, and millions of dollars in tourist revenue (no, I do not exaggerate). These attractions—such as the Tenement Museum, the Museum of the Moving Image, the American Museum of Folk Art, The Frick Collection—while lesser known, can add immensely to a New York City visit. And therefore it's important occasionally to step off the tourist treadmill (Empire State/Times Square/Statue of Liberty) and try one of the so-called secondary sights.

See chapters 7 through 10 for my insights on New York's outdoor spaces, the vital New York theater scene, the city's nightlife, and historic walks.

Finally, don't forget to page through chapter 6, "The Other New York," for sights and activities that should help you get "under the skin" of the city, allowing you to actually meet New Yorkers and see how they work, play, and learn. From tango lessons at the Argentinean Embassy to erudite lectures by world leaders to nights of bawdy excess at the city's Russian nightclubs, these are the types of experiences you'll find in that chapter to help give your vacation depth and flair.

MAKING THE MOST OF YOUR TIME

If you have just 1 day in New York: You have my condolences. First thing you're going to want to do is slam your shoe into your fanny for giving yourself far too little time to experience the city. Then go directly to the Ferry Terminal at Battery Park City (try to get there at 9am to avoid the crowds) and spend 2 to 3 hours touring **Ellis Island** (p. 128). You'll see the Statue of Liberty from the ferry, but with only 1 day, you have no time to tour it. From the ferry terminal, walk north to **Ground Zero** (p. 130) to pay your respects. Then head over to **Chinatown** (p. 83) for lunch. From Chinatown, catch a subway up to the **Metropolitan Museum of Art** (p. 135), where you should spend the remainder of the afternoon. Head next across the park to the Upper West Side for dinner, and after dinner down to **Times Square** (p. 131) to see the lights and take in a show (with just 1 day in town, book your tickets in advance; go to chapter 10 to learn how to do so at a discount). If you have the stamina, head over to the **Empire State Building** (p. 119)—open until 2am—for a fond farewell to the city, which will be glittering and throbbing with a million tiny lights after dark.

> **❝** *Other cities consume culture. New York creates it.* **❞**
>
> —Paul Goldberger,
> *The City Observed*

If you have 2 days: You can slow down . . . a little. Start the day as you would have if you had only 1 day, with a ferry trip to Ellis Island. This time, however, hop off at Liberty Island to tour the small museum and base of the **Statue of Liberty** (p. 127) before going on to the **Immigration Museum at Ellis Island.** This will require 3 to 4 hours, so take the subway directly up to **Chinatown** for a late lunch, then double back to Ground Zero. From there, head to Midtown for an afternoon visit to the **Museum of Modern Art** (p. 139). Alternately, you can spend the afternoon on **Fifth Avenue** (p. 245) between 56th and 48th streets, window-shopping and taking in **St. Patrick's Cathedral** (p. 194) and **Rockefeller Center** (p. 133). About an hour and a half before sunset, head over to the **Empire State Building** to see the city at twilight, and catch the moment when thousands of lights spark to life (a thrilling sight). End your evening with dinner down in the **Village** (East or West, your choice), and if you're really ambitious, pop over to a music, dance, or comedy club (see chapter 9 for info on the city's evening entertainment) before collapsing into bed.

Day Two should begin at the **Metropolitan Museum of Art** (which opens at 9am; p. 135) for a morning of culture; take one of the guided tours or pick up a self-guided audio tour. Then stroll across Central Park, following one of the narrow winding paths (there are many) until you find yourself on the Upper West Side, where you should have lunch. Spend the rest of your afternoon at the **American Museum of Natural History** (p. 137) and **Rose Planetarium** (p. 139). After all of your museum-hopping, treat yourself to a nice dinner near the museum or in Midtown, and then take in a **Broadway** or **Off-Broadway** show.

If you have 3 days: You now have time to breathe both in and out. You'll also have time to divide the city into efficiently visited areas. Spend Day One downtown, taking in **The Statue of Liberty, Ellis Island,** and **Ground Zero,** and visiting **Chinatown** for lunch. Then take a **walking tour of the Financial District** (p. 211) or visit **The Tenement Museum** (p. 155), the **Museum of Jewish Heritage** (p. 154), or the **NY Police Museum** (p. 151). If you have the time, walk across the **Brooklyn Bridge** (p. 134). Dine in SoHo, Greenwich Village, the East Village, or the Lower East Side.

Day Two can be devoted to Midtown. Start your day at the **Museum of Modern Art** (p. 139), have lunch there, and then either take a stroll on **Fifth Avenue,** visiting **Rockefeller Center** or **St. Patrick's Cathedral,** or simply window-shopping. Or spend the afternoon at either **The Museum of American Folk Art** (p. 150) or the **Intrepid Sea, Air and Space Museum** (p. 150). An hour before sunset, make your way to the **Empire State Building** so you can take in the views at dusk. Eat downtown (if you have time; the food is so much better there) or in the Theater District, and take in a show.

Day Three will be your Uptown day: The **Metropolitan Museum of Art** (p. 255) should occupy your morning, and you can eat lunch there or at a nearby restaurant. If it's a nice day, you may want to spend the afternoon exploring **Central Park** (p. 198). Alternately, make it a full museum day by visiting either **The Guggenheim** (p. 141), the **Frick** (p. 142), the **Whitney Museum** (p. 146), or the **American Museum of Natural History.**

If you have 4 or more days: Follow our itinerary for the 3-day visit and work in the sights you have missed on the other days. You may wish to devote 1 day to exploring an outer borough: Perhaps make a pilgrimage to the **Brooklyn Museum** (p. 157) and **Botanical Gardens** (p. 206); or, alternatively, take an outing to the **PS 1 Contemporary Art Center** (p. 165) and the **Museum of the Moving Image** (p. 156) in Queens. Take in a few shows, a jazz concert, a dance club, or a lounge. For ideas on more idiosyncratic ways to spend your time, scan "The Other New York" (p. 176).

NEW YORK'S 12 ICONIC SIGHTS

Of all the sights of New York, an even dozen are must-sees:

KONG'S-EYE VIEW: There's no better introduction to New York than a visit to the **Empire State Building** ✸✸✸ (350 Fifth Ave., at 34th St.; ☎ 212/736-3100; www.esbnyc.com; $18 adults, $16 seniors and kids 12–17, $12 under ages 6–12, free to military in uniform and toddlers; daily 8am–2am; ❷, ❹, ❺, ❻, ❼ to 34th St.). The apex of the New York skyline, both literally (at 102 stories and 4,563 ft.) and figuratively, the view from its Observation Deck is at once instructive and exhilarating. From your bird's-eye perch, you orient yourself geographically and see, with a clarity not possible on the ground, the miracle of Manhattan, that runt of an island that couldn't get much wider or longer, and so did what no other city before it had done and expanded to the skies, becoming a dense, pulsating city of boxy stalactite-like towers set on a painfully narrow strip of land.

Look first to the south, where the Financial District's powerful skyscrapers loom over the field of lower, mostly residential housing that stands between it and Midtown. Beyond the Financial District, in the harbor, are the Statue of Liberty to the right and the Brooklyn Bridge (the most graceful of the three bridges you'll

The Empire State Building, in Brief

- Opened in 1931 after just 14 months of construction (total cost: $25 million)
- Tallest building in the world from 1931 to 1970, when the World Trade Center took the title. It is now the seventh tallest building on the planet.
- The oddly shaped spire at top was meant to be a landing port for blimps, but high winds kept dirigibles from ever being able to anchor here.
- In 1945, a plane accidentally crashed into the building, killing 17 people.
- Every Valentine's Day, 14 couples are married for free on the Observation Deck.

see in this direction). Right below you will be the triangular Flatiron building, one of the most thrillingly odd in Manhattan (it was Frank Lloyd Wright's favorite building), wedged between Broadway and Fifth Avenue at the point where they form an "X," and looking, as many have said, like the prow of a ship. Just to the side of it are the glittering gold roof of the Metropolitan Life Tower and the World Life Insurance Towers, once centers of New York's high society and now just part of the landscape. Drift to the north side of the building and you will be among a riot of skyscrapers, thrown up in a manner that seems wildly chaotic from this vantage point. This strip of Midtown contains more office space per acre than any other area in the world. Peer through the curtain of buildings to catch a glimpse of Central Park, looking like a modest lawn from this great height. To your right, take a good look at the shining, scalloped spire that is the top of the Chrysler Building (many have said that it was designed to look like the grillwork of 1930s-era Chrysler cars). If you dare, stick your head through one of the large holes in the suicide prevention fence to gaze at the ever-moving current of yellow cabs below.

The Empire State Building keeps longer hours than any other tourist attraction in the city, opening at 9am and closing at 2am to accommodate the close-to-four-million visitors who troop through yearly. As you may have heard, the lines here can be epic. In fact, you'll have stood in four separate lines before you reach your goal of the 86th-floor or the 102nd-floor (extra $15) Observation Deck. On very crowded days, this can take up to 2½ hours. Some ways to "game the line" include:

- Arrive promptly at 9am or during the dinner hour, which are relatively uncrowded times.
- Plan to visit on a Tuesday or Wednesday, the least popular days of the week. You'll encounter the biggest crowds on Saturday and Sunday, followed closely by Monday and Friday.
- Bite the bullet and buy an "Express Ticket" (pricey but possibly worth it), which will allow you to jump to the head of all of the lines and get to the top in 20 minutes flat.
- Purchase and print out a ticket from the Empire State Building website, which will allow you to skip the ticket line (though *not* the lines for security or the elevators). Purchase of the **City Pass** (p. 138) brings the same perks. The **New York Pass,** which also covers the ESB, is not quite as good a deal,

Downtown Manhattan Attractions

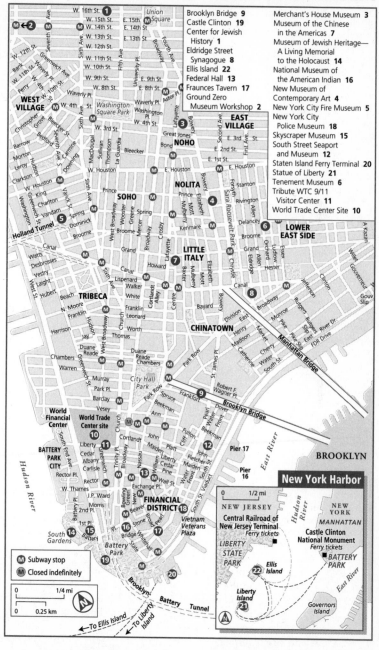

Brooklyn Bridge **9**
Castle Clinton **19**
Center for Jewish
  History **1**
Eldridge Street
  Synagogue **8**
Ellis Island **22**
Federal Hall **13**
Fraunces Tavern **17**
Ground Zero
  Museum Workshop **2**

Merchant's House Museum **3**
Museum of the Chinese
  in the Americas **7**
Museum of Jewish Heritage—
  A Living Memorial
  to the Holocaust **14**
National Museum of
  the American Indian **16**
New Museum of
  Contemporary Art **4**
New York City Fire Museum **5**
New York City
  Police Museum **18**
Skyscraper Museum **15**
South Street Seaport
  and Museum **12**
Staten Island Ferry Terminal **20**
Statue of Liberty **21**
Tenement Museum **6**
Tribute WTC 9/11
  Visitor Center **11**
World Trade Center Site **10**

Ⓜ Subway stop
Ⓜ Closed indefinitely

0   1/4 mi
0   0.25 km

Midtown Manhattan Attractions

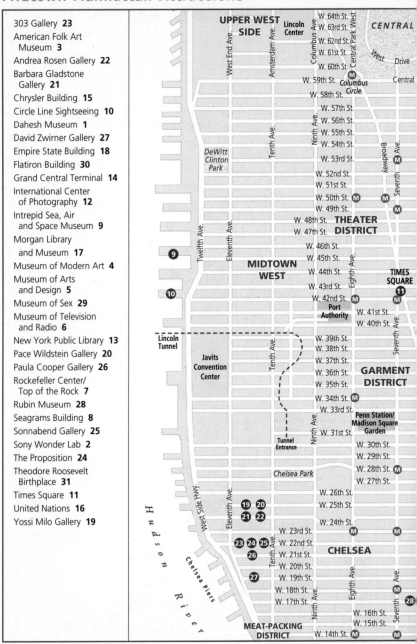

UPPER EAST SIDE

E. 64th St.
E. 63rd St.
E. 62nd St.
E. 61st St.
From Lower Level
First Ave.
York Ave.
E. 60th St.

Roosevelt Island Tram

Queensboro Bridge

E. 59th St.
E. 58th St.
To Upper Level
E. 57th St.
E. 56th St.
E. 55th St.
E. 54th St.
E. 53rd St.
E. 52nd St.
E. 51st St.
E. 50th St.
E. 49th St.
E. 48th St.

MIDTOWN EAST

Rockefeller Center

Sutton Pl. South

Beekman Place
Mitchell Pl.

E. 47th St.
E. 46th St.
E. 45th St.
E. 44th St.
E. 43rd St.
E. 42nd St.
E. 41st St.
E. 40th St.

Grand Central Terminal

New York Public Library

Bryant Park

United Nations

MURRAY HILL

E 39th St.
E. 38th St.

Tunnel Exit

Queens–Midtown Tunnel

FDR Drive

E 37th St.
E. 36th St.

Tunnel Entrance

E. 35th St.
E. 34th St.
E. 33rd St.
E. 32nd St.
E. 31st St.
E. 30th St.
E. 29th St.
E. 28th St.
E. 27th St.
E. 26th St.
E. 25th St.
E. 24th St.
E. 23rd St.
E. 22nd St.
E. 21st St.
E. 20th St.
E. 19th St.
E. 18th St.

Empire State Bldg.

Madison Square Park

Gramercy Park

FLATIRON DISTRICT

GRAMERCY PARK

East River

ROOSEVELT ISLAND

QUEENS

Peter Cooper Village

Stuyvesant Town

Asser Levy Pl.
Ave. C
Second Ave.
First Ave.

Pl.
Irving Pl.
N.D. Perlman Pl.

E. 17th St.
E. 16th St.
E. 15th St.
E. 14th St.

Union Square

M Subway stop

Center Drive
PARK
East Drive
The Pond
Park South
Grand Army Plaza

Fifth Ave.
Madison Ave.
Park Ave.
Lexington Ave.
Third Ave.
Second Ave.
Vanderbilt Ave.

Sixth Ave. (Ave. of the Americas)

Broadway

Park Ave. South

0   1/4 mi
0   0.25 km

UPPER MANHATTAN
Central Park
UPTOWN
Area of detail
DOWNTOWN

123

Uptown Manhattan Attractions

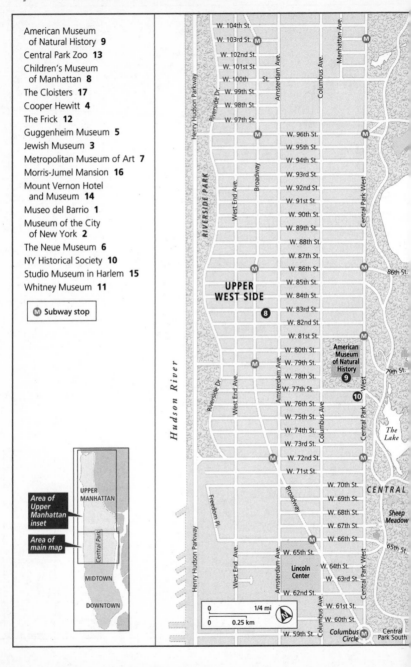

American Museum
  of Natural History **9**
Central Park Zoo **13**
Children's Museum
  of Manhattan **8**
The Cloisters **17**
Cooper Hewitt **4**
The Frick **12**
Guggenheim Museum **5**
Jewish Museum **3**
Metropolitan Museum of Art **7**
Morris-Jumel Mansion **16**
Mount Vernon Hotel
  and Museum **14**
Museo del Barrio **1**
Museum of the City
  of New York **2**
The Neue Museum **6**
NY Historical Society **10**
Studio Museum in Harlem **15**
Whitney Museum **11**

Ⓜ Subway stop

UPPER
WEST SIDE

Area of
Upper
Manhattan
inset

Area of
main map

UPPER
MANHATTAN

MIDTOWN

DOWNTOWN

Hudson River

Henry Hudson Parkway

Riverside Dr.

RIVERSIDE PARK

West End Ave.

Broadway

Amsterdam Ave.

Columbus Ave.

Manhattan Ave.

Central Park West

Central Park

Freedom Pl.

Lincoln
Center

American
Museum
of Natural
History
9

10

8

The
Lake

CENTRAL

Sheep
Meadow

Columbus
Circle

Central
Park South

86th St.

79th St.

65th St.

W. 104th St.
W. 103rd St. Ⓜ
W. 102nd St.
W. 101st St.
W. 100th   St.
W. 99th St.
W. 98th St.
W. 97th St.
W. 96th St.
W. 95th St.
W. 94th St.
W. 93rd St.
W. 92nd St.
W. 91st St.
W. 90th St.
W. 89th St.
W. 88th St.
W. 87th St.
W. 86th St.
W. 85th St.
W. 84th St.
W. 83rd St.
W. 82nd St.
W. 81st St.
W. 80th St.
W. 79th St.
W. 78th St.
W. 77th St.
W. 76th St.
W. 75th St.
W. 74th St.
W. 73rd St.
W. 72nd St.
W. 71st St.
W. 70th St.
W. 69th St.
W. 68th St.
W. 67th St.
W. 66th St.
W. 65th St.
W. 64th St.
W. 63rd St.
W. 62nd St.
W. 61st St.
W. 60th St.
W. 59th St.

0   1/4 mi
0   0.25 km

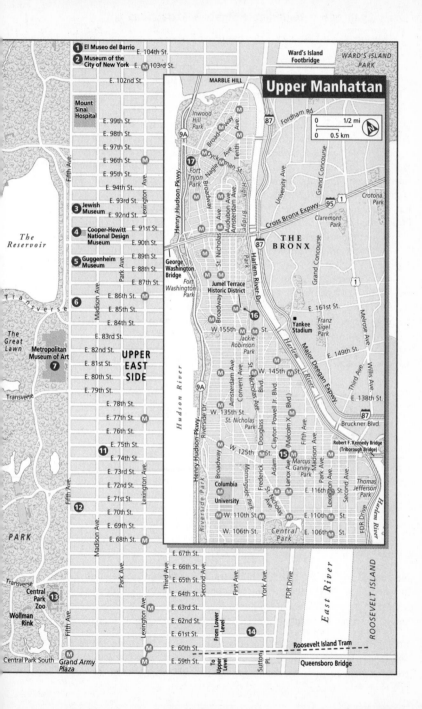

1 El Museo del Barrio · E. 104th St.

2 Museum of the City of New York · E. (M) 103rd St.

E. 102nd St.

MARBLE HILL

Upper Manhattan

Mount Sinai Hospital

E. 99th St.

E. 98th St.

Inwood Hill Park

87 Fordham Rd.

0   1/2 mi

E. 97th St.

9A

0   0.5 km

E. 96th St. (M)

E. 95th St.

17

E. 94th St.

Fort Tryon Park

E. 93rd St.

95 1

Crotona Park

3 Jewish Museum · E. 92nd St.

Claremont Park

4 Cooper-Hewitt National Design Museum · E. 91st St.

E. 90th St.

Cross Bronx Expwy

THE BRONX

5 Guggenheim Museum · E. 89th St.

E. 88th St.

George Washington Bridge

Grand Concourse

The Reservoir

E. 87th St.

E. 86th St. (M)

Fort Washington Park

Jumel Terrace Historic District

6 E. 85th St.

E. 84th St.

16

E. 161st St.

E. 83rd St.

Franz Sigel Park

The Great Lawn

Metropolitan Museum of Art

7 E. 82nd St.

UPPER EAST SIDE

W. 155th St.

Yankee Stadium

E. 81st St.

Jackie Robinson Park

E. 80th St.

E. 149th St.

Transverse

E. 79th St.

9A

E. 78th St.

W. 145th St.

E. 77th St. (M)

St. Nicholas Park

E. 138th St.

E. 76th St.

W. 135th St.

E. 75th St.

87

11 E. 74th St.

Bruckner Blvd.

E. 73rd St.

E. 72nd St.

W. 125th St.

15

Robert F. Kennedy Bridge (Triborough Bridge)

E. 71st St.

Marcus Garvey Park

12 E. 70th St.

Columbia University

E. 116th St.

Thomas Jefferson Park

E. 69th St.

Central Park

E. 110th St.

PARK E. 68th St. (M)

W. 110th St. (M)

E. 106th St.

E. 67th St.

W. 106th St.

E. 66th St.

E. 65th St.

ROOSEVELT ISLAND

Transverse

E. 64th St.

Central Park Zoo **13**

E. 63rd St.

Wollman Rink

E. 62nd St.

14

East River

E. 61st St.

From Lower Level

E. 60th St.

Roosevelt Island Tram

Central Park South

To Upper Level

Queensboro Bridge

Grand Army Plaza

because you'll have to wait in the ticket line to change your voucher into a ticket.

◆ If it's the view you're seeking and not just the experience of being at the Empire State Building, consider **Top of the Rock** (p. 134) which has instituted timed tickets and therefore never has a wait.

WE ARE THE WORLD: Make your way along 42nd Street towards the East River, where you'll find the 7-block stretch of international territory that makes New York City the capital of the world. Step through the visitors entrance gate and you will be leaving the United States behind and entering the **United Nations** ✰✰✰ (First Ave., at 46th St.; ☎ 212/963-8687; www.un.org/tours; tours $12 adults, $8.50 seniors, $7.50 students, $6.50 children 5–14; children under 5 not admitted; tours Mon–Fri 9:30am–4:45pm, except for the last week of Sept, first week of Oct when the U.N. is closed to visitors; ❹, ❺, ❻, ❺ to Grand Central Station).

It's become fashionable of late in some political circles to denigrate the U.N. Though some reform is obviously necessary, a tour here will remind you of just how much the United Nations has done since its inception. It was founded, after all, with the express purpose of ensuring that there would never be another world war, and it has accomplished that, no small task. Perhaps more importantly, a visit here will remind you of how much potential the U.N. still has for effecting meaningful progress in numerous fields, from the elimination of disease and poverty to the resolution of ethnic conflicts.

Those who take the 45-minute tour will visit not only the General Assembly (where Khrushchev once famously pounded his shoe in anger) and the Security

United Nations, in Brief

The grounds: John D. Rockefeller purchased the land the U.N. now occupies for $8.5 million and then presented it as a gift to the organization. The buildings, appropriately enough, are all designed in the so-called "International Style"— uncluttered boxes of glass and stone meant to have an "elemental" or "international" look, completed in 1950. The 39-story glass building that looks a bit like a cigarette pack is the Secretariat, where every nation has offices, and much of the nitty-gritty work of the U.N. gets done. At a right angle to the Secretariat is the Dag Hammarskjold Library, the newest of the structures, opened in 1961; on the other side of Secretariat is the General Assembly building.

Membership: When the United Nations was chartered in 1945, it originally had 51 members. Today, 191 countries are represented, their flags snapping in the wind in a most impressive display along First Avenue. Flags are ordered alphabetically in English starting with Afghanistan (on 48th St.) and ending with Zimbabwe.

An international experience: Meetings at the U.N. are conducted in 6 official languages: English, Mandarin, Spanish, French, Russian, and Arabic. Tours are conducted in 20 different languages by a bright young cadre of guides from approximately 25 countries.

Council, but the less well-known Economic and Social Council Room that oversees the work of UNICEF, the World Health Organization, and 28 other U.N. programs of development (little-known fact—it's thanks to recommendations by the WHO that most countries have expiration dates stamped on milk). It's in this room that officials are working to create standardized tests for avian flu, vaccinate the world's children against polio, and promote the cause of world literacy. The Nobel Peace Prize won by the U.N. Peacekeeping forces in 2001 is displayed just outside the council room, along with an enlightening exhibit on the important work these troops are still doing throughout the world.

If you don't want to pony up $12 for the tour, you can still visit, taking in the lobby of the General Assembly building, with its free, changing exhibits (photojournalism mostly), meditation room, and the memorial stained-glass window Marc Chagall created for former Secretary General Dag Hammarskjöld in 1964 (to the right of the entrance). An international gift shop with trinkets from across the globe and the U.N. post office are in the basement. The sculpture garden is no longer open to the public, nor is the gallery at the Security Council when it's in session, but ordinary Joes can once again dine side by side with diplomats in the Delegates' Dining Room (call in advance for a reservation; men are required to wear jackets). My father was actually married at the U.N., so I can vouch for the food, which is quite good, especially if you hit it when a nation is sponsoring a celebratory buffet of its specialties.

LIBERTY BELLE: The great harbor of New York and the grand lady who guards it are, after the Empire State Building, the city's top must-visit attractions. You'll follow in the footsteps of the millions of immigrants and visitors who came here before you, their way lighted by the torch of the **Statue of Liberty** ★★ (Liberty Island, NY Harbor; ☎ 866/STATUE4 or 212/269-5755; www.nps.gov/stli; daily ferry departures 9am–3:30pm, extended hours summer; ferry fees: $12 adults, $10 for seniors, $5 for children 4–12; ❶ to South Ferry or ❹, ❺ to Bowling Green, or ❷, Ⓦ to Whitehall St.) and the promise inscribed on her base: that the "teeming masses yearning to breathe free" would find succor, freedom from persecution, and economic opportunity in this new land.

You will have a fine view of Lady Liberty from the shores of Battery Park, but if you have the time, it's worth it to board a ferry out to Liberty Island and take the official ranger tour of the monument. The tour includes a small museum on the history of the statue, and the chance to stand just feet from the original torch, which had to be replaced in the mid-1980s due to severe water damage. In pre-9/11 days, this tour concluded with a thrilling, exhausting climb up a circular stairway to the crown of the statue, but due to security concerns visitors now can only get to the statue's base. From there, you peer through a glass ceiling at the intricate metal work that French engineer Gustave Eiffel (of the Eiffel Tower) created to anchor the statue; it acts like a spring, allowing the "skin" of the structure to adjust to different temperatures and sway up to 3 inches in 50-mph winds.

If you do want to take the tour—and I recommend it—it's extremely important to order timed tickets in advance, either by phone or through the website (see above). Some 3,000 visitors take the tour each day, but on certain days, in summer and around the holidays in particular, nearly 15,000 show up and have to be turned away. This is the one major New York site you really do have to plan ahead for, as only a small number of tickets are held for day-of-sale tours.

The Statue of Liberty, in Brief

The French connection: Dreamed up at a dinner party of French intellectuals in 1865, the statue was first proposed as a hundredth birthday present from France to the U.S. (and as a not-so-subtle jab at France's then-authoritarian Second Empire). Fundraising woes kept it from being completed in time for that anniversary, but in 1881, after over a decade of begging for money (a lottery finally did the trick), sculptor Auguste Bartholdi was able to finish the massive work.

The battle for the base: Though the statue was completed in 1881, it took another 2 years for the Americans to keep their half of the bargain and create a pedestal for it. Newspaperman Joseph Pulitzer finally stepped in, and in a series of angry editorials condemning the wealthy for not contributing, he finally convinced thousands of lower-income Americans to send in what they could to get the job done. Thanks to their dimes and nickels, the pedestal was finally built (designed by Richard Morris Hunt) and the statue was dedicated on October 28, 1886.

Crafting the Lady: *Repousse,* a technique of hammering and shaping thin strips of copper, was used to create Lady Liberty. Though the statue is massive at over 151 feet (47m) from base to torch, the "skin" of the piece is just 3/32 of an inch thick (or 2.38mm). It is thought that the ancient Colossus of Rhodes was built using this method.

A key to the symbolism: Every piece of the statue has meaning. The seven rays in the crown represent the seven seas of the world, and the 25 windows there give a nod to the 25 gemstones found on earth. On the tablet Liberty is holding are inscribed the Roman numerals for July 4th, 1776. And though it's difficult to see, Liberty is breaking shackles with her right foot.

Those without tickets to the monument can take a ranger-led tour of the island, but the better option may be to simply stay on the ferry, which slows down as it approaches the statue, giving those on board a good view of Lady Liberty in all of her surprisingly delicate beauty. Spend the time you'll save to go on to Ellis Island (see below), Liberty's sister monument, with no entrance quotas. I think Ellis is ultimately the more rewarding of the two.

THE GOLDEN DOOR: If you decide to get off the boat and tour **Ellis Island** ★★★ (www.nps.gov/elis; ferry fees: $12 adults, $9.50 seniors and children 4–12; daily ferry departures 9am–3:30pm, extended hours in summer; ❶ to South Ferry, or ❹, ❺ to Bowling Green, or ❷, ❿ to Whitehall St.)—and you really should—you'll be visiting what was the epicenter of the largest migration in human history. In near-continuous use from 1892 to 1954, this was the point-of-entry processing center for the majority of immigrants (including my grandmother) hoping to settle in the U.S. during those years. Over 12 million people passed through its halls, sometimes as many as 12,000 in a single day.

The stories of these immigrants—what they were escaping, what they found once here, and what their short time in the purgatory that was Ellis Island was like—is movingly told here in a number of ways. First off, there's a short film narrated by Gene Hackman which wraps the story up in a half-hour nutshell; but I think you'll find it much more enlightening (and fun) to follow the path that the immigrants themselves took, seeing the tale unfold room by room. Start in the second-floor Grand Hall (officially titled the "Registry Hall"), awe-inspiring with its massive white tile-vaulted ceiling (created by the same firm that did the ceiling in Grand Central Station's Oyster Bar). The room would have been filled with benches back in the day, but today there are just a handful of original ones that you can rest on while imagining what it must have been like for a voyage-weary Russian or Italian or Irishman to encounter this monumental, intimidating room—probably larger than any church or temple they had attended in their home village—on their very first day in America.

Behind the Grand Hall is a warren of small rooms where immigrants were tested for mental competency, literacy, and communicable diseases. How these tests were done—and the fear they inspired—is chronicled in historical photos, wall text, and most poignantly at listening stations, where immigrants share their memories of their time on the island. Illuminating exhibits on the role of immigrant aid societies, the place of women, the types of work immigrants tended to do in the U.S., and other issues, complete the floor.

The top floor of the museum chronicles the history of the processing facility itself, its problems with corruption, its physical structure, and the history of the island. These exhibits can be skipped if you're short on time, but don't miss the **"Treasures from Home"** exhibit, also on this floor, which features 2,000 of the possessions that were brought through Ellis. Somehow seeing the china dolls, the precious wedding photos, the native costumes, and the letters home brings the immigrant experience more vividly to life than any other part of the museum. If you have time, return to the first floor, and browse through the **"Peopling of America"** exhibit that discusses the ethnic makeup of the U.S. today. In all, you should allot a minimum of 2 hours for a visit here; there's a cafeteria on-site should you need a break, along with the **"American Family History Center,"** where American visitors can track their genealogical history online with the help of on-site librarians.

I am one of the 40% of all Americans who had a relative come through Ellis Island, and I find it difficult to tour this museum without tearing up at some point. I have no doubt that even those visitors without this direct a connection will find the journey through Ellis to be one of the most moving experiences of their New York visit.

SITE OF THE UNTHINKABLE: The boat from Ellis and Liberty Island will deposit you in Battery Park City, just a short walk through the canyons of the Financial District to Ground Zero (along the way, you may want to take my walking tour (p. 211), which will introduce you to the gems of the neighborhood). Seeing these sights over the course of a single morning or afternoon is a moving and highly logical way to tour the tip of Manhattan.

I wonder if it's as difficult for visitors to gaze upon the **World Trade Center** site (the open space btwn Church, Barclay, Liberty, and West sts.; www.nycvisit.com

Ground Zero In Depth

The reverberations of September 11, 2001—historic, cultural, economic—continue to affect life in New York and across the nation. Understanding their impact is a massive task, and so, wisely, the two museums that have recently opened to commemorate the attacks take a "micro" approach, concentrating on the stories of the people who were directly involved when the towers came down and during the massive cleanup and investigative efforts afterwards.

On Liberty Street, directly across from Ground Zero, the **World Trade Center Tribute Center** ★★ (120 Liberty St.; ☎ 866/737-1184 or 212/393-9160; www.tributewtc.org; ⓒ,ⓔ to World Trade Center; Wed–Sat and Mon 10am–6pm, Tues noon–6pm, Sun noon–5pm; $10) is an effort to convey a "person to person" history of the event by the 9/11 Families Association. Along with a scale model of the World Trade Center and various artifacts from the site (twisted metal forks from the restaurant at the top, a plane window from one of the jets that hit the towers, papers that fluttered from the towers like snow) are highly personal audio exhibits on what it was like to work at the Towers; photos of the deceased; and a wall plastered with the heart-rending, homemade posters that popped up about town after the attacks, made by friends and family members searching for their loved ones. Most affecting are the superb tours the Center offers several times daily of the area immediately adjacent to Ground Zero, all of which are led by people directly affected by the attacks—survivors, family members of the deceased, rescue workers, residents of lower Manhattan. The one I recently took was led by an extraordinarily eloquent former firefighter and structural engineer who was badly injured trying to get people out of the lobby of one of the towers before it collapsed (a blast of air threw him clear of the building). "I feel a moral obligation to present this tour," he began, and then enthralled our group with his discussion of the construction of the towers, how they were financed, and finally his own experiences on 9/11 and afterwards.

The **Ground Zero Museum Workshop** (14th St. btwn Ninth Ave. and Washington St.; ☎ 212/209-3307; suggested donation $25 adults, $19 seniors, students, and children; Sun–Mon noon, 2pm, 4pm, Thurs–Sat and Tues tours at 11am, 1pm and 3pm; ⓐ, ⓒ, ⓔ, ⓛ to 14th St./Eighth Ave.) shifts its focus to the recovery efforts after the attacks. Created by Gary Suson, the photographer who was hired by the Firefighters Union to document the cleanup and investigation, it's, in many ways, an even more personal account of this tragedy. After a short video, visitors don headphones to hear Suson narrating stories about the artifacts he salvaged (according to Suson, thousands were simply being tossed in the trash) as well as his moving photos of the firefighters at work. And it really is an untold story: After the first 24 hours, photographers were banned from the site, so many of the images you'll see here will be totally new to you. Unlike most museums, Suson allows visitors to touch many of these artifacts—glass from the airplane, twisted metal from the site. His narration, too, is unorthodox, inserting a good deal of his spiritual philosophy into the proceedings. Some will find that appropriate; others may be turned off by it. Though it's just a one-room museum, allot about one hour to an hour and a half to listen to most of the 80 short stories and watch the video.

for further information; ⓒ, ⓔ to World Trade Center), as it is for me to write about it. For those of us who live in New York and lost friends to the terrorist attacks on September 11, 2001, the site is a haunted place, a vast, windy hole that I personally find difficult to look at. The grayness of it, the immeasurable emptiness of this rectangular cavern, remains an open wound.

Most visitors who come are surprised by its size. Though the World Trade Center towers were not the tallest buildings in the world at the time of the attack, they had the greatest volume, supplying over 12 million square feet of office space and housing 350 different firms and organizations. In any one day, approximately 50,000 people came to work here and another 70,000 visited the towers, either for business purposes, to shop in the vast underground mall at its base, or to go to the observation deck. One of the few blessings of 9/11 was the timing of the attacks; had they occurred just 1 hour later in the day, hundreds of tourists would likely have been trapped on the observation decks, thousands of additional office workers would have been killed, and the death toll—already horrific at nearly 3,000—would have risen even higher.

As a New Yorker I have memories of that day that are seared into my brain as if by branding iron. I was in my Midtown office when the first plane struck the towers at 8:45am and will never forget the 2½-mile trudge home, walking into the crowds of businessmen and women, painted gray, head to toe, with ashes from the towers. I will never forget the painful, burning smell that enveloped me the farther downtown I went and hung over our neighborhood for months; the military vehicles patrolling the streets in my area, all cars banished; the crowds at the supermarket, snapping up water and trading rumors. But what stays with me most of all was the sight of those towers crashing to earth. I happened to be standing on the street by a bar with a TV on when the second tower fell, surrounded by a group of people trying to get home. Strangers all, we cried out as one when it happened, hands reaching towards the screen as if we could stop the descent of glass and steel. To my right was a young Hispanic woman, desperately dialing her cellphone, trying to get through to someone who worked at the World Trade Center. I've always wondered if her call ever got through.

A logistical note: Fabric now covers the fence surrounding the World Trade Center site, making it difficult to see in. For the best views, head towards the river to the World Financial Center (200 Vesey St.). On the second floor are large windows overlooking Ground Zero that offer unobstructed views.

See the box p. 130 for two museums dedicated to 9/11.

CROSSROADS OF THE WORLD: On to happier matters. At some point in your stay you're going to want to see **Times Square** ★ (Broadway and Seventh Ave., btwn 42nd and 47th sts.; www.timessquarebid.org; ❶, ❷, ❸, ⓝ, ⓞ, ⓡ, ⓦ, ⓢ to Times Sq.), if only briefly, a touchstone for the New York experience. As Adam Gopnik wrote in *The New Yorker,* "No other part of New York has had such a melodramatic sensitivity to the changes in the city's history, with an image for every decade." Think for a moment and those visions of Times Square should start flooding your mind: snazzy clubs and peroxide blond chorus girls in the 1920s and '30s, sailors kissing girls at the end of World War II, the wisecracking small-time hoods of *Guys and Dolls* in the '50s, and, of course, the bleak urban decay of the '60s and '70s when, as Gopnik put it, "everything fell apart and Hell wafted up through the manhole covers."

Times Square, in Brief

What's in the name: Originally known as Longacre Square, it was the center of the horse-and-carriage trade until the early 1900s, when theaters started claiming the neighborhood. In 1904, the *New York Times* took up residence on the Square, a half-mile up from the (then) much more developed Herald Square named for the *Times*'s big competitor, the now defunct *New York Herald*.

The lullaby of Broadway: Today there are 38 theaters in the Times Square area, though only 4 front Broadway itself.

Ringing in the new: At the northern end of the square, the skinny skyscraper that stands between Broadway and Seventh Avenue (there's been a steaming CUP A SOUP billboard on it for a number of years now) is the famed building where the ball drops down on New Year's Eve. A 1,070-pound crystal ball is placed at the top and then lowered by computer near midnight (the computerization of the ball has actually led to its being late or early for the past several years, as the handlers have less control than they did when they could shout at the fellows who were pulling the ropes, "Hurry up." The speed of descent is now set in advance). To read more about "doing" Times Square on New Year's Eve, go to p. 309.

Times Square is back on the upswing now, the porn shops banished and crime held (mostly) at bay. To get the full effect of today's Square, it's imperative you visit at night. It's then that the rainbow glitter of the flashing lights from the dozens of billboards, giant TV screens, electronic news crawls, and headlights of cars whizzing by wash over the Square, sweeping all of the litter and crowds into the background. The effect is like watching fireworks.

(This tradition of massive "spectaculars" is codified into law. In the 1980s, ordinances were passed requiring that new buildings abutting the Square have 16,000 square feet of light shows on their facades, with "moving elements" that are sufficiently bright—and the city monitors the brightness using a measuring system they called LUTS or Light Unit Times Square).

Beyond this theater of the streets is the legitimate theater, and Times Square still has more playhouses per acre than any other area in North America. For full information on the theater scene, visit chapter 10, "A Night at The Theater."

Other attractions by the dozens crowd Times Square, but only three should be visited, to my mind: The Virgin Megastore (largest media store in the world), Toys "R" Us (with its kid-pleasing Ferris wheel), and Sephora (where you can spray on perfume until you faint from the fumes at no cost whatsoever). And while you can't "visit" the following sites, you can peer into the sidewalk-level television studios of *Good Morning America* (44th and Broadway) and the NASDAQ (43rd and Broadway). If you hear the piercing screams of preteens, look up and you may see the cameras of MTV's *Total Request Live* scanning the area from the second-floor studios between 44th and 45th Street on Broadway.

What else occupies Times Square? Only spots that should be avoided, like the expensive and kitschy **Madame Tussaud's** (234 W. 42nd St., btwn Seventh and

Eighth aves.; ☎ 212/719-9440; www.nycwax.com; $29 adults, $26 seniors, $23 children 4–12; Sun–Thurs 10am–8pm, Fri–Sat 10am–10pm)—if you must visit it, be sure to go to its website first for a discount coupon. Also to be avoided are half a dozen overpriced, downright bad chain restaurants; and stores that you'll see in every mall in America, but that are more expensive here.

GET A PIECE OF THE ROCK: Once you've done Times Square, repair immediately to the area that outclasses it by a mile, and has more to interest fans of architecture and city planning: **Rockefeller Center** ★★ (btwn Fifth and Sixth aves., 48th to 51st St.; ☎ 212/632-3975; www.rockefellercenter.com; ⑧, ⑩, ⑪ to Rockefeller Center), Gotham's splendid "city within a city." Built in the 1930s at the height of the Depression—thanks to the jobs it gave construction workers, it was the second largest employer in the city after the federal Works Progress Association (or WPA) at the time—it remains a marvel of elegance and aspiration, a several-blocks-wide collection of 19 buildings that, despite their mass, create a space that is airy and light, a welcoming haven for both tourists and city residents. No matter how many times I come here, I still get goose bumps on the walk from Fifth Avenue through the gardened central walk—called "The Channel," as it runs between the French and the British buildings. Follow this path down to the **ice-skating rink** (the first commercial one in the world), and the golden statue of *Prometheus,* or "Leaping Louie" as wits have called him over the years, his prone position under the soaring vertical of the RCA building making him look like he just jumped. If you'd like to skate here, the tab will be $10 weekdays, $14 weekends and holidays ($7.50–$8.50 for children and seniors), plus $8 for skate rental, but the charm of the experience makes it well worth the price (the rink is open Oct to early Apr, Mon–Thur 9am–10:30pm, Fri–Sat 8:30am–midnight, Sun 8:30am–10pm).

There's much to see at the Rock. Directly behind the statue is where the yearly 70-plus-foot Christmas tree is set on November 20th each year, a plaque marking the space. In warmer months this plaza is often used for art exhibits, craft fairs, and other public exhibitions. Take a left and walk towards 49th Street to the small side street with the glassed-in TV studio on the corner. This is where NBC's *Today Show* is taped, the small street the area where sign-waving crowds gather every weekday morning, as early as 5:30am, to attempt to get their faces on TV. (When the show has musical performances, guests play on a stage in this narrow alley—it looks much bigger on TV, doesn't it?) Stroll next to Fifth Avenue between 50th and 51st streets, where *Prometheus's* brother, mighty *Atlas,* the finest piece of art in the complex (by artist Lee Lawrie), hoists a giant globe on his shoulders, muscles rippling. From the back, *Atlas* looks a bit like a Christ figure, especially superimposed on St. Patrick's Cathedral across the street (which, in case you were wondering, is a copy of Cologne Cathedral in Germany). Go into the lobby behind *Atlas* for a peek at one of the most magnificent public spaces in the city, the walls bedecked with a rare, swirling Greek marble; the gold "curtains" at the side creating an ever-changing dance of shadows on the ceiling.

Although I don't recommend the Rockefeller City tour (it doesn't go anywhere you can't yourself, and the guides are a dull lot), the **NBC Studio tour** (☎ 212/664-7174; www.shopnbc.com; $18 adults, $16 seniors and children ages 6–16; under 6 not admitted; Mon–Sat 8:30am–5:30pm, Sun 9:30am–4:30pm; ⑧, ⑩, ⑪ to Rockefeller Center) will be of interest to *Saturday Night Live* and Conan O'Brien fans—both studios are usually visited. Other than that, it's a relentless commercial for NBC and can get wearying. Better is a trip to **Top of the Rock** ★★ (30 Rockefeller Plaza; ☎ 212/698-2000; www.topoftherocknyc.com; $13 adults, $12 seniors, $9 children 6–12; daily 8:30am–midnight; ❸, ❿, ❺ to Rockefeller Center), the 70th-floor Observation Deck at Rockefeller Center. While not as high as the one in the Empire State Building, it gives the latter a run for its money with its own striking views (you have a much better vista of Central Park from here, a grand bumpy green blanket, laid at your feet) and its use of timed tickets, which eliminate the painful waits that can sour the experience at its rival. The Rock reopened in November of 2005, re-creating very closely the cruise ship–themed look of the deck from the '30s, when it was first constructed. It's a wonderful addition to the Rockefeller Center experience.

Finally, **Radio City Music Hall** (1260 Avenue of the Americas at 50th St.; ☎ 212/247-4777; www.radiocity.com; $50–$250 show tickets, tour $17 adults, $14 seniors, $10 children 12 and under; ❸, ❿, ❺ to Rockefeller Center) remains the kitschy, thrilling delight it's always been: the Christmas and Easter shows both marvels of excess, with hundreds of people and hooved animals on the stage at one time; orchestras magically rising from the pit; laser lights throwing patterns around the theater; and best of all, the Rockette chorus line, that superhuman all-leg dancing machine. The precision of the Rockettes' routines, the dazzling white of their smiles, the sight of all of those legs in a row—being a native New Yorker, there's nothing else that says "Christmas" quite so loudly for me.

Those who don't want to shell out for a show, or who visit when the theater is dark, can take the tour, which is well worth it, to see the exquisite Art Deco features of this sensational pleasure hall.

A MAN, A PLAN, A SPAN: New York has a grand Gothic cathedral in St. Patrick's, but for many New Yorkers, the city's true cathedral, the point at which earth and water join and thrust upwards towards the heavens, is the **Brooklyn Bridge** ★★★ (entrance at Centre St. in lower Manhattan; ❿, ⓜ, ❷, ❹, ❺, ❻ to Brooklyn Bridge). The greatest engineering feat of its day, it remains one of the most breathtaking structures in the city.

To fully appreciate its dazzle, you must walk the bridge. Start on the Manhattan side and walk first to one of the great Gothic towers that hold up the bridge's cables. It took 7 years and massive heartbreak to build these two structures. Architect John A. Roebling died surveying the area in 1869 (just 2 weeks after the project had been approved): he was standing on a pier when a ferry accidentally rammed into it, crushing his foot. He died of lockjaw 3 weeks later. His son Washington took over and created a method of sending pneumatic caissons, basically large pressurized pine boxes into which compressed air was pumped to keep the water out, down to the river bed. This allowed six workers at a time to descend and lay the foundation for these towers. Because they didn't have a good understanding of the effects of underwater pressure on the human body (known to scuba divers as "the bends"), many were killed or injured in the caissons, including Washington Roebling. In 1872 he had to be carried out of the chamber, partially paralyzed. He remained an invalid for the rest of his life, and his wife Martha took over directing the job, learning advanced mathematics in the process. Washington watched the progress of the bridge through binoculars from his apartment, and when the bridge was competed after 13 years, Grover Cleveland (then president), the governor, and the mayor all came to his home to personally thank him.

Walk to the center of the bridge and take in the spectacular views of both Brooklyn and Manhattan. When the bridge was built, its span—1,595 feet—was the longest leap across an open space of any on Earth, and the first bridge to connect Manhattan with any of the lands that surrounded it. Take a look up at the cables; these, too, were an innovation, the first steel cables to be used on a bridge (before then cables were iron). It took 2 years to string the cables back and forth before work could begin building the suspension bridge. The cables each contain 5,434 wires and weigh 870 tons. Take a moment at the Brooklyn side to read the plaque on the construction of the bridge.

When you depart the bridge, consider taking a stroll in brownstone-heavy Brooklyn Heights, the first neighborhood in the city to be landmarked. You can catch the ❶ train at Cadman Plaza/High Street back to Manhattan.

ICONIC MUSEUMS

As I've noted before, there are scores of museums in New York. But four are so grand in scope and ambition, so profound in their impact upon the visitor, that they have to be counted as iconic experiences.

THE GREAT HOME OF CLASSIC ART: The **Metropolitan Museum of Art** ★★★ 🄺 (1000 Fifth Ave., btwn 80th and 84th sts.; ☎ 212/536-7710; www. met.org; suggested donation $20 adults, $15 seniors, $10 students; Tues–Thurs and Sun 9:30am–5:30pm, Fri–Sat 9:30am–9pm; ❹, ❺, ❻ to 86th St.) is the giant among New York museums, and the finest art museum in this hemisphere, the equivalent of the Louvre in Paris, the Prado in Madrid, the Uffizi in Florence, and the British Museum in London. Among all the "must-visit" sites of New York, this is the one that simply can't be skipped. Whatever your interest in art—and even if you usually have no interest in art—you will find something here to astonish you, to enlighten and enrich your life. I solemnly promise. No, really, I do.

The Met was founded fairly late, as great museums go, conceived in 1870 by a group of wealthy businessmen and artists; a decade later, the museum's collection had grown so rapidly that Calvert Vaux, one of the architects of Central Park, was brought in to create the first red-brick building on this site (you can see that facade still—it's the side wall of the European Sculpture Court). A little over a decade later, another expansion was necessary, so famed architect Richard Morris Hunt was tapped to create the majestic, Indiana limestone, neoclassical edifice that still stands today, awing the visitors who climb its mountain of steps and walk past its redwood-height pillars. (One oddity of the facade: Because money ran out during construction, the square pediments on the front that were meant to house statuary were left empty. The building was landmarked and locked into its current appearance before that deficiency could be addressed.) Never a static institution, the museum and its collection have continued to grow, with the Met currently the owner of three million works of art spanning 5,000 years. The building has expanded accordingly, taking over acre upon acre of former parkland to reach its current size—a quarter of a mile long, encompassing 2 million square feet of floor space.

Obviously, there's no way to see it all in one, two, or even five visits. So you must choose carefully among the 18 curatorial departments and decide what interests you most. One way to do so is by taking one of the hour-long scholarly "Highlight" tours—free with admission and offered five times a day—led by volunteer docents. These enthusiastic art lovers are a treasure in and of themselves, highly trained and well spoken. They'll run you all over the museum, pointing out and expounding upon the various gems of the collection, offering a quick taste of the museum's highlights so that you can come back yourself and feast upon what really interests you.

If I had a gun to my head and had to pick the top five highlights, I'd select:

- **The European paintings collection** on the second floor, with such jewels as Velazquez's truer-than-life portrait of Juan de Pareja (the slave whom the painter respected enough—you can see it in the painting—to set free); El Greco's brooding landscape of Toledo; the 20 Rembrandts here, including *Aristotle Contemplating the Bust of Homer* (three great Greeks in one painting—notice the pendant of Alexander the Great hanging from his shirt); five light-kissed Vermeers; five rooms of Degas; a roomful of van Goghs; and works by Manet, Monet, de Goya, Breughel, van Eyck, and every other master you read about in your college art-history course.

- **The period rooms,** which re-create dozens of important rooms, including Louis XIV's state bedroom in Versailles; and the stunning Cubiculum from Boscoreale, a perfectly preserved, brilliantly colorful room from a villa a mile from Pompeii that was buried by the eruption of Mount Vesuvius in A.D. 79. Other highlights: Frank Lloyd Wright's Arts and Crafts Living Room, and a serene 16th-century Ming Scholar's audience hall from China. Whenever I visit these rooms I'm always reminded of the terrific children's novel *From the Mixed Up Files of Mrs. Basil E. Frankwiler,* in which the protagonists slept each night in a historic bed. Share it with your tweens and they'll be dying to come here.

- **The American Collection,** the most comprehensive in the world, features masterworks by Sargent, Homer, Tiffany, Leutze (his sentimental but rippingly fun *Washington Crossing the Delaware*), and many more.

- **The Egyptian Collection** includes some pieces discovered by the Met's own teams of archaeologists, such as the miniature figures found in a tomb in Thebes that show in intricate detail what daily life for a wealthy Egyptian was like. There are also elaborate statuary, mummy cases, jewelry, wall paintings, and the Temple of Dendur, an actual temple to the goddess Isis (c. 15 B.C.) that was saved from the rising waters of the Nile after the construction of the Aswan Dam.

- The hidden **Hall of Art from Japan,** with its famed Iris Screens (on many Metropolitan Museum products), is also home to architectural-looking suits of armor, delicate woodcuts, and dazzling kimonos. To my mind, this is one of the most ravishingly beautiful sections of the museum.

These five are what I'd pick if my life were at stake, but the truth is, I'd be just as happy exploring other areas of the museum. As I said before, there's just no way to go wrong here.

Along with all the art, the Met has half a dozen pricey cafes and restaurants; wonderful gift shops and bookstores; and tremendously engaging art and culture programs for children of all ages (mostly on the weekends; visit the website for more information).

PLANETS, PRIMATES, & OTHER DELIGHTS: Since 1869, **The American Museum of Natural History** ★★★ 🎈 (Central Park West, btwn 79th and 81st sts.; ☎ 212/769-5100; www.amnh.org; suggested donation $15 adults, $11 seniors, $8.50 children; daily 10am–5:45pm; **B**, **C** to 81st St.) has served as both the country's preeminent private scientific research facility and its top museum for paleontology, zoology, anthropology and, in recent years, astronomy. It's this constant flow of energy and insight between the research side and the curatorial side that has kept the museum fiercely vital, fresh, and unique. Just a few years ago, for example, scientists concluded that dinosaurs had not dragged their tails as had long been thought but waved them in the air as they walked. The curators responded, painstakingly dismantling the Museum's famed dino skeletons and reassembling them with tails erect. Then, in a brilliant stroke, they placed one skeleton atop a section of a Texas riverbed where they had found fossilized dino footprints (sans tail-dragging marks), giving museum-goers a peephole into how new scientific theories emerge.

This double spotlight on the science itself and on how science is "made" is one of the pleasures of a visit here, with many of the exhibits focusing on the current "educated guesses" and the scientists who are making them. An extraordinarily interactive museum, it challenges visitors to figure out which theories make the most sense via computer stations, wall text, videos, soundscapes, and, of course, the artifacts themselves.

Start your visit by exploring the dinosaur rooms on the fourth floor, as these tend to get most crowded later in the day. The museum has the largest such

---

Planning tips for the Museum of Natural History

Timing your visit: Because the museum is so popular with school groups, it's difficult to predict when the museum will be crowded. In general, attendance is in inverse proportion to the weather: When it's lovely outside, the crowds will be sparse within. When it's blustery or rainy . . . watch out. Weekdays tend to be less crowded than weekends.

An overview tour: First-time visitors should consider taking one of the guided introductory tours that begin at 15 minutes past the hour throughout the day. Led by highly knowledgeable and well-spoken volunteer guides (they take classes for 6 months), tours vary by guide and will often hit different highlights of the museum.

Especially for kids: Families with children will want to visit the **Discovery Room,** an educational center where kids can pretend to dig up dinosaur bones, do a scavenger hunt, work with microscopes, and more. Timed tickets are given for admission here, so be sure to grab one early in the day before they run out.

Parsing the sightseeing passes

Let's start with **City Pass** ✦✦✦ (☎ 208/737-4800; www.citypass.com) the most selective of the passes, allowing entry to just seven attractions (The **Museum of Modern Art**, The **Circle Line Sightseeing Cruise** or The **Statue of Liberty/Ellis Island Ferry**, The Observatory Deck of the **Empire State Building**, The **Guggenheim Museum**, The **American Museum of Natural History**, The **Cloisters**, and The **Metropolitan Museum of Art**). That said, all seven attractions are superb and more than worthy of your time.

The cost of the City Pass is $74 for adults, $54 for kids between the ages of 6 and 17, which may sound like a lot, but if you visit only the first four attractions on the list above, you'll save about $20. Visit all seven and the discount will come to about $65. Travelers have 9 days to use all their passes, which is a generous amount of time. Additional bonus: The passes work as tickets, so you'll be able to breeze right into the attractions, standing only in the security inspection line at the Empire State Building.

The **Explorer Pass** ✦ (☎ 800/887-9103; www.explorerpass.com) works a bit differently. Of a long list of options, which include tours along with museums, you pick five. You then have a full 30 days to use the pass. Explorer Pass costs $109 for adults, $69 for kids 3-12, but, depending on how you pick, you could be looking at savings of between $20 and $40. That being said, I think that some of the pickable attractions aren't worth your time, and only some of them seem to include a "skip the line" option. I'd still rate City Pass, higher, but if you really want to do a bus tour, then this is the pass for you.

My least favorite, the **New York Pass** (☎ 888/714-1999; www.newyork pass.com), grants admission to a full 55 sites and tours but (and this is a big *but*) it doesn't really give the bearer enough time to see these sights. So, you may end up spending more on the pass than you save. Its 1-day pass is a whopping $69 for adults ($49 for kids) and you'd have to move at action hero speed to get your money's worth. Buy a 2-day pass and the tab goes to $99, with 3 days at $125 and 7 at a whopping $165. Though the New York Pass does give you "line skipping" rights, as the City Pass does, you'll need to go to the admissions window and exchange your voucher for a ticket—a real time-waster (especially at the Empire State Building).

Still, the New York Pass does cover many important sites that the others don't, including the Bronx Zoo and the United Nations Tour. My advice? Create an itinerary and then crunch the numbers to see which option will work best for you.

collection in the world, and the hot questions surrounding dinosaurs—How did they die out? Did they care for their young? Did they live in organized herds?— are fully explored. Also on this floor is the equally fascinating "Wallace Wing of Mammals and Their Extinct Relatives" exhibit; make time for it if you can.

Floors two and three are diorama driven, with half the floors devoted to the anthropological study of the various peoples of the world; the other half to African and North American mammals. If you're short on time, take the mammal route, which features the poetic work of taxidermist/zoologist/sculptor Carl Akeley, who eventually died in Africa while collecting animals to stuff and display. Akeley pioneered a new technique of sculpting papier maché, which he would then cover with actual animal skins, antlers, and hoofs, often using the animal's bones for structure as well. The results are remarkably lifelike. The exhibit also fulfills his mission to conserve these animals and their environment for future generations—some of the wilderness areas depicted have changed beyond recognition in the past 50 years.

Other highlights of the older three-quarters of the museum include the dazzling Hall of Minerals, with its Fabergé-carved gems and the largest star sapphire in the world; the Hall of Ocean Life (with its famed 10-ton blue whale replica hanging from the ceiling); and the new Spitzer Hall of Human Origins, an extraordinarily persuasive argument for the theory of evolution.

One of the newest sections of the museum, the **Rose Center for Earth and Space** ✭✭✭ has been widely hailed as one of the most architecturally important new buildings in New York—a monumental 120-foot-high glass box enveloping a colossal sphere, which is the new virtual reality theater, the Hayden Planetarium. When you first enter the museum, be sure to get one of the timed tickets to a planetarium show, a highlight of any visit. Its show on collisions in space could be the first planetarium show ever that could double as an action flick. After or before the show, you'll want to explore the Cullman Hall of the Universe, which is devoted to discoveries in astrophysics; and the spellbinding Hall of Planet Earth, which tackles the issues of how our planet evolved and what makes it habitable.

I WANT MY MOMA: In 2004, a $425-million expansion designed by Japanese architect Yoshio Taniguchi nearly doubled the space at the renowned **Museum of Modern Art** ✭✭ (11 W. 53rd St., btwn Fifth and Sixth aves.; ☎ 212/708-9431; www.moma.org; $20 adults, $16 seniors, $12 students, free for kids 16 and under; Sat–Mon and Wed–Thurs 10:30am–5:30pm, Fri 10:30am–8pm; **E**, **V** to Fifth Ave.), thought by many to be the most important art museum of its kind in the world. Thanks to that expansion, a larger chunk of the museum's collection is now displayed in the 125,000 square feet of gallery space available for contemporary art, prints, and illustrated books (on the 2nd floor); architecture, design, and drawings (3rd floor); and all of the old favorites in the painting and sculpture collection (4th and 5th floors). The sculpture garden was also expanded from 18,400 square feet to 22,400 square feet, and there's more room as well for special exhibitions (on the 6th and 3rd floors).

Along with all of this growth is a palpable feeling of excitement that you'll notice as you wander the halls. This seems to be where all the "cool people" are hanging out, those bright, design-savvy New Yorkers with the architectural glasses and spiky haircuts. As you go from gallery to gallery, or visit the on-site restaurant

Museum-Hopping with children

Going to museums with children shouldn't be a medicinal experience: healthy for all, but hard to swallow. There *are* ways to make museums fun, especially the varied, rich museums of Gotham. Here are a few suggestions to keep in mind for your next visit with the kids:

1. **Timing:** Don't plan on staying for more than 2 hours at any museum with children under 10, and follow your sightseeing with a "kidcentric" activity, such as kicking back in a playground in Central Park (near most of the art museums).

2. **Advance planning:** Go to a museum's website before your visit to see if there are any special children's programs scheduled on the day of your visit. The Metropolitan, the Museum of Natural History, the Guggenheim, and others all offer kids' tours and art sessions free with the cost of admission.

3. **Fun and games:** Create a scavenger hunt for your child. With kids over 7, go into the gift shop as soon as you enter the museum and have them pick out three postcards. Then have your child search the museum until he or she finds those pieces of art. Your child can then use the postcard to write to family or friends about their experience. With younger children, give them a sheet of paper on which you will have drawn a bird, a dog, a baby, and a crown (or other symbols if you prefer); give the child the task of making a mark next to that symbol every time they see it and then count up the number of "scores" at the end of the visit. Trust me, these games work, and they're sneaky ways to get the kids to pay attention to the art.

4. **The talking cure:** Consider investing in the headphone tour if the museum has one for children. The one at the Museum of Modern Art, in particular, is extremely fun (in fact it's better than the adult's audio tour . . . but that's another story all together).

5. **Stroller strategy:** Check to see what the stroller policy is before you get to a museum. Some museums don't allow them at all; others only allow them on certain days of the week—and there's nothing worse than having to lug a squirming toddler (who could be napping peacefully in a stroller) through a crowded museum.

(which, by the by, has the best quality food of any museum in Manhattan), the chatter among visitors has an intensity and passion that are quite unusual.

But not all is rosy at the new MOMA. The entrance fee is a painful $20, higher by far than any other museum in the city (remember: the Metropolitan's admission fee is only "suggested"). And the museum itself has been redesigned and curated in a manner that's not necessarily friendly to the visitor. Pride of place has been given to the Contemporary Collection (which will be the first space you'll encounter after the lobby), a decision sure to challenge the navigational skills of the vast majority of visitors who have come here expressly to see the Picassos, van Goghs, and Matisses hidden far up on the fifth floor. Galleries, too, can be confusingly laid out, with four exits often leading out of one gallery; I spent my last visit worrying that I was missing galleries as I stumbled through white box after white box, with little sense of where each exhibit began and ended.

These factors make it important (more than at almost any other New York museum) to sit down with a map of the facility (ask for it when you pay the entrance fee) and map out what you want to see—you've paid a lot of money and if you don't have a plan, you'll run out of time for what really interests you. If you haven't been here before, get an audio tour (it's free) and begin with the Modern Masters, art work from 1840 to 1945, which is on the fifth floor. Several "Mona Lisas" grace this area:

- Vincent van Gogh's *Starry Night,* which has an even more vivid impact when viewed in person, the thickness of the brush strokes making it as much sculpture as painting. Created a year before his suicide, when van Gogh was in an insane asylum, the painting is filled with premonitions of what was to come, the foreground taken up with a soaring cypress tree, symbol of death.
- Pablo Picasso's *Desmoiselles d'Avignon,* a massive brothel scene in which Picasso experimented with a number of art styles—look closely and you'll see that one of the women's heads looks like an African mask, another profile is taken from Egyptian art, the woman in the middle assumes a classical Venus-like pose, and a leg of one of the figures devolves into cubist abstraction. Reportedly, Picasso painted the work when he was suffering from syphilis, which may be why the women appear so threatening.
- Salvador Dalí's *Persistence of Memory,* in which watches melt and a long-nosed figure (some say it was a self-portrait of Dalí; others think it represents an unborn baby) lies prostrate on the ground. You may be surprised at how small this seminal work is.

Soaring sculptures by Brancusi, intensely colorful masterpieces by Matisse, absurdist creations by Deschamps, and painted metaphors by Magritte are among the other wonders of the museum's collection, the most important in the world for art of this era.

FRANK LLOYD WRIGHT'S MASTERPIECE: New York is the city of the rectangle, of the sharp right angle. Our streets form a severe grid; our buildings are boxy and regular. Until you get to **The Guggenheim Museum** ✹✹✹ (1071 Fifth Ave., at 89th St.; ☎ 212/423-3500; www.guggenheim.org; $18 adults, $15 students and seniors, ages 12 and under free; Sat–Wed 10am–5:45pm, Fri 10am–8pm; ❹, ❺, ❻ to 86th St.), that is. Frank Lloyd Wright's delirious spiral of a museum sits among the towers of Fifth Avenue like a steroidal peacock among guinea hens. Architectural critic Herbert Muschamp described the look best when he wrote, "What else but a building brought back from a dream would be windowless, have walls and floors that tilt and twist, begin on the top floor, and spiral in toward the center like an enigma."

Visiting the center of this 1959 masterpiece and trudging up the ramps of curving halls transforms the standard museum experience into a profound journey (and sometimes a battle against vertigo), no matter what artworks are on display. Early critics dismissed the museum (*Newsweek*'s insipid review was headlined

"Museum or cupcake?"), but I think today even the most jaded visitor will feel the power of the place, the symbolic weight of infinite circle upon circle upon circle.

New York's museum is now one among five Guggenheims (in Venice, Berlin, Las Vegas, and most famously Frank Gehry's Bilbao), making it the "McDonald's" of the art world, a chain of museums that has managed to remain terrifically popular wherever it hangs its architecturally daring shingle. Part of that popularity, beyond the buildings, has resulted from its ability to formulate blockbuster retrospectives on topics that combine art with history and in some cases sociology—shows on Aztec culture, motorcycles, and Brazilian art, to mention just a few that have created headlines in the past few years. In her review of 2005's "Russia! Exhibit"—a tour de force of art, ranging from Byzantine icons all the way to the installation art of today—Roberta Smith of the *New York Times* wrote that the museum now has an "increasingly foolproof formula for presenting engrossing, impeccably installed spectaculars that, flaws and all, offer a lot to all levels of the art-viewing public, from bikers to the cognoscenti." I'd add that it's a very different sort of experience from other NY museums—populist, yes, but also engrossing, sweeping, and usually just plain fun.

Aside from the architecture and changing exhibits, the Guggenheim is known for its concentration of artworks by Kandinsky (150 in all), Brancusi, Picasso, Miró, and Mondrian, among other modernists. These pieces are always on display in the second-floor Tannheuser Collection room.

And to answer the question that nobody ever voices aloud: No, there haven't been any suicide jumps from over the low-slung rails, nor has anyone ever accidentally fallen to their death.

THE 13 RUNNERS-UP TO THE ICONIC SIGHTS

Thirteen institutions just barely miss inclusion on the list of places you simply have to visit when in town. But each one can add a special dimension to your New York visit. If you have the time, try to supplement the 12 iconic sights with these 13 runners-up.

A ROBBER BARON'S LEGACY: Arguably the best small museum in the nation, the **Frick Collection** ★★★ (1 E. 70th St. at Fifth Ave.; ☎ 212/288-0700; www.frick.org; $15 adults, $10 seniors, $5 students; children under 10 not admitted, those under 16 must be chaperoned; Tues–Sat 10am–6pm, Sun 11am–5pm; ❻ to 67th St.) provides a deeply satisfying experience on a number of levels. There's the highbrow fun of seeing some of the world's greatest masterpieces; the lowbrow kick of getting a firsthand peek at the home of one of the super-rich; and the somewhat macabre thrill, akin to a séance in a way, of communing with someone long dead through his choices in art. In the end, the Frick Collection is as much about Henry Clay Frick and the world he created as it is about the art itself.

And that's a good thing, as Frick (1849–1919) was a fascinating figure, an entrepreneur in the steel and coke industries with only 3 years of formal schooling, who became a self-made millionaire by the time he was 30. In some ways the typical "Robber Baron" (his violent methods for strike-breaking resulted in a number of deaths and injuries), he was nonetheless influenced by his friendship with Isabelle Gardner (of the Isabella Stewart Gardner Museum in Boston) to try and do a little bit of good for the common man after his death. So he bequeathed his enormous art collection and the grandly colonnaded neoclassical mansion that housed it (built by Carrere and Hastings, architects of the N.Y. Public Library) to the formation of a public museum for the purpose of "encouraging and developing the study of the fine arts" in the United States.

It's not a large museum, but in each of the 16 galleries there are wonders to behold, paintings and sculptures from nearly every great artist in the Western canon. Because Frick wanted viewers to have their own experiences of the art, there is very little wall text posted (which makes the collection feel more like a home than an institution), nor is the art arranged in any "instructive" manner—different periods of art are mixed together, as are artists of various nationalities. Unlike the Barnes Collection in Philadelphia, Frick gave his trustees the right to change the arrangement of the works, and acquire new ones; a full third of what you'll see was purchased after Frick passed away.

But most of the great pieces are from Frick's era and they are a testament to his astute taste as a collector. This is a man who not only collected Rembrandts (a trifecta of them!) but chose none but the most intriguing works, such as the painter's portrait of fur merchant Nicholas Ruts, Rembrandt's first commissioned portrait and the one that launched his career. Showing an edgy, dignified, intelligent-looking man wrapped in the softest, furriest ermine (look at it closely; many of the brush strokes are thinner than a hair), it's clear why Frick would have chosen it: As critic Simon Schama notes, it's one of the greatest renderings of a "businessman as hero" (and what self-made millionaire wouldn't want that in his home?). Rembrandt's self-portrait of 1658 is another transcendent pick, painted when the artist was at the lowest point in his life, having been excommunicated by the Church, financially bankrupted, and written off by the arts community. But instead of portraying himself as a failure, there's a challenge in his gaze and an upright quality to his carriage that seems to say, "Make my day." You may just laugh out loud when you see it. Both works are in the West Gallery.

Masterpieces by Vermeer (3 of the meager 36 that still exist today), Renoir, Degas, Velazquez, van Eyck, Brueghel, Whistler, Pierro della Francesca, Fra Filippo Lippi, Ingres, Frans Hals, El Greco (his *St. Jerome,* of which the Metropolitan Museum's version is a copy), Gainsborough, Fragonard, David, Cimabue, and more, are also on view. The most famous painting in the collection, Holbein's portrait of Sir Thomas More, hangs next to the mantle in the Living Hall, though in an ironic move, Frick also hung Holbein's portrait of Thomas Cromwell—More's longtime political rival, who was also executed by Henry VIII—on the other side of that mantle, so that the two can stare each other down through eternity.

An erudite audio tour, free with admission, serves as a pleasant companion for a walk through the museum. Every hour on the half-hour, a short but interesting movie on the life of Frick is screened. And if you have the foresight, you may wish to visit the Frick website to learn if a classical music concert will be taking place during your time in New York—the collection has a history of hosting some of the best up-and-coming talents.

THE BEAUTY OF WORDS: Famed Canadian scientist George Mercer Dawson once wrote that a great library contained "the diary of the human race." With that definition, very few libraries come as close to greatness as the **Morgan Library & Museum** ✹✹ (225 Madison Ave. at 36th St.; ☎ 212/685-0008; www.morgan library.org; $12 adults, $8 seniors, students, and children, free on Fri nights after

Attractions in Brooklyn, Queens & the Bronx

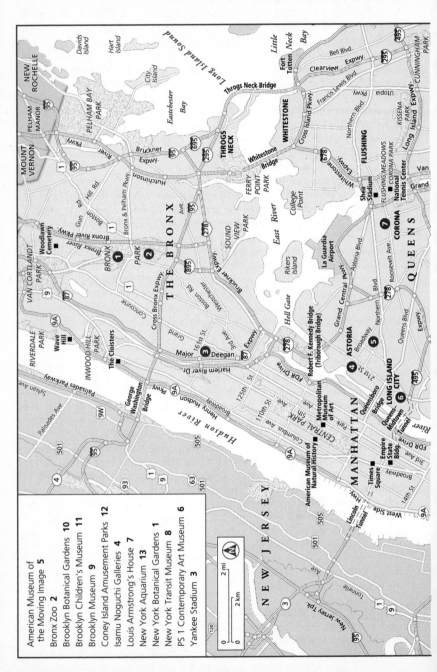

American Museum of
the Moving Image **5**

Bronx Zoo **2**

Brooklyn Botanical Gardens **10**

Brooklyn Children's Museum **11**

Brooklyn Museum **9**

Coney Island Amusement Parks **12**

Isamu Noguchi Galleries **4**

Louis Armstrong's House **7**

New York Aquarium **13**

New York Botanical Gardens **1**

New York Transit Museum **8**

PS 1 Contemporary Art Museum **6**

Yankee Stadium **3**

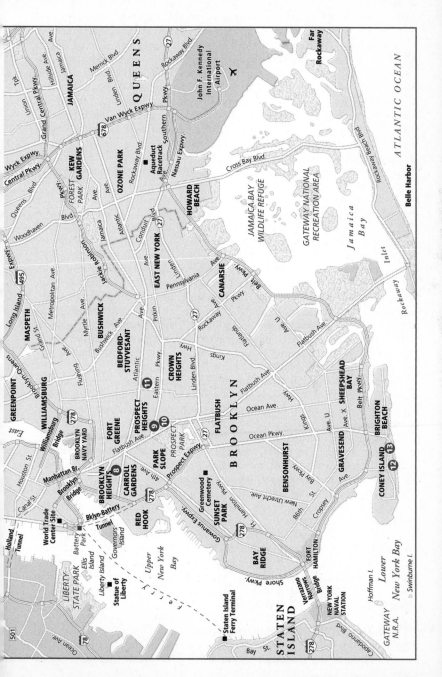

6pm; Tues–Thurs 10:30am–5pm, Fri 10:30am–9pm, Sat 10am–6pm, Sun 11am–6pm; ❹, ❺, ❻, ❼ to Grand Central) which contains examples of the written word from the beginning of recorded time—pictorial Mesopotamian cylinder seals (4th millennium B.C., a precursor to writing) to papyrus rolls from ancient Egypt, Greece, and Rome to brilliantly colored medieval illuminated manuscripts. Its crowning jewels are three editions of the Gutenberg Bible, the first book to be created using moveable type. (This is the only collection in the world to boast three; scholars come from across the globe to study them, as each is unique.) Also in the collection today are manuscripts by Mark Twain, Jane Austen, Charles Dickens, the Bronte sisters, Galileo, Bob Dylan, Alexander Calder and James Joyce. One of the 25 known surviving copies of the Declaration of Independence is another highlight along with a First Folio of Shakespeare. (The fragility of these treasures means that they cannot be constantly on display, but when you visit you'll usually see one of the Gutenbergs along with other exquisite books.)

The Morgan in the name of the library was another 19th-century billionaire but unlike Henry Clay Frick (see earlier in this chapter), J. Pierpont Morgan (1837–1913) was a collector who relied heavily on experts to guide him—most notably his nephew Junius Spencer Morgan (1867–1932), a rare books and manuscripts aficionado; and his remarkable librarian, Belle da Costa Greene (1883–1950), a woman who was not only one of the most powerful female rare books scholars of her day, but also hid the fact, for her entire life, that she was half-black (her father was the first African American to graduate from Harvard). They advised the millionaire, but to be fair, Morgan turned so heavily towards books for another more pragmatic reason: taxes. In 1897, the U.S. government imposed a 20% tariff on all foreign works of art entering the country. Books and manuscripts were exempted from this tax, and so these were the first treasures that Morgan brought into the U.S.

I don't mean to imply that Morgan only collected books—like Frick and Isabella Gardener (of Boston), he was a voracious buyer of all manners of artworks, from paintings by the great masters to prints and drawings to musical scores. Like his contemporaries, he felt that it was his duty to bring the world's great art home for Americans to enjoy. But many of his greatest artistic acquisitions were donated to the Wadsworth Atheneum (in Hartford) and the Metropolitan Museum after Morgan's death, so the heart of the collection today (I would argue) are the literary works (you will, of course, find great works of art there today, but not in the same number as at the Frick).

When you visit, be sure to put aside at least an hour and a half to take in the ever-rotating special exhibitions, along with the exquisite architecture. The original library, a marble villa in High Renaissance style, was designed by Charles Follen McKim (of the famous firm of McKim, Meade, & White). An expansion by lauded architect Renzo Piano, completed in 2006, added massive steel and glass pavilions, doubling the size of the facilities without diluting their Italianate flair. Along with a gift store, a terrific cafe and restaurant were added (so you may want to combine your visit with lunch).

THE HOME-GROWN ART OF AMERICA: "The Whitney"—you utter those two words with respect. Artists coming up in the world dream of having their work displayed at **The Whitney Museum** ★★★ (945 Madison Ave. at 75th St.;

☎ 800/WHITNEY; www.whitney.org; $15 adults, $10 students and seniors, free Fri btwn 6 and 9pm and for children under 12; Wed–Thurs and Sat–Sun 11am–6pm, Fri 11am–9pm). Art aficionados consider the curatorial work done here to be the most intellectually rigorous, risky, and exciting of any in the city. And over the years, a number of artists discovered by this institution—Alexander Calder, Edward Hopper, Georgia O'Keeffe, and others—have gone on to create works that then entered the canon of American art. Yet if you ask the average tourist about the museum, most won't even know it exists.

Which is a tremendous shame, because this institution, the only major museum in New York devoted to collecting *only* American fine art, consistently puts on astonishing shows. In 2005, for example, it assembled a team of experts to create a "floating island" filled with trees and shrubs that would circle Manhattan, a piece dreamed up by the now-deceased artist Robert Smithson. The Whitney, with the aid of Smithson's widow, made that dream a reality, timing it to coincide with a retrospective of Smithson's work, and for 3 weeks city dwellers bore witness to a floating mirage in the Hudson River—a tiny wedge of Illyria pulled by a tugboat.

Every 2 years the Whitney pushes the envelope even further, hosting its famed **Biennial,** a show of the best American art of the past 2 years. Curators scour the country for artists in every medium—sculpture, painting, video, installations, you name it—mixing the work of established artists with that of newcomers (whose careers are made by being picked). "Love it, hate it, see it" was the slogan for 2004, and that pretty much covers the experience every year.

Along with these changing exhibits (which usually take up two-thirds of the space at the museum), the Whitney showcases its fine permanent collection of American works on the fifth and second floors. Here you'll find the many mournful works by Edward Hopper (who always insisted—in vain—that his paintings were not meant to have emotional content); the desert-scoured paintings of Georgia O'Keeffe; the intricate, undulating sculptures of Louise Nevelson; and my favorite, Calder's famed *Circus* on the mezzanine level, a one-ring wonder with tiny circus figures made of wire, fabric, cork, and thread, accompanied by a video of the artist gleefully making the sculpture "perform." Calder's magical mobiles, a type of sculpture that didn't exist until he dreamt it up (marrying sculpture with movement for the first time), are a highlight of the top floor.

(***Note to parents:*** If you're visiting with kids, take them first to the *Circus* and then to the stairwell between the second and third floor. There you'll see a tiny adobe city by artist Charles Simonds. Walk down to the window and see if the kids can spot the "sister city" on the bank building across the street from the museum.)

In the basement is a swell cafe and a gift shop stuffed with chic, expensive items. The Whitney has a satellite gallery, the **Whitney Museum of American Arts at Altria,** on 42nd Street across from Grand Central Station.

TWO CENTURIES OF AMERICANA: Across the park from the Whitney sits **The New-York Historical Society** ★ (170 Central Park West, at 79th St.; ☎ 212/873-3400; www.nyhistory.org; $10 adults, $5 students and seniors, free Fridays from 6pm–8pm; Tues–Thurs and Sat, 10am–6pm, Fri 10am–8pm, Sun 11am–5:45pm; Ⓑ, Ⓒ to 81st St.), which must have the most misleading name of any institution in New York. First off, this is a full-blown museum with four floors of immense exhibition halls, not some sort of private society. More importantly, the museum's gaze extends far beyond New York as it displays one of the oldest collections of Americana in the country, which it started amassing in 1804 (the only other institution doing so at the time was the Massachusetts Antiquarian Society). It has pieces of unequaled importance from all parts of the United States, including one of the largest collections of Tiffany lamps in the nation (135 of them, all on view); Gilbert Stuart portraits of George Washington; the largest collection in the world of paintings from the Hudson Valley School; hundreds of Audubon prints; and a huge store of artifacts from the Gold Rush. These are all housed on the fourth floor in the Luce Center, an innovative open-storage facility of glass exhibition cases in which 70% of the Society's collection is on view. And though it can be daunting to muddle through case after case of, say, historic silver urns, jewelry, children's toys, or portrait busts, the free audio tour is helpful in pinpointing the gems of the collection. "We're a living *Antiques Roadshow*," says the Society's Public Historian Kathleen Hulser. "The kind of charge you can get ransacking your own attic, you can also get by ransacking the city's attic."

The most interesting pieces, to my mind, are to be found in the case just in front of you and to the right as you enter the Luce center. It holds a number of relics, from FDR's leg brace to the chair George Washington sat in at his inauguration to pieces taken from the World Trade Center site in the months after the attack. And don't miss the large model bust that sculptor Daniel Chester French created in preparation for the Lincoln Monument.

On the first two floors, the Society houses changing exhibits on a number of subjects, usually pairing a lighter topic with one of more substance. Exhibits planned for 2008 and 2009 include a large retrospective of the museum's watercolors; a comparison piece on the lives of Civil War Generals Grant and Lee; and an exhibition on the effect of cholera on the history of New York City.

THE STUFF OF DESIGN: Architect Mies Van der Rohe famously said, "God is in the details." That could be the motto for the **Cooper-Hewitt National Design Museum** ✬ (2 E. 91st St., at Fifth Ave.; ☎ 212/849-8400; www.cooperhewitt. org; $15 adults, $10 students and seniors; Mon–Thurs 10am–5pm, Fri 10am–9pm, Sat 10am–6pm, Sun noon–6pm; ❹, ❺, ❻ to 86th St.), which has made a name for itself by taking simple subjects in the world of design—say sample books, wallpapers, or super-strong textiles, to note three recent exhibits—and dissecting them to the point not of exasperation, but of fascination. The textiles exhibit, for example, showcased what looked like crocheted bags that are actually used in reconstructive heart surgery; entire fabric-covered kayaks that weigh less than 20 pounds; the materials used in space suits; and artistically strung netting used to stop soil erosion. Because the Cooper-Hewitt, which is a branch of the Smithsonian, is the only design museum in the nation to cover both contemporary and traditional design, its exhibits have a breadth and depth that's quite unusual for this type of subject matter.

The collections—textiles; wall coverings; product design and decorative arts; and drawings, prints, and graphic design—are housed in steel baron Andrew Carnegie's former home, a two-story mansion with a grand central staircase, elaborately carved wooden paneling, and 9,000 feet of exhibition space (plus a chichi gift shop). There are no permanent exhibitions; instead, pieces from the 250,000-object collection are removed from storage based on the subject matter of the show. Check the website before you go, as the museum tends to host facility-wide shows, meaning that for 6 weeks or so a year, the museum goes dark while the next exhibit is being installed.

A JOURNEY BACK TO THE MIDDLE AGES: Of the four museums in upper Manhattan, one towers above the rest, making it more than worthy of the some-times hour-long trek it takes to get there. I'm speaking of **The Cloisters** ★★ (Fort Tryon Park; ☎ 212/923-3700; www.metmuseum.org; suggested donation $20; Tues–Sun 9:30am–5:15pm Mar–Oct, 9:30am–4:45pm rest of year; **Ⓐ** to 190th St.), the only museum in the United States devoted wholly to medieval art and one that not only displays masterpieces of that era, but does so in a setting that appears to have been airlifted, utterly intact, from some remote corner of the Pyrenees, or from a castle-bound town in Bavaria.

Opened in 1934, the museum was, in fact, constructed in the United States, but 30% of the architectural elements—columns, pedestals, naves, door frames, exquisite stained-glass windows—were salvaged from medieval European struc-tures. It's a stunning mirage—even the land across the river was bought by patron John D. Rockefeller to thwart development and ensure that the Cloisters' views would forever have a medieval face. At its heart are four cloisters, ancient garden areas centered with a fountain and surrounded by covered walkways of the type that appear in every monastery and abbey in Europe. Off these tranquil gardens are galleries devoted to different periods of art and architecture—a peak-ceilinged Gothic chapel here; a squat, square Romanesque-era hall there—each housing the treasures of that time period.

Though you can see the entire museum in a bit over an hour, pay special atten-tion to the Unicorn Tapestries, one of only two full sets with a unicorn theme in the world (the other's in Paris). These richly detailed tapestries can be enjoyed on a number of levels today, just as they were back then. Many scholars see the uni-corn as a symbol of Christ, and the hunt to slay it as evocative of the Passion. Others write that the work is a metaphor for courtly love, with the hunt itself courtship, and the last tapestry of the unicorn trapped inside a wedding ring–like fence symbolizing marriage (despite this captivity, the unicorn does look happy). Whatever you decide, they are strikingly beautiful, an evocative slice of the past, when nobles only hunted in packs of six, and unicorns were thought to be real (hence the long Narwhale tooth next to the fireplace in this room, which medieval men thought came from unicorns).

The other examples of must-see art are kept in the climate-controlled Campin Room (bring a sweater), where you'll view Robert de Campin's breakthrough Merode altarpiece (c. 1425), which placed the Annunciation—the moment when the Virgin Mary is informed by the angel that she will be bearing the child of God—in a secular setting rather than a church. It's also quite dramatic for its use of Jewish objects, including a prayer shawl and a vase with Hebrew-looking let-tering, to establish Mary's background. To the right diagonal of the triptych is the so-called Cloisters Cross, another highlight; it's one of only three ivory crosses from the 12th century and the most complex of the three, with over 90 figures and inscriptions painstakingly carved into the unyielding walrus-tusk ivory.

I highly recommend timing your tour to coincide with one of the curator-led gallery talks or garden walks (usually held midday); they're absolutely worthwhile.

SELF-TAUGHT SAVANTS: You'll be surprised by the powerful impact the **American Folk Art Museum** ★★ kids (45 W. 53rd St., btwn Fifth and Sixth aves.; ☎ 212/265-1040; www.folkartmuseum.org; $9 adults, $7 seniors and students, free after 5:30pm on Fri and for kids 12 and under; Tues–Thurs and Sat–Sun 10:30am–5:30pm, Fri 10:30am–7:30pm; **E**, **V** to Fifth Ave.) makes. Dedicated to "self-taught" artists, the museum weaves its spell in much the same way Scheherazade did: by telling odd, intriguing, haunting stories. These stories—bits of history, personal history, and anthropology, really—are told through sculpture, paintings, weather vanes, quilts, painted furniture, collages, and the most entertaining wall text of any museum in the city. You may, for example, view the sketchbook of a Civil War–era prisoner of war; or a "Freedom Quilt" harkening back to the legendary "Underground Railroad quilts" that may have had routes to freedom imbedded in their patterns. You'll see the kooky but beautiful *Gold Tower* of Eugene Von Bruenchenhein, on floor five, created entirely from the turkey and chicken wings he ate at local fast-food restaurants (monetary problems kept him from being able to afford more traditional sculptural materials). Also on floor five is a phantasmagorical paper mural by Henry Darger, who spun his nightmares and obsession with his adopted sister into a series of disturbing novels with accompanying watercolors (à la William Blake) featuring poignant, odd subjects—hermaphrodite children, strangely frozen soldiers, and doll-like girl warriors.

It's great fun, and because the museum usually organizes its exhibits by theme, you'll see works from all eras, in all mediums, in one room, which helps with the "museum fatigue" some visitors experience after seeing too many Impressionist paintings in a row, or room after room of ancient Greek statuary.

Start at the top where the permanent collection is housed, and you can see the whole shebang in less than 2 hours, meaning that a visit here could be easily paired with a visit to the Museum of Modern Art right next door. There are numerous classes and tours for children, and those who visit in between these programs should request a copy of the "scavenger hunt" of animals in the museum, an engrossing activity for children between the ages of 5 and 11. A small cafe and gift shop are housed respectively on the second and first floors.

WAR—UNDER THE SEA AND IN THE AIR: The only tourable nuclear submarine in the world, an assortment of grounded jets, and a World War II–era aircraft carrier make up the attractions at the **Intrepid Sea, Air and Space Museum** ★★ kids (Pier 86 at W. 46th St., off Twelfth Ave.; ☎ 212/245-0072; www.intrepid museum.org; $17 adults; $13 veterans, reservists, seniors, and students; $12 ages 6–17; $4.50 ages 2–5; 50% discount for persons with disabilities; Mon–Fri 10am–5pm, Sat–Sun 10am–6pm; **A**, **C**, **E** to 42nd St.). It's quite a lineup and one that's guaranteed to engage the attentions and imaginations of visitors of all ages.

You'll want to begin your visit at the USS *Growler* submarine, built in 1958 and so narrow that only small groups can enter at a time (which keeps the lines here long). You'll be taken on a brief, thrillingly claustrophobic tour introduced by a short video. Children under the age of 6 are not admitted.

Next, make your way to the Concorde, the oversized luxury lawn dart that, after flying half-empty for a number of years, was finally taken out of commission in 2003. (The jet isn't in the classic bent-nosed pose; that was only used for take-offs and landings.) This ultra-deluxe flying bus carried a mere 100 passengers at a time, most of them paying $6,000 each way for the privilege of crossing the Atlantic faster than the speed of sound (it went from 0 to 165mph in just 2.5 seconds). Take a close look at places A and B, the seats reserved for Queen Elizabeth II and Prince Philip of England.

The *Fighting I,* the main focus of your visit, is a 40,000-ton aircraft carrier that had one of the greatest survival stories of World War II. Though it was hit by five kamikaze planes (two of them in a single day) during its tours of duty, it continued to serve (the Japanese called it "The Ghost Ship" because it couldn't be sunk). You can wander through the ship on your own, but you'll get more out of the experience with the hour-long guided tour, led by highly informed docents, most with military backgrounds. They'll take you through the World War II planes stored on this deck (take a look, too, at the Revolutionary War version of a submarine); and the planes on the flight deck, such as the McDonnell Douglas F-4 Phantom, the most widely used plane during the Vietnam war, and the "Tomcat," which you may remember from the movie *Top Gun.* The tour guide will also explain how the crew navigated and docked the boat, the procedures for briefings before missions, even mess-hall etiquette.

I also recommend the 25-minute-long video detailing the history of the ship (interviewed on it is John McCain, who served aboard the *Intrepid*), which starts every half-hour; and the "Intrepid Experience," which begins on the hour, and is a sound, smoke, and video re-creation of what it would have been like to be aboard the ship when it was attacked by a kamikaze fighter. For those who like interactive exhibits, there are two nausea-inducing (for me anyway) space and flight simulators (for a small extra charge).

As I write this, the *Intrepid* is in dry-dock for repairs but is scheduled to reopen to the public on November 11, 2008.

COPS ON THE BEAT: The New York City Police Museum ★★ (100 Old Slip, btwn Water and South sts.; ☎ 212/480-3100; www.nycpolicemuseum.org; suggested donation $5, $3 for seniors, free children under 5; Mon–Sat 10am–5pm; ❹, ❺ to Bowling Green, ❷, ❸ to Wall St., or ®, ◐ to Whitehall St.) packs an emotional wallop because it deals with the events of 9/11 in an intricate, thoughtful manner. The museum was being created at the time of the attacks; it opened just 6 months later, and many of the exhibits conclude with a bit of information that will pull you directly back into that harrowing time. You'll read, for example, of how cadets were pulled out of the police academy to patrol the streets; or how overwhelmed 911 operators waded through the torrent of frantic phone calls, both on the day itself and in the weeks that followed.

Start your visit on the top floor at the 9/11 exhibit (on the right as you enter), which profiles the actions of two officers who died on that day. Video of the attack accompanies this exhibit, so if you're traveling with small children you may wish to skip this room. Next to the 9/11 room is a space for changing exhibits, and then on the left end is the sobering "Hall of Heroes," dedicated to the 700-plus officers over the years who have lost their lives in the line of duty (the

Chelsea Calling: Meet the new SoHo

In the past decade, more than 250 galleries have moved onto the blocks spanning 20th to 29th streets between Tenth and Eleventh avenues in West Chelsea, effectively making the Big Apple the planet's premiere marketplace for contemporary art. Gallery after gallery has taken over the former warehouse and industrial spaces of this dusty old 'hood, creating an eminently walkable new arts district.

Although you can have a perfectly lovely time simply getting lost in the area and wandering blindly from one space to the next, you could hit a lot of clunker exhibitions (just as with any collection of new art, some are better than others). If you want to take this course of action, start on 24th Street, which has the largest assortment of "name" galleries. A better tack might be to catch a tour of the area (see below) or to concentrate on the following 10 galleries, which have made their reputations with consistently thought-provoking shows.

Note: The standard schedule for all Chelsea galleries is Sept–May Tues–Sat 10am–6pm and June–Aug Mon–Fri 10am–6pm. Your best subway option is to take either the **C** or **E** to 23rd St.

- **303 Gallery** (525 W. 22nd St.; ☎ 212/255-1121; www.303gallery. com). The Whitney biennial has come calling recently, picking up the works of the young to mid-career, cutting-edge photographers and painters who present shows here. For a good look at the artists the gallery represents, visit the website first.
- **Paula Cooper** (534 W. 21st St. and 521 W. 21st St.; ☎ 212/255-1105; www.paulacoopergallery.com). Cooper used to be one of the biggest names in art, the dealer that everyone wanted. Though she's slipped in the last 5 years or so and lost some of her big-name clients, she still has the exquisite taste she's always had, and exhibits a number of prominent artists, including: Jennifer Bartlett, Donald Judd, Sol LeWitt, and Andres Serrano.
- **Gagosian** (555 W. 24th St.; ☎ 212/741-1111; www.gagosian.com). A massive, important family of galleries (one uptown, one in Los Angeles, another in London), it presents blockbuster shows of works from such major 20th- and 21st-century figures as Roy Lichtenstein, Francis Bacon, Nan Goldin, Cindy Sherman, and Cy Twombly.
- **Barbara Gladstone Gallery** (515 W. 24th St.; ☎ 212/206-9300; www. gladstonegallery.com). Come here to see the artists who have emerged as big honchos in the last 5 years or so, such as Ilya Kabakov, and Richard Prince. Gladstone tends to feature conceptual, often highly political art—most prominently photography and videos, but also sculpture and paintings.
- **Yossi Milo** (525 W. 25th St.; ☎ 212/404-0370; www.yossimilo gallery.com). One of my personal favorites, Milo works almost exclusively with photographers and has a terrific eye for the next big thing. He also runs a very friendly gallery, and he and his staff are always happy to talk with interested patrons. Because he represents photographers, some of them selling multiple editions of their work, you just may be able to afford to buy something here.

- **Pace Wildenstein** (534 and 545 W. 25th St.; ☎ 212/929-7000; www. pacewildenstein.com). Another "Blue Chip" gallery, with two outposts in Chelsea (see above) and one in Midtown (32 E. 57th St.), Pace Wildenstein has been a powerhouse since the 1960s, when it was founded in Boston. Shows in 2007 and 2008 featured the works of such biggies as Chuck Close, Robert Rauschenberg, Claus Oldenberg, and Jim Dine.
- **The Proposition** (559 W. 22nd St.; ☎ 212/242-0203; www.the proposition.com). A gallery geared towards the "insiders" of the art world, those engaged in the sometimes obscure dialogue of new ideas. If you're part of the game and know the lingo, you should enjoy it. If not, viewing the downright odd photos, paintings, installations, and sculptures might be a baffling experience.
- **Andrea Rosen** (525 W. 24th St.; ☎ 212/627-6000; www.andrearosen gallery.com). The Rosen gallery is a terrific place to see emerging artists, especially those who are "installation happy" and like to create entire environments for their viewers. It seems that each time I come here I'm stepping into some new type of utopia (or dystopia); the experience can be chilling and exciting.
- **Sonnabend Gallery** (536 W. 22nd St.; ☎ 212/627-1018; www.art net.com/sonnabend.html). Maybe I've just hit it right, but I find that the Sonnabend has something that's missing from so many galleries: a sense of humor. Most of the work I've seen here has been purposefully funny—odd *Star Wars* sculptures, videos of Germans singing along to Madonna songs—and after all of the "serious art" at other places, coming into this playful atmosphere is a delight. Sonnebend is one of the more established galleries, founded by the former wife of famed dealer Leo Castelli.
- **David Zwirner** (519, 525 and 533 W. 19th St.; ☎ 212/727-7020; www.davidzwirner.com). Owned by an ex-pat German, this gallery has a reputation for showing the best up-and-coming Teutonic art, some of it quite racy. This is not the place for people with delicate sensibilities, but if you don't mind seeing art that's really on the edge, you'll often find something here that will get your adrenaline pumping.
- **A gallery tour:** Allowing an expert to lead you through this ever-shifting maze of art is a good idea. And New York's foremost expert in the Chelsea Gallery scene—he visits 50 to 70 shows a week just to keep current—is Raphael Risemburg of **NY Gallery Tours** ★ (☎ 212/946-1548; www.nygallerytours.com). Risemburg, a professor at Keane College in New Jersey, has a droll, friendly manner and leads his tours in Socratic fashion: He'll tell you what he thinks of the art at the 10 to 20 galleries you cover on your tour, and then ask your opinion on the unanswered questions the art poses. His open tours are offered one Saturday per month (the cost is $15, but you can get $3 off by going to the website first), and he also leads private tours for $200 (though you can bring along up to 15 people on those).

recorded bagpipe music and recitation of names goes on even when the museum is closed in an attempt to ensure that the sacrifices of these men and women are never forgotten).

The second floor is largely devoted to illustrating how officers do their jobs today. The New York City Police Department (NYPD) has 38,000 officers plus 20,000 civilian employees, making it the largest police force in the world. To put into perspective just how gargantuan the department is, consider that the Los Angeles Police Department has just 12,000 officers and 8,000 civilians—added together, that's less than half the number of uniformed New York officers. How the NYPD's various units interact and the highly specialized nature of their jobs is explored in a series of interactive, video-taped interview/montages with current members of the force: housing police, mounted police, undercover detectives, the vice unit . . . you name it. You'll learn about the precautions an officer needs to take before entering a roof area, the types of disguises employed by subway decoys, what it's like to infiltrate a gambling ring—fascinating, in-depth depictions more interesting and inspiring than any TV drama (in fact, I left thinking, for the first time in my life, that perhaps I should consider a career change to law enforcement—you may feel the same way). To the left of this exhibit is a macabre room dedicated to mug shots, famous criminals, and all of the weapons confiscated over the years (including the first machine gun to be used in a crime, by a member of Al Capone's gang).

The ground floor covers transportation and communication methods that the force has used over the years. Gloss over it quickly and spend the majority of your time here upstairs.

REMEMBERING THE HOLOCAUST: Though they're located close to each other, don't try to visit the Police Museum and **The Museum of Jewish Heritage— A Living Memorial to the Holocaust** ★★ (36 Battery Place, in Battery Park City; ☎ 646/437-4200; www.mjhnyc.com; $10 adults, $7 seniors, $5 students, free admission Wed 4–8pm; Sun–Tues and Thurs 10am–5:45pm, Wed 10am–8pm, Fri and the eve of Jewish holidays 10am–3pm; ❹, ❺ to Bowling Green, ❷, ❸ to Wall St., or ❽, ❿ to Whitehall St.) on the same day. Not only will you run out of time (it takes at least an hour and a half to see the Jewish Museum), but both can be emotionally draining experiences, particularly the Museum of Jewish Heritage, which deals in explicit fashion with the Holocaust. To be fair, the museum is not in any way a showcase of horrors; its curators have been very careful to create a rounded picture of what life was like before, during, and after World War II, and visitors are sent back out into New York dwelling not only on the first part of the museum's mantra—"Never forget"—but also on the vibrant lives these Jews lived and on the resilience of the Jewish people.

Your tour will begin in the older section of the museum—an elegant six-sided building by architect Kevin Roche, meant to evoke both the Star of David and the six million Jews who were murdered during the Holocaust. The first floor covers life before the war with a sensitively constructed exhibit detailing the various aspects of daily existence, from the professions Jews entered, to the various ideologies that were popular at the time, to the rituals surrounding seasons of the year and days of the week. Each artifact shown has two stories attached to it: the explanation of what it would have been used for at that time, as well as a bit of history about the person who once owned the piece—the latter giving the whole enterprise a wonderfully personal tone.

The second floor is dedicated to the war years, and as might be expected, many of the images shown are quite graphic and disturbing. (People with children under 12 would be well-advised to skip this floor by taking the elevator directly from the 1st floor up to the 3rd.) In addition to photos, objects, and text, the museum is a repository for videos from Steven Spielberg's Shoah Foundation's Visual History project, and these vivid accounts of life in the camps and ghettos are the highlight of the museum.

The final floor discusses the Diaspora, with exhibitions on Jewish life in the United States, Israel, and Europe. There are also changing exhibits, and programs of lectures and music. For those looking for a very in-depth experience, there is a self-guided headphone tour (an additional $5) narrated by Meryl Streep and Itzhak Perlman. On-site, too: a kosher cafe.

THE IMMIGRANT EXPERIENCE: As narrow in its focus as the Jewish Heritage Museum is broad, the **Tenement Museum ★★★** kids (108 Orchard St., off Delancey; ☎ 212/431-0233; www.tenement.org; $17 adults, $13 students and seniors, free for children; Tues–Fri 1pm–4:45pm tours, Sat–Sun 11am–4:45pm tours; **B**, **D** to Grand St., or **F** to Delancey St.) looks at just one building on the Lower East Side. In exploring the personal histories of the people who called this tenement home between 1863 and 1935 (and there were well over 7,000 of them from 25 different countries), it is able to give a remarkably in-depth snapshot of what it must have been like to be an immigrant in New York City during that period, when the housing itself could be a hazard.

Visits to the museum are by 45-minute guided tour only, and visitors have a choice of three programs: The "Getting By" tour, which tells the dramatic tale of how two immigrant families survived the Great Depressions of the 1870s and the 1930s; the "Piecing it Together" tour, about the life of the garment industry workers of the area; and the "Confino Family Apartment," which is less tour than interactive experience in which a costumed character, teenaged Victoria Confino, instructs new immigrants (the people on the tour) in a candid, revealing, and totally improvised manner on how to get along in New York. (The last one sounds hokey, I know, but to my mind it's the most vivid of the three.) The Confino program is especially appropriate for children and seniors, as there's little walking involved, visitors get to touch objects in the room, and this is the only apartment in the building that's air-conditioned (an important consideration in July and Aug). The Confino experience is offered on weekends only.

Choosing between the other two tours is more difficult. In the Garment District program, visitors get a peek at artifacts that were found in the building, see a small in-apartment sweat shop, and learn about the practice of "sitting Shiva" when a member of a Jewish family dies. The "Getting By" tour is pegged on the heart-rending story of the disappearance of one of the tenants in the building and how his family was able to survive without the breadwinner of their household (be sure to ask your guide to tell the story of what happened to this man's descendents). It's possible to take both tours for $20, though there is some overlap between them.

The museum also offers walking tours of the neighborhood, between April and November each Saturday and Sunday at 1pm and 3pm ($12); and free post-tour "Kitchen Conversations" after some tours, to allow participants a bit of extra time to explore the issues raised over coffee and cookies.

If you visit the Tenement Museum on a Sunday or mid-week, take the opportunity to stroll over to the nearby **Eldridge Street Project** ✸ (12 Eldridge St. btwn Canal and Division sts.; www.eldridgestreet.org. Sun–Thurs 10am–4pm; $10 adults, $8 seniors and students, $6 children 5–18, toddlers free; ⓑ, ⓓ to Grand or ⓕ to W. Broadway). It's an 1887 synagogue, the oldest house of worship in the city for eastern European Jews, and has the kind of grandeur and beauty that you normally associate with the cathedrals of Europe. There's a poignancy to the place as well, as the building was abandoned for 40 years before restoration began in the 1990s, and it's crumbling picturesquely away in places. An hourly "From Bottom to Top" tour takes you through the history of the synagogue and the issues involved in its restoration.

FROM MAGIC LANTERN TO X-BOX: Head to the borough of Queens, more easily accessible than you'd think, for a major museum experience that must be included on any list of must-sees. For sheer, unadulterated fun, there's no museum in town that can beat the **Museum of the Moving Image** ✸✸✸ 🄺🄸🄳🄸 (35th Ave. at 36th St., Astoria; ☎ 718/784-0077; www.movingimage.us; $10 adults, $7.50 students and seniors, $5 children ages 5–18; free Fri 4–8pm; Wed–Thurs 11am–5pm, Fri 11am–8pm, Sat–Sun 11am–6:30pm; ⓡ, ⓥ to Steinway St.). The first museum anywhere to look at TV, film, and video games together (a heretical concept when the museum was opened in 1988), it's not simply an archive of past shows. Instead, it explores the craft and technology behind these arts with startlingly imaginative interactive exhibits, commissioned art works, video sequences and, of course, artifacts. Just how much fun is all this? Well, Citysearch ranked it the best place in the city for a family outing, and *Time Out* magazine called the museum the #1 place to go when you're "baked" (and if that doesn't hit all the bases, I don't know what does).

Start your visit on the third floor with the museum's core exhibit, "Behind the Screen," which explores the many technical issues behind moving images, from explanations of how the eye is tricked into seeing movement in rapidly repeating images, to the intricacies of sound and film editing. You'll have a chance to dub your own voice into such classics as *My Fair Lady*, create original computer animation, transmute the musical score of a famous film scene, and more. Several times a day, working editors, animators, and educators give demonstrations of how these techniques are used on actual productions.

On the second floor the focus shifts from technical issues to design issues, with exhibits devoted to the makeup, costumes, sets, and publicity stills that help create the image the director (or studio) is looking for. So you may see the rubber masks that transformed Dustin Hoffman into a very old character in the film *Little Big Man,* or the dazzling costumes from the movie *Chicago*. Walls and walls of marketing ephemera—lunch boxes of the Fonz, cookie tins with the faces of silent film stars, Muppet memorabilia—complete the floor, along with "Tut's Fever Movie Palace," a wacky '30s-style theater, created by artist Red Grooms; the theater screens classic silent serials.

And if you've been harboring a secret yen to play Galactica just one more time, you'll have your chance on the ground floor exhibit "Digital Play: Reloaded," which pairs the classic arcade games of the '80s with their contemporary counterparts (I've known folks who've spent their entire afternoon just at this exhibit). Also on the first floor is the museum's full-sized movie theater, which offers free screenings of feature films from around the world. "We don't draw a line in the sand and say, "'This is art and this is not,'" says New Media curator Carl Goodman. "We screen it all here so we get to look at the artistic side of a commercial film, followed by an obscure art film. It gives us a much broader scope than most institutions." Screenings are often followed by discussions with the artists involved, including such big names as Glenn Close, Tim Burton, David Cronenberg, and Jennifer Connelly.

As we went to press, the Museum of the Moving Image was closed for renovations. It will partially reopen in early 2009, with the full reopening scheduled for winter 2009/10.

OUTER BOROUGH BONANZA: Some Manhattan-centric residents downplay the remarkable **Brooklyn Museum** ✹ (200 Eastern Pkwy., Brooklyn; ☎ 718/683-5000; www.brooklynmuseum.org; suggested donation $8 adults, $4 seniors and students, free children under 12; Wed–Fri 10am–5pm, Sat–Sun 11am–6pm; ❷, ❸ to Eastern Pkwy.) as the "mini Met." It has a grand, neoclassical facade—but not quite as grand as the Metropolitan Museum's (especially now that much of it is masked behind a large, modern glass-and-steel canopy/walkway/entryway). It gets smaller crowds than the Metropolitan, meaning you can stroll through on a weekday and often have an entire gallery all to yourself. And though it covers every period in the history of art in its 560,000 square feet of galleries (on five floors), it has far fewer objects per era or region than the Met does, which dwarfs it with a whopping 2 million square feet. (An interesting aside: Its smaller size is an accident of history. The original plans by esteemed architects McKim, Meade & White called for a space 16 times as large, but when Brooklyn was annexed by New York City in 1898, funds for what was now just a borough, rather than a city museum, dried up.)

That being said, what the museum does well, it does superbly. Its Egyptian Collection, while not as big as the Met's, arguably has more masterpieces. In fact, when an ancient Egyptian piece comes up at auction, dealers often ask, "Is it Brooklyn quality?"—the Brooklyn Museum's collection being the benchmark for this sort of artifact. Among the collection's many wonders are a tiny 5,000-year-old, pre-dynastic terra-cotta sculpture of a woman, which curators have nicknamed "Birdwoman" for her beaklike face, one of the very few intact sculptures from this long-ago era. Why she looks so much like a bird, and what the statue was used for, remains a mystery to this day. The Cartonnage of Nespanetjerenpere is another highlight, a mummy case that looks like it was swiped from the set of *Revenge of the Mummy,* its colors electrically bright and unfaded. I highly recommend getting the audio tour ($3) for this gallery, as it will explain how these works were created, what the symbolism means, and what they reveal about life in ancient Egypt.

Second most popular among the museum's offerings are the Decorative Arts Galleries (on the 4th floor), which re-create important rooms from different eras of American history, including John D. Rockefeller's "Moorish Smoking Room," an extravagantly over-the-top Victorian version of the Middle East, every single bit of space lavishly carved, gilded, inlaid, or embroidered. Also worth a look are the Museum's American Collection and the Rodin Sculpture Gallery, both on the top floor. The American Collection jumbles together fine art, folk art, and decorative arts by theme rather than era, creating a dense, rich viewing experience, with works by such American masters as Albert Bierstadt, Thomas Eakins, Winslow Homer, and Georgia O'Keeffe. The Rodin is one of the museum's newest acquisitions, containing modern castings of Rodin's original molds, two dozen or so, from such masterpieces as the *Burghers of Calais* and the *Gates of Hell.*

And one final thing that the Brooklyn does better than the Met: Party. On the first Saturday of each month, the museum throws open its doors, hires deejays and performers of all sorts, and throws a "First Saturday" fiesta that is free to the public. Two free movies are screened and there's always a gallery talk or two by curators or visiting artists. It's usually a good time, and a great evening activity for families, as there are many kids' activities. Festivities commence at 6pm, ending at 11pm, but because many of the special activities require free tickets, which are handed out early in the evening, it's a good idea to get there at 6pm.

MUSEUMS FOR VISITORS WITH SPECIALIZED INTERESTS

Have endless reserves of energy—and time? Or are you interested in seeing some of the city's more off-beat sights? There are two dozen other museums which will delight those with the following specialized interests.

AFRICAN-AMERICAN, CARIBBEAN & HISPANIC ART

Though it's not a large museum, **The Studio Museum in Harlem** (144 W. 125th St., btwn Lenox Ave. and Adam Clayton Powell, Jr. Blvd.; ☎ 212/864-4500; www.studiomuseum.org; suggested donation $7 adults, $3 students and seniors, free children 12 and under; Wed–Fri and Sun noon–6pm, Sat 10am–6pm; ❷, ❸ to 125th St.) is one of the most respected in Gotham, known for presenting challenging, intricate shows of African-American and Caribbean-American art (contemporary and from the 19th and 20th centuries). In addition to two floors of galleries that host changing exhibitions, there's a space right off the lobby for the semi-permanent "Postcards from Harlem" wall, on which famous artists share their own memories of the neighborhood through text, photography, paintings, and drawings.

Uptown, on the East Side, **El Museo del Barrio** (1230 Fifth Ave. at 104th St.; ☎ 212/831-7272; www.elmuseo.org; suggested donation $6 adults, $4 seniors and students, free children; Wed–Sun 11am–5pm; ❻ to 103rd St.) serves as a showplace for the art of Latin America and the Caribbean. Among its collections are hundreds of pre-Columbian pieces, contemporary and modern paintings and sculptures, and, most significantly, 500 Santos de Palo, mostly from Puerto Rico. These hand-carved, wooden saints are very beautiful and well worth a visit. The museum also throws fun parties for every Latin and Caribbean holiday, and hosts changing exhibits.

AUSTRIAN & GERMAN ART

The Neue Gallery (1048 Fifth Ave., entrance on 86th St.; ☎ 212/628-6200; www.neuegallery.org; $10 adults, $7 students and seniors; Sat–Mon 11am–6pm,

Fri 11am–9pm; ❹, ❺, ❻ to 86th St.) is most notable for its six jewel-toned paintings by Gustave Klimt, its "Didn't I sit on that in the '70s?" Bauhaus furniture, and its collection of drawings by such Teutonic masters as Dix, Schiele, and Klimt. Because some of these drawings are a bit racy, children under the age of 12 are not admitted, and those 16 and younger must be accompanied by an adult. Also on-site: a Viennese cafe (p. 114), a small theater for lectures and films, and a pricey gift shop.

CHINESE-AMERICAN HISTORY

A now expanded **The Museum of Chinese in the Americas** (211–215 Centre St.; ☎ 212/619-4785; www.mocanyc.org; $3 adults, $1 students and seniors; hours to be determined; ❶ to Grand St.) is the only one of its kind in the world. It displays its collection of ethnic artifacts in changing exhibits. Unfortunately, the new museum had not yet opened at press time, so it's impossible for me to give a full review.

COLONIAL, REVOLUTIONARY & EARLY AMERICAN NEW YORK

Far uptown, and looking like it should be in the midst of some grand Virginia estate, **Morris Jumel Mansion** (65 Jumel Terrace btwn 161st and 162nd sts.; ☎ 212/923-8008; www.morrisjumel.org; $4 adults, $3 seniors, free children under 12; Wed–Sun 10am–4pm; ❸ to 163rd St.) served briefly as George Washington's headquarters during the Revolutionary War. Built in 1765, it was later bought by French immigrant Morris Jumel and his wife (who became the wife of Vice President Aaron Burr after Jumel's death) and is furnished with Second Empire and Colonial furnishings of the type the Jumels would have had. While the house has an interesting history, the lack of original furnishings and guided tours reduce its appeal, making it a must-visit only for die-hard American Revolution aficionados.

   Mount Vernon Hotel Museum and Garden (421 E. 61st St. btwn First Ave. and York St.; ☎ 212/838-6878; www.mvhm.org; $8 adults, $7 seniors and students; Tues–Sun 11am–4pm; ❹, ❺, ❻, ❶, ❷ to 59th St.) is a better historical house experience, thanks to the talents of the guides who lead visitors through this 1799 carriage home. Attached at first to a country manor, it became a fashionable resort hotel in 1826. The story of that hotel and life in 1820s and '30s make up the bulk of the tour. The fact that this little house still exists among the high-rises of Midtown, and that there's a tranquil garden where you can retreat and regroup, gives the museum special appeal.

   Fraunces Tavern (54 Pearl St., near Stone St.; ☎ 212/425-1776; www.fraunces tavernmuseum.org; $4 adults, $3 seniors and students, free kids 5 and under; Mon–Sat noon–5pm; ❷, ❶ to Whitehall, or ❹, ❺ to Bowling Green) is more notable for what happened on its premises than what the museum actually houses. This is the famed watering hole where the Sons of Liberty planned their moves against the British, where George Washington bade farewell to his troops, and where Alexander Hamilton toiled (with his small staff) as the first secretary of the treasury for 2 years. The highlight is the "Long Room," a re-creation of the dining hall where Washington gave his famous farewell. Look for the handwritten diary, on the third floor, in which one of his generals gives an account of that emotional dinner; in a case diagonally across from the diary, you'll see an actual lock of the great man's hair (he was a redhead!). The museum is administered by the Sons of the Revolution and contains a number of Revolutionary War paintings and memorabilia. On the website you'll also find information about weekly history programs.

You may want to pair your visit to Fraunces Tavern with nearby **Federal Hall** (26 Wall St., off Broad St.; ☎ 212/825-6990; www.nps.gov/feha; Mon–Fri 9am– 5pm; free; ❻, ❷ to Whitehall St. or ❹, ❺ to Bowling Green), the severe Greek temple–like structure that stands on the site where George Washington took the oath of office, the Congressional Congress passed the Bill of Rights and, much earlier, the Peter Zinger trial established de facto freedom of the press in Colonial America (and may have hastened the Revolution thanks to the incendiary articles the press started writing after that time). Inside you'll find a grandly ornamental rotunda and two floors of exhibits chronicling all of the important events that took place here.

CONTEMPORARY ART

Perhaps the greatest sign of New York City's ever increasing prosperity is the fact that now, even the gritty, grimy Bowery (birthplace of the term "Bowery bums" for the homeless people who used to swarm its cheap bars and bunk in its missions) now has a museum. And a bright and shiny one at that, a massive steel and glass tower, called the **New Museum of Contemporary Art** (235 Bowery btwn Stanton and Rivington Sts; ☎ 212/219-1222; www.newmuseum.org; Wed, Sat– Sun noon–6pm, Thurs–Fri noon–10pm; $12 adults, $8 seniors, $6 students, free ages 18 and under; ❽, ❿, ❺, ❻ to Broadway-Lafayette). As with much of the art of the moment, the exhibits range from the sublime to the silly (I was stopped dead in my tracks at a recent exhibit by a cardboard box and a big plastic bag among all the sculptures—was it art, or the container the art came in? I knew the answer intellectually, but my heart kept crying out: Recycle that bag and box, and do something useful with it!). Wall text is hard to find, so buttonhole one of the gallery guides wearing big "Ask Me" buttons; sometimes their explanations— about the melting candle sculpture, or that branch with snow hats on it—are more interesting than the art itself.

DECORATIVE ARTS

Just across the street from the Museum of Modern Art, **The Museum of Arts and Design** ✦ (40 W. 53rd St. btwn Fifth and Sixth aves.; ☎ 212/956-3535; www.mad museum.org; $9 adults, $7 students and seniors, free Thurs 6–8pm; Fri–Wed 10am–6pm, Thurs 10am–8pm; ❺, ❻ to Fifth Ave.) is only now recovering from a decades-long identity crisis. Formerly known as the American Craft Museum, it never showcased only American works, nor did it restrict itself to crafts. Instead, the museum's mandate has always been to collect and display contemporary decorative arts (objects that are part of our everyday lives) from around the world and has done so with vigor, creating exhibits that are at once aesthetically pleasing and instructive, focusing on the interaction between materials and technique. "We want visitors to leave with a new curiosity of how things are put together," says Chief Curator David McFadden. The museum is on the cusp of being able to achieve this goal even more consistently thanks to a planned move in late 2008 to a much larger space at 2 Columbus Circle, which will allow it to house permanent exhibits. Until then, it will focus on such changing exhibits as "Pricked: Extreme Embroidery," "Inspired by China" (contemporary furniture inspired by Chinese traditions), and "Radical Lace and Subversive Knitting" (a contemporary art installation by artists who are using these traditional crafts in highly unusual ways).

HIMALAYAN ART

Travelers who need a break from the bustle and stresses of New York can escape to **The Rubin Museum** ★ (150 W. 17th St. btwn Sixth and Seventh aves.; ☎ 212/ 620-5000; www.rmanyc.org; $10 adults, $7 students and seniors, free for children under 12 and on Fridays btwn 7pm and 10pm; Sat and Sun 11am–6pm, Mon and Thurs 11am–5pm, Wed 11am–7pm, Fri 11am–10pm; ❶ to 18th St.), a serene, contemplative museum of art from the Himalayas. Secular in origin—the museum was founded by an American millionaire and his wife who fell in love with the art of this region—its effect is nonetheless tremendously spiritual, as the paintings, drawings, sculptures, and artifacts shown are all religious items, many used by traveling monks to teach Buddhism or to help worshippers deepen their meditation (that's why so many of the works are done on fabric—they're meant to be rolled up and carried). Many tell the stories of the various Buddhas, portraying meditating men with halos, snarling demons, teachers, and commoners in the deepest blues, ruby reds, emerald greens, and dazzling golds. For sheer beauty, the 1,500 works housed in this museum are hard to top.

The museum itself is one of the youngest in the city, opened in October 2004 on the site of the former Barney's Department Store (the Rubins chose it because the central circular stairway looked like a mandala, a never-ending circle surrounded by a square, which is the Tantric Buddhist diagram of the cosmos). Programs are held each weekend for children, and the museum even trains teens to lead other teens on tours. There are also lectures, musical performances, and a Friday night "Cinema Cabaret" each week, where patrons can sip wine, dine, and watch a Hollywood movie that has some connection—sometimes tenuous—to the Himalayas. The only disappointment here is the audio guides, which are free with admission but poorly done. Don't waste your time with them; instead, ask questions of the knowledgeable guides, wearing big red ASK ME buttons.

HISTORIC HOMES

New York City has never been very good at preserving its past (perhaps we have too little room . . . or patience), but on East 4th Street one precious sliver of the Victorian era has survived utterly intact. Called **The Merchants House Museum** (29 E. 4th St. btwn Bowery and Lafayette; ☎ 212/777-1089; www.merchants house.com; $8 adults, $5 seniors and students, free children 12 and under; Thurs–Mon noon–5pm; ❻ to Bleecker, ❻, ❻ to 8th St.), this handsome Greek Revival town house was once the home of the Tredwell family, who furnished it in the highest style of the day, all mohair couches, crystal chandeliers, and deep red curtains. These furnishings, the clothing of the 10-person family, their cookware, and anything else you might want to see, are all on display thanks to the efforts in 1936 of a preservationist (before there really was such a thing) named George Chapman, who had the foresight to buy the house and then safeguard it as it was (some of the rooms have been restored back to their mid-1800s look). A lovely garden and frequent ghost sightings add to the home's appeal. It's a good stop for history buffs, as this is the *only* Victorian-era house in New York City preserved intact, both inside and out.

Close to a mile uptown from the Merchant House, we have the **Birthplace of Teddy Roosevelt** (28 E. 20th St. btwn Broadway and Park Avenue South; ☎ 212/260-1616; www.nps.gov/thrb; $3 adults; Tues–Sat 9am–5pm, tours on the hour; ®, ◎ to 23rd St.). While it's a delight to see his original Rough Riders uniform and the many family portraits and photographs in the two gallery spaces, the house itself is not the place where T.R. was born (that was torn down and replaced by this copy); and only about 20% of the furniture in the five period rooms is original. The last time I visited, the ranger on duty seemed surprised to see a visitor and had to hastily run through the museum turning on the lights so that I could tour the place. For die-hard Roosevelt fans only.

My personal favorite among the historic bunch would have to be the **Louis Armstrong House and Museum** ★ (34–56 107th St. in Corona, Queens; ☎ 718/478-8274; www.satchmo.net; $8 adults; $6 seniors, students, and children; Tues–Fri 10am–5pm, Sat–Sun noon–5pm; ➐ to 103rd St.), a visitor experience as gracious, warm, and intriguing as the man himself, thanks to the marvelous guides (all ex-musicians and jazz historians) who lead visitors through the home every hour on the hour. The only house that this traveling musician ever owned, it was perfectly preserved after the death of his wife Lucille in 1983 (Armstrong himself passed away in 1971), and opened to the public in 2003. The sense that someone still lives here is so eerie that you may find yourself expecting Satchmo to emerge from the kitchen, turn on the stereo, and tell a joke. In the course of your tour, you'll hear about Louis's rags-to-riches history (son of a prostitute, learned to play trumpet in the juvenile detention center, made his name in mobster-owned clubs), and see the fairly modest two-story home that he and his wife lavished with every luxury, from custom-made, 24-karat bathroom fixtures—they were featured in a *Time* magazine article called "How the Other Half Bathes"—to Baccarat chandeliers and a state-of-the-art audio system. The highlight: recordings of everyday life that Armstrong made on his tape-recorder; your guide will play them as you wander through, allowing you to hear the family and visiting musicians talking, laughing, and jamming together.

TWO MORE JEWISH MUSEUMS

The "modest" goal of the **Jewish Museum** ★★ 🧒 (1109 Fifth Ave. at 92nd St.; ☎ 212/423-3337; www.thejewishmuseum.org; $12 adults, $10 students and seniors, free Thurs after 5pm and for children under 12; Sat–Wed 11am–5:45pm, Thurs 11am–8pm; ❹, ❺, ❻ to 86th St.) is to explore 4,000 years of Jewish culture through art, and surprisingly, it succeeds much of the time. Its two-floor permanent exhibition (which starts on the fourth floor) gently guides viewers from the biblical era, and the many clashes of the day over such issues as animal sacrifice and the role of the Temple (Jesus wasn't the only one up in arms over that), through the *Diaspora,* when the Israelites, forced out of their home by successive conquerors, became "wandering Jews," spreading to every part of the known world. The modern section brings the exhibition up to today, with only the briefest of mentions of the Holocaust (if that's what interests you, you'll be better served by the Jewish Heritage Museum downtown; p. 154). The story is told through a mixed marriage, so to speak, of nearly 800 exquisite artifacts and works of art, and by a variety of storytelling devices, including a free audio tour (narrated by Leonard Nimoy among others), interactive computer programs, videos, television clips, and wall texts. What finally emerges is a portrait of a people who have not only managed to survive against the steepest of odds but have become magnificently diverse in the process. In fact, the second half of the exhibit could be seen as a survey of world art styles as seen through Jewish eyes, making the museum of interest to a wide audience.

The fourth floor also houses a nifty playroom for kids (my daughters love it). On the first and second floors are galleries for changing exhibits, which have housed blockbuster shows on William Steig and Chagall in the past. There's also a so-so kosher cafe and two handsome gift shops.

Persons interested in tracing their Jewish ancestry can visit the **Center for Jewish History** (15 W. 16th St. btwn Fifth and Sixth aves.; ☎ 212/924-8318; www.cjh.org; free admission; Mon–Thurs 9:30am–5pm, Fri 9am–3pm, Sun 11am–5pm; ❹, ❺, ❻, ❶, ❶, ❶ to Union Sq., or ❶ to 18th St.), which is the largest repository of Jewish records, artifacts, books, and letters in the world—100 million archived documents in all—and a state-of-the-art genealogical library open to all. Three to four temporary exhibits, drawn usually from these vast archives, are housed in three large, on-site galleries. Cultural programs are held in the small auditorium three or four times a week.

NATIVE AMERICAN CULTURE

National Museum of the American Indian (One Bowling Green, btwn State and Whitehall sts.; ☎ 212/514-3700; www.americanindian.si.edu; free admission; daily 10am–5pm, Thurs until 8pm; ❹, ❺ to Bowling Green, or ❶, ❶ to Whitehall St.) is usually overshadowed by the American Indian Museum in Washington (the two are actually branches of the Smithsonian Institution) and often overlooked by visitors because it has no permanent collection on-site. Nevertheless, the museum plays host to a number of impressive touring exhibits (and to be truthful, some duds as well). Its stated mission is to "strengthen the voice of native peoples," and to that end, it usually includes wall text along with objects created by members of the Native American nations. Next to a basket, for example, you're as likely to read a tale told by the niece of the woman who made the piece as you are some dry explanation as to what the basket is used for. Housed in the magnificent Customs House, designed by architect Cass Gilbert (see our chapter on walking tours for a complete write-up on the architecture), the museum hosts a series of performances, lectures, and courses each year.

NEW YORK CITY HISTORY

People interested in New York City history will enjoy the **Museum of the City of New York** ★ (1220 Fifth Ave. at 103rd St.; ☎ 212/534-1672; suggested donation $9 adults; $5 students, seniors; free for children under 12; Tues–Sun 10am–5pm; ❻ to 103rd St.), the only cultural institution in the city that has no other purpose than to chronicle the life of the Big Apple. Its heartbeat is a masterful 25-minute video on New York history that affectingly recounts the tale of the city's growth from tiny Dutch colony to world capital. Along with rooms from historic homes, displays of children's toys, and a razzle-dazzle overview of New York theater (with costumes and photos from a number of current and past Broadway productions), the museum mounts numerous temporary exhibits on topics such as the influence of Paris on the look of the city, the role commissioner Robert Moses had in reshaping NYC, and the effect of various ethnic communities on city life.

PHOTOGRAPHY

Founded in 1974 by Cornell Capa, brother of eminent war photographer Robert Capa, the **International Center of Photography Museum** ★ (1133 Avenue of the Americas at 43rd St.; ☎ 212/857-0000; www.icp.org; $12 adults, $8 seniors and students, free children 12 and under; Tues–Thurs and Sat–Sun 10am–6pm, Fri 10am–8pm; **B**, **D**, **F**, **V** to 42nd St.) has a definite grounding in photojournalism. So when you visit this handsome white box of a museum, you can expect to see probing, investigative photography that will illuminate some destination, social ill, or recent conflict. In the last few years it has also started creating exhibitions that explore the world of art photography, with video pieces, collages, and other works that test the bounds of photography in interesting ways. I only wish that the entrance fee was a bit lower, as you can easily see the three or so exhibits (the normal maximum) in 45 minutes or less. Still, those interested in photography or current events should enjoy this intelligent, small museum.

A SEAFARING MUSEUM & MALL

The South Street Seaport Museum and Seaport Area (12 Fulton St., btwn Front and South sts.; ☎ 212/748-8590; www.southstseaport.org; $8 adults, $6 students and seniors, $4 children 5–12; Apr–Oct Tues–Sun 10am–6pm, Nov–Mar Fri–Mon 10am–5pm; **2**, **3**, **4**, **5**, **J**, **Z**, **M** to Fulton St.), with its massive collection of, well, sailing stuff—20,000 pieces of scrimshaw, models, maritime paintings, and other ephemera—doesn't normally excite me; I'm too much of a landlubber. Better are the daily tours of the three humongous historic sailing vessels the museum has moored off Pier 16, and the 1895 schooner cruises that often take place at sunset. To be fair, the museum often goes "off message" with worthy exhibits on topics tangentially related to the seaport area (in 2005, it hosted a fine one on Walt Whitman). The Seaport Museum also sponsors daily walking tours of the area, concerts, and lecture series. The area surrounding the seaport I find equally as uninspiring, a sad case of an historic area transformed into a tawdry mall. Except for the TKTS booth, the historic sailing vessels, and occasionally interesting shows at the museum, there's no real reason to make the trek here.

SEX—YES, SEX

Though it tries hard to avoid a carnival atmosphere, with voluminous and often soporific wall text accompanying each hard-core film clip, sex toy, "intercourse machine," and erotic photo, **The Museum of Sex** (233 Fifth Ave., entrance on 27th St.; ☎ 866/MOSEXNYC or 212/689-6337; www.museumofsex.org; $15 admission, but go to website for a $3 discount coupon; Sun–Fri 11am–6:30pm, Sat 11am–8pm; **R**, **O** to 28th St.) still has a major "wink, wink, giggle, giggle" quotient. Not that I'm complaining; at a recent exhibition of objects from the permanent collection, I learned about fetishes and saw some, er, sexual "enhancers" that I never imagined existed. But if you're interested in the subject from an anthropological perspective, you may be disappointed. For the rest of us, including all of the folks who seemed to be out on dates (or perhaps they met there?), the museum is good, dirty fun. (Do I need to mention that the museum's exhibits are far too graphic to take children to?)

SKYSCRAPERS

The Skyscraper Museum (39 Battery Place; ☎ 212/945-6324; www.skyscraper. org; $5 adults, $2.50 seniors and students; Wed–Sun noon–6pm; ❶ to Rector St.) is more interesting than you'd expect. An architecturally innovative space in and of itself (notice how the shiny metals, ascending ramp, and mirrored surfaces give the smallish room its own skyscraper aspect), the museum explores not only the structural feats behind these soaring structures, but also the economic forces that shaped them and their sociological impact. A well-curated gallery that even non-architecture buffs should enjoy.

QUEENS MUSEUMS & SIGHTS

Queens has recently developed into a museum powerhouse, home to half a dozen fine institutions. Along with the Louis Armstrong House (p. 162) and the Museum of the Moving Image (p. 156), I highly recommend the following art museums.

It's a difficult museum to get to, but the **Isamu Noguchi Museum** ★ (32–37 Vernon Blvd. entrance on 33rd St.; ☎ 718/204-7088; www.noguchi.org; $10 adults, $5 seniors and students, free for kids under 12; Wed–Fri 10am–5pm, Sat–Sun 11am–6pm; ❶, ❿ to Broadway) is certainly worth the trek. Utterly unique, it's the only museum in the nation to be founded by an artist in his lifetime, dedicated to his work, and curated by him. As Noguchi (1904–1988) was a genius in a number of fields—sculpture, architecture, ceramics, furniture design—he was more than up to the task, and created a space that is at once sublimely balanced and (often) rapturously beautiful. The first floor consists of three large galleries housing monolithic sculptures in stone, marble, and steel; a video room (where footage of the artist at work is on a constant loop); a small cafe/bookstore; and an updated Zen sculpture garden (one of the most serene spots in the city). The second floor is dedicated to changing exhibits from the collection of smaller pieces—chess sets, set design pieces, furniture, lamps, and more. Gallery talks, free with admission and held at 2pm each day, are helpful for those not familiar with Noguchi's work, as they illuminate the complex engineering issues and intentions behind his large, sometimes slablike, non-representational works.

*A **word on transportation:*** Those who visit on the weekends can take a free shuttle bus that leaves at regular intervals from the **Asia Society** (725 Park Ave. at 70th St.) in Manhattan, but if you plan on visiting during the week, a subway ride will either have to be paired with a substantial walk (about a half-mile) or a bus once you're in Queens. Allow an hour for transportation to and from the museum.

More than any other museum in New York, with the possible exception of the Whitney, **P.S. 1 Contemporary Art Center** ★★ (22–75 Jackson Ave. at 46th Ave., Long Island City; ☎ 718/784-2084; www.ps1.org; suggested donation $5 adults, $2 seniors; Wed–Sun noon–6pm; ❼ to 45th Rd./Courthouse Sq., or ❤ to 23rd St./Ely Ave.) has been, since its founding in 1976, a proving ground for young artists. That means the work you're going to see here will be challenging, right of the moment, and sometimes downright wacky. "P.S. 1 is mythological," says Assistant Director Brett Littman. "Wherever I go, people know that there's this crazy building in Long Island City where you see crazy art. They come here to put a notch on their culture belt."

That "crazy building" was once a public school (hence the name), and its somewhat decrepit charm is part of the experience. Because it's not a fancy white box of a space (like its sister institution, the Museum of Modern Art), P.S. 1 allows its artists to create full-blown, sometimes invasive, installations in the space (one summer several years ago, an artist blasted holes in the brick wall of a gallery). It also uses all kinds of unusual spaces to house art, such as the boiler room in the basement, where dusty old equipment stands side by side with sculptures and neon displays. One of my favorites of the few permanent pieces in the museum is a small hole in the floor of the lobby area with a video of a tiny artist shouting "help me!" in a number of different languages. (Look for the wall text about artist Pipoleti Rist's *Selfless in the bath of lava* to locate the hole.)

The bulk of the work you'll see here will be in changing exhibits, as the museum does not collect art. Instead, visitors are greeted with as many as 14 different shows in all parts of the building, and some can be quite, well, bizarre. In its retrospective of New York City art recently, one framed sculpture turned out to be the actual hand of the artist who was sitting on the other side of the wall, personifying her art. Now if that's not worth $5, I don't know what is.

NEW YORK'S ARCHITECTURAL STANDOUTS

The Cathedral of St. John the Divine ✦✦ (1047 Amsterdam Ave. at 110th St.; ☎ 212/316-7490; www.stjohndivine.org; Mon–Sat 7am–6pm, Sun 7am–7pm; ❶ to 110th St.) leads the list of Gotham's most significant structures. Little-known fact: The largest cathedral in the world is *not* St. Peter's in Rome (which is actually not officially a cathedral), it's St. John the Divine up in Harlem. Odder fact: Despite the popish name, it isn't Catholic, it's Episcopalian. Oddest fact: Though construction began on the cathedral in 1892, the building is yet to be completed, and many estimate that it will take another 100 years for that to happen.

All of which makes this a fascinating building to visit, as you'll see a bit of how the ancient cathedrals of Europe might have been built. The 121,000-square-foot structure, a blend of Romanesque and Gothic elements (thanks to the varying tastes of the architects who have worked on it over the past century), is being built without steel, in the classic Gothic manner. To that end, a master stonecutter was brought in from Europe to help train a cadre of American stonecutters in the necessary work in 1979. There's still much work to be done (including a lot of fundraising!). For over a hundred years a temporary dome has kept parishioners dry; that will eventually be replaced. And an unfortunate fire in one portion of the building has also added to the load of work. But what is in place—and there's a lot—is quite beautiful, especially the Rose Window in the apse, the largest in North America. A daily 11am tour (1pm on Sun) of the cathedral explains the construction work and jumbled history of the place.

You may also want to attend a service here, as these tend to be among the most musical, progressive services in the city. I particularly recommend the New Year's Eve service, featuring original work from some of the best composers in town; and the Blessing of the Animals (on the feast day of St. Francis of Assisi, usually Oct 4), a ceremony in which New Yorkers bring their pets—ranging from puppies to pythons to thoroughbred horses—to be blessed.

In the **Chrysler Building** ★★★ (405 Lexington Ave. at 43rd St.; **4**, **5**, **6**, **S** to Grand Central Station), we see the last burst of what Alan Greenspan would call the "irrational exuberance" that sent stocks and buildings soaring to the heavens before the thudding crash of 1929. Throughout the previous decade, real estate speculators had been throwing up building after building in lower Manhattan and Midtown, adding almost 100 skyscrapers of 20 stories or more, and utterly transforming the skyline of the city. Automaker Walter P. Chrysler commissioned architect William Van Alen to top them all, instructing him that he wanted a building "higher than the Eiffel Tower," the tallest in the world at that time. What Chrysler would soon learn was that the gentlemen behind the Bank of America had the same ambition, and they had hired Van Alen's former partner (and sworn enemy) H. Craig Severance to build them the tallest building on the planet down on Wall Street. Soon the race was on, as each architect returned continually to the drafting board, adding 10 more stories of penthouses here, a lantern there, a 50-foot flagpole. In the fall of 1929, Severance was sure he had won, so he completed the Bank of America building at 927 feet. Van Alen then unveiled the coup de grace that he had been hiding in an elevator shaft—a silver spike to crown his building, making it, at 1,046 feet, an unbeatable 117 feet higher than his rival's.

Not only taller, the Chrysler was the more striking of the two buildings, its scalloped spire set like a jaunty jester's cap atop a sleek tower. Take a look at the sharp stainless steel eagles that jut out just below the roof; the "gargoyles" below those on the 61st floor are actually modeled after the hood ornament of the 1929 Chrysler Plymouth.

The Chrysler remains one of the most impressive Art Deco buildings ever constructed, but it wasn't the tallest for long. Less than a year after it was completed, the Empire State Building assumed that mantle and held it until the World Trade Center came along.

The Flatiron Building ★★★ (23rd St. btwn Broadway and Fifth Ave.; **R**, **Q**, **6** to 23rd St.) is smaller than the Chrysler but just as distinguished. You'll probably know the Flatiron Building even before you see it thanks to the famous photos of the building taken by Alfred Stieglitz, who snapped it numerous times, calling the Fuller Building (its original name) "a picture of new America still in the making." Many consider it the first skyscraper in New York; it certainly was one of the first to use a steel frame, the classic skyscraper structure. Its unusual triangular shape was architect Daniel Burnham's solution to a space problem: The building rests on the bow-tie intersection where Broadway and Fifth Avenue cross each other. In order to produce a decent amount of rentable space, he built it to a towering 375 feet on every sliver of land he had available to him. The apex is just 6 feet across at its narrowest point. When it was first erected in 1902, crowds used to gather in Madison Square Park across the street to wait for it to fall down! Later men were drawn here by the urban myth that the building's shape caused strange wind patterns that were effective in blowing up women's skirts. The cops who dispersed these groups of gaping men would call out "23 skidoo!," and so a slang term was born. One of the most beloved buildings in the city, it has been compared by many to a mighty ship sailing up Fifth Avenue.

In ancient Roman times, the entrances to great cities were framed with monumental arches, meant to awe all who passed through. When **Grand Central Terminal** ★★★ (42nd St. at Park Ave.; ☎ 212/340-2210; www.grandcentral terminal.com; ④, ⑤, ⑥, ⑨, ⑦ to 42nd St./Grand Central Station) was being built at the turn of the last century, it was recognized that our railroad terminals were our grand gateways, the first view a traveler would have of the metropolis. So the architects of both Grand Central and the late great Pennsylvania Station (the original, torn down in the 1960s) conspired to create as much pomp and stateliness as possible, filling these spaces with the symbols and architecture of imperial Rome. On Grand Central's facade, 10 colossal Doric fluted pillars tower over Park Avenue; above them a massive statue of Mercury, the god of travel, spreads his arms in welcome as Hercules and Minerva, gods of strength and wisdom, lounge at his feet. (The face of the clock below the sculpture is the largest piece of Tiffany glass in the world.)

The station's interior is no less impressive, its concourse soaring the equivalent of nine stories to a vaulted ceiling on which the signs of the zodiac are created from 59 fiber-optic lights and 2,500 painted stars (created by Paul Helleu—now, that was some paint job!). The side walls feature massive windows that throw shafts of light onto the acre-long Indiana marble floor. Not that the station needed them: One of its innovations was the use of electric lights, so you'll see bare bulbs sprinkled throughout the station and on the massive chandeliers that overhang the concourse. Two hundred buildings were demolished to make way for the station, which opened on February 2, 1913, bearing a price tag of $80 million.

As you walk through, take in all of the trendy shops housed in the arteries of the main concourse; the dining concourse below, with the famed Oyster Bar at its heart (p. 79); the Campbell Apartment, former office of a finance tycoon and now a fab bar (p. 284); and Vanderbilt Hall (towards 42nd St., off the main concourse), which houses seasonal markets and special exhibitions. If you're traveling with children, take them to the "whispering gallery" right outside the Oyster Bar. Stand on one side of the arch there and have your child stand on the other, and then whisper to each other back and forth; a trick of acoustics allows sound to travel from one side of the vault to the other.

Free tours of the station are offered every Wednesday at 12:30pm (meet at the information booth in the center of the concourse) and Friday at 12:30pm in front of the Whitney at Altria, across 42nd Street from the station. For more information, go to the Grand Central Station website (see above).

The **New York Public Library** ★★ (Fifth Ave. at 42nd St.; ☎ 212/930-0830; www.nypl.org; Mon and Thurs–Sat 11am–6pm, Tues–Wed 11am–7:30pm, Sun 1pm–5pm; ④, ⑤, ⑥, ⑨ to Grand Central Station) is another masterwork; many art historians consider it to be the finest Beaux Arts building in the United States. It certainly is one of the grandest, completed in 1911 at a cost of over $9 million. The library was the result of a merger in 1895 of the three largest private libraries in the city—the Astor, Tilden, and Lenox libraries—and each carried an endowment significant enough to warrant the creation of this grand institution (it didn't hurt that Andrew Carnegie was persuaded to kick in $5.2 million in 1901). Built by the firm of Carrere & Hastings, the exterior takes its inspiration from the twin palaces on the north side of the place de la Concorde in Paris and is done in the same French Renaissance style, a perfect harmony of columns, pediments, and statuary. Famous stone lions guard the entrance and are said to roar whenever a virgin passes by. Want to use the library? Well, you will be "reading between the lions" (sorry, I couldn't resist).

The library itself holds thousands of volumes, many of which are housed underground below what is now Bryant Park. A "no-browsing" facility, it uses an ancient dumbwaiter system for retrieval of books in which the tomes are stacked into a small elevator and sent up when requests are made. Along with books, **Gottesman Exhibition Hall** (1st floor) often houses interesting exhibits on literary and New York history. Entrance is always free, and the palatial interior, with its expanses of marble and carved oak ceilings, is worth a look-see. For a more formal tour, time your visit to occur at 11am or 2pm, Tuesday through Friday, when guides lead visitors through the building.

Simplicity, clarity, and the most elemental forms: Those are touchstones of the "International Style" of architecture that came to the fore in the 1950s, and Mies Van Der Rohe's 1958 **Seagram Building** (375 Park Ave. at 53rd St.)—along with the slightly less impressive Lever House across the street—were its poster children. If the Seagram building looks familiar, that's because it inspired a craze for this style, with dozens of look-alikes thrown up in city after city around the world. But the Seagram is more detailed and handsome than most of those that followed it, featuring ornamental bronze beams (meant to reveal the structure of steel beams underneath) and topaz-tinted windows. It was revolutionary not just for its simple shape but for its re-direction of New York's zoning laws. Instead of using set backs (the cascading layers found on early skyscrapers) to create enough open sky for those on the sidewalk, it was built straight up, with a large plaza for open space. City planners liked the design so much that they created a new zoning law in 1961 allowing owners to add floor space to their new buildings only if they, too, created plaza space at the base.

And though I discuss them elsewhere in this book, **Trinity Church** (p. 219); the **U.S. Customs House,** now the **Museum of the American Indian** (p. 163); and the **Woolworth Building** (p. 221) are all noteworthy architectural sights.

ESPECIALLY FOR KIDS

While children will enjoy most of the attractions listed in this chapter—especially those with our handy, dandy "kids" symbol attached—there are a handful of museums, zoos, and aquariums especially geared to the tastes of the Sponge Bob set.

Obviously, there's much to keep children busy in Central Park—from playgrounds every 5 blocks or so (always on the perimeter of the park, rarely in the interior) to the carousel at 64th Street off the park's baseball field to rowboats on the lake. But the **Central Park Zoo** ★ (behind Fifth Ave. at 64th St.; ☎ 212/439-6500; www.nyzoosandaquarium.com; $6 adults, $1.25 seniors, $1 children over 3; Apr–Oct daily 10am–5pm, Nov–Mar daily 10am–4:30pm; ❻ to 68th St., or ❿, ❶ to Fifth Ave.) tops them all, a delicious little jewel box of a zoo, with just enough animals to keep everyone entertained until their feet begin to tire. Founded in 1864 and completely overhauled in 1988 to make it a more animal-friendly environment (with glass and moats replacing cages), the zoo actually has two halves.

The main section, at 64th Street, has a seal pond in the middle (look at the schedule for feeding show times) and three areas representing different climactic zones. Because you're going to be moving from zone to zone, it's important to dress in layers, as you'll be sweltering in the rainforest exhibit with its fluorescent frogs, melancholy Colobus monkeys, and parrots; and freezing in the arctic zone as you watch the penguins waddle and polar bears pace (the bears here are famous for being manic-depressive, so behaviorists were brought in to stop their compulsive behavior by creating hunting games). There's also an outdoor woodlands area, where you'll see badgers, beavers, and the like.

About 1 block's walk from the main zoo, still in the park, is the "Children's Zoo," featuring animal encounters where the kids get to interact with animals that don't bite, and a lot of fun places for children to climb, run, and blow off steam.

As the mother of two young daughters (aged 5 and 9 as I write this), I've probably spent more time in New York's children's museums than some of the staff. I'm very grateful to both the **Children's Museum of Manhattan** ★ (kids) (212 W. 83rd St. btwn Broadway and Amsterdam Ave.; ☎ 212/721-1223; www.cmom.org; Tues–Sun 10am–5pm; $9 adults and children, $6 seniors; ❶ to 86th St.) and the **Brooklyn Children's Museum** ★ (kids) (145 Brooklyn Ave. at St. Marks St.; ☎ 718/735-4400; www.brooklynkids.org; $5 children and adults; July–Aug Tues–Thurs noon–6pm, Fri noon–6:30pm, Sat–Sun 11am–6pm; Sept–June Wed–Fri 1–6pm, Sat–Sun 11am–6pm) for the shelter and excitement they've brought to rainy days over the years, and we patronize both on about an equal basis since I live fairly far downtown.

There are significant differences between the two. The Brooklyn Museum involves much more of a trek; families have to make either a half-mile walk from a subway station, or catch one of the infrequent trolleys that the museum provides on weekends. Despite this inconvenience, the Brooklyn Museum has a blessed serenity that the Manhattan one lacks, getting half as many visitors in a space that's a bit larger (thanks to a recent expansion). The oldest children's museum in the nation (in fact it started the movement), Brooklyn was designed from the ground up to delight kids and has such whimsical touches as a small enclosed stream that runs along the ramp that leads from floor to floor, allowing kids to splash and dip their fingers as they go; and a small greenhouse with a tiny zoo of snakes and lizards attached (it's here where nature classes are given). Plus large spaces for changing exhibits, most created by the museum and usually quite engrossing.

The Manhattan Museum is a glitzier affair of changing exhibits that highlight the kiddie zeitgeist of the moment: Dora the Explorer, Maurice Sendak, and William Wegman's dog art were just a few of the recent exhibit themes. Those with toddlers should go directly to the Child Development Center on the fourth floor, where young 'uns can finger paint to their hearts' delight, play with little stoves, and send rubber balls rocketing down a twisted tube from a loft to the floor (there were days when I never got past this room). Older children will want to take part in the classes and special exhibits, and since these fill up fast, it's important that you stop by the small desk in front of the elevator on the first floor where you sign up for these options. *One word of warning:* Although the museum is easy to get to from anywhere in Manhattan, there will often be quite a wait just to get in, or to check your stroller. Try to arrive here early in the day on weekends, or plan your visit for a weekday afternoon when the place tends to be deserted.

What kid can resist a big red fire engine roaring by, or a room full of swooping red fire hats? You'll see both in abundance at the **New York City Fire Museum** kids (278 Spring St. btwn Varick and Hudson sts.; ☎ 212/691-1303; www.nycfire museum.org; suggested donation $5 adults, $2 seniors and students, $1 children under 12; Tues–Sat 10am–5pm, Sun 10am–4pm; **C**, **E** to Spring St.), which has one of the largest collections of firehouse memorabilia in the nation. It also has the good sense to hand out a free scavenger hunt map on arrival, which should keep even the most restless of youngsters amused.

I'd say the **New York Transit Museum** ★ (corner Boerum Pl. and Schermerhorn St., Brooklyn; ☎ 718/694-1600; www.mta.info/mta/museum/index.html; Tues–Fri 10am–4pm, Sat–Sun noon–5pm; $5 adults, $3 seniors and those under 17; **2**, **3**, **4**, **5** to Borough Hall) is pretty irresistible too, for both kids and adults. Heck, how many other museums are set wholly underground in a recreated subway station? Along with dozens of interactive exhibits on the history and engineering behind the city's trains and busses (my daughters love pretending to be bus drivers here), are actual and gorgeous antique subway cars in the sub-basement leading me, for one, to long for the days when the windows opened and the straps were leather. The Museum is the largest in the U.S. devoted to the topic of public, urban transportation.

Sony Wonder Lab kids (E. 56th St. and Madison Ave.; ☎ 212/833-8100; www. sonywondertechlab.com; free admission; Tues–Sat 10am–5pm, Sun noon–5pm; **R**, **O** to Fifth Ave.) is one big ol' commercial for Sony products, and yes, it dumbs down its explanations of the technology to a sad level at points. But if you happen to be in Midtown with someone, say, under five feet tall who loves to press buttons and play computer games, this four-level museum can be a welcome distraction. Filled with interactive experiences that allow users to play at environmental engineering, ultrasound technology, and sound editing, the experience is a lively one and certainly right for the price. Advance reservations are recommended as the museum does fill up; expect to spend about 1 hour tops in the museum. If you're truly interested in this subject, or would like your child to have a deeper educational experience with technology, head out to Queens to the superb Museum of the Moving Image (p. 156).

If you count number of animals as well as acreage, **The Bronx Zoo** ★★ kids (Fordham Rd. and Bronx River Pkwy.; ☎ 718/367-1010; www.bronxzoo.com; $14 adults, $12 seniors, $10 children, pay what you wish on Wed; Mar 26–Oct 29, Mon–Fri 10am–5pm, Sat–Sun 10am–5:30pm; Oct 30–Mar 25 daily 10am–4:30pm; **2**, **5** to E. Tremont Ave./West Farm Sq.) is still the largest zoo in the United States and an innovative, unbeatably entertaining place to spend the day. But with over 4,000 animals and 24 exhibits, you need to strategize your time wisely so you can see what you want without meltdowns from the younger set. When I visit with my girls, I most often make a direct path to the **Congo Forest** first ($3 extra; it gets mobbed), a remarkable exhibit of 24 silverback gorillas that begins with a short film. Once the film is over, curtains dramatically part to reveal floor-to-ceiling windows, with cavorting gorillas galore (unlike other animals at the zoo, the gorillas are always awake if you visit in the daytime; along with the adults there always seem to be half-a-dozen baby gorillas in sight as well). From here we hop over to the nearby "bug carousel" or the butterfly exhibit (a tent with thousands of beautiful butterflies fluttering about your head), or to lunch at nearby Flamingo Park. Then we blow off steam for a bit at the children's zoo—with all the usual farm animals, a spiderweb jungle gym, and a prairie dog park where children crawl into tunnels and pop their heads up right next to the critters. There are dozens of other animals, a fun monorail ride, feeding shows, and more to keep you entertained.

A word on transportation: Although you can take the subway (see above), I prefer to take the BXM11 Express Bus that runs up Madison Avenue, going express after 99th Street. It usually is faster than the subway, though be sure to check the bus schedule at **www.mta.nyc.ny.us**, as it runs only every half-hour or so (the schedule varies by day and time of year).

Finally, you can use a visit to the **New York Aquarium** ★ 🧒 (Surf Ave. and W. 8th St.; ☎ 718/220-5100; www.nyaquarium.com; $12 adults, $8 seniors and children; hours vary seasonally, but in general it's open daily 10am–5pm; **F**, **Q** to W. 8th St., Coney Island) as a great excuse for taking in the gritty delights of **Coney Island.** Take the subway out here for a day that's partially educational, partially nostalgic, partially beachy (if you visit in summer), and a heck of a lot of fun.

The aquarium is (obviously) the educational component of the adventure and it fulfills that role magnificently, with over 8,000 animals from all parts of the globe spread across a 6-acre complex. There's a performing sea lion show, a mesmerizing exhibit on stingrays (some in a tank where you can touch them), exhibits on every variety of fish and mollusk, plus regular craft activities for children on weekends. Because this is an indoor/outdoor facility, it's important that you dress appropriately for the weather, as part of your visit will be spent outdoors. It's also a good idea to get a schedule of feeding times when you arrive—a highlight of any visit here.

Once you're done with the aquarium, you can wander down the boardwalk to the honky-tonk paradise that is Coney Island. It's currently in the midst of a major upgrade, but it's still possible to ride some of the classic attractions from times past, including the **Cyclone** (a huge wooden roller coaster, one of the scariest you'll ever ride because you'll do so with the knowledge that nearly a dozen people have been killed on it over the years), and the **Wonder Wheel** (a Ferris wheel with gliding compartments). Prices on rides vary but average between $2 and $5; most rides are open roughly between Easter and Labor Day (the weather is a factor). The best food in the 'hood is **Totonno's Pizza,** one of the first parlors in the city; it's located at 1524 Neptune Ave. between West 15th and 16th streets.

If you visit in summer, don't skip the Freak Show, which features the tattooed man, a snake charmer, a man who hammers nails up his nose, and other odd performers. It's one of the last shows of its kind in the U.S., and though it sounds unsavory, it's G-rated. You also have the beach itself here, a motley swatch of sand where gaggles of Brooklynites gather daily in summer to pitch their umbrellas, practice kung fu, listen to boomboxes, picnic, and swim. It's a very social scene, with many different ethnic groups represented, and fascinating in its own way.

TOURS OF THE BIG APPLE

If you'd prefer a guide at your side as you explore the city, you have a number of options, each of which involves a different mode of transportation and varying levels of coverage.

WALKING TOURS

For the most intellectually stimulating, complexly realized tours, you have to put on your sneakers and hike. Only at the slow pace of a walking tour is it possible to really do justice to the unique architecture, history, and culture of the city. There are a number of different tour companies, each with a unique approach to the subject at hand. Know that each offers tours of approximately 2 hours, usually rain or shine, and that each company will also set up private tours, if requested (though you'll pay more for those).

More personal than any other tours in the city, **Big Apple Greeters** ★★★ (☎ 212/669-8159; www.bigapplegreeter.org; free) pairs untrained New York volunteers with visitors who have similar interests. Host and guest spend a few hours touring the host's neighborhood and learning about life there from a native's point of view. To read about this unique experience in more depth, see chapter 6, "The Other New York."

Big Onion Tours ★ (☎ 212/439-1090; www.bigonion.com; $15 adults, $12 seniors, $10 students) are led by local graduate students, most of them studying history, with a few sociologists and literature majors thrown in. The emphasis therefore is on the history of the area you may be visiting—Greenwich Village, Times Square, Central Park—and the lectures tend to be complex, illuminating portraits of those places. My only problem with these tours is that the talk is often only tangentially related to the building or park you may be viewing at the time, so the walking tour can feel more like a classroom lecture than an afternoon's exploration.

Joyce Gold History Tours ★ (☎ 212/242-5762; www.nyctours.com; $15 adults, $12 seniors) also have an academic bent, as they're led by Ms. Gold, an instructor at both New York University and the New School for Social Research. Ms. Gold was formerly a real estate agent, and so you'll also hear a lot on this tour about the shocking prices of NYC real estate. These are in-depth, entertaining tours, though here, too, I wish there were just a bit more emphasis on the architecture of the sites visited.

There are few more pleasant activities than meandering through Central Park, and the free **Central Park Conservancy** (www.centralparknyc.org; free) tours give you an excuse to do just that. Along the way, you'll learn how the park was designed and constructed, of the protests that have taken place here, and about the social activities the park has hosted over the years. Tours vary widely in quality, as they're led by volunteers (not licensed tour guides), but if you get a good one, they can be quite fun.

I'll Take Manhattan Tours ★★ (☎ 732/270-5559; www.newyorkcitywalks. com; $15) are my favorite of the bunch, led by curmudgeonly Anthony Griffa. A remarkable storyteller, Griffa is able to weave together architecture, cultural tidbits, and decades-old gossip (as well as history, of course) into an enjoyable afternoon's stroll. Unlike the other tour companies, he does not cover Harlem, and his tours tend to be more sporadically offered (check the website for a schedule).

The hippest, most exciting (and sometimes scary) walking tours around, **Soundwalk** ✦✦✦ (www.soundwalk.com; $12 to download, $19 in stores) is a series of self-guided audio tours to neighborhoods across Manhattan, Brooklyn, and the Bronx. For a full description, go to p. 197 in chapter 6.

Street Smarts (☎ 212/969-8262; www.streetsmartsny.com; $10) offers the most sensationalistic view of the city, concentrating on ghost stories, famous gangsters, and ladies of the evening. It also hosts quite a fun pub tour each evening (drinks are extra).

BOAT TOURS

Despite the fact that this is a thoroughly commercial tour, in its 60-plus years of cruising round New York, **The Circle Line** ✦✦ (Pier 83 at W. 42nd St. and the Hudson River; ☎ 212/563-3200; www.circleline42.com; prices vary by tour, see below; tours depart 2–4 times daily, depending on season, beginning at 10am) has become as much a tourist attraction as the United Nations, and deservedly so. Led by witty, informed guides (many are also actors), the cruise takes travelers round the harbor on 3-hour, 2-hour, and 75-minute cruises. The longest makes a complete circle of the city ($30 adults, $25 seniors, $17 children), but I'd recommend the 2-hour tour instead ($25 adults, $21 seniors, $14 child). You'll miss Yankee Stadium and the view of the Palisades (the wooded cliffs of New Jersey) on that one, but all of the other highlights—the Statue of Liberty, the lower Manhattan skyline, the Empire State Building, the Chrysler Building—are included. Make sure to arrive at the dock early because you'll want to grab a good seat: on the right-hand side of the boat, facing inward as you enter (that's the side that faces Manhattan; ask the staff if you're unclear). It can get very chilly on the water, so be sure to dress in layers, or take a seat inside.

From the most famous boat tour to . . . the cheapest. Most visitors—and even some New Yorkers—don't know that the **Staten Island Ferry** ✦ (Whitehall ferry terminal, southern tip of Manhattan; ☎ 718/815-BOAT; www.siferry.com; daily, 24 hr.; ❶, ❷ to Whitehall St., ❹, ❺ to Bowling Green, ❶ to South Ferry) makes its own daily excursion within Polaroid distance of the Statue of Liberty, Ellis Island, and Roosevelt Island. And riders pay absolutely nothing for the great views. You simply board the ship (be sure to wait for one of the older orange-and-green boats, because the newer ones don't have decks for viewing) and, as with the Circle Line, sit on the right-hand side (stay at the back of the ferry for the best view of the Manhattan skyline). It's a joke in New York that this is the best "cheap date" in the city, so don't be shy about toting along a bottle of wine, some bread, and cheese. But be sure to dress warmly: In winter the outdoor decks can be frigid. One-way, the trip takes approximately a half-hour, after which you'll need to disembark and take the next ferry back.

HOP-ON, HOP-OFF BUS TOURS

If you were to climb aboard any public bus (cost $2), turn to the person next to you, and ask, "What building is that?" you'd probably get a response as informative, accurate, and interesting as what you'll find on the much pricier, hop-on, hop-off bus tours of New York City. Upon 2 full days riding one after another, I was drenched in misinformation. One guide informed our bus that "most of the

American Revolutionary battles took place in New York" (wrong!); another suggested we go to the ESPN Zone because the ancient Romans would have loved it since they "invented sports" (not!); yet another tour guide described Greenwich Village as an inexpensive haunt of bohemians and artists (not anymore). I also hopped on and off three different buses that passed the Empire State Building, and each gave a different answer for the total number of months that it took to complete the building (only one said 14, the correct number).

And when the information was correct, it was usually along the lines of "That's the building where the ball drops on New Year's Eve," a cursory statement made as we whizzed by, the guide not having time enough to give further details before moving on to the next sight. I also found that a lot of the commentary could be construed as commercials for some of the bigger tourist traps—Jekyll and Hyde, ESPN Zone, and so forth—leading me to wonder (I really don't know) whether there was some sort of sponsorship deal between the bus companies and these restaurants.

This is all a long way of saying: Don't take these tours. Yes, it's fun to sit high up as the city whizzes by, but the experience is so utterly superficial and so misleading (at points) that it is unworthy of the time or the considerable expense.

If you're still determined to try one of these companies, the major operators are:

◆ **Gray Line** (777 Eighth Ave., btwn 47th and 48th sts.; ☎ 800/669-0051 or 212/445-0848; www.newyorksightseeing.com; $37 per hop-on, hop-off loop, all day; $50 for all loops—uptown, downtown, Brooklyn, and the night tour—in 1 day; ®, ⓞ, ©, ⑤ to 50th St.). The most popular of the companies and the only with its own indoor visitor center, Gray Line offers a number of different tours to all parts of the city. As with the other companies, it's possible to buy tickets at any of the stops the bus makes.

◆ **CitySights** (☎ 212/812-9000; www.citysightsny.com; $37–$79 per hop-on, hop-off tour). City Sights offers fewer itineraries, although it does offer one unusual combo bus tour/walking tour (you borrow headphones and walk independently). Its salespeople, who work only on the streets in front of the bus stops (identify them by their bright yellow jackets), seem more willing to bargain on the price, possibly because these tours get far fewer takers than Gray Line.

◆ **On Board New York Tours** (☎ 877/UTOUR-NY or 212/277-8019; www.new yorkpartyshuttle.com), formerly known as the Party Shuttle, is a bit different than the other two. Groups are driven around in vans with large windows and instead of hopping off to explore on their own, a guide goes with the group to narrate on the streets as well as on the van.

6 The "Other" New York

Your chance to experience the city as the locals do

IN BUENOS AIRES THEY TANGO. IN PARIS, THE PREFERRED DIVERSION IS still conversation, in cafes, with cigarettes dangling. In Japan, the scorching bath is the pastime of choice, and Japanese flock in huge numbers to soak, relax, and socialize in bathhouses around the country.

From your point of view, as a traveler, these are wonderful touchstones, because you, too, when you visit these places, can make a few fumbling attempts at the tango, hang out in a cafe airing your broken French (cigarettes optional!), or slide ever so carefully into a Japanese bath heated to the temperature of lava.

But what do you do when you go to New York? What is the one activity that you, the visitor, can try that will instantly give you insight into the life of the city, the mindset of its locals, the frisson that binds residents to New York . . . even after high real estate prices have driven them out?

I wish I knew.

The truth is this is a city without a center, with hundreds of small communities, dozens of ethnic groups, and thousands of ways of passing the time. That makes it extremely difficult for tourists to get even a small insight into life here, let alone to meet and get to know locals. In fact, I know of no other city where the tourist experience is so vastly different from that of the locals'. Even the areas we hang out in are different (get a slingshot, load it up in Times Square, and you'll hit a visitor; do the same in the East Village and you'll soon have a very angry mob of downtowners chasing you back to your hotel).

This chapter will introduce you to some parts of the city that tourists rarely see and activities in which only locals engage. How we work, how we play, how we worship—these topics and more are covered. I would encourage you to try at least one or two of the suggested activities, along with the standard tourist activities, as they should give you a more profound experience of the city and its unique riches . . . for those willing to dig a bit beneath its surface.

HOW WE LEARN

Many people move to New York in the hopes of changing their lives in some way. Often this involves taking classes, and consequently there are dozens of learning opportunities available for adults every day of the week. I've tried to highlight some of the most accessible and interesting, starting with single-evening lectures.

EVENING LECTURES

As the home base of the American news media, New York is matched only by London in the number of free or inexpensive **lectures, readings, and one-night**

classes ★★★ held each evening, year-round. The folks in charge of creating buzz for a new book, product, or even a policy decision know that by getting it in front of the opinion makers here, they have a better chance of getting their message out to the rest of the world. You become their witting audience, not just by attending a lecture but by becoming part of the opinion-making machine (for all the good and the bad that implies).

What types of events will you see? Well, during a single week in February of 2008:

- Former Poet Laureate Billy Collins interviewed songwriter Paul Simon on the art of lyric writing
- Actress Kathleen Turner gave a reading of her autobiography (smokily)
- Clinton White House Press Secretary Dee Dee Myers got grilled by author Tina Brown about the importance of female leadership
- Famed conductor/musician/composer Andre Previn did a Q&A
- Deepak Chopra signed his new book, *The Third Jesus*
- "Sexpert" Ducky DooLittle taught the "Art and Nature of Being Sexy" at the Museum of Sex
- A free panel was held on medical ethics in this era of technological innovation and new life-sustaining techniques

These are just a small fraction of the hundreds of events that saturated the city that week, drawing crowds of locals and, I would guess, not one tourist. Why no visitors? Because nothing in the tourist literature that is customarily handed out at hotels ever mentions these less-commercial, quirkier offerings. It's necessary to seek them out, and you can do so easily by going to the following sources:

- *Time Out* **Magazine** ($3.99 on newsstands): The city's most comprehensive listings of lectures, signings, and other events of the mind; go to the "Around Town" and "Books" sections for details on the week's events.
- *The New Yorker* ($2.95 on newsstands): Has a listings section similar to the one in *Time Out* up front, but one that is infinitely more selective, promoting only the most intellectually stimulating programs.
- **92nd Street Y** ★★ (1395 Lexington Ave. at 92nd St.; ☎ 212/445-5100; www.92y.org; $26 ticket average): The top venue in the city for lectures and "conversations" of all types, the 92nd Street Y (originally called the Young Men's Hebrew Association) has been a fixture of the Jewish community since 1845. And though a number of programs are devoted to Jewish topics, the vast range of talks (open to all) in Monday, Tuesday, and (sometimes) Thursday lecture series are more far-reaching, covering issues of health, politics, gastronomy, ecology, and the arts. Some of the distinguished guests who have spoken here include philosopher Bernard Henri Levy, Nobel Laureate Elie Wiesel, newsman Dan Rather, actors Alan Alda and Ralph Fiennes, domestic diva Martha Stewart, and musician Billy Joel.
- **Columbia University** (www.columbia.edu/cu/news/calendar) and **NYU** (http://events.nyu.edu): Gotham's two mega-universities present excellent evening lectures, usually open to all, on all sorts of topics (most notoriously, Columbia invited President Ahmadinejad of Iran to speak in 2007).

ACTING CLASSES

One of the brightest, shiniest dreams about the Big Apple is to come here and make it big as an actor. To see a small slice of that world, audit an acting class at **Herbert Berghof Studio** (120 Bank St.; ☎ 212/675-2370; www.hbstudio.org; $10 to audit). The school, established in 1945 by Broadway diva Stella Adler and her husband, is one of the most highly regarded in the city. It's also the only one I know of that allows outsiders to sit in on classes. Watching these young and often seriously talented students work is an object lesson in how difficult something as seemingly simple as appearing natural in front of a large crowd of people can actually be. And watching the teachers, many of whose faces you'll recognize from film and TV—Earle Hyman, Austin Pendleton, and Anne Jackson are all on the faculty—is another lesson showing how near-impossible it is to make a living just as an actor. Each day there are approximately 30 classes, given in disciplines as widely varied as Musical Performance, Scene Study, and Acting on Camera.

COOKING CLASSES

Though ideally you should be interested in cooking to take a class here, the **Institute of Culinary Education** ✦✦✦ (50 W. 23rd St., btwn Fifth and Sixth aves.; ☎ 212/847-0700; www.iceculinary.com) has another trait that makes it a star of this chapter: It has to be one of the easiest places to meet and actually get to know New Yorkers in the city. That's because since its inception, originally as the Peter Kump School in 1976, the emphasis here has been on "hands-on" classes. You won't be sitting in some dim lecture hall among a group of strangers. Instead, your class will be divided into small groups of two, three, or four, and for 3 to 4 hours, you'll cook or bake with your partners, poring over recipes, consulting with the teacher, and chatting away. Recreational classes, while serious (the school is known for engaging some of the most expert chefs in the city), are tremendously social. At the start of the class, crudités are put out, as at a cocktail party, so that you can snack while listening to the instructor's opening lecture. And, as at any good cocktail party, the crowd is well-mixed: the classes draw people of all ages and at night the ratio of men to women is pretty close to 50/50 (though in the daytime women predominate).

If you're serious about cooking, you won't find a better school in the city. The instruction here is highly practical, and it aims to teach you as much about the principles of cooking as specific recipes. The classes in which I recently sat taught me the technique of putting my thumb and forefinger on the blade of a knife to stabilize it (it works like a dream); when it's important to buy expensive ingredients and when it won't matter; and how to choose fresh herbs. From the esoteric to the basic, it's all on offer here; in fact, I.C.E. offers over a thousand recreational classes a year, more than any other cooking school in the world. They're taught in nine, state-of-the-art, gleaming, stainless-steel kitchens (you'll feel like you're the star of some Food Network show). Class prices range from $90 to $125 for a good 4 hours of instruction, plus a feast at the end, including wine. The tuition may seem steep, but as staffer Annie McBride pointed out to me, "You'll be paying what you'd pay for a gourmet meal in a New York restaurant, but you'll leave with the knowledge of how to cook it yourself."

DANCE CLASSES

Hundreds of lithe young things come to New York each year expressly to dance. It's a major preoccupation among certain Big Apple tribes, some of whom do it for fun, and others who dream of becoming the 21st-century's Gwen Verdon, Mikhael Baryshnikov, or Martha Graham. And because this is such a fluid, changing world, very few centers require that students sign up for more than one class at a time. Taken on an ad hoc basis, they offer secret windows into this sheltered (and sheltering) world. In fact, it can be fascinating to simply stand outside and peer through the glass doors at dancers in training, so take this section as not only an invitation to pull on some tights, but as an opportunity to simply stand and watch in amazement at the things some human bodies can do.

I'll start with a non-hard-core option for beginning dancers, or for those who prefer ballroom to ballet. Every Tuesday and Wednesday at noon, **The Argentine Consulate** ✪ (12 W. 56th St. off Fifth Ave.; ☎ 212/603-0400; **E**, **V** to Fifth Ave.) recruits. It's not looking for new citizens, but in an oddly appropriate show of patriotism it seems determined to add new tango dancers to the world with free dance lessons. About 40 novices show up at each class in a difficult-for-tango ratio of three women to every man, but because the first hour is spent mastering steps alone, it doesn't much matter. The tutorial is sometimes led by a former ballet dancer: a woman in her 60s with a throaty accent, upright bearing, and the ability to break down steps in such a way that even a clod like myself could follow them. As the wailing of the violins swelled, I slowly went through my paces, concentrating on not looking at my feet, on keeping my movements as pantherlike and steady as possible, and on moving with "pride." It's ultimately a very Zen experience, akin to tai chi, and surprisingly relaxing. During the second hour, the real tango fanatics show up, and for a rippling hour, men and women stalk one another, feet darting this way and that, hip to hip, adding a bit of heat to the sunny glare of midday. *One note:* A consular employee will ask for your name, phone number, and e-mail address when you enter, but this is simply so they can alert you if the next week's class is cancelled. You can decline if you don't want to share this information.

For a more challenging—some might say downright scary—experience, attempt a dance class at the **Broadway Dance Center** ✪ (221 W. 57th St. btwn Seventh and Eighth aves.; ☎ 212/582-9304; www.broadwaydancecenter.com; $14–$18 per class), which is where New York's legions of chorines go for their daily ablutions of stretches, steps . . . and a check of the competition. One of the largest dance schools in the world, with over 350 classes on offer at any one time, it covers everything from ballet to tap to theater dance to hip-hop. Most are taught by big-name dancers and choreographers (from the world of music videos and theater). Pack your leotard; appropriate attire is required, as well a good dose of attitude—the beginner classes here are as rigorous as intermediate classes anywhere else. **Steps** (2121 Broadway, btwn 75th and 76th sts.; ☎ 212/874-2410; www.stepsnyc.com; $16 per class) on the Upper West Side is a smaller studio but just as serious, and the bonus here is that you can wander in and watch a class from the doorway without having to participate yourself (there's a less strict door policy here).

HOW WE WORK

As in the rest of the country, most of the work done in New York City takes place in offices honeycombed with cubicles or behind the counters of restaurants, shops, and salons. You won't really be able to see these New Yorkers at work, nor would you really want to. But New York is also one of the two media capitals of the country (the other being Los Angeles), so some of our jobs have a bit of glitz to them, meaning that they need an audience in order to exist. Below, I'll tell you how to become part of the many audiences needed around town, as well as how to get a peek at some other working folks and their fascinating jobs.

ATTENDING A TV TAPING

There's no job as glitzy—or accessible to the visitor—as TV production. Literally dozens of shows are taped in the Big Apple each day, many of which require an audience. Though it may seem odd to take time out of your vacation to do what you do at home—watch TV—it's the behind-the-scenes elements that make the experience here: the scurrying grips and cameramen, the "warm-up act" before the show, and seeing what the host does when the camera isn't on.

Attending tapings is a very popular activity, so it's important that you request tickets in advance, *far* in advance. Six months ahead of time is not too early for a cult hit such as *Saturday Night Live* or *Late Night with David Letterman*. If you can't plan that far ahead, or are rejected for an advance seat, all hope is not lost— stand-by seats are distributed for most shows. To snag one of these, you'll need to get up early and do a lot of waiting, but many people on the stand-by list do get in. *One warning:* Stand-by tickets are given out by person, not by couple, so if you're traveling with someone else, both of you have to brave the line to attend the show.

Some of the available tapings include:

The Daily Show with Jon Stewart

The best show on TV, to my mind, this hilarious news parody is a very hot ticket.

> **Tapes:** Monday through Thursday at 5:45pm; audience arrives between 4pm and 5pm; doors open at 5pm.
> **Online information:** The show makes very few tickets available to the general public (in a recent 12-month period, they only opened up 14 dates). So as soon as you know when you'd like to attend, go to **www.thedailyshow. com** and click on the ticket link which will give you the calendar of available dates and an e-mail address to contact. *Note:* The Daily Show spin-off **The Colbert Report** is an even more impossible ticket to get. I'm not including it here because in 2008 they gave out NO advance tickets to the general public whatsoever.
> **Last-minute tickets:** Call ☎ 212/586-2477 on Friday between 11am and 11:30am a week prior to the date you wish to attend.
> **Stand-by tickets:** Occasionally, people who line up outside the studio (733 11th Ave., between 51st and 52nd sts.) at 5pm are admitted, but this method is very iffy.
> **Fine print:** No one under 18 admitted.

TV Taping Tips

1. **Doll up.** If you're hoping to get your face on camera, dress nicely. Seats are not given out at random; instead, on shows where audience participation is key, they place the well-coiffed folks wearing attractive, vibrant colors at the front.

2. **Layer up.** To keep the camera equipment in top shape, TV studios are kept the temperature of the Arctic Circle. You're going to want to bring something warm to wear, even in August.

3. **Own up.** When you apply for a seat, be sure to give them all the information they want, including your full name, daytime phone number, address, e-mail address, and requested dates (be flexible on dates if you can). Leave out any of this information and you won't be attending the show.

Late Night with Conan O'Brien

If Marcel Duchamp had been a comedian with a talk show, it might have turned out something like this one, which features an hour of absurdist humor alternating with celebrity interviews (two per show is the norm).

Tapes: Tuesday through Friday 5:30 to 6:30pm; audience arrives at 4pm.
Books audience: Approximately 6 months in advance.
Call: ☎ 212/664-3036 (and keep pushing the numbers for more info until you get a live person).
Online information: www.nbc.com.
Stand-by policy: Would-be audience members show up at 9am to pick up stand-by tickets and then return at 4:30pm. Usually a handful of stand-bys will get into each show.
Fine print: No one under 16 admitted. Audience members can book up to four tickets at a time. Those who show up earliest get the best seats (those in front may be scanned by cameras).

The Late Show with David Letterman

Wry, sardonic, and usually funny, the Letterman talk show is the second hottest ticket in New York (after *The Daily Show*). A far larger auditorium, however, means that many more people get to see Dave live each week than Jon Stewart. The audience often becomes part of the show, so come prepared to entertain.

Tapes: Monday through Wednesday at 5:30pm and Thursday at 4:30 and 6:30pm; audience arrives 90 minutes before the show.
Books audience: As far as 6 months out, though you can snag a ticket on the day of the show.
Apply online: At www.cbs.com. You will receive a follow-up call from a staffer who will ask you trivia questions about the show, so bone up if you want to get in.

Apply in person: At the Ed Sullivan Theater (1697 Broadway, btwn 53rd and 54th sts.; Mon–Fri 9:30am–12:30pm, Sat–Sun 10am–6pm). Using this method, you can apply for that day's show, or any other show in the upcoming month. You will be told by phone whether or not you've gotten the tickets. Be aware that this is really an audition: You'll be asked how often you watch the show, what your favorite moments have been, and trivia questions about the show. Those who perform best, get in.

Stand-by: Numbers are assigned starting at 9am, day of show, and if there's room in the audience, stand-bys get in on a first come, first-served basis.

Fine print: No one under 18 admitted. Thursday is audience participation night, so come prepared if you want to get on camera. And this theater makes the rest seem warm, so bring a jacket.

Live with Regis and Kelly

Bubbly blond and gruff old guy chat with famous people, on one of the most popular of the daytime offerings.

Tapes: Monday through Friday at 10am; audience arrives 90 minutes prior to show time.

Books audience: This show can sell out a year in advance. Send in your request as soon as possible and no later than 4 weeks before your requested date.

Apply by mail: Write to "Live Tickets," Ansonia Station, P.O. Box 230-777, New York, NY 10023-0777.

Online information: http://tvplex.go.com/buenavista/regisandkelly/show info/tickets.html.

Stand-by policy: Numbered stubs given out starting at 7am; holders get in on a first-come, first-serve basis if seats are available.

Fine print: Kids ages 10 to 18 are admitted but must be accompanied by an adult.

The Morning Show with Mike and Juliet

The poor man's Regis and Kelly, this Fox chatter-fest features two unusually bawdy hosts (this is morning TV?), who flirt and insult one another. "Relationship experts" are most likely to be the featured guests, though occasionally celebrities drop by as do chefs, doctors, and stylists.

Tapes: Monday through Friday, 9am–10am. Audience arrives at 7:45am and is treated to a free breakfast.

Book audience: As they go along. It's not a difficult ticket to get; if you don't plan ahead, you can probably get in off the stand-by line.

Apply by phone or email: Call 877/FOX-TKTS or log on to www.mandj show.com.

Stand-by policy: Arrive at the Fox Studios, 133 West 47th St. (btwn 6th and 7th aves.) no later than 7:30am.

Fine print: Ages 18 and over only.

Morning Mayhem

The Today Show, Good Morning America, and *The Early Show*—in that order—are the most popular taping events for tourists to NYC. With the exception of *Good Morning America* (see below), none give out tickets in advance. Instead "audience" members line up outside the studios, in all sorts of weather, bearing all sorts of signs, and stand for hours hoping to be scanned by the TV cameras. I personally don't think it's as interesting an experience as actually watching a taping in a studio, but many find the experience exciting, partially because it's such a challenge to find and then hold your position in the crowd. If you want to try it, get up at dawn, dress for the elements and go to:

- Fifth Avenue and 59th Street (for *The Early Show*)
- 30 Rockefeller Center, on 49th Street, between Fifth and Sixth aves. (for *The Today Show*)

For *Good Morning America* get reserved tickets at http://abcnews.go.com/GMA.

Rachael Ray

Yum-O! Watch this manic sprite cook in person, and with celebs as her sous chefs, on this popular morning talk show.

Tapes: Tuesdays, Wednesdays, and Thursdays at noon and 4pm. Audience arrives at 10:15am and 12:15pm.
Books audience: Through its website only, and up to 2 years (!) in advance.
Apply online at: www.rachaelrayshow.com.
Stand-by policy: Stand-by vouchers are given out at the studio at 10:15am and 12:15pm, then you wait again to see if you get in.
Fine print: Ms. Ray only admits audience members 16 and older and reserves the right to deny admission to anyone wearing shorts, T-shirt, busy patterns, and other "inappropriate" clothing (there's a list on the site). Chewing gum is a no no, too.

Saturday Night Live

It's been great, it's been less-than-great, and then near-great again. I personally think this comedy sketch show is in a valley right now, but occasionally it's still funny, and seeing the live taping with the mad dash of set changes, costume changes, and general hysteria is a kick.

Tapes: About every other Saturday, September through May, at 11:30pm (there are also tickets to an 8pm dress rehearsal that night); audience arrives at 10pm.
Books audience: In the month of August for the upcoming season. Your e-mail is your contact information at that point and is entered into a ticket lottery. If you are chosen, you hear from SNL; if not, you don't.
Apply by e-mail: Send your request to SNLtickets@nbcuni.com.

Stand-by policy: Arrive no later than 7am at the 50th Street side of 30 Rockefeller Center (under the NBC marquee) to get stand-by tickets. Come back at 10pm, and if there are seats you may get in.

The View

Popular once more (thanks to the controversies sparked by the departed Rosie O'Donnel and now Whoopie Goldberg), this talk show features four chatty host-esses, and usually one celebrity guest. Very little audience participation, though the camera scans the audience for reaction shots, so look your best.

Tapes: Every weekday, 11am to noon; audience arrives at 9:30am.
Books audience: 6–9 months in advance.
Apply by mail: Send a postcard to Tickets, The View, 320 W. 66th St., New York, NY 10023.
Apply online: http://abc.go.com/daytime/theview/tickets.html.
Stand-by policy: Numbered stand-by stubs are distributed between 8:30am and 10am. Holders then return by 10:20am and wait in the hopes of getting in. The earlier you pick up your numbered stub, the better your chances.
Fine print: Must be age 16 or older. Tickets are distributed on a first-come, first-served basis; if you arrive late you may not get in as they do sometimes overbook.

BACKSTAGE AT THE METROPOLITAN OPERA OR *WICKED*

Have you ever toyed with a car engine or taken apart a clock? The **backstage tour of the Metropolitan Opera** ★★ (at Lincoln Center, off Columbus Ave. btwn 61st and 65th sts.; ☎ 212-769-7020; www.operaed.org; Oct–June, Mon–Fri 3:30pm, Sun 10:30am; $15) offers the same kind of fascination. You don't even have to care a whit about opera to enjoy it. This is simply the best showbiz behind-the-scenes tour in New York, as it guides you through all the meticulous steps it takes to put on a show—or 22 shows (the Met's seasonal average). The 1¾-hour tour will whisk you through half of the 10 stories that make up the backstage area. You'll see carpenters re-creating Roman forums in plywood, following plans that have them methodically sawing out pieces down to the sixteenth of an inch; wigmak-ers creating hairpieces from scratch, shaping a cap and then pulling the hair (imported from Sweden) through it one strand at a time; seamstresses sewing reams of beads; prop masters sculpting severed heads (for Salome); and—most fun—you'll get to peek into rehearsal rooms and listen to trumpet-voiced singers practicing their arias and gestures. In fact, watching the hundreds of people toil-ing backstage to bring these operas to life is a show in and of itself. *One warn-ing:* The tour involves non-stop walking, often in slippery, sawdusty areas, so wear sneakers or shoes with good treads.

Behind The Emerald Curtain (Gershwin Theater, 222 W. 51st St.; www.emerald curtain.com; $37) touts itself as a tour, but is in reality more of a Q&A session with current and former members of the *Wicked* cast, with a video thrown in for excitement. You never actually get behind the curtain (the experience takes place entirely in the lobby and auditorium of the theater). That being said, these are some of the Great White Way's best talents, and they know how to wring every laugh out of an anecdote and sell information that could be dry (the types of fabrics used in the Emerald City costumes—gasp!—are upholstery fabrics). If you're a fan of the show, or have an intense curiosity as to how a Broadway show is put together, you'll enjoy it. Otherwise, I think the Met tour trumps it.

FACTORY TOURS

New York's industrial heyday is long gone, but a handful of factories do remain in the Big Apple. Three periodically open their gates to the public, and when they do, they have a Wonka-like appeal—the ultra-cool factory tour!—introducing you to the intricacy, effort and, yes, art that goes into creating their products.

People come from all over the world to tour the premises of **Steinway & Sons** ✮ (19th Ave. and 38th St., Astoria, Queens; ☎ 718/721-2600; www.steinway.com; free admission; Ⓝ to Ditmars St.), the famed piano manufacturer. These very special tours take place only on Monday and Tuesday mornings from September through June (call for details). In the course of the 2½-hour tour, you'll witness the yearlong painstaking process of handcrafting a piano, watching workers delicately sawing, rubbing, voicing, and stringing the instruments. If you're lucky, you'll be there as I was, when the workers bend the huge planks of wood around an iron press that creates the distinctive grand piano shape, a method invented by C. F. Theodore Steinway. (Sounds dull, but it's actually a strangely balletic process to witness.) One of the final stops is the "Pounder Room," where a machine methodically bangs all of the keys of a piano up to 10,000 times, looking for any possible flaws.

Fewer than 5,000 Steinway pianos are created per year (other manufacturers produce 100,000 per year), yet over 98% of the world's top classical pianists use these instruments exclusively. After witnessing the loving care these pianos get, you'll understand why.

Less a tour than a 40-minute lecture, the **Brooklyn Brewery Tour** (79 N. 11th St., Williamsburg, Brooklyn; ☎ 718/486-7422; www.brooklynbrewery.com; free admission; Sat noon–6pm; Ⓛ to Bedford St.) offers a witty introduction to the world of hops and yeast, and a nice overview of the underdog history of this particular company, now the 24th largest brewery in the United States. You'll hear about how a former journalist went from bar to bar, selling his beer from the back of a van; why this brew is better known in Denmark than it is in Colorado; and how beer should be made (and isn't at Budweiser, Coors, or Miller). Best of all you'll get a ticket for a free pint. Behind me, while standing in line at the bar, one slacker 20-something remarked to another: "We'll drink these, then take the tour again!"

Making money, quite literally, is the job of the economic factory that is the **Federal Reserve Bank** ✮✮✮ (33 Liberty St. at the corner of Nassau; ☎ 212/720-5000; www.ny.frb.org; free admission; Mon–Fri 9:30am, 10:30am, 11:30am, 1:30pm, and 2:30pm; reservations required 5 days in advance; ❷, ❸, ❹, ❺, Ⓐ, Ⓒ, Ⓙ, Ⓜ, ❷ to Fulton St.). Although you won't see the currency being printed—that function was moved from this site to New Jersey in 1992—you will likely see more lucre than you ever will again in your lifetime when you descend 80 feet down to the basement of this financial fortress, where a gold vault right out of *Mission Impossible* is housed. Down here, behind a door that's a good 5 feet thick, the Fed keeps $100,000 billion worth of gold bars, a full 25% of all the gold reserves in the world, and far more than is housed in Fort Knox. Ninety-five per-cent of the gold stored here belongs to foreign nations, who use this facility, embedded in the bedrock of Manhattan and guarded by a small army of marks-men (they have their own on-site firing range for practice), because it's considered the safest place in the world for this type of storage. I wish I could give you more details, but the security here is so spandex-tight that my reporter's notebook was confiscated at the door.

The gold is supplemented by precious coins (one worth $7 million), in an exhibit in the lobby by the Numismatic Society in partnership with the Fed. Also featured are brief videotapes detailing the work of the Fed, and an interactive exhibit explaining what the massive, semi-governmental agency does (it's an inter-esting topic). The entire tour takes a bit less than an hour.

LAW & ORDER: THE REAL THING

After years of watching cop movies and TV shows set in Gotham, you may feel like you've already been inside a **New York City courtroom.** The reality, however, is vastly different: weirder, with scruffier characters, lawyers so young they look like high schoolers, and an offhand, almost casual atmosphere that somehow underscores even more grippingly the life and death issues faced by the defen-dants. And with the sheer volume of cases coming in and out of the courts, you're almost guaranteed to find an engrossing trial to watch.

Your best bet is to go to **100 Center St.,** at the corner of Leonard St. (❹, ❺, ❻ to Brooklyn Bridge/City Hall), Manhattan's busiest criminal courthouse. Jury trials, several per day, are held from 10am to 5pm Monday through Friday, and night court is on from 5pm to 1am (meal breaks at noon–1pm and 10–11pm). If you visit during the daytime, go directly to the 10th floor, Room 1000, where the clerk will be able to direct you to the day's felony trials. You can simply walk in and sit down in any courtroom; no one will question you or think it odd. Arrive at night, and simply go to one of the two first-floor courtrooms where any-one arrested after the sun goes down is arraigned, from people caught driving under the influence all the way up to accused rapists and murderers.

Watching the trials and arraignments is a lesson in how our system works . . . admittedly a chilling one at times. Though I've seen many good lawyers and com-petent judges, I've also witnessed sessions of name-calling between the two that would embarrass a kindergartner; and night court prosecutors so obviously unable to distinguish one case, or prisoner, from another that the whole process raises goose bumps of sympathy for the defendants, no matter how guilty he or she may actually be. A fascinating, sometimes disturbing look at the underpinnings of the city.

HOW WE PLAY

You'll find an extensive list of nightlife options in chapter 10, with a bar and lounge section that uncovers many of the local hangouts, places where tourists rarely venture. This section covers the more unusual types of nightlife (and four playful daytime experiences), such as Russian nightclubs and parties that pop up in different places each month.

RUSSIAN BATHS

After a night of questions and cocktails, a little schvitz might be in order. That's Yiddish for "sweat" and it's what you'll do copiously at the **Russian & Turkish Baths** ⚡ (268 E. 10th St., btwn First Ave. and Avenue A; ☎ 212/674-9250; www. russianturkishbaths.com; $30 admission; Sat–Sun 8am–10pm, Mon–Tues and Thurs–Fri noon–10pm, Wed 10am–10pm; ❶ to First Ave.), the last holdout from the years when the Lower East Side and the East Village were swimming in such establishments—wet clubhouses where newly arrived eastern European immigrants (primarily) met to gossip, raise a glass of vodka, and then flush the alcohol out of their systems with a sauna. Of course, when this bathhouse was established in 1892, only men came; today, it's co-ed most of the week, with special men-only hours on Sunday from 7:30am to 2pm and women-only Wednesday from 9am to 2pm.

Little else has changed—the little restaurant at the front continues to dole out borscht and beer (no more vodka, sorry); and in the basement, people of all ages, nationalities, shapes, and sizes peer at one another through mists of steam and do what they've always done here: talk. And talk. And talk—about their children, about the weather, about food and politics and television. First and foremost this is a social scene, open to all, and totally different from the serenity-obsessed, beauty-promulgating spas elsewhere in the city. The facilities are defiantly old (but clean); everyone is issued the same robes and shorts, a great leveler; and the body obsessions that seem to haunt spas are refreshingly absent. (Women who are modest may want to bring along a bathing suit, as the armholes on these one-size-fits-all robes often reach down to the bottom of the rib cage, exposing all.)

Though you can spend your time drifting from cloudy room to room—there's a Swedish sauna, a Turkish steam room (the steam scented with lavender and eucalyptus), and another tiled steam room—to be instantly transported back to the early 1900s you'll want to opt for the *platza* treatment (an additional $35). Nicknamed "Jewish Acupuncture," it takes place in an actual Russian sauna (one of the few in the U.S., it's heated by 2,000 pounds of rocks that are baked in an oven overnight, giving off an intense radiant heat). You'll lie down on one of the wooden piers as an attendant scrubs/whips you with oak leaves doused in olive oil soap. The oil in the leaves is an astringent, which is then massaged in, to open your pores and cleanse your skin. Just when you're feeling utterly relaxed, the attendant douses you with frigid water. If you want to have a tale to bring home to your friends, this is it. If you're not that adventurous, you can simply wander into the Russian Sauna, take a seat, and watch someone else getting the treatment. Massages, Dead Sea salt scrubs, and black mud treatments are also available.

A TEA CEREMONY

At the bathhouse, you'll experience the old Eastern European East Village. To experience the new East Village, trade the bathhouse for a teahouse, where you'll learn about the latest immigrant group to transform the neighborhood: the Japanese. At a very authentic tea *kaiseki* (Japanese version of tapas) restaurant, **Cha-an** (230 E. 9th St.; ☎ 212/228-8030; $15 per person; call in advance for reservations; ❻ to Astor Place), a traditional Japanese tea ceremony is performed each Friday. It's an unusual opportunity, because in Japan a guest at such a ceremony would be expected to know *Sadu*, the correct way to take the tea, and the comments and gestures to make during the ritual.

I knew none of this, nor did my then 6-year-old daughter, when we were graciously waved into the small, tatami-matted hut in the center of the restaurant by a murmuring woman in a sherbet-colored kimono. She was our hostess for the next half-hour and patiently took us through the ceremony, explaining softly that samurai performed the tea ceremony before they went into battle to center themselves, and that each move was part of the ritual, one that is deeply meshed with Zen Buddhism. We learned that the process celebrates the moment of the encounter between the host and guest, one that will never again be repeated in just the same way. And as we ate our small treat (made of sticky rice) and drank the bitter tea, the sounds of traffic and the pace of the street retreated for that short while and all was reduced to the miniature world of the hut. It was an otherworldly way to spend a half-hour, and even my sometimes rambunctious daughter walked away calmed and refreshed by the experience.

THE GAMES LOCALS PLAY

This next experience is a classic, one of the few holdovers from the '50s and '60s Greenwich Village, when it was still a hotbed of intellectuals and would-be revolutionaries (you've seen cartoons of them, all long hair and berets). I'm speaking of chess, which is avidly played today in the small Village "Chess District" consisting of the southwest corner of Washington Square Park and the chess shops along nearby Thompson Street. Here, as they've done for decades, intense clusters of men (primarily) gather for intense games, speaking little, grunting a lot, occasionally flipping through the paper between moves, or gathering in clusters to watch the really expert players (Grand Masters sometimes show up).

You may have seen the park players featured in the movie *Searching for Bobby Fischer*. While they're fun to watch, if you want to play yourself I'd recommend going to the **Village Chess Shop** ✪ (230 Thompson St; ☎ 212/475-9580; www.chess-shop.com; games 11am–midnight) instead, where gambling is forbidden—you can lose your shirt in the park, those guys are sharks. Games cost a whopping $1, making this one of the cheapest pastimes in the city. Watch your temper, though: Profanities incur a fine of $3. Along with selling tea, coffee, and small snacks, the Village Chess Shop has all sorts of chess sets for sale, many of them collectors' items.

Table tennis is beloved in China, and when you visit **Wang Chen Table Tennis Club** ✪ (250 W. 100th St., just off Broadway; ☎ 212/864-7235; www.wangchenttc.com; Mon–Fri 3pm–10pm, Sat 10am–10pm, Sun 10am–7pm; ❶, ❷, ❸ to 96th St.), you'll feel like you've been transported there as you watch Asian, sweat-spouting (mostly) men, women, and children pace the tables here, slamming down the balls with an intensity that would impress Andre Agassi. Arguably the best place in the nation to learn to play table tennis—the top-ranked female player in the U.S. is an instructor here, and her male colleagues are ranked 16th and 17th respectively (you gotta wonder what kind of mind games happen around the water cooler here)—Chen's is open 7 days a week and will accept short-term students. If you have just 1 hour to devote to improving your game, that's okay: $40 will buy you a session with one of these masters. It's also possible to simply drop by for a couple of games at a cost of just $8 an hour or take part in their weekly Wednesday night tournament (7:45pm, $15).

SURPRISE PARTIES . . . FOR ALL

Next is a legendary **roaming party** ✪✪✪ that pops up unexpectedly about once a month in all sorts of odd locations. One night a thousand revelers gather on a summer evening in a waterside park in Brooklyn for a renegade street festival of music, dance, and exotic partywear. Another time, a set of modern dance studios is taken over for a night of "new circus" performances and bawdy burlesque (I attended that one and watched as a hula dancer wearing a bra made of fake skulls performed a very funny trio with her breasts . . . you had to be there). And most famously, the A train mysteriously becomes a disco at midnight, as several hundred board at a pre-arranged stop, boomboxes in hand, and boogie through the boroughs until dawn. If it sounds outrageous, it's meant to be. "In the New Lost City, you are the performer and the night is your stage," write the anonymous party-givers. "We create these events to wake the wild inside, to remind you of the infinite possibilities of your nightlife vision made real." When I recently e-mailed them to find out whether these fests are open to all, one of the party-throwers named Will e-mailed me back saying, "We love outsiders. In fact, I think all of us are outsiders." To find out when the next one's happening and if there's a charge (most are free, but some cost btwn $9 and $20 to attend), head online to **www.thedanger.com** and join the list (free).

DIVAS BELTING IT OUT

Even Broadway stars like to do karaoke. The difference is, when they do it, they bring sheet music so that top musicians can accompany them live . . . and about 250 people show up to listen. Or at least that's the case at **Jim Caruso's Cast Party** ✪✪✪ (at Birdland, 315 W. 44th St.; ☎ 212/581-3080; www.castpartynyc.com; Mondays at 10pm–1am), a daffy, joyous night of music and jokes that spontaneously erupts every Monday night (the dark night for most Broadway shows). Along with the Broadway types, both known and wannabe, are top talents from the world of jazz, cabaret, and comedy. (When I was last there, an inventive, awesomely synchronized a capella quartet performed.)

Jim Caruso, the host, is hilarious, an affable gossip who reminds me of a modern-day Paul Linde. He keeps the show moving, deciding who gets to sing and the tension in the room just before the next name is announced can be palpable. You'll likely meet some showbiz types while there. Last time I went, I sat at the bar next to a would-be jazz singer who squealed with delight when Marilyn Mayes took the mic (when I asked who she was, my neighbor said with indignation "Who's Marilyn Mayes?!? Why she appeared on the Ed Sullivan show more than any other singer!" A moment later she grabbed my arm and moaned tragically "She's singing the song I was going to do!!!"). Along with Mayes, the second actor to play Tony in "West Side Story" sang a duet with his daughter from that show; famed cabaret performer Billy Stritch tickled the ivories; and a whole host of folks who I'd never heard of made a very good case that they should have careers in show biz. It feels like a combo of the ultimate insider's night and the best cocktail party you've ever been to. Best of all, it's an adrenaline rush thinking: Should I? If you've got the courage (and the sheet music) you could get up and sing, too.

VEGAS VIA MOSCOW IN BROOKLYN

Up to this point, my "Other New York" selections have been activities that pretty much any local can engage in. The Russian nightclubs of Brooklyn are a bit different. While they're certainly open to all (and once the vodka starts flowing freely—as it will—everyone gets quite chummy), these nightclubs have a clientele that's almost entirely made up of Russian immigrants. They also have an earnestly kitschy sensibility—think showgirls with perma-grins in feathered bras and Russian-mafia-looking types boozily singing along to top-40 hits—that's quite unique. Interestingly, the clubs offer these émigrés something that doesn't really exist in their homeland: a supper club, where a lavish, multi-course meal is the opener to a night of entertainment, with a floor show and dancing until the wee hours (according to Russian friends of mine, restaurants are never dance halls in Russia; they're strictly separated).

It's not a cheap experience: A night at one of these clubs can easily run to $150 or more per couple. But I'd say it's the most worthy splurge in this book. In fact, it may well end up being your most memorable evening in the city. To keep costs in check bring your own liquor: it's allowed and will cut your final tab dramatically.

Of the dozen or so nightclubs in Brighton Beach, three are universally considered to be the finest. **Tatiana Restaurant** (3162 Brighton at 6th St.; ☎ 718/891-5151; Fri–Sun for dinner and show; ❸ or ❹ to Brighton Beach) is right on the boardwalk, so if you get there early enough you'll have the fun of walking the sand and seeing the sun set. Like the other two, it has a floor show of dancers and singers, but its entertainment (at least when I last saw it) is a bit weirder and more amateurish than the others. For top-notch entertainment, including a singer who's the Russian doppelganger of Celine Dion, there's **Rasputin** ✯✯ (2670 Coney Island Ave.; ☎ 212/332-8111; Fri–Sun for dinner and show; no decent public transportation options), which has the largest dining room and stage of the three, as well as the most lavish stage show, with 12 talented and enthusiastic singers and dancers, dozens of costume changes, and clever choreography (including numbers where cast members were swinging from the ceiling when I was last there). My favorite, however, is the oldest of the bunch, **The National** ✯✯✯ (2730 Brighton Beach Ave.; ☎ 718/646-1225; Fri–Sun for dinner and show; ❸ or ❹ to Brighton Beach), which somehow best captures the joyous spirit of this community—along with top-40 and swing dancing, people in the crowd periodically request Russian folk dances, and suddenly the dance floor will be filled with men and women clasping one another's shoulders and kicking their ways across the floor. If you're looking for a younger crowd, though, go with Rasputin. *One note:* Dress appropriately, or you'll feel very awkward. For men, that means suits or very upscale casual wear; women should wear an outfit they might don for an evening wedding.

HOW WE PRAY

A city that many have denounced as the next Sodom and Gomorrah, New York is in reality brimming with well-subscribed churches, mosques, synagogues, and temples of all types. Attending a service—even of a religion other than your own—is a marvelous way of meeting locals and getting a peek at the zeitgeist of that particular community.

Note: There are dozens of religious services of every stripe to attend across the city. I only have space enough for a few in this section, and so have chosen those that readily accept visitors and are, to my mind at least, particularly fascinating for outsiders. If you're interested in attending another type of service, beyond those listed here, the front desk clerk at your hotel should be able to direct you.

A GOSPEL SERVICE IN HARLEM

I'll start with the disclaimer that this is hardly a non-touristy activity. In fact, the subway up to Harlem on Sunday mornings is a regular train car of Babel, with visitors from all over the world making the trek Uptown. Most are going to the **Abyssinian Baptist Church** ★★ (136–142 W. 138th St., btwn Lenox Ave. and Adam Clayton Powell Blvd.; www.abyssinian.org; Sun 9am and 11am; ❷, ❸ to 135th St.), the best-known of Harlem's churches, and a center of the African-American community. In fact, at the service I first attended, the new president of the NAACP spoke to the congregation, as did New York's chancellor of education. The only disappointing element of the service was the music, which was subdued and lackluster. But for those who value the word (every service includes an eloquent sermon) over the melody, there's no better place than this church, still the most important in Harlem (see p. 227 for more on the church's architecture and history). *One note:* Abyssinian is extremely popular. To get into the 9am service, you'll need to arrive no later than 8:30am; and for the 11am service, arrive at 9am. If you're not a member of the congregation, you'll be placed in the visitors' line and then in a special visitors' seating section in the balcony.

Better music, in fact seriously wonderful music, is at the heart of the services at **Canaan Baptist Church** ★ (132 W. 116th St., off Lenox Ave.; Sun 11am; ❶ to 116th St.), where a 30-person-strong, red-robed choir is ably backed by a hot septet of piano, organ, bass, electric guitar, organ, drums, and bongos. By the halfway point of the service, the congregation is swaying, jumping, and swooning from the weight of the emotions this non-stop music machine is pumping out (in fact, there's very little preaching here). Problem is, visitors are not admitted until after the 11am service commences, and then they are shepherded up to a steep balcony with only limited views of the stage. I have always felt very removed from the action, though the music is by far the best you'll hear anywhere.

The most welcoming of the gospel churches is the **Greater Refuge Temple** (2081 Adam Clayton Powell, Jr. Blvd; ☎ 212/866-1700; Sun 11am; ❷, ❸ to 125th St.), which has no specific area for outsiders; here guests sit side by side with parishioners. The church itself is a massive, '60s structure that looks more like an auditorium than a church, but with excellent acoustics and an enthusiastic all-male choir who make up in spirit for what they sometimes lack in talent (the choir actually is terrific, the soloists less so). Like Canaan, they, too, have a complete band grooving with the singers. And for anyone who wants to see the holy-roller spirit of Harlem, this is the place to come: Parishioners bring their own tambourines, wear elaborate hats, and jump up and dance whenever the spirit calls.

A BUDDHIST TEMPLE IN CHINATOWN

At the entrance to the Manhattan Bridge, a giant smiling Buddha with a blue neon halo blesses all who approach. He presides over the largest Chinese Buddhist temple in New York, a building that once housed a kung fu movie house but now

Other Prominent Houses of Worship

Beyond the Baptist, Catholic, and Buddhist churches and temples discussed in this section, here are some notable houses of worship that hold services you may wish to attend.

Armenian Apostolic

◆ **St. Vartan Armenian Cathedral** (630 Second Ave., at 34th St.; ☎ 212/686-0710; Divine Liturgy services Sun at 10:30am). Built to resemble the Cathedral of Holy Echmidiazen (4th c.), the first cruciform church in the world, this cathedral was consecrated in 1968, the first of its kind in the U.S.

Episcopalian

◆ **Cathedral of St. John the Divine** (1047 Amsterdam Ave., at 110th St.; ☎ 212/316-7490; services Mon–Sat 8am, 8:30am, 9:30am, 12:15pm, 5:30pm; Sun at 8am, 9am, 9:30am, 11am, 6pm; ❶ to 110th St.). This architectural masterpiece, still under construction (p. 166), is the largest cathedral in the world.

Hindu

◆ **Hindu Temple Society of North America** (45–57 Bowne St, Flushing; ☎ 718/460-8484; www.nyganeshtemple.org; Mon–Fri 8am–9pm, Sat–Sun 7:30am–9pm; ❼ to Main St., Flushing). Dedicated to the god Ganesh, this was the first Hindu temple built in the United States. It's still the place visited by all Indian Hindus during their first week in New York City. Dress appropriately: Those wearing shorts, ripped jeans, or very short skirts will not be admitted.

Interdenominational Christian

◆ **Riverside Church** (490 Riverside Dr., btwn 120th and 122nd sts.; www.theriversidechurchny.org; services Mon, Tues, and Thurs 6pm; Wed 7pm, Sun 8:15am and 10:45am; ❶ to 116th St.). An architecturally important church (modeled on Chartres Cathedral in France), it's known for the progressive views of its clergy and its proudly interracial congregation.

trades in serenity instead of jaguar-claw punches. Like all Buddhist temples, **Mahayana Buddhist Temple** (133 Canal St. just at the entrance to the bridge; ❻, ❼, ❽, ❾ to Canal St.) is open to all at most hours of the day. The few formal ceremonies they offer are tied to the lunar calendar and thus difficult to anticipate.

When you enter, you'll see a statue of Kwan Yin, the Goddess of Mercy (the most famous and beloved of the Buddhist deities, you may have seen her likeness at your favorite Chinese restaurant). All around her are bamboo fortune-telling

Jewish

- **Congregation Emanu-El** (1 E. 65th St., off Fifth Ave.; ☎ 212/744-1400; www.emanuelnyc.org; services Sun–Thurs 5:30pm, Fri 5:15pm, Sat 10:30am; ❻, ❻ to Fifth Ave). This reformed Jewish temple boasts the largest Jewish congregation in the world. After the Saturday services there are architectural tours of the sanctuary.
- **Congregation Shearith Israel** (Central Park West at 70th St; ☎ 212/873-0300; www.shearithisrael.org; services Mon–Fri 7:15am and 6:30pm, Sat 8:15am, Sun 8am; ❶ to 66th St.). This Orthodox synagogue (also known as the Spanish and Portuguese Synagogue) is home to the oldest Jewish congregation in New York. I also think it's one of the loveliest houses of worship in the city.

Methodist

- **Christ Church United Methodist** (520 Park Ave., at 59th St.; ☎ 212/838-3036; www.christchurchnyc.org; services Wed at 7:30pm and Sun at 9am, 9:30am, and 11am). This eye-poppingly beautiful church has a Byzantine/Romanesque sanctuary adorned with seven million Venetian tiles.

Mormon

- **Manhattan New York Temple** (125 Columbus Ave., at 65th St.; ☎ 917/441-8220; ❶ to 66th St.). Non-Mormons not admitted to services. Call for service times.

Muslim

- **The Islamic Cultural Center of New York** (201 E. 96th St., at Third Ave.; ☎ 212/722-5234; Fri prayers held at 12:30pm in winter, 1pm summer; ❻ to 96th St.). This striking modern mosque was built in the mid-1980s and is very much at the center of Muslim life in the city.
- **Masjid Manhattan** (12 Warren St. btwn Church St. and Broadway; ☎ 212/866-1765; prayer services 6 times daily at approximately 5am, 6:30am, noon, 3pm, 5:45pm, and 7pm; ❻, ❿, ❹, ❺, ❻ to City Hall). Established in 1970, this was one of the pioneer mosques in New York and is busy night and day; come early for Friday services.

sticks—100 different sticks, each with a number that will refer to a devotional story. Worshippers will ask a question—something along the lines of "Is this a good year to open a business?"—pick a stick at random, and then approach the man behind the counter, who will know what story has been referenced and will help the worshipper by giving his interpretation (only in Chinese, however). You can have a simpler and somewhat ersatz experience by asking your own question, making a donation of a dollar, and then pulling out one of the tiny paper scrolls at the entrance to the main hall.

The main hall is flanked on both sides with memorial pictures, surrounding the Boddhisatva of hell, the god who helps souls pass quickly through hell to be reincarnated once again (and in Chinese Buddhism, everyone is expected to spend some time atoning in hell). Family members bring offerings (the fruit that you'll see) and light incense to appease the gods. If there's a ceremony going on, you're welcome to enter quietly but don't approach the main table where the chanting takes place. You'll know a ceremony is over when the large gong is rung.

NEW YORK'S CATHOLIC CATHEDRAL

Catholics, and anyone who appreciates the solemn theatricality of the Catholic Mass, will enjoy the service at **St. Patrick's Cathedral** ★★ (Fifth Ave. btwn 44th and 45th sts.; ☎ 212/733-2261; www.saintpatrickscathedral.org; Sun Mass at 7am, 8am, 9am, 10:15am, noon, 1pm, and 5:30pm; daily Masses during the week at various times; ❸, ❹ to Rockefeller Center). It's an imposing, handsome house of worship, with the classic Rose Window (26 ft. in diameter), flying buttresses, and attenuated columns of prototypical European Gothic cathedrals. You may want to call in advance to learn at which services the choir will perform (they don't do them all) because they have a glorious one here, its sound magnified by that of a massive organ (7,855 pipes; it's in the balcony behind the congregation). Watching the service through the wavy air (from the hundreds of candles always glowing in the transepts and along the walls) and listening to the choir can be a transporting experience. *Two small notes:* To get a seat, you'll want to arrive at least 15 minutes in advance for any of the midday Sunday services. It's also not considered appropriate for non-Catholics to take Communion.

A COOL NEIGHBORHOOD STROLL

New York City's residents make a home for themselves across the five boroughs, but there are certain residential neighborhoods that offer you more than just a peek at people scurrying to the laundromat or corner deli. I've picked one particularly interesting area to recommend, as it offers a tantalizing window into how some of the most artistic among us live.

Colonized by cheap-rent-seeking artists from the late 1970s through the early '90s), the North Side of **Willamsburg, Brooklyn** ★★ (take ❶ to Bedford St.) is a neighborhood that's saturated with art. Formerly an industrial area, it's now speckled with small galleries every other block, coffee shops brimming with serious 20-somethings hunched over computers, and high-design restaurants, as artful in decor as they are in food. What's charming is the home-grown nature of it all. At many other galleries, these former factory spaces are still so rough that you literally climb little mounds in the flooring to get around. Visit the **Temporary Museum of Painting** (118 N. 11th St. off Berry St.; $3 admission; Sat–Sun noon–5pm; www.thetemporarymuseum.com), and you'll be stepping into the cathedral-like apartment of the curator (amazing vaulted ceilings and brickwork), who will offer you mint tea, and ask you to pick your favorite and least favorite of the paintings so that she can share your thoughts with the artists. **Art 101** (101 Grand St. off Wythe; Fri–Sun 1pm–6pm; www.art101brooklyn.com) is also a home gallery, so you'll not only see the art, but get to peek at the curator's spotless kitchen and

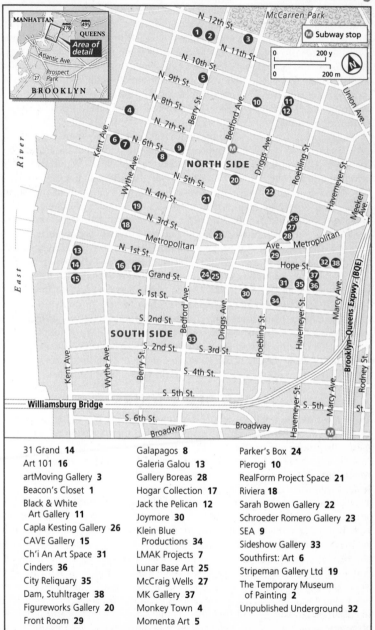

MANHATTAN
QUEENS
Area of detail
Atlantic Ave.
Prospect Park
BROOKLYN

McCarren Park

Ⓜ Subway stop

N. 12th St.
N. 11th St.
N. 10th St.
N. 9th St.
N. 8th St.
N. 7th St.
N. 6th St.
N. 5th St.
N. 4th St.
N. 3rd St.
Metropolitan Ave.
N. 1st St.
Grand St.
S. 1st St.
S. 2nd St.
S. 2nd St.
S. 3rd St.
S. 4th St.
S. 5th St.
S. 6th St.
Broadway

NORTH SIDE
SOUTH SIDE

Williamsburg Bridge

Kent Ave.
Wythe Ave.
Berry St.
Bedford Ave.
Driggs Ave.
Roebling St.
Havemeyer St.
Meeker Ave.
Union Ave.
Marcy Ave.
Rodney St.
Hope St.
Metropolitan Ave.
Brooklyn-Queens Expwy. (BQE)

River
East

31 Grand **14**	Galapagos **8**	Parker's Box **24**
Art 101 **16**	Galeria Galou **13**	Pierogi **10**
artMoving Gallery **3**	Gallery Boreas **28**	RealForm Project Space **21**
Beacon's Closet **1**	Hogar Collection **17**	Riviera **18**
Black & White Art Gallery **11**	Jack the Pelican **12**	Sarah Bowen Gallery **22**
	Joymore **30**	Schroeder Romero Gallery **23**
Capla Kesting Gallery **26**	Klein Blue Productions **34**	SEA **9**
CAVE Gallery **15**	LMAK Projects **7**	Sideshow Gallery **33**
Ch'i An Art Space **31**	Lunar Base Art **25**	Southfirst: Art **6**
Cinders **36**	McCraig Wells **27**	Stripeman Gallery Ltd **19**
City Reliquary **35**	MK Gallery **37**	The Temporary Museum of Painting **2**
Dam, Stuhltrager **38**	Monkey Town **4**	
Figureworks Gallery **20**	Momenta Art **5**	Unpublished Underground **32**
Front Room **29**		

dining room (I guess you would keep it ultra-clean knowing that strangers will be tramping). At the **City Reliquary** (corner of Grand and Havermeyer sts.), the gallery is simply three large windows that you view from the street, filled with historical detritus of New York City, from bits of stone from famous buildings to souvenirs from ages past to pieces of wreckage from the World Trade Center—an oddball, fascinating collection and utterly of a piece with the neighborhood. Because these are emerging rather than established galleries, the prices for art are within the reach of the average Joe. I've seen wall-worthy paintings for $500, and photos for even less.

An ideal visit to the neighborhood would take place on a sunny weekend afternoon (many of the galleries are only open weekends). Get off at the Bedford stop and immediately walk to the **Figureworks Gallery** (168 N. 6th St., off Bedford St.; www.figureworks.com; Fri–Sun 1–6pm) to see the art and pick up a copy of *WagMag*, a free gallery guide that will tell you what's on at all of the galleries (there's also a helpful map). After a few hours of gallery-hopping, stop by **Galapagos** (70 N. 6th St.; ☎ 718/782-5188; www.galapagosartspace.com) for a drink and a performance (local bands, burlesque shows, performance art, you name it), and then visit one of the area's many excellent Thai restaurants—**SEA** (114 N. 6th St; ☎ 718/384-8850) is ultra-chic, cheap, and darn good. Or if you want to continue your foray into the art world, go to **Monkey Town** (58 N. 3rd St., btwn Wythe and Kent sts.; ☎ 718/384-1369; Tues–Sun 4pm–midnight; ● to Bedford St.), a "performance art/video restaurant" where you dine on excellent Asian fusion food (main dishes from $10) while surrounded by 20-foot-high movie screens on all four walls. As you eat, you watch video art, or live performances, or a combination of both. When I last dined there, we watched slowed-down segments from the TV show *America's Funniest Pet Videos* as a man in the restaurant's center got an elaborate massage from another man. It was a unique experience.

INSIDER'S TOURS

Though it may seem odd to include tours in this "Other New York" chapter, the following two experiences so successfully bridge the gap between native and tourist that they must be discussed here.

The **Big Apple Greeters** program ★★★ (☎ 212/669-5159; www.bigapple greeter.org; free) is the more straightforward of the two. It pairs friendly New Yorkers (no, that's not an oxymoron) with visitors of similar tastes and interests. After a phone discussion, the host, an unpaid volunteer, devises a 2- to 4-hour walking tour of his neighborhood or a neighborhood he knows well. The two meet at the visitor's hotel and then spend the afternoon or morning together walking the streets, and getting to know one another. For some visitors, the experience becomes a short tutorial on how to navigate the subways or pick a locals-only restaurant. Others find the experience more profound. "I was nervous about hanging out with a stranger for the afternoon, but I left feeling like I'd made a true friend," Mei Wong, a visitor from Ohio told me. "It was also so moving when we talked about 9/11 and his experiences of it. After our time together, I felt like the city was my own, like I had a better understanding of it than I ever would have gotten in my short visit."

I had a similar experience. To prepare for this book, I did a Greeters tour with a roly-poly banker from Queens named Teddy, picking an area of the city that I don't know that well: Jackson Heights. A Colombian-American, Teddy was able to offer insights into the neighborhood that I never could have gleaned on my own: the ways in which the different Hispanic groups in that neighborhood interact; the single-family homes that house four or five immigrant families; and the people who were buying the "miracle waters" sold at the local *botanicas* we passed. Even for me, a native New Yorker, the experience was an eye-opener.

Big Apple Greeters can accommodate families with children and people with disabilities, and sends visitors to every part of the five boroughs (Harlem is the most requested tour). It currently has about 350 active volunteers, but because requests often exceed that number per week, it's important to call at least 2 weeks in advance to secure a tour.

Soundwalks ✮✮✮ (www.soundwalk.com; $17 for CD at Barnes & Noble or Amazon, $12 downloadable onto an iPod from the website) is the disembodied version of the Greeters program. Here, too, you have a native New Yorker squiring you around the city's most interesting neighborhoods, but in this case your companion is in your head, his voice coming through your headphones from an iPod or CD player. The speaker is backed by appropriate music and sound effects. And your guide is a provocateur, a scamp, an adventurer, wheedling you to go into places you normally wouldn't dare enter. "We are living in such a well-planned way," says founder Stephen Crasneanski, "we don't really push ourselves to try new things. So when we have a chance to step out of our lives for 10 minutes, push a door that we wouldn't normally push, that's a strong experience. These Soundwalks bring you places where you'd never normally go."

That's certainly so. In the four Soundwalks I have tried, I:

◆ keyed in a door code to get into a forbidding-looking building in Brooklyn, and then keyed in another code to take the elevator up for a spectacular view of the Manhattan bridge;
◆ stood on tiptoe to peer through a grated window at a sculptor hard at work, the narration telling me who the man was;
◆ descended a flight of stairs from the sidewalk and under a shop into a litter-strewn back alley, to the site of owner Meyer Lansky's notorious speak-easy;
◆ and surreptitiously entered a crumbling Chinatown tenement, to peer through the cracks in a second-floor door at the former Chinese Mafioso who plays mahjongg there on a daily basis.

My heart was pounding each time, the scary music and sound-effects in my ear blurring the line between reality and fiction. Suddenly, I wasn't just on a walking tour, I was starring in my own thriller.

These are the hallmarks of the Soundwalks genre, which plays up all of the adrenaline-pumping aspects of New York City—the danger, the sex, and the greed (in the Wall St. walk), in a way that may sometimes be exaggerated, but is certainly never dull. The series features walks to nearly every neighborhood you'd want to explore and some you might not have considered, including Chinatown (my favorite walk), Wall Street, Ground Zero, the East Village, Times Square, Little Italy, the Meat-Packing District, DUMBO (Brooklyn), Hasidic Williamsburg (one version for men, one for women), and the Bronx.

7 Sports & Relaxation in a Tense Town

In parks and stadiums, indoors and out

THOUGH GOTHAM MAY SEEM ALWAYS TO BE ON THE GO GO GO, THE opportunities for restful and relaxing pursuits are surprisingly numerous. The five boroughs of New York have more than 2,700 acres of parks, playgrounds, beaches, and other assorted recreation facilities—more "green" spaces than in any other city of the United States.

If you prefer to watch from the sidelines rather than swing for the fences, the city is one of the best in the world for spectator sports. Gotham boasts not one, but two adored (and despised—especially if you hail from Boston) major league baseball teams in the Yankees and the Mets. Gridiron fans will find two major football teams (though, ironically, both actually play their games in neighboring New Jersey)—the Giants and the Jets. Local pro-basketball fans flock to the down-on-their-heels Knicks and the WNBA's talented Liberty. And the N.Y. Rangers, the local hockey team, has the supernatural effect of turning ordinary fans into raving lunatics the minute they hit Madison Square Garden. Although going to a game won't be as relaxing a pastime as a park visit, it is a great way to blow off steam and meet locals (be sure to root for the home team), and is thus another highly recommended NYC experience.

CENTRAL PARK, THE CLASSIC GREEN

Central Park ★★★ (60th St. to 105th St., btwn Fifth Ave. and Central Park West; ☎ 212/360-6600 for recorded info or 212/628-1036 for live help; www.central parknyc.org; free admission; too many subway stops to list) is the logical starting place for this discussion. Manhattan's 843-acre oasis is the yin to the city's neon, concrete, and office tower yang. It serves as the city's backyard, its concert hall, its daytime pickup bar and, in the summer, when dozens don bathing suits to soak up the rays, its green beach. The marvel of the park, besides its size (a full 6% of the total area of Manhattan), is its ability to provide just the right sort of experience for the myriad of very different personalities who think of it as their own. I think it's that flexibility, that chameleon-like quality, that makes it such an interesting place for visitors to tour. Seeing it from an outsider's perspective, it's much easier to recognize what a great mirage and paradox the park is.

Because, let's face it, very little here is natural. Every tree, every shrub, every lake, and most of the rolling hills were designed, planted, or blasted into existence by landscape architects Frederick Law Olmsted and Calvert Vaux back in the 1850s, and their efforts still shape our experiences today. These two geniuses took

Central Park

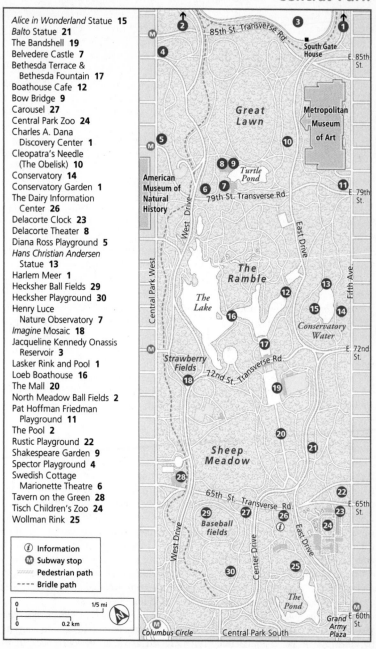

ⓘ **Information**
Ⓜ **Subway stop**
⋯⋯ **Pedestrian path**
- - - **Bridle path**

0 ————— 1/5 mi
0 ————— 0.2 km

a 2½-mile tract of swampland, farms, and suburban towns and created an Arcadia that had no resemblance whatever to what had come before. Below the park, 95 miles of drainage pipes were installed, many to both fill and periodically empty the four lakes that were created; at ground level the site was transformed using six million bricks, 65,000 cubic tons of gravel, 26,000 trees, and 250,000 shrubs. Even the dirt was imported; the natural topsoil was so poor that 500,000 cubic feet of topsoil was shipped in from New Jersey. As Olmsted once wrote, "Every foot of the park, every tree and bush, every arch, roadway and walk, has been fixed where it is with a purpose."

And what was that purpose? No less than the health of the city. Those who rallied for its creation felt that it was crucial to create a place where New Yorkers could blow off steam, get away from the stresses of urban life. Moreover, Olmsted wanted to create a park that would be a bridge between classes. "There needs to be places and time for re-unions," Olmsted wrote, "[where] the rich and the poor, the cultivated and the self-made, shall be attracted together and encouraged to assimilate." Though that didn't happen when the park was first finished—it was too far from the homes of poor New Yorkers for them to visit it—that ideal was realized when the city itself began to wrap around the park, making it finally a true *central* park.

In your own strolls around the park, you'll encounter three different types of landscapes: pastoral vistas, such as the Sheep's Meadow, which are meant to evoke a cultivated countryside; primitive portions where dense forest shuts out any view of the city; and the promenade zones, which were once used by the city's aristocracy as an extension of their parlors, a place to strut and be seen. An ideal visit here will include all three, and I've created a relatively brief list of highlights, along with the activities you can engage in once in the park, that should allow you to do just that. Feel free to ignore the following list altogether and just wander the curving paths of the park, exploring its hidden nooks, surprise vistas, ball fields, and dog runs. There's no right way to see or do this park; you'll enjoy yourself however you approach it.

CENTRAL PARK HIGHLIGHTS

◆ Actually two zoos in one—an interactive kids' zoo and the zoo for all ages—the relatively small **Central Park Zoo** ✹ (btwn 62nd and 66th sts., right off Fifth Ave.; see p. 169 for full details) is one of the oldest zoos in the U.S. A few years back, one of its polar bears made national headlines when he was treated for obsessive-compulsive disorder and depression. The cure: All the bears now hunt for their food, which is hidden daily. You can watch them do so when you visit.

◆ Completed in 1871, **The Dairy** (at roughly 65th St., a short walk into the park from the zoo), a froufrou laden Gothic structure, was an actual dairy set up to give city children access to fresh milk. Today it serves as the park's visitor center. Most of the Central Park Conservancy's tours (p. 173) start from this point. From the dairy you should be able to see **Wollman Rink** ✹ (☎ 212/439-6900; www.wollmanskatingrink.com; mid-Oct to mid-Apr; admission $9.50 adults, $4.75 seniors and children weekdays, $12 adults, $8.25 seniors, $5 kids Fri–Sun; skate rental $5), a wonderfully scenic place to skate. (You may remember it from the movie *Love Story*.) In the summer, the rink is transformed into a mini-amusement park called **Victorian Gardens.**

◆ **The Carousel** ✹ (at approximately 65th St., in the dead center of the park; www.centralparkcarousel.com; Apr–Nov 10am–6pm, Dec–Mar 10am–dusk; $1 per ride), a Victorian spinner, is most children's favorite park stop (it certainly is my daughters'). Though it's not the original carousel (the first burned down in the 1950s), it's a beaut', built in Coney Island in 1908, and features some of the tallest merry-go-round horses in the United States. It's also a much more humane carousel than the original, which was rotated by a blind mule and horse toiling in the basement.

◆ **Sheep Meadow** (btwn 64th and 68th sts., towards the west side) is the premier see-and-be-seen spot for New York's teenagers, who turn this expanse of grass into a sunbathing party come spring and summer. They're following a long tradition: This is where New York's hippie "be in," a day of non-political grooviness created by Abbie Hoffman, took place in 1967. The meadow got its name in 1864 when park commissioners set sheep to graze here in an attempt to stop the First Division of the NY National Guard from using the meadow as a parade ground (it didn't work). In 1934 the sheep were exiled to Prospect Park in Brooklyn.

Just next to Sheep Meadow, to the West, is **Tavern on the Green** (Central Park West at 67th St.; www.tavernonthegreen.com; ☎ 212/873-3200), a rococo restaurant with terrible food and service but an interior that is among the most romantic in the city (stop by for a drink or for ballroom dancing Saturday nights in the summer). It's interesting to note that this extremely expensive restaurant was originally the smelly sheepfold for the meadow next door.

◆ In their original plans for the park, Olmsted and Vaux called the area known today as **The Mall** (just east of Sheep Meadow, btwn 62nd and 68th, approximately), the Promenade, an "open air hall of reception." Today when you visit you'll be greeted by a grand elm tree–lined walkway bedecked with statues. At its Uptown end is an underused band shell, and west of that is one of the park's premier party places: an unofficial roller-blading rink where regulars dance-skate for hours each weekend to blasting disco music. It's quite a scene. **Bethesda Terrace** ✹✹ is at the Uptown end of the mall (just across the road) and is, without a doubt, the architectural heart of the park. You're likely to see a bride or two here, as many use this extraordinarily lovely area of the park as a backdrop for wedding photographs (the practice is particularly common among Chinese-American couples). If you approach it from The Mall, you'll come to a ravishingly carved gate with symbols representing day and night (the side with the witch on a broom is "night"). Take a look as well at the carvings on the stairs down to the fountain area; they represent the four seasons, and no two are alike. Bethesda Fountain was erected to celebrate the opening of the Croton Aqueduct, which finally solved New York's water problems in 1842. Sculpted by Emma Stebbins, the first woman to receive this type of commission from the city, the statue represents the angel Bethesda. She blesses the water with one hand, carrying a lily—the symbol of purity—in the other.

◆ Added to the park in 1874, **Loeb Boathouse** ✹ (approximately 74th St., off Park Dr.; ☎ 212/517-2233; boat rentals: $10 1st hr., $2.50 every 15 min.

thereafter) is where you rent the boats that you see bobbing on the lake. It's also the best place in the park to eat, with a decent fast-food counter and a very good (and more expensive) restaurant, for which you'll need a reservation. Carrie and Mr. Big, of *Sex and the City,* fell into the water together at the end of a disastrous date on the dock that pushes forward from the cafe.

◆ Darting west for a second to 72nd Street just off Central Park West is **Strawberry Fields,** a memorial to John Lennon, who was shot to death in front of the **Dakota apartment house** (1 W. 72nd St.) just across the street. A mosaic spells out "Imagine" on the ground; many come here to play music and leave flowers.

◆ Back on the East Side at around 74th Street, you'll find the **Conservatory Waters** ★, the model-boat pond where Stuart Little had his fabled race. Here you can rent a model boat to float around (via remote control), take a look at the Hans Christian Andersen statue (where storytelling takes place on weekends in summer), or visit the Alice in Wonderland statue, an artistic jungle gym for the city's youth.

◆ Walk farther into the center of the park to **Belvedere Castle,** Olmsted and Vaux's "folly" (or fantasy building), a turreted castle that sits atop the second-highest elevation in the park. Inside is a nature observatory with good rainy-day activities for children. In front of the castle is the **Delacorte Theater** (☎ 212/539-8500; www.publictheater.org; free), where the famed **Shakespeare in the Park** is performed, a star-studded and free evening of theater staged in the summer months only. If you decide to take in a show, know that you could end up spending 4 or more hours standing in line to get tickets; they're passed out at 1pm in front of the theater, but depending on the popularity of the show, crowds have been known to show up hours before that, and even camp overnight at the gate to the park. From Belvedere, you'll also look down on the **Great Lawn,** which has gone through a number of incarnations, first as a reservoir and later in the 1930s as "Hooterville," the shantytown where hundreds of homeless families lived out the Depression. Today it's most famous as a concert space: Simon and Garfunkel reunited here in the early 1980s in a widely televised concert.

◆ **Cleopatra's Needle** ★★ is next. The obelisk standing near the Metropolitan Museum of Art was a gift to the United States from Egypt in 1881, in recognition of the help this country gave in the construction of the Suez Canal. Transporting the 200-ton pillar took 38 days from Alexandria to New York by ship, and then another 144 just to get it from the Hudson River to Central Park. It originally stood at the Temple of the Sun in Heliopolis, and is believed to have been erected in 1600 B.C. The Romans moved it in the 12th century to the front of a temple built by Cleopatra, hence the name. Look for the plaque at the base, which translates the hieroglyphics.

◆ Far Uptown at 105th Street and Fifth Avenue is the park's only formal gardens, the **Conservatory Gardens** ★, and they're simply stunning. Each of the gardens' three sections was designed in the style of a different country (France, England, and Italy). Another major spot for wedding photographers (and weddings, for that matter), there are few more fragrant and lovely places in the city.

Central Park, in Brief

A word on playgrounds: With a few exceptions, most of the park's playgrounds are located on the rim of the park near the entrances. They tend to pop up every 5 blocks or so, with some of the more elaborate playgrounds located on the south end of the park (which was conceived as the children's side of the park because it was nearer to where the lower income families would have lived at the time of the park's opening).

Transportation within the park: The park is open to car traffic on weekdays only from morning to mid-afternoon. At other times, the park is a haven for cyclists, and it's quite easy to rent a bike at the Loeb Boathouse (see above) for $6 to $15 per hour. Outside the park, you can rent bikes most conveniently at **Eddie's Bicycle Shop** (490 Amsterdam Ave., at 83rd St.; ☎ 212/580-2011; www.eddiesbicycles.net; $35 per day, $10 per hr.) or at **Metro Bicycles** (1311 Lexington Ave., at 88th St.; ☎ 212/427-4450; $35 per day, $45 overnight, $7 per hr.).

Wildlife in the park: Birdwatchers from all over the city flock to the park for the variety of species it hosts, the most coveted sightings being of the endangered red-tailed hawks that make their nest on Woody Allen's Fifth Avenue building (at Fifth Ave. and 74th St.).

Though the places I list above are just a few of the wonders of the park, there are many others. And many may feel familiar if you're American. Central Park was and remains the most influential piece of landscape architecture in the United States, and many parks around the country were directly copied from this one.

OTHER MANHATTAN PARKS

Central Park was not the only green space Olmsted and Vaux created in New York City. In fact, many consider Prospect Park in Brooklyn (see later in this chapter) and **Riverside Park** (72nd to 158th sts. along the Hudson River; www.nycgov parks.org) to be their true masterworks. As its name suggests, Riverside Park has always had one advantage over Central Park: glorious river views. Many of the garden-laced promenades make the most of these vistas, as does the lovely boat basin and rotunda area at 79th Street (go to p. 280 to read up on the bar that enlivens summer evenings here). As in Central Park, there is a smattering of playgrounds; a skate park with assorted ramps and half-pipes; and a handful of monuments, including Grant's Tomb, the largest mausoleum in the United States at 8,100 square feet. (And the answer to who's buried in Grant's tomb is: No one. Ulysses S. Grant and his wife are not buried; their sarcophagi lie aboveground.)

Just behind the New York Public Library, **Bryant Park** (40th to 42nd sts., btwn Sixth Ave. and the back of the library; www.bryantpark.org; ❸, ❹, ❺, ❻ to 42nd St.) is a welcome respite from the endless high-rises and crushing crowds of Midtown, a 4-acre lawn surrounded by London plane tree–shaded promenades (like the Tuilleries Gardens in Paris), benches, and statuary. It's notable for its extensive programs of public concerts, movies, and even book loans. Weather permitting, a small "reading room" is set up outdoors on the 42nd Street side of the block Monday through Saturday from 11am to 5pm, with movable furniture; kiosks with loaner books, periodicals, and children's books (no library card or ID is required); and free Wi-Fi connection for those who want to use this tiny outdoor library to get on the Internet. From roughly May through October, the Sixth Avenue end of the park is set up as a stage, where Broadway performers are often invited to give concerts, free movies are shown in the summer (Mon nights), and other events are held. In winter a small "pond" is erected for free ice-skating; it stands where the tents for Fashion Week (p. 305) usually do. On the 40th Street side is **Le Carousel** ($2 per ride, summer Mon–Fri 12:30–6:30pm, Sat–Sun 11am–6pm; winter Thurs–Sun 11:30am–6pm), an elegant little merry-go-round that spins to the sounds of French cabaret music. A good spot for a picnic, Bryant Park has an excellent sandwich kiosk, **'wichcraft** (p. 76). There are also two pricey, so-so restaurants on the north side of the park (visit the picturesque setting for drinks but not dinner).

The spirit of the 1960s is still very much alive in two downtown New York parks that have been havens for protesters and folk singers for many decades. I'm speaking of **Union Square Park** (14th to 18th sts. btwn Broadway and Union Park East; ❹, ❺, ❻, Ⓛ, Ⓝ, Ⓞ, Ⓡ to Union Sq.) and **Washington Square Park** (Ⓡ, Ⓦ to 8th St., or Ⓐ, Ⓑ, Ⓒ, Ⓓ, Ⓔ, Ⓕ to W. 4th St.). Union Square Park's tradition of political activism goes back to the first Labor Day Parade in 1882, which ended in the park. Since that time, it has become soap box central, a place where orators come on a daily basis to blast whatever current administration is in power, weighing in on all the big topics of the day (visit nowadays and you're likely to witness someone holding forth on the plight of the Palestinians as well as U.S. foreign policy). Beyond these individual speakers, masses of people regularly congregate here to protest. In 1927, 5,000 peaceful marchers gathered to decry the execution of Sacco and Vanzetti; in 2001, several thousand gathered here in anti-war protests; and masses of bike riders regularly gather here to stage impromptu—and illegal—mass rides through the city to call attention both to what they call the city's unfair traffic laws, and the importance of turning to more ecologically conscious forms of transportation. A statue of Gandhi, a gift of the Indian people, calmly watches over these proceedings, a fresh wreath of flowers always draped about his neck. Along with the political folk, Union Square hosts the finest **greenmarket** in the city (on the northern and western sides of the park) every Monday, Wednesday, Friday, and Saturday. Most days you'll find about 100 vendors hawking locally grown produce, organic wines, cider, flowers, artisan cheeses, even gourmet pickles. It's a lot of fun to visit. Three playgrounds, a dog run, a very fine equestrian statue of George Washington, and a warm-weather bar/restaurant (p. 280) are also on-site.

While only intermittently political, **Washington Square Park** is nothing if not tuneful, and this has long been a place for amateur musicians to gather in groups, lugging along instruments for impromptu concerts each weekend. The round fountain in the center of the park serves as a stage for a dozen-or-so regular comedians, acrobats, impressionists, and dancers who are good enough to draw crowds of 100 people or more to their sidewalk shows. These go on year-round on weekends and often on Thursday and Friday afternoons as well, depending on the weather.

All Hail the Highline

For years, a secret, untamed garden hovered above the cityscape of Chelsea and Hell's Kitchen. Formed from the wild grass, flower, and weed seeds that randomly blew onto the tracks of a 1½-mile abandoned elevated railway, it became a hidden-in-plain-sight oasis for those New Yorkers brave (and limber) enough to scale the tressils. (It runs from Gaansevoort to 34th street over Tenth and Eleventh aves.) When the city started planning to tear down the historic rail structure (constructed 1929–34), a movement was born to save it and create a "grand public promenade," with easy access from the street, for all to enjoy. If all goes as planned, the **Highline** (as it's been dubbed) will soon be a 6½-acre river of green flowing through some of the boxier areas of the city. Meandering paths, some of the old railway tracks, and many of the same flora will (hopefully) give it a similar aura to what it had when it was a clandestine garden. Betting on the popularity of the park, many developers are erecting swank new buildings with gallery, restaurant, and even concert hall space, in its shadows. When it will open is anybody's guess (apparently there have been construction delays); I'm predicting no earlier than spring of 2009.

Entertaining as well are the intense chess matches (p. 188) played in Washington Square Park from noon to sundown on the southwest corner of the park (the regulars here are real sharks). Children will enjoy the two playgrounds on the north side of the park and watching the bocce ball players practice their ancient game on the south side of the park.

For information on Washington Square's long and eclectic history, go to p. 234 in chapter 8.

Tompkins Square Park (Avenues A to B btwn 7th and 10th sts.; ❶ to First Ave.) probably rates as New York's funkiest outdoor space. It's seen its share of political protests—in 1988 a stand-off between police and the homeless living here culminated in 5 days of small-scale rioting and charges of police brutality—but today it's better known for the very free expression it gives a home to. It's here every summer that the **Howl Festival** (www.howlfestival.com) is held. It's a spiky mix of spoken word performances and music, often political in nature. Best is the daily sidewalk catwalk of pierced, tattooed, fashion-forward locals—from punk to slacker to new boho, you'll see all sorts of fashion statements parading by. Incorporated as a park in 1878, Tompkins Square has a number of meditative green spaces, four playgrounds, a swimming pool, and a scattering of undistinguished monuments. It used to have a bandshell where an early version of the Grateful Dead made their East Coast debut, but that has since been torn down.

At the southernmost tip of Manhattan, **Battery Park** (West St. to Chambers St. on the Hudson River; www.bpcparks.org; ❹, ❺ to Battery Park) has been growing kudzulike for the past several decades and is now really a string of eclectic park spaces that hug the waterfront from just above the original Battery Park (where the ferry terminal for the Statue of Liberty is located) all the way up to Chambers Street. To read about the history of the original "battery," check out the walking tour on p. 215; there are a number of stirring war monuments to peruse. Walking Uptown from the original battery, you'll encounter expansive lawns, a promenade along the river that runs the length of the park, brand-new playgrounds, and a yacht marina. My favorite parts are the South Cove (on the Esplanade between First and Third places), an artfully varied collection of quays, bridges, and meandering walkways with great river views; and the Irish Hunger Memorial, a grassy outcropping direct from Ireland, complete with a real Irish stone fence.

VISIT-WORTHY PARKS IN
THE BRONX & BROOKLYN

Right next to the Brooklyn Museum, **Brooklyn Botanical Gardens** (1000 Washington Ave. at Empire Blvd.; ☎ 718/623-7200; $5 adults, $3 seniors and students; Apr–Nov Tues–Fri 8am–6pm, Sat–Sun 10am–6pm; Oct–Mar closes daily at 4:30pm; ❸, ❹ to Prospect Park, or ❷, ❸ to Eastern Pkwy.) is not only one of those necessary green safety valves, it's also quite an innovative garden in many ways. It was the first in the world to have a "children's garden," allowing local kids to develop green thumbs (it's still here, along with a fun play area for youngsters). There's also a "fragrance garden" for sight-impaired visitors, where everyone is encouraged to sniff and touch the plants; and an authentic Japanese garden, complete with a large pond, pagodas, and plants from that area of the world. The best time of year to visit is spring, when the gardens' many cherry trees are in bloom, though there are seasonal displays, both outdoors and in the on-site greenhouses, year-round.

An equal to the Brooklyn Botanical Gardens in both scope and interest, **The New York Botanical Gardens** ✦ (Bronx River Pkwy., at Fordham Rd.; ☎ 718/817-8700; $13 adults, $11 seniors and students, $5 children; Apr–Oct Tues–Sun 10am–6pm; Nov–Mar Tues–Sun 10am–5pm; ❹, ❹ to Bedford Park Blvd.) boasts the world's largest Victorian greenhouse, a "home gardening" section with classes and demonstrations for all the green thumbs out there, a children's garden and play center, and a 50-acre native forest. If there's any difference between the two gardens—they're both wonderful—it may be the wealth of hands-on programming here. Other than that, if you're interested in visiting one of these world-class gardens, you have a difficult choice to make.

A forest grows in Brooklyn, or at least it does in **Prospect Park** ✦✦ (at Grand Army Plaza; www.prospectpark.org; ❷, ❸ to Grand Army Plaza, ❺ to Seventh Ave., ❹ to Parkside Ave., ❸ to Prospect Park), the 575-acre greensward that many consider to be Frederick Law Olmsted's and Calvert Vaux's true masterpiece. While not as large as Central Park, it has nearly as many attractions, including a large lake where people pedal boats when the weather is agreeable; its own small zoo; the 90-acre Long Meadow (thought to be the largest meadow of any city park in the nation); a carousel; an ice-skating rink; and the nation's first urban Audubon Center, which is a wellspring of nature classes for both adults and children, year-round.

RECREATIONAL SPORTS CENTERS

Back in Manhattan, **Bowlmor Lanes** (110 University Place, btwn 12th and 13th sts.; ☎ 212/255-8188; www.bowlmor.com; $7.45–$8.95 per game, depending on hour, $5 for shoe rental; Mon 11am–3am, Tues–Wed 11am–1am, Thurs 11am–2am, Fri–Sat 11am–4am, Sun 11am–midnight; ❹, ❺, ❻, Ⓝ, Ⓞ, Ⓡ, Ⓛ to Union Sq.) is an outstanding bowling alley. Two facts you should know before you even attempt to bowl there: **1)** It's one of the most profitable bowling alleys in the United States, and **2)** It's also one of the oldest, having opened in 1938. That means dozens of people daily try to jam into a fairly small facility, with the result that lines can sometimes snake onto the street. Once inside, it's tremendous fun, from its "Down with Love"–style decor, to Monday's Night Strike party, which features glow-in-the-dark pins and a deejay spinning house music (unlimited bowling and shoe rental cost $20).

Chelsea Piers (btwn 23rd and 19th sts. at the Hudson River; ☎ 212/336-6800; www.chelseapiers.com; ❻, Ⓔ to Eighth Ave.) is New York's premiere indoor sports and recreation center—it really has no rival—located along the waterfront on the former luxury piers where the *Titanic* would have docked had she completed her voyage. Overhauled in the mid-'90s at a cost of $100 million, Chelsea Piers offers nearly every type of sports opportunity there is, but because many of these options are only available to those taking classes or members of the competitive leagues here, I'll list only those that are open to the short-term visitor. They are:

◆ **Bowling:** At the state-of-the-art **AMF Bowling** (☎ 212/835-2695; $5.50–$8.25 per person, per game, depending on the time of day; $4.50 for shoe rental), there are 40 lanes. In the evenings, management cranks up the pop music, puts out Day-Glo pins, and starts swirling the laser lights, making this a real party place. It's not as chic a place to bowl as the **Bowlmor Lanes** (see above)—yes, even bowling can be chic in New York—but it's more spacious than its rival and well maintained.

◆ **Golf:** The **Golf Club at Chelsea Piers** ($20 for 80–118 balls depending on the time of day; Oct–Mar 6:30am–11pm, Apr–Sept 6am–midnight) is perhaps the most popular attraction at the Piers and is crowded night and day. A 15-story-high net encloses the 200-yard driving range, which juts into the Hudson River on a pier, for some of the most scenic swinging anywhere in the state. The area for the players is covered and heated, meaning it's possible to tee off in all sorts of weather (though the range usually does close when it snows or during heavy rainstorms). In addition, the club has two swing-simulator booths where you can improve your play with a lesson.

◆ **Skating:** **Sky Rink** (☎ 212/336-6100; $10 adults, $7.50 children; $5 skate rental) comprises two massive indoor rinks that are open year-round, though most of their schedules are taken up by hockey leagues and ice-skating classes. Open skating is offered in the afternoons only, though if getting roughed up is your idea of a fun Saturday night, there's an open adult hockey game every Saturday beginning at 10:30pm. (Readers interested in outdoor ice-skating should go to p. 133 for information on the rink at Rockefeller Center; and p. 200 for details on Wollman Rink in Central Park.)

NEW YORK'S OUTSTANDING SPECTATOR SPORTS

When it comes to spectator sports, New York's die-hard fans can rarely be called "spectators." They yell, they stomp, they jerk forward as a ball is being hit or caught—in short, they're almost as entertaining to watch as the game itself. While we don't have the same level of hooliganism as the Brits do, the passions run just as high. Attending a game—particularly baseball, hockey, or football—is an adrenaline-pumping experience (especially if the home team wins) and highly recommended.

BASEBALL

It's been 8 l-o-o-o-ng years without a title for the New York Yankees and if you listen closely, you may hear the sound of quiet weeping in some quarters of the city. The star power of Jeter, Matsui, and Giambi is keeping seats filled nonetheless: So if you're planning to enjoy a session at **Yankee Stadium** (161st St. and River Ave., Bronx; ☎ 718/293-6000; www.yankees.com; ❹, ❷, ❹ to Yankee Stadium), purchase tickets online at the Yankees site well in advance; you'll also skip the line at the stadium that way, as you can print out your own ticket. If you don't have that much forethought (or a printer), it's often possible to get bleacher seats on the day of a game for about $14, and that's the best way to experience our, ahem, outspoken fans up-close-and-personal. There are no longer the same types of problems with drunkenness as existed a decade ago (the stadium now stops selling beer after the sixth inning), but things can get rowdy. The "House that Ruth Built" doesn't have a bad seat in it, but if you'd like something a bit closer in than the bleachers, I'd recommend the Upper Deck behind home plate, rather than front row outfield. It's cheaper ($30 vs. $48), you get a more panoramic view and, best of all, it usually sells out later. Attempting to get anything closer to the action may be futile, as those seats are usually sold out far in advance to season ticket holders—but you might try StubHub (see "StubHub," below). Very occasionally you'll see discount coupons for the games in the *Daily News*, but these are rare and usually only for early-season games. *Note:* The Yankees are currently building a new stadium adjacent to the old one and set to open in 2009. Sorry, I don't yet have info on the quality of seating there.

Persons visiting New York out of season (baseball is played Apr–Oct) can still visit this historic 1923 stadium on one of the **near-daily tours** ($20 adults, $15 for students and children) that take visitors into the clubhouse, the dugout, the press box, and Monument Park (where the team's historic greats are commemorated), and then right onto the field. Tours usually begin at 11am; a schedule is posted on the Yankees website (see above).

New York's secondary baseball team (and I know I'll receive angry letters for that disrespect) is the **Mets.** You can catch their home games at **Shea Stadium** (123–01 Roosevelt Ave., Flushing, Queens; ☎ 718/507-TIXX; http://newyork.mets.mlb.com; ❼ to Willets Point/Shea Stadium), and because their record doesn't usually compare with that of the Yanks (despite the valiant efforts of Pedro Martinez), you shouldn't have problems getting a seat for their games. Cheap seats go for between $5 and $23 depending on the game; to get out of the nosebleeds expect to pay between $38 and $62.

One other oddball place to watch games is Central Park, especially if you're into celebrity-spotting. Every Thursday afternoon from May through September, the Broadway Show league plays softball at the diamonds just south and to the east of Tavern on the Green. Along with techies and unknown chorus guys and gals, Denzel Washington, Matthew Broderick, and Hugh Jackman have played here during their turns on the Great White Way.

StubHub

An auction site for sporting events tickets, **StubHub** (www.stubhub.com) out-eBays eBay in this realm, usually offering more sporting events tickets at better rates than its larger competitor. And because the site gives a small percentage of the resale price to the sports teams involved, these transactions can in no way be construed as scalping. In fact, StubHub guarantees that the tickets will be usable. This is a top resource for game tickets, even for near-sold-out sporting events.

BASKETBALL

As any basketball fan knows, the **Knicks** (www.nyknicks.com) have suffered a huge decline over the past few years, and though fans hope that new coaching will bring about a revival, many have simply stopped attending games altogether. Which is good news for you, the visiting sports fan, as it means that you should be able to stroll up to the window at **Madison Square Garden** (Seventh Ave., btwn 31st and 33rd sts.; ☎ 212/465-6741; www.thegarden.com; Ⓐ, Ⓒ, Ⓔ, ❶, ❷, ❸ to 34th St.) and snag a good seat the day of the game at a reasonable price. The key here is to check the seating map carefully before you buy. There will often be $12 upticks in price for seats that are only a row apart and have an identical view of the action. The cheapest seats start at just $10 (and whenever you see Spike Lee courtside, know that either he or his publicist paid upwards of $2,000 for those seats).

For higher quality basketball, at even cheaper prices, you want to go with the dames. The **New York Liberty** are a gaggle of high-jumping, fast-scoring, strategy-savvy women led by such All-Stars as Becky Hammon and Elena Baranova. They play in the summer months May through fall. Bring your daughter and get a seat for just $10 at the top of the stadium, $15 to $25 a little farther down. Courtside seats are just $70 at these games.

FOOTBALL

The Meadowlands (50 State Rte. 100, Rutherford, NJ; ☎ 201/935-3900; www.meadowlands.com) is the stadium the **NY Jets** (www.nyjets.com) share with the 2008 Super Bowl champs, the **NY Giants** (www.nygiants.com), and because both teams usually play only eight games a season in their home stadium, games always sell out. The solution? You can show up and try to purchase a ticket on the spot from a scalper, but I'd turn instead to sites such as StubHub (see "StubHub," above) where fans trade tickets and stick within the legal $5 mark-up on price. When you're searching for a seat, take the weather into account. If it looks like it's going to be an ugly day, sacrifice the panoramic view for a more sheltered seat in the covered lower level. Blue skies and balmy breezes? Go with the upper level, which will give you a bigger view of the game (for less money, usually). More than 45 million fans have attended games here since the stadium opened in 1976.

HOCKEY

Hockey's another terrifically popular sport in the Big Apple (Canadian ex-pats perhaps?), with arguably the rowdiest fan base of the lot (so expect some shenanigans if you go to a game). **New York Rangers** games tickets tend to go quickly, and games do sell out. The top ticket price for a game at **Madison Square Garden**, where home games are played, is a whopping $1,004, but it's possible to pay much, much less in the upper level, where seats start at $40.

MARATHONS

The New York City Marathon is one of NYC's most exciting yearly spectacles and one of the world's great marathons, drawing 35,000 competitors. Runners visit each borough, crossing the finish line in Central Park, near Tavern on the Green, at approximately 68th Street. The marathon always takes place the first Sunday in November, beginning in the early morning, though you'll often see stragglers finishing up just as the sun is setting. You can see the marathon in many parts of Manhattan and in the other boroughs (visit www.nycmarathon.org to see the full route), but my favorite place to watch it is at Cat Hill in Central Park at approximately 76th Street, right off East Side Drive (you'll recognize it from the sculpture of the wild cat on the hill). It's not too crowded, and because it's at the top of a hill, you'll witness the heroic efforts of runners who have already gone nearly 26 miles, fighting to climb this last obstacle and finish the race.

TENNIS

Once a year, Gotham becomes the center of the tennis universe as thousands of fans descend on the Arthur Ashe Tennis complex for the **U.S. Open** (Corona Park, Queens; www.usopenseries.com; ➐ to Shea Stadium). And once you're in the gate, it's tennis lifestyle all the way, from the Polo store set up on the grounds, to fancy food courts dishing up sushi and pad Thai, to the 18 smaller courts where those who just happen to wander by can sometimes watch Roger Federer, Maria Sharapova, and the Williams sisters in their preliminary matches or warming up once the semifinals and finals are on. In fact you'll get the best views on the outside courts during the opening days of the tournament; the cheap seats in the main stadium are true nosebleeds, and though you won't have to contend with vendors clogging the aisles and blocking your view, you may want to invest in a pair of binoculars or opera glasses if you sit at the top.

The Open is played over the course of 2 weeks, starting at the end of August (on Aug. 25 in 2008) and not surprisingly, it's much easier to get tickets to the first week of play before the small fry have been weeded out. On the first 3 days, stadium seats cost as little as $22; later, the lowest prices for stadium seating is in the $50-to-$64 range for the cheapest seats, up to $80 for the finals. Grounds passes are sold for the first week for $46. These special tickets allow holders to roam the smaller courts and see as many preliminary matches as their hearts desire.

Tickets go on sale in early June (Amex holders and United States Tennis Association members get first crack at them), but except for the finals, the U.S. Open rarely sells out. You should be able to get seats or grounds passes for the first week within that week; for second-week play, you'll need to book ahead (2–3 weeks, to be safe).

Walkabouts

Enjoy a unique curbside view of the city's life and history

WHY SHOULD YOU CONSIDER TAKING WALKING TOURS OF MANHATTAN? Because they are a different sort of experience, each offering special rewards. They introduce you to the history of the city, up close and personal. They reveal the special essence of the city, and create memories that will last long after you have returned home. And unlike the motorcoach tours or a sightseeing boat, they introduce you to all this slowly and at your own speed. You teach yourself, so to speak, instead of accepting the memorized patter of the out-of-work actors who generally supply the spiel on escorted group tours.

In the pages ahead, you supply the feet and the eyes, and I supply the commentary. I've picked three neighborhood walks that will envelop you in the sweep of the city's history, architecture . . . and gossip. The tour of Lower Manhattan, the oldest area of New York City, obviously has the most historical resonance, but the Harlem tour touches on Revolutionary War history, along with 20th-century issues; and the tour of Greenwich Village and SoHo quickly moves from the Colonial era, through the early days of the Republic, to the Civil War, to the industrial era, and all the way to the art scene of the 1970s.

I'm willing to bet that one of these itineraries will be the highlight of your visit. And if you happen to be a resident, a walking tour of one of these special areas of Manhattan is a fine exercise for natives, too.

Walking Tour 1: Lower Manhattan

Start: National Museum of the American Indian (One Bowling Green, btwn State and Whitehall sts.; take ❹, ❺ to Bowling Green)

Finish: The Woolworth Building

Time: Allow approximately 2 hours, not including time spent in restaurants or shops

Best times: Weekdays, during the daytime so that you can take in the hustle and bustle of the area

Worst times: At night, when you won't be able to discern many of the sights

If you have time for only one walking tour of New York, make it Lower Manhattan. Not only is this the most historic part of the city—in fact, the city reached no farther than Wall Street for its first 100 years of existence—it also affords the best overview of architectural styles in the city. Buildings range from jazzy Art Deco structures, to pseudo-Greek temples, to the soaring glass rectangles of the "International Style" heyday, one rubbing up against the other like guests at a fantastic costume party where Martha Washington cha-chas uninhibitedly with Donald Trump. All the sites inhabit a compact, eminently walkable area.

More importantly, Lower Manhattan is the area of the city that has seen the most tragedy, having endured not one but four terrorist attacks over the years (I describe them below), terrible fires, epidemics, and a cruel occupation by the British during the Revolutionary War that left the city in rubble. The scars of these events, the weight of the tears shed, and the lives lost give this area a resonance and presence unlike those found any other place in the United States.

❶ Bowling Green Park

We begin our tour facing the city's first official park (est. 1733). Had you been a soldier during the British Colonial era, you would have been stationed at the fort that once stood here, Fort George, and likely you'd have passed your leisure time lawn bowling where the park now stands (hence the name Bowling Green Park).

On July 9, 1776, the Declaration of Independence was read aloud (near City Hall) and a small battalion of agitated colonists marched here to behead the statue of King George that stood in the center of the park. It had been erected just 5 years previously by many of these same men, in gratitude for the king's part in repealing the odious Stamp Act (the one that provoked the "no taxation without representation" movement). Though it can't be proven, legend has it that the lead statue was then melted down and used for cannon balls and bullets in the war against the British. The gate that rings the park is the original, one of the few Colonial structures of any sort left in Manhattan (when it was first erected, its spokes had royal crowns at their tips; these, too, were destroyed by the colonists).

Even earlier, the area that became the park was the site of New York's first great real estate deal: the "selling" of Manhattan by members of the Canarsie tribe (probably) to Peter Minuit of the Dutch East India Company, for 60 guilders (the equivalent of $24). It's a transaction that has been plagued by controversy for decades. Did the Indians know they were selling the island, or did they think that they were simply accepting shiny trinkets as part of a welcome ceremony? Were the Canarsie even in a position to sell it, as it had long been a communal hunting ground, used by a number of tribes? We'll never know the truth of the matter, but here is where it all likely happened; the event is marked by a small bas-relief sculpture on a flagpole in nearby Battery Park.

Look north to the great skyscrapers that now shadow the park. On your left, the building with the Egyptian motif (5 Broadway) was the headquarters of the White Star shipping line. It is here that distraught relatives came to learn the fate of their loved ones after the sinking of the *Titanic* (there's a famous photo of a stricken Jacob Astor exiting the building after learning that his son had perished). Across the street, to your right, is the former headquarters of Standard Oil, the company that made John D. Rockefeller his millions. As you step back out of the park you should be able to see the elaborate oil lamp at the top.

Walking Tour: Lower Manhattan

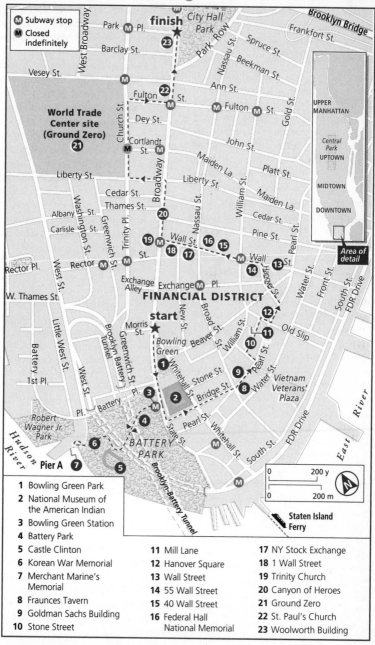

1 Bowling Green Park
2 National Museum of
  the American Indian
3 Bowling Green Station
4 Battery Park
5 Castle Clinton
6 Korean War Memorial
7 Merchant Marine's
  Memorial
8 Fraunces Tavern
9 Goldman Sachs Building
10 Stone Street

11 Mill Lane
12 Hanover Square
13 Wall Street
14 55 Wall Street
15 40 Wall Street
16 Federal Hall
   National Memorial

17 NY Stock Exchange
18 1 Wall Street
19 Trinity Church
20 Canyon of Heroes
21 Ground Zero
22 St. Paul's Church
23 Woolworth Building

Retrace your steps out of the park and gaze up at the

② National Museum of the American Indian

Designed by Cass Gilbert, the architect responsible for the Woolworth Building (which we'll visit later in this tour), this was one of the most important buildings in the city when it was built—the Alexander Hamilton U.S. Customs House. Before 1913, when the federal government instituted the personal income tax, the federal government's revenue came almost entirely from customs on goods imported into the States. And a full 75% of this revenue came from the Port of New York, where it was processed in this appropriately grand Beaux Arts colossus, completed in 1907, and comprising over 450,000 square feet of interior space.

It's a wedding cake of a structure, with dozens of bright white sculptures adorning the gray granite facade. Daniel Chester French was the sculptor—he also did the moving sculpture of Lincoln at the Lincoln Memorial—and his choice of symbols could be used as a treatise on the prejudices of Victorian America. The four women seated at the front represent the four "great" continents of the world. From left to right as you look at them, they are Asia, the Americas (South America, barely present, is tellingly represented by the Aztec-like structure that North America has her foot on), Europe, and Africa. America and Europe look full of vigor and purpose, but Asia has her eyes closed (perhaps in meditation?), and Africa—in a metaphor for her lack of vision and power?—is in a deep slumber. America is sheltering a new immigrant who crouches to her left, and the immigrant is pushing forward a wheel with wings on it, those of the Roman god Mercury, the divine overseer of commerce (a comment, some think, on the essential role immigrants were playing in the expanding economy).

At the top of the building are 12 more figures, this time meant to represent the great trading nations of history: Greece, Rome, Phoenicia, Genoa, Venice, Spain, Holland, Portugal, Denmark, England, France, and Belgium. Why Belgium, you ask? The official story is that during World War I, "vandals" carved BELGIUM across the shield of the figure that had originally been "Germany." No explanation has ever been given on how vandals could surreptitiously make such a big change to one of the most visible and heavily guarded buildings in the city.

If you have the time, go inside the building for a peek at the marvelous WPA murals in the rotunda (depicting the great conquistadors, ironic as the building now houses the National Museum of the American Indian); the staircase on the right as you enter (meant to evoke the look of the inside of a nautili shell); and in what is now the study center of the museum, the elaborate, imposing rows of teller windows where merchants would pay their Customs taxes.

You should be facing the museum, so take a right and cross the street to the larger park there, stopping at the little house that serves as an entry to the subway.

③ Bowling Green Station

This 1904 structure is one of only two surviving subway "control houses" in New York City. When the subway was first opened in 1904, all stations had these little houses; now riders simply descend a staircase directly from the sidewalk.

Enter Battery Park and walk to the large, partially crushed *The Sphere*.

❹ Battery Park

Named for the battery of guns the British kept here (trained on the river), this park is landfill, created immediately after the American Revolution. It has a long history as a military training ground, but in front of you is a non-military sight and one of the most moving in Lower Manhattan: *The Sphere,* designed by Fritz Koenig, a sculpture that once stood in the plaza area of the World Trade Center. When the towers came crashing down upon it, at a speed of more than 60 mph, *The Sphere* tore apart and many pieces were irreparably bent. It was reassembled and now rests here as a monument to the cause of world peace (which was also the original theme of the sculpture). *Note:* As we go to press, there's word that the Sphere may be moved, but no definite plans yet.

Make your way towards the water and you should come upon a round stone building, the spot where tickets are now sold for the ferry to Liberty and Ellis Island.

❺ Castle Clinton

Though it doesn't look like much now, this circular structure (it was taller in some earlier incarnations) has, over the years, been at the center of New York life. In 1807, the "West Battery," as it was then called, was built as a fort on a landfill island in the water off Manhattan to ward off British invasions; it never saw action—the Brits attacked Washington, D.C., instead during the War of 1812. In 1823, the federal government ceded the site (renamed Castle Clinton in 1817, in honor of the city's mayor, De Witt Clinton) to the city and it became an extremely popular entertainment center called Castle Gardens (the "Swedish Nightingale," Jenny Lind, was a headliner here in 1850) until 1855 when the space was transformed once more into the city's first immigrant processing center. Over eight million new arrivals, a full two-thirds of those who came to the United States at this time, spent their first hours in the United States here registering their names with the government, exchanging money, and getting information on jobs, medical care, and lodgings. In 1890, the vast number of immigrants—and the growing problem of outsiders scamming them—necessitated a move to a larger and more easily patrolled space, Ellis Island. The famed architectural team of McKim, Mead & White then stepped in and transformed the site into the nation's first aquarium, visited by about 90 million people until it was moved in 1941 to Coney Island. After the site stood empty for many years, the National Parks Service took it over and restored the Castle Clinton of the original fort.

Turn right to face the

❻ Korean War Memorial

Because so many nationalities fought in the Korean War, the government decided to erect a memorial celebrating the "Universal Soldier." The Welsh-born artist Mac Adams, who created the piece, does this neatly by showing only the outline of the soldier within the imposing obelisk of black granite; you, the viewer, fill in what the soldier looks like. Around the base of the monument are inscribed the nations that participated in this war.

Walk towards the water until you come to the

❼ Merchant Marine Memorial

Based on a famed photograph, taken by a German serviceman, of sailors on a sinking lifeboat after the attack on the S.S. *Muskogee* (off the east coast of the U.S.), this dramatic sculpture group commemorates the nearly 7,000 Merchant Marines who perished during World War II. It was created by Marisol Escobar, and it's interesting to visit at different times of the day: at low tide, you'll see the bottom figure from his knees up, by high tide he's drowning up to his neck in water.

If you have the time, walk farther around the park to see the other war memorials scattered here and there.

Retrace your steps and leave the park, walking around to the back of the National Museum of the American Indian on Bridge Street. Cross Whitehall Street and continue walking on Bridge away from the river until your reach

8 Fraunces Tavern (54 Pearl St., at the corner of Broad St.)

The bad news first: This is not what Fraunces Tavern actually looked like, but a hopeful reconstruction completed in 1904 and based on the architectural styles of the period (about 40% of the building is original). Nonetheless, it was here that the Sons of Liberty met on dozens of occasions to discuss plans for evicting the British. Once the Revolutionary War was over, Fraunces Tavern was the place where George Washington delivered his famous "Farewell to the Troops" and where Alexander Hamilton set up his first Office of the Treasury. Inside is a rather mediocre restaurant and an interesting museum (you can read more about it on p. 159).

On a more sobering note, in 1975 Fraunces Tavern was bombed by the Armed Forces of Puerto Rican National Liberation. Four people were killed and dozens injured. The choice of this site for the bombing had dual reasons: Not only

is it a symbol of American ideals, it is one of the few important historic buildings in New York that has a Caribbean connection, as Samuel Fraunces was an immigrant from the West Indies.

Look behind you and you'll see

9 Goldman Sachs Building

Directly across the street from the tavern is the headquarters of Goldman Sachs, the massive glass and brownstone skyscraper that cuts Stone Street in two. When it was being constructed, crews found the foundations of old **Governor Lovelace's Tavern,** another Colonial-era watering hole, and briefly seat of the Colonial government. In a compromise with local archaeologists, part of the site was left open with a glass-viewing pane atop it. If you walk around the perimeter of the skyscraper in the same direction that you've been going, you should be able to see these excavations through glass panels in the sidewalk (they're at the end of the rows of benches, one under the colonnade, one in the open air). Take a moment to read the plaques and gaze down.

Continue to walk north and then curve around the Goldman Sachs Building until you spot

10 Stone Street

Here you'll have a remarkably accurate snapshot of what the city looked like in about 1837. This narrow winding street (it's the next street west from Pearl St.) was the first to be paved in New Amsterdam and the only street that is thought to still be where the Dutch colonists originally placed it. All of the buildings were constructed in the period immediately following the great fire of 1835, which devastated the city, wiping out 20 square city blocks. Many blamed the volunteer firefighters of the time who, working in rival squads for cash payment, spent more time fighting one another than fighting the flames (Martin Scorsese's 2002 film, *Gangs of New York,* dramatically re-creates a similar firefighter battle).

The buildings we see today are classic Greek Revival structures of straight up-and-down brick with granite bases. They were built as counting houses and warehouses for local merchants. **57 Stone St.,** you'll notice, has a very Dutch step-like gable, added in 1908 by architect C. P. H. Gilbert as a nostalgic nod to New Amsterdam.

Continue to the middle of the street and then step to the left onto

⓫ Mill Lane

Mill Lane has the distinction of being the shortest street in Manhattan (and, yes, there was once a mill on this block). It was here, records show, that Peter Stuyvesant reluctantly surrendered the city to British troops in 1664, once he found that none of the pragmatic Dutch merchant-citizens of New Amsterdam wanted to stand and fight against the invaders (capitalism trumped patriotism—a battle would have hurt business, after all).

Take a break

Grab a sweet treat at the patisserie, **Financier** ★ **(62 Stone St.; 8am–8:30pm; $).** There are both indoor and outdoor tables, and every French delicacy you could want—from fruit tarts to Napoleons just oozing cream. Espresso, cappuccino, and soft drinks are also available.

At the end of Stone Street lies

⓬ Hanover Square

One of the only places in New York City to retain its "royalist" name after the American Revolution, it was named for the House of Hanover, from which the era's British monarchy was descended. Once the center of the social and political life of the city, this was where the colony's first newspaper was published, and the cotton exchange dominated one corner. When he was still considered a respectable citizen, notorious pirate Captain Kidd lived here in bourgeois splendor with his wife (they were known for their grand dinner parties). India House, on the west side of the square, is a perfectly preserved example of a brownstone banking house from the 1850s; it's now an expensive restaurant.

Continue walking to the uptown point of the triangle that is Hanover Square and hook a left onto Hanover Street. Walk until you come to

⓭ Wall Street

You are now standing at what was the boundary of the city during Dutch Colonial times. If you had been alive then, you'd be staring at a 9-foot-high wooden wall erected to keep out local Native Americans as well as British invaders, who were by then vying with the Dutch and French for land in the Americas. To your right, when you face north, would have been the largest slave market in the United States (approximately at the corner of Pearl and White sts.), a bastion of inhumanity that held more auctions than any other in the U.S. in the 18th century. Slavery was not fully outlawed in New York until 1827, making it one of the last two northern states to do so.

Take a left and walk to

⓮ 55 Wall St.

This building is one of the area's most impressive renovation jobs. Originally built to house the Merchant Exchange and finished in 1842, it was a grand example of Greek Revival architecture, most notable for the 12 massive columns that graced the front, each carved from a single block of stone. In 1907, the noted architectural firm of McKim, Meade, & White was hired to enlarge the space; instead of tearing it down and starting anew, as so many lesser architects would have done, they brilliantly built up, adding another level of columns to the second story (this time in the more ornamental Corinthian style) to harmonize with the first. The building is now a hotel, one of the poshest in the city.

Stroll a few steps west to

⑮ 40 Wall St.

New York's greatest monument to thwarted ambitions. Architect William Van Alen had a dream: He wanted to build the tallest building in the world, taller than the Woolworth Building (which held the record from 1917 to 1930). Problem was, his former partner and archrival H. Craig Severance had the same aspirations, and in the summer of 1929, at the height of the bubble that preceded Black Tuesday (the great stock market crash), they began a "race to the top," Van Alen at 40 Wall St., and Severance at the Chrysler Building. In a record 11 months, Van Alen completed 40 Wall St., then the Bank of Manhattan building, certain that the Chrysler building was completed and his structure would be the tallest. But once Van Alen finished construction, Severance administered the coup de grace that he'd been hiding in the elevator shaft of his building: the Chrysler Building's iconic, Art Deco spire, which added an unbeatable 125 feet onto the building. I can only imagine that Van Alen felt some small measure of satisfaction when the Chrysler's title was snatched from it one short year later by the Empire State Building. Take a moment to gaze up at 40 Wall;

it's still an impressive achievement and a beautiful building, with all of the ziggurat-like stepbacks (cascading layers) of the prototypical late '20s skyscraper.

Keep walking in the same direction until you get to the corner of Wall Street and Broad Street. Our next stop is

⑯ Federal Hall National Memorial

The most historically significant piece of land in the city. What you will see is a quintessential Greek Revival edifice, a modified version of the Parthenon, actually (can't get much more Greek than that!) that was completed in 1842. Note the statue of George Washington; it was here, perhaps on the very spot where the statue now stands, that George Washington took the oath of office to become president (though not in this actual building, but in an earlier one located on this spot). That monumental occasion would be enough to secure its place in history, but matters just begin there: The Bill of Rights was drawn up in this former British City Hall (transformed into "Federal Hall" when the Brits quit the city); the famous Zenger Trial (which helped secure freedom of the press) took place in a court in the hall; and before the Revolutionary War, the Stamp Act Congress met here and railed against "taxation without representation." If the building is open, do take a moment to step inside. You'll quickly see that despite its very square outward appearance there's a magnificent rotunda within, one of the loveliest public spaces in the city.

Note the austere, somewhat anonymous-looking building across the street from the hall; it was the headquarters of banker J. P. Morgan (the window of his former office is above the flagpole). If you look closely at the side of the building that faces Federal Hall, you'll notice that it is pocked with small indentations. These are the scars of the Financial District's first terrorist attack, which occurred in 1920. One bright and sunny morning (isn't it odd that these events always seem to occur on beautiful days?), a horse and carriage loaded with explosives parked here. Moments later a huge explosion shook the street, killing 31 people and wounding scores more. The blast was so powerful that all that was ever found of the horse was its horseshoe, and the police used this piece of evidence to trace the blacksmith who made it. He had vague recollections of shoeing the horse of an Italian man, and on this scanty piece of evidence the police (and press) decided that the blast must have been the work of Italian anarchists. No one was ever charged with the crime.

Walk around the corner until you're facing the

⑰ New York Stock Exchange

You are now gazing at the most famous (some would say infamous) financial institution in the world, the New York Stock Exchange. The building's towering columns, crowded ornamental pediment, and huge flag trumpet louder than any opening bell that this is a place of incomparable might and prestige (interestingly, it's a much more imposing building than the government's plainer Federal Hall across the street). In front of the Stock Exchange is a scraggly buttonwood tree, meant to invoke the buttonwood that New York's first traders stood under in 1792 when they met to begin brokering the Revolutionary War debt—the first stock market in America.

One odd fact about the Stock Exchange: Though it's associated in the popular imagination with Wall Street, its facade actually fronts Broad Street, not Wall.

Continue crosstown on Wall Street towards Broadway until you arrive at

⑱ 1 Wall St.

Take a moment to gaze at 1 Wall St., an absolutely stunning Art Deco building, once one of the priciest addresses in the city. The beautifully fluted, curtainlike limestone of the facade; the spiderweb pattern of the cathedral window above the entry; and the sumptuous, soaring lobby remind us of a time when such excess and exquisite workmanship were the norm for places of business (which were, literally, in the heady times before the Stock Exchange crash, conceived as temples of commerce).

Cross the street to

⑲ Trinity Church

This is actually the third Trinity Church to stand on this site. The first version was destroyed in the fire set by fleeing colonists in 1776 to thwart British occupiers (it ended up razing one-third of the structures in Manhattan). The second was poorly constructed, and its roof collapsed in a heavy snowstorm. But the third was a keeper and is considered by many to be one of the best, if not *the* best, Gothic Revival buildings in the United States.

Designed by Richard Upjohn, the religious structure can be seen as the stone and mortar embodiment of a theological movement that was sweeping the Anglican Church at that time, one that attempted to invigorate the Church by harkening back to its Catholic roots. Specifically, it paid heed to the idea that the Church needed a strong hierarchy to survive. So instead of creating a boxy, continuous space, like so many churches of the period (and like St. Paul's farther down Broadway), Upjohn used self-consciously medieval features designed to underscore the sacred nature of the clergy's space, including a chancel. Normally, in a Gothic cathedral, the chancel (which is the area behind the altar, reserved for the clergy and choir) is marked off by railings, but that idea was quite controversial in Democratic New York, so Upjohn created a subtle solution, raising this area a few feet above the ground, to give the feeling of an exalted place, without prominent barriers in place. Other Gothic features include the towering 280-foot spire, which was the tallest structure in the city until the piers of the Brooklyn Bridge were built; the flying buttresses; and the lovely stained-glass windows. The doors were modeled after Ghiberti's famous bronze doors for the Baptistery of Florence and were designed by noted American architect Richard Morris Hunt, though the sculptures on them were done by Austrian immigrant Karl Bitter. You can see the latter's self-portrait in the knoblike head sticking out of the lower-right-hand corner of the door; above him is Richard Upjohn and above him Richard Morris Hunt (who also designed the base of the Statue of Liberty).

Don't miss touring the graveyard, which holds the remains of many Revolutionary War–era New Yorkers, including countless babies and toddlers felled by the various epidemics that swept the city each summer during that period. Among the notables are Captain James Ludlow, who uttered the famous command, "Don't give up the ship," in the War of 1812; he's buried in the tomb that looks like a ship, on the southern side of the church, surrounded by a fence made from captured British cannons. Behind Lawrence and to the right a bit is the most famous tomb here, that of Alexander Hamilton; beside Hamilton is the grave of steamboat designer Robert Fulton.

Exit the churchyard and continue north toward Liberty Street and the

⑳ Canyon of Heroes

Look down as you amble along. You've entered what used to be known as the "Canyon of Heroes," and the brass plates with names and dates list the ticker tape parades that have been held along this swatch of Broadway. Had you been here on one of those occasions in the 1930s or '40s, the crowds around you would have been shoulder to shoulder, and above your head, hundreds of men would have been standing at the windows, showering the street with the long paper ribbons of stock market quotations that spewed from their machines, marking the dance of the stock market. Read the plates. The catalogue of names is an interesting reread of American history and political alliances; along with athletes, astronauts, and presidents, you'll find parades for the American hostages released from Iran (1982), pianist Van Cliburn (1958), and the controversial President Sukarno of Indonesia (1956).

Take a left on Liberty Street and walk to

㉑ "Ground Zero"

Take a moment to read the **"Wall of Heroes"** postings along the fence. To read more about this site, go to p. 130.

Facing north, take a right on Fulton Street and walk to

㉒ St. Paul's Church

Built in 1766, this is not only the oldest church in the city, but the only public space to be in continuous use since the Colonial era. The design of the church, with its Ionic columns and huge pediment, was based on that of St. Martin-in-the-Fields in London, though I think the overall effect of this church is not nearly as graceful. Still, the church is redolent with history: George Washington had a pew here (now marked by a plaque), and he came directly here after his inauguration to pray and give thanks.

The church miraculously survived a rain of fiery metal when the Twin Towers collapsed, and served as a focal point for the volunteer effort that ensued as hundreds of people came from all over the world to search for survivors and then human remains. Many slept at St. Paul's, on the pews or in cots, and took their meals here; an exhibition detailing the saga of these volunteers is housed at the rear of the church.

Continue walking up Broadway until you reach the

㉓ Woolworth Building (233 Broadway, btwn Barclay Street and Park Place, opposite City Hall Park)

From tragedy to triumph. We end our tour in front of what is arguably the most dramatic skyscraper ever built, a lacy late-Gothic tower that goes straight up, with none of the stepbacks of the sleek Art Deco skyscrapers that were to follow it. Instead, architect Cass Gilbert took his inspiration from Rouen Cathedral in France, building directly to the sky and covering the facade with snarling gargoyles, sharply angled flying buttresses, and spires, all faced in creamy terra cotta. As F.W. Woolworth intended, it was the tallest building in the world from the year it was built (1913) all the way until 1930. Woolworth, an inveterate collector of nickels and dimes, paid for the building in cash.

The interior is as grand as the exterior, with a vaulted mosaic ceiling, glowing gold-leafed cornices, and humorous gargoyles of Woolworth counting his coins and Cass Gilbert embracing a model of the building. Unfortunately, the lobby has been closed to the public since 9/11, but catching a glimpse of this beautiful interior space is worth getting yelled at. I've been able to manage a good minute and a half of gazing before security guards have shooed me out.

Walking Tour 2: Harlem

> **Start:** 138th Street and Amsterdam Avenue (❶ Train to 135th St.)
>
> **Finish:** The Lenox Lounge
>
> **Time:** Allow approximately 3½ hours, not including time spent in restaurants or shops (or divide the tour in half—see below—for a shorter walk)
>
> **Best times:** Tuesday through Sunday in the daytime
>
> **Worst times:** At night, as you won't able to see the architecture clearly

More than in any other place in the city, you need to have a strong imagination and social sense to really enjoy touring Harlem. The tragic fact is that much of what made this area unique, lively and . . . well, Harlem, during the fabled Jazz Era (aka The Harlem Renaissance), crumbled beneath the wrecking ball decades ago. What you do see here—the wide avenues, the rows of brownstones, the elegant apartment buildings—are somewhat an accident of history, the physical face of an area that housed a people, but wasn't necessarily "of" that people (I'll explain below). But despite all this, Harlem remains the African-American capital of the United States (sometimes called the "capital for Africans throughout the world"), a one-of-a-kind area with much to recommend it. Architect and author Zevilla Jackson Preston best sums up the appeal of the area in the book *HarlemWorld*, in which she writes, "Ultimately it is the energy on the street, the beat on the street—all of the beautiful black people on the streets—that make the experience unique."

Harlem was settled by a number of different groups over the years—Dutch farmers first, followed by their British counterparts, then poor Irish and Italian immigrants. But development of the area only took off in the years just prior to 1904, when the city's first subway line opened, a 9½-mile snaking tunnel, connecting Lower Manhattan with points as far north as 145th Street. In anticipation of this event, an unprecedented housing boom hit the neighborhood, with developers slapping up Victorian row house after row house for the crowds of upwardly mobile immigrants—middle-class Jews and Germans, pri-

> " Harlem is the Negro metropolis and as such is everywhere known. In the history of New York, the name Harlem has changed from Dutch to Irish to Jewish to Negro: but it is through this last change that it has gained widespread fame. "
>
> —James Weldon Johnson, 1917

marily—they were certain would soon flood this newly commutable neighborhood. What they didn't anticipate were recessions and panics in 1893, 1907, and 1910, which deflated the housing market; and the development of large numbers of homes on the Upper West Side.

Because of these miscalculations, property owners were left with hundreds of unrentable homes and soon began doing what nobody else had done in the history of the United States: renting or selling brand-new, often beautifully appointed buildings to the race that had, until that point, always made do with the tumble-down, ghetto housing no other group would accept. In 1905, a pioneering real-estate agent named Philip Payton persuaded a white landlord to rent him 31 W. 133rd St. so that he could re-lease it to African Americans. The landlord accepted the offer because Payton promised to pay far more than the going rate, a substantial $5 more per tenant per month (a lot of money in those days). Several other white landlords panicked and bought the buildings in order to evict the black tenants, but by then it was too late. Payton had the funding to buy several other buildings, and black migration into the area began in earnest.

So what you'll see in Harlem are homes and businesses that were not created by or for African Americans. These lovely buildings, however, did allow for a standard of living and security, primarily in the '20s, '30s, and '40s, that was unprecedented for African Americans living in the United States.

Another thing you won't see in Harlem today are the Jazz Era nightclubs and theaters for which the area was famed. Tragically, those historic sites were torn down. But we will visit places where the great political figures of Harlem, men such as Alexander Hamilton, Malcolm X, Eubie Blake, and Marcus Garvey lived, worked, and made history.

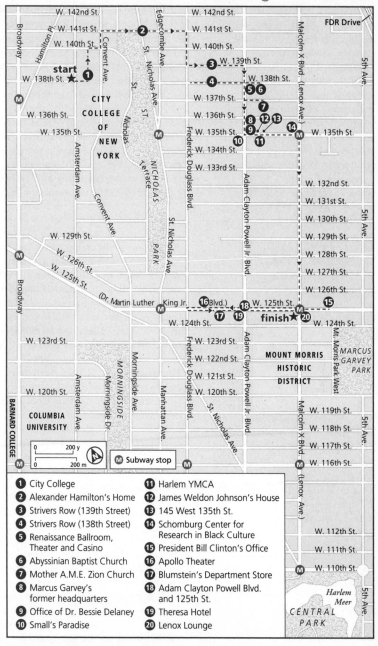

1 City College
2 Alexander Hamilton's Home
3 Strivers Row (139th Street)
4 Strivers Row (138th Street)
5 Renaissance Ballroom, Theater and Casino
6 Abyssinian Baptist Church
7 Mother A.M.E. Zion Church
8 Marcus Garvey's former headquarters
9 Office of Dr. Bessie Delaney
10 Small's Paradise
11 Harlem YMCA
12 James Weldon Johnson's House
13 145 West 135th St.
14 Schomburg Center for Research in Black Culture
15 President Bill Clinton's Office
16 Apollo Theater
17 Blumstein's Department Store
18 Adam Clayton Powell Blvd. and 125th St.
19 Theresa Hotel
20 Lenox Lounge

And now is an excellent time to visit, as the homogeneity of the neighborhood has been changing of late, with more and more "downtowners" of all races moving into Harlem, drawn by the beauty of its historic buildings, plummeting crime rates, and, most importantly, the relatively lower cost of living up here. According to Douglas Elliman Real Estate, a 4,500-square-foot town house in Harlem sells for $1.5 million today; a town house of a similar size in Greenwich Village would go for at least $7 million. Visit now before the neighborhood loses more of its character (and current residents).

A note about this tour: Harlem is the largest neighborhood in Manhattan by far, stretching from approximately 116th Street all the way up to the river. The walking tour I've devised, therefore, is a lengthy one divided by a subway ride in the middle. If you're ambitious, you can do the whole thing in an afternoon; or simply limit yourself to one half, starting either at the beginning and ending before the subway ride (stop 13); or going directly to 125th Street to begin your tour at stop 14.

---

① City College (138th St. and Amsterdam Ave.)

We'll start at Harlem's own City College, established in 1847 (the oldest college in today's City University of New York, known to locals as CUNY) as the "Free Academy," with a mandate to educate the children of immigrant and working-class New Yorkers. In 1897 it moved to this site, changed its name to the present one, and built itself a Gothic quadrangle a la Harvard or Yale, a symbolic way of saying that this institution of higher learning for New York's "underclass" was just as good, if not better, than those more prestigious universities (and it proved that point in years to come). But though the Gothic buildings of City College have all of the requisite spires, lacy stonework, and arch gargoyles, they don't look like any Gothic structure you've ever seen before, do they? Looming and dark, like buildings from the kingdom of Mordor in *Lord of the Rings,* these halls were created from mottled black schist (Manhattan bedrock), a dense, 5-million-year-old rock hard enough to bear the weight of all the heavy skyscrapers that were soon to emerge downtown.

At the time of the college's construction these blocks were abundant and cheap, having been recently excavated from the nearby Broadway subway line. You won't see this type of schist used in this quantity on any other major structure in New York. The original buildings were designed by George Post, the architect of the New York Stock Exchange (see p. 219 for more on this building).

Since its inception, City College has been a remarkable center of learning, its policy of giving free tuition to gifted scholars (in place until 1977) helping to draw the brightest students in New York. Scientist Jonas Salk, who invented the polio vaccine, studied here, as did Supreme Court Justice Felix Frankfurter, lyricists Ira Gershwin and Yip Harburg, Colin Powell, former Mayor Ed Koch, Pulitzer-Prize winning novelist Oscar Hijuelos, muckraking journalist Upton Sinclair, and many others. In all, City College has nine Nobel Prize winners among its alumni, more than any other public university in the nation.

Wander down the hill (you'll be on the top as you enter through the college

A short detour around Sugar Hill

If you have time, instead of descending the hill leading away from Hamilton Grange immediately, you may want to stroll around "Sugar Hill," the surrounding area, so named because this is where African Americans with money, or "sugar," resided in the 1930s and '40s, living the "sweet life." Duke Ellington had a home here, as did Ethel Waters, Lena Horne, Thurgood Marshall, and Ralph Ellison.

gate), and take a closer look at the gargoyles in the archways of the buildings—these are caricatures of students and professors engaged in the subjects each hall was meant to house. Take a left when you reach the street at the bottom of the hill and walk towards the Convent Avenue gate.

Follow the signs to Hamilton Grange. If you miss the signs, simply walk out the gate and downhill on Convent Avenue until you see the large statue of Alexander Hamilton.

❷ Hamilton Grange

I'm at a bit of a loss to direct you at this point, because the **home of Alexander Hamilton** (Wed–Sun, 9am–5pm; free admission), hero of the American Revolution and first secretary of the treasury, is scheduled to be moved from its current location sometime in 2008 or 2009. So when you read this, you'll either be able to visit it at 141st Street and St. Nicholas Avenue or it will be closed to visitors.

If it is open, take the tour, as it's an intriguing place, the home Hamilton retreated to, in disgrace, after his adulterous affair with a woman named Maria Reynolds was exposed in a Republican newspaper. Seeking to ease the strain on his marriage and appease his wife, Elizabeth (who grew up on a grand country estate), he transferred his family to this midsize farm, named Hamilton Grange for his ancestral

manor in Scotland, 8 miles from the center of the city. Most days he traveled 2 hours by coach to his work in "the city," making him one of New York's first commuters. But distance didn't keep him out of trouble. On July 11, 1804, after living at the Grange only 2 years, he was mortally wounded in his famous duel with Vice President Aaron Burr. He died the next day.

The building is the oldest in New York, an elegantly simple, wooden Federalist-style farmhouse. Step inside to catch the video on Hamilton's life, and see a bit of the house. The first floor is where the reception rooms would have been, but these were moved to the second floor (which housed the bedrooms in Hamilton's day). The Louis XVI–style chairs are original; most of the other furnishings are simply period pieces.

Walk down 141st Street to Frederick Douglass Boulevard, past Hamilton Terrace, St. Nicholas Avenue, and Edgecombe Street (this will be your longest walk of the tour). Turn right at Frederick Douglass Boulevard make a left at 139th Street.

❸ Striver's Row

You have now reached "Striver's Row," one of the most famous neighborhoods in Harlem, actually comprised of four rows of houses on 138th and 139th streets. The neighborhood was the brainchild of developer David H. King (he'd earlier overseen the construction of the pedestal for the Statue of Liberty), who had the dream of creating a dignified neighborhood for people of modest means. So he purchased 9 acres of land from the Equitable Insurance Company, and bought all of the building materials at once and in bulk, thus obtaining reasonable prices for the very finest of woods, brick, stone, and other materials. In a creative move, he hired not one but three architectural firms for the project. Each chose a different architectural style but kept the scale of the buildings the same, creating one of the most harmonious and interesting-looking cityscapes in Manhattan.

As you walk east on 139th Street, look right to take in the eight row houses designed by architects Bruce White and Clarence Luce, built between 1891 and 1893 (buildings #202–252). There was a fascination in the 1890s with all things Colonial, and that's reflected here in the traditional stoops and measured proportions of these brick buildings. On the other side of the street are 32 even lovelier homes, done in buttery sandstone. Famed architect Stanford White designed these himself in neo-Italian Renaissance style (horizontal lintels over the windows, circular ornamentation across the facade).

You'll note that the block is punctuated every so often by gates that lead to a small back alley. King felt that residents would be willing to give up a traditional backyard for a back alley where trash could be collected and deliveries made. As a result, this is one of the very few streets in the city that is never disfigured in the early morning by big garbage cans and plastic sacks of trash. On 138th Street (our next stop), many of these gates still read: PRIVATE ROAD: PLEASE WALK YOUR HORSES.

So all of this innovation and quality should have been a sweeping success for King, right? Wrong. He sold only nine houses, and in 1895 a national depression forced him to sell the remaining ones back to Equitable, his mortgagee. Most of the homes remained empty until 1919, when Equitable, after many years of refusing to do so, finally began selling the homes to African-American buyers.

As you stroll along, look out for the homes of the "Father of the Blues," composer **W.C. Handy** (232 W. 39th St.); orchestra leader **Fletcher Henderson** (228 W. 139th St.); and famed boxer **Harry Wills** (245 W. 139th St.). Though Wills was the best boxer of his day, he was never allowed to vie for the heavyweight title because of racism—champion Jack Dempsey, not wanting to fight a black man, paid Wills a forfeit of $50,000 rather than enter the ring with him.

Turn right on Adam Clayton Powell, Jr. Boulevard and make a right onto

④ 138th Street

Architects Edwin R. Will and J. Averit Webster are responsible for the look on the second block of Striver's Row—the north side of the street filled with Queen Anne–style domiciles, the south all neo-Renaissance. Among the notables housed on the block were songwriter **Eubie Blake** (236 W. 138th St.) and the **Black Swan Recording Company** (257 W. 138th St.). Black Swan was the first company to make records by African-American artists, scoring big hits with Ethel Waters and Fletcher Henderson. Ironically, it was the success of these records that ultimately led to the company's demise—mainstream companies, sniffing cash, started publishing recordings by African-American singers and musicians.

Though I've constantly mentioned the famous people who lived here, this really was home, for most of its existence, to lower-middle-class African Americans: teachers, janitors, bank clerks, and waiters. Many lived in the boarding houses that these homes soon became, but all were thought to be "striving" to better themselves—hence the name "Strivers Row."

Walk back towards Adam Clayton Powell, Jr. Boulevard and cross the street. On the corner of 138th, look up to see what remains of the famed

5 Renaissance Ballroom, Theater, and Casino

From the 1920s through the 1950s, this now-decrepit, boarded-up building on the corner was a center of Harlem nightlife, a club where residents could not only work (as they did at the "whites only" Cotton Club) but also party, as the casino was open to all. Music was provided by, among others, famed bandleaders Chick Webb and Fletcher Henderson. Built by Afro-Caribbean owners, another rarity at that time, its gimmick was an in-house basketball squad that played with portable baskets in the ballroom. Called the Rennys, it was the first African-American basketball team anywhere, precursors to the Harlem Globetrotters and one of the winningest teams ever (it won 80% of the nearly 3,200 games it played before disbanding).

Walk east towards the yellow sign that says BUMP AHEAD until you come to the

6 Abyssinian Baptist Church (136–142 W. 138th St.)

Abyssinian Baptist was founded in protest. In 1808, a group of free Negroes left the First Baptist Church of New York, angered by its segregated seating policy. With the help of Ethiopian merchants, they formed their own church downtown, which pastor Clayton Powell, Sr. eventually moved to Harlem. Powell's son, Clayton Powell, Jr., took his place in 1937, and the church remained at the forefront of the then nascent civil rights movement thanks in large part to Powell, Jr.'s legendary oratorical skills and community activism. In 1944, Powell, Jr. became the first African American to represent Harlem (or any other district in New York State, for that matter) in the U.S. Congress and served there until 1970, eventually becoming chair of the Education and Labor committees. His career was cut short by a corruption scandal, and though he was ultimately cleared by the Supreme Court, he lost his seat to Charles Rangel, who still holds it today. Later pastors of the Abyssinian—Samuel DeWitt Proctor (a mentor to Dr. Martin Luther King, Jr.) and Calvin O. Butts, Jr.—also were heavily engaged in the civil rights movement and local politics. Today, this is the largest black congregation in the United States.

The unimaginative neo-Gothic building that houses the church was created by architect Charles W. Bolton, and completed in 1920 (and it's a sign of those times that this all-black church put up stained glass featuring blond-haired, blue-eyed angels).

Before you walk on, look across the street to 133 W. 138th St., where blues singer Alberta Hunter (1895–1984) lived. She was an extremely successful entertainer from the 1920s through the 1940s; in fact she was the first black singer to be backed by a white band. She recorded and performed music with Fats Waller, Louis Armstrong, Bessie Smith, and Fletcher Henderson, and toured with the U.S.O. during

World War II. In 1959, she quit music to study nursing, working in that profession for the next 20 years, until a comeback in 1982 led to a brief but stellar cabaret career before her death at the age of 84.

Retrace your steps to Adam Clayton Powell, Jr. Boulevard and take a left on the corner, going south to 137th Street. Take another left and walk to

7 Mother A.M.E. Zion Church (140–148 W. 137th St.)

Founded in 1796, Mother Zion Church is the oldest black church in New York State and was one of the stops along the Underground Railroad (legend has it that it sheltered runaway slave Frederick Douglass). In 1850, when the church was located in Lower Manhattan, 1,500 people gathered there to protest the capture of an escaped slave named James Hamlet. The crowd managed to raise $800 to free Hamlet and keep him from being sent back to Maryland. Harriet Tubman, Sojourner Truth, and Paul Robeson were all members of the congregation. This is the fifth home for "Mother Zion," and one of the few major churches in Harlem to have been designed by an African-American architect, George W. Foster, Jr.

Walk back to Adam Clayton Powell, Jr. Boulevard and turn left, then head south to

8 2305 Adam Clayton Powell, Jr. Blvd. (btwn 136th and 135th sts.)

Though his legend has dimmed in recent years, in the 1920s and '30s Marcus Garvey was one of the most controversial, colorful, and important figures in Harlem and across the Americas, the founder of the first black nationalist movement the U.S. had ever seen. Called the Universal Negro Improvement Association, it was located on the second floor of this building. UNIA advocated economic self-sufficiency for African Americans and, ultimately, a return to Africa, which Garvey hoped would one day be one vast empire, controlled by Negroes (rather than colonial whites).

Though Garvey was unsuccessful in his goal of shipping large numbers of African Americans back to Africa, his Negro Factories Corporation at one point employed hundreds of workers across Harlem; and branches of the UNIA in other parts of the United States and the Caribbean were also successful in creating black-owned businesses of many types. Garvey was arrested on trumped-up charges of mail fraud in 1923 and deported in 1927. He died penniless in London several years later, but his ideas inspired a generation of American and African leaders.

Walk a few steps south to

9 2303 Adam Clayton Powell, Jr. Blvd.

At the age of 102, Dr. Bessie Delaney and her sister Sadie became national celebrities, thanks to their best-selling autobiography, "Having Our Say." The daughters of a former slave, the two women were both college graduates, with Bessie spending the majority of her life practicing dentistry in this very building. Always socially aware, Bessie was known in the neighborhood for her reasonable rates: In fact, she didn't raise her prices for more than 30 years.

Pause for a moment at the

⑩ **Corner of 135th Street and Adam Clayton Powell, Jr. Boulevard**

You are standing on the spot that once was the heart of Harlem. Diagonally across from you, the castlelike building that is now oddly topped by a middle school (Thurgood Marshall Academy) was once Smalls Paradise, one of Harlem's most popular nightclubs from the 1920s to the 1940s, attracting a crowd of mixed races and some of the top jazz musicians in the city. Malcolm Little, later known as Malcolm X, worked here briefly as a waiter until he was fired for giving the number of a prostitute to a customer, thus beginning his downward plunge into criminal activities (before his conversion to Islam). His experience is detailed in his renowned autobiography. In the 1960s, basketball star Wilt Chamberlain bought the place and briefly brought it back to life as "Big Wilt's Small's Paradise."

Down the street from Smalls at 244 W. 135th St. was the headquarters of the National Association for the Advancement of Colored People (NAACP). It was here that W. E. B. DuBois edited *The Crisis* (1909–1934), the monthly NAACP magazine, which at its peak had over 100,000 subscribers. Along with DuBois's searing editorials, *The Crisis* was the first major magazine to publish the works of Langston Hughes and James Weldon Johnson. In 1917, the NAACP organized a famous silent march in which 10,000 people walked down Lenox Avenue to protest the East St. Louis Race Riots in which 200

African Americans were killed and over 6,000 burned out of their homes. Walked in dignified silence, this march is widely seen as one of the precursors to Dr. Martin Luther King, Jr.'s peaceful marches in the 1960s.

Turn left and head east down 135th Street, stopping in front of the

⑪ **YMCA (180–181 W. 135th St.)**

It's difficult to underestimate the importance of the YMCA to Harlem. Its hotel facilities housed many prominent visiting African Americans who were excluded from white hotels downtown (including Langston Hughes, when he first arrived, and James Baldwin). The earlier branch (at 181 W. 135th St., on the south side of the street), had a renowned theater program that trained a number of black performers, including Eartha Kitt, Sidney Poitier, James Earl Jones, and Cicely Tyson. And in the gyms you'd often find baseball greats Willie Mays and Jackie Robinson working with local youth (now, how many Ys can boast that?).

Next to the YMCA is

⑫ **187 W. 135th St.**

Poet, scholar, lawyer, composer, and NAACP leader James Weldon Johnson lived here between 1925 and 1938. The first African-American lawyer admitted to the Florida bar, the multi-talented Weldon authored "Lift Every Voice and Sing," which is known as the African-American National Anthem; and Teddy Roosevelt's campaign song, "You're all right, Teddy!" (for which he was rewarded with posts as consul to Venezuela and Nicaragua).

Take a few more steps until you're standing in front of

⑬ **145 W. 135th St.**

In 1911, another barrier was broken when Reverend Hutchinson Bishop of

St. Philip's Episcopal Church persuaded the owners of the row of tenements you see before you to sell them to him for his parishioners. Bishop was a light-skinned man, the developer thought he was white, and soon nearly half a block of formerly restricted real estate was in the hands of black homeowners. The buildings were sold for $640,000, the largest real-estate transaction by an African American in the city's history up to that point. Though the paper, the *Harlem Home News,* entreated homeowners to "wake up and get busy before it is too late to repel black hordes," more and more African Americans came to Harlem and by the 1920s, 70% of the blacks living in New York City were in Harlem.

At the end of the block, on the corner of Lenox Avenue, stop in front of the

⑭ Schomburg Center for Research in Black Culture

This groundbreaking branch of the New York Public Library, the largest repository for African-American documents and artifacts in the world, was founded by Arturo Schomburg of Puerto Rico. When in elementary school, Schomburg asked his teacher why they never learned anything of the black history of Puerto Rico. His teacher responded that blacks had never done anything worth studying, and he vowed to prove her wrong. When the N.Y. Public Library bought his collection (and brought him on to manage it), it consisted of 5,000 items; today, the Schomburg has more than five million.

If you have a moment, enter the building and take in whatever special exhibition the center has on tap (they're usually quite well done). Langston Hughes asked that his ashes be buried in a library, and you'll find them here, in the main entry hall.

You can end your walking tour here, or you can hop a ❷ or ❸ train (or stroll) downtown to 125th Street. From the subway station, walk west (the numbers should be descending) to

⑮ 55 W. 125th St.

Do you hear the faint whine of a saxophone? That could mean that Harlem's most famous tenant, former President Bill Clinton, is in his office on the top floor of this out-of-place high-rise building. You may remember that he decided to move to Harlem after a public outcry over the taxpayer-supported rent on his proposed Carnegie Hill office space (a whopping $850,000 per year, more than all of the other presidential offices combined) sent him scurrying uptown. He pays a little over $350,000 a year here. It is, of course, highly appropriate that he's here, as Harlem is one of the Business Empowerment Zones his administration created. The decor of the office was created by Sheila Bridges, who also designed for rap mogul Sean "Puffy" Combs.

Two blocks from the office is **Mount Morris Park,** named for Gen. Roger Morris in honor of the very first American victory in the Revolutionary War. It was in the vicinity of where you're standing now, on Sept. 16, 1776, that George Washington engaged in what he called a "brisk little skirmish" with the Redcoats. Just 1 month earlier, the largest British expeditionary fleet in history had sailed into New York Harbor, bringing with it 21,000 troops, a full 40% of all of the men engaged by the Royal Navy at that time. In quick order, these trained soldiers slaughtered approximately 2,800 American militiamen at the Battle of Brooklyn, forcing Washington to escape Brooklyn under cover of night and hightail it to the northern reaches of Manhattan. At the small battle on this site, called the Battle of Washington Heights, enemy buglers taunted the colonists by playing the call that traditionally ended a foxhunt. Enraged, Washington called for reinforcements and drove the Redcoats back to what is now the Upper West Side. It was the first time his soldiers had won an engagement and did much to boost morale. It also bought Washington the time to escape Manhattan altogether and "live to fight another day."

Retrace your steps and keep walking west on 125th Street until you reach Adam Clayton Powell, Jr. Boulevard. Cross the street and continue walking west; you're now strolling the

⑯ "Great Black Way"

Like its counterpart downtown (Broadway's "Great White Way"), this was the theater district of Harlem. Only a few of these great show palaces still exist, but right in front of you should be the most famous and influential: **The Apollo Theater** (253 W. 125th St.). A whites-only burlesque house until 1934, it changed its policy and its lineup, becoming a music hall in January of that year and introducing the legendary "Amateur Night" a few months later. Among the many big names who jump-started their careers at Amateur Night: Sarah Vaughn, Lauryn Hill, James Brown, and most famously Ella Fitzgerald, who was planning to dance but fortuitously changed her mind backstage right before she went onstage. Amateur night continues here every Wednesday night at 7:30pm, and it's as raucous as ever, with wild cheers for the performers the audience enjoys and painfully cruel shouts and boos for those who get the axe.

Look across the street to what is left of

⑰ Blumstein's Department Store

When it opened its doors in 1900, this was the neighborhood's largest and most exclusive store, built at a cost of $1 million (notice the beautifully worked copper ornamentation on the facade, a mix of Art Deco and Spanish Renaissance in its patterning). In 1934, the Urban League began a campaign, spearheaded by Reverends John H. Johnson and Adam Clayton Powell, Jr., to boycott and picket the store until it changed its hiring practices. Up until that point, though the vast majority of its clientele was African American, Blumstein's refused to hire any black store clerks (a particularly maddening policy as this was the Great Depression and jobs were scarce). The action lasted 2 months, with picketers carrying signs with the simple but effective request DON'T BUY WHERE YOU CAN'T WORK. Blumstein's finally relented, hiring 34 African-American women as clerks. Dr. Martin Luther King, Jr., often spoke of this strike in his speeches, as an example of the power of nonviolent protest.

In 1958, Dr. King himself was at the center of history at Blumstein's. He was seated at a table signing copies of his book *Strides Towards Freedom* when an African-American woman named Izola Ware Curry got to the front of the line. After asking, "Are you Martin Luther King?" she pulled a letter opener out of the book she was carrying. Shouting "You Communist, you Communist!" she stabbed him in the chest. Dr. King was rushed to Harlem Hospital with the blade still in (had it been removed he would have bled to death) and underwent surgery. The next morning the *New York Times* reported that had King sneezed, he would have died, as the blade was touching his aorta. From his hospital bed, King issued a letter of forgiveness to Wade, who was committed to an insane asylum for the act (she had had a long history of mental instability).

Retrace your steps and walk back to Adam Clayton Powell, Jr. Boulevard, crossing the street so that you're standing on the corner of the block that houses the massive State Office Building.

⑱ Adam Clayton Powell, Jr. Boulevard and 125th Street

Abuzz with history, this intersection is one of the most important in Harlem. Look over first at the windswept northwest corner, the spot where Malcolm X spent many long hours lecturing to Harlem residents on behalf of the Nation of Islam. His message—"We are blacks first and everything else second"—was such a powerful one, and he was such an effective orator that before he left the NOI that organization had nearly half a million members (it dwindled rapidly after his resignation). His message, which rejected nonviolence and condemned integration as cultural suicide, was a controversial one that went directly against the goals of the NAACP, the largest civil rights organization of the time.

Now, gaze up at the former

⑲ Hotel Theresa (2090 Adam Clayton Powell, Jr. Blvd.)

If your olfactory glands have any imagination, you may detect a hint of Cuban cigar smoke in the air. In 1960, a young Fidel Castro was scheduled to speak at the United Nations but no hotel in town would take him and his contingent. After he threatened to set up camp on the lawn of the United Nations, the government ordered the city hotels to accommodate him, but Castro got into an argument with the hotel he had picked, the Shelburne. So, after a conversation with Malcolm X, he moved up here to the Hotel Theresa, the tall white building with geometric

patterns climbing up its facade (you may want to cross the street to get a better look). It was a dramatic gesture, and one he hoped would show his solidarity with Black Americans (and perhaps encourage a few to register with the Communist Party). Repeated clashes between the pro- and anti-Castro forces outside the hotel kept the 258-police contingent assigned to Castro busy. On his second day at the Theresa, Nikita Khrushchev came to visit, and his police contingent plus Castro's created the greatest show of force Harlem had ever witnessed (to this day it hasn't been matched).

Four years later, when Malcolm X broke with the Nation of Islam to found his own Organization of Afro-American Unity (open to people of all religions), he held his press conference at the Theresa and soon afterwards moved his offices here. When he was assassinated in 1965, just 1 year later, this is where crowds gathered to mourn until they were dispersed by the police.

If you have the time, walk 1 block east and end your tour with a cocktail at the

⑳ Lenox Lounge (288 Malcolm X Blvd., just south of 125th St.)

This is the only major Harlem jazz club still operating from the days of Fats Waller, Duke Ellington, and Louis Armstrong. Stop in for a drink, or just take a peek at the faux zebra-skin walls and Art Deco frills that served as a backdrop to most of the Jazz Era greats, especially Billie Holliday, who was a regular here.

Note: You may also want to stop in at the **Studio Museum** (p. 158), Harlem's major art museum, which you'll pass along the way to the Lounge.

Walking Tour 3: Greenwich Village & SoHo

Start: Under the arch at Washington Square Park (take the **R** or **W** to 8th Street, or the **A**, **B**, **C**, **D**, **E** or **F** to West 4th Street)

Finish: The Little Singer Building, 561 Broadway

Time: 2½ hours

Best times: On the weekend, when the Village and SoHo are alive with musicians, shoppers, and stylish downtowners lounging at sidewalk cafes

Worst times: It's never a bad time to take a stroll in these two areas

Harlem and Lower Manhattan, the first two walking tours in this chapter, have had relatively stable identities over the years. Though originally farmland, Harlem for the last 2 centuries has been primarily a residential neighborhood of some sort, never a center for commerce or industry. Lower Manhattan began as both a residential and commercial zone, but it morphed into a center of commerce and industry in the 19th century, and has remained that way over the years.

But SoHo and Greenwich Village? Identity whiplash. Most tend to think of these two neighborhoods as havens for artists, eccentrics, and bohemians, but that's only part of the story.

Greenwich Village started as its own village, a place where, as in Boccaccio's *Decameron,* the well-to-do fled on a near-yearly basis to escape the plagues of colonial Nieuw Amsterdam and New York (recurrent bouts of yellow fever mostly). Building began in earnest in the 1820s and 1830s, as wealthy families threw up row house after row house in what was supposed to be a suburb of the city. Soon, of course, the city had caught up, the hoi polloi were living just down the block, and the blue bloods did the 19th-century version of urban flight and moved a mile uptown to the newest suburbs. Their swank one-family houses were subdivided into cheap apartments and boarding houses, or torn down entirely to create factories, and the neighborhood became one of immigrants and later, artists. The Village always retained its status as a place apart, however, thanks to the confusing configuration of its streets, a jumble of twisting byways and narrow streets.

"The streets have run crazy and broken themselves . . . into strange angles and curves," O. Henry wrote. "One street crosses *itself* a time or two." In the 1960s and '70s it was the charm of this urban topography, the quiet of the tiny streets cut off from the bustle of upper Manhattan, that brought the well-to-do back, and the neighborhood reverted to its 1830s self as a hideaway for wealthy New Yorkers (with some exceptions).

A similar do-si-do of social movements ran its course in SoHo, with town houses becoming factories becoming artist's lofts becoming homes for mega-millionaires. I hope in this walking tour to give you a taste of all the varied groups of people and social movements that shaped these two neighborhoods over the years.

Stand at the arch in Washington Square Park, someplace where you can get a good view into the interior of the park.

❶ Washington Square Park

Hangings, protests, burials, parades . . . if there's another spot in New York that's seen as many different types of drama as Washington Square Park has, I've yet to hear of it. Located above the boundaries of the first Dutch settlement in Manhattan, the area was originally a marshland, fed by the stream that still runs under nearby Minetta Lane. Its first settlers were Nieuw Amsterdam slaves who were given partial freedom in 1641 in return for farming this then-dangerous and remote land. Older men and women were the primary settlers, as their usefulness to the colony was diminished, and the freedom was a mixed blessing. They were required to give over a large part of their harvests to the colony; and perhaps more disturbingly, were human watchdogs set here to alert the Dutch should local Indians or British forces try to attack.

In 1797, the land was designated a potter's field; it was put to good use a year later when yellow fever swept through what was by then New York City, part of the brand-new United States of America. Over 5% of the population of the city died that muggy, mosquito-infested summer (it was these pests that spread the illness), the poorest of whom were buried here in the drained swamp. Before it became a parade ground for the military in 1826, nearly 20,000 New Yorkers were laid to rest here. Tales are still told today of soldiers doing their maneuvers on the field, boots slipping through the crust of the dirt and crunching down on shroud-covered skeletons. If all this weren't enough of an invitation for hauntings, the square was often used for public hangings, the condemned strung up on the massive elm tree that still stands on the northwest corner of the park.

The magnificent white marble arch that you should be facing was designed by Stanford White, the second such arch he created for the city (the first, made of wood and plaster, was erected in 1889 to mark the centennial of George Washington's inauguration and to raise funds for this permanent one, which was completed in 1892). *Washington as President, Accompanied by Wisdom and Justice* is the sculpture on the right side of the arch, added to the arch in 1918 by Alexander Stirling Calder, father of the great modern artist and mobile-maker Alexander Calder. On the other side, we see *Washington as Commander-in-Chief, Accompanied by Fame and Valor* by Herman Atkins MacNeill (note the sword), also tacked on in 1918.

Over the years, the arch has become a choice target for protesters looking for something big and tall to seize. Dada-Daddy Marcel Duchamp made his way up the 110 interior steps (accompanied by other members of the Liberal Club, including a woman who liked to call herself "Woe," so she could declaim, "Woe is Me!") carrying Chinese lanterns, food, wine, and cap guns to declare Greenwich Village an "independent republic" in 1918. They were soon brought down by an unamused constable. A less lighthearted takeover took place in 1968 when the Students Against Racism and War barricaded themselves inside to hang a banner protesting the Vietnam War. Don't you try to capture the arch: The door to the inner stairway has been bolted ever since.

❷ Washington Square North (btwn Fifth Ave. and University Place)

Walk towards Washington Square North and gaze at the elegant line of

Walking Tour: Greenwich Village & SoHo

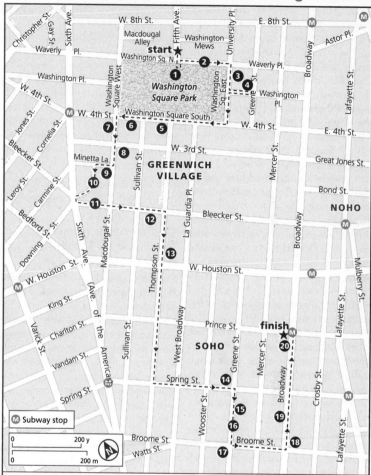

1 Washington Square Park
2 Washington Square North
3 Silver Center
4 Former Triangle Shirtwaist Factory
5 Judson Church
6 New York University Law School
7 Provincetown Playhouse
8 Former home of Louisa May Alcott
9 Minetta Tavern
10 Minetta Street
11 Bleecker Street

12 Former home of Theodore
   Dreiser & Allen Ginsberg
13 Former home of Frank Zappa
14 Manhattan Bistro
15 72 Greene Street
16 Greene Street
17 Gunther Building
18 Haughwout Building
19 Former St. Nicholas Hotel
20 Little Singer Building

town houses fronting the square between Fifth Avenue and University Place. You should be looking north now at what is the longest unbroken string of Greek Revival town houses anywhere in the United States. Aren't they lovely? New York University owns most of these (in fact, it owns much of the neighborhood), but in the 1830s, when these were built, they were strictly for individual owners of the highest social class. Novelist Henry James's grandmother lived here and he used the pretensions of off-Park living as the centerpiece of his famed novel *Washington Square* (which was later turned into the movie *The Heiress,* starring Olivia DeHavilland). "The ideal of quiet and of genteel retirement, in 1835, was found in Washington Square," wrote James. "It has a kind of established repose which is not of frequent occurrence in other quarters of the long, shrill city; it has a riper, richer, more honourable look than any of the upper ramifications of the great longitudinal thoroughfare—the look of having had something of a social history."

The use of Greek Revival architecture for the area was in no way accidental. In the mid-1820s, support for the Greeks in their fight for independence against the Ottoman Empire was all the rage among the upper echelons of Manhattan society. Balls were held, collections taken, special theatrical performances given, all to help this Christian nation, inheritor of the mantle of classical Athenian democracy, win freedom from the Turkish "heathens." Because so many wealthy New Yorkers identified with this struggle, seeing America as the current iteration of ideal Greek democracy, classical columns started popping up on buildings all over town, with Greek symbols incorporated into fences (as you'll see in front of you), pedestals added to facades, and so on.

By the early 20th century, the strip had become rundown and many of the Village's best-known "bohemians" moved in, including painter Edward Hopper. He lived at 3 Washington Sq. N. from 1913 all the way through 1967. Other residents of that building over the years have included writer John Dos Passos and painter Thomas Eakins.

Walk east towards University Place (on your left if you're facing Fifth Ave.) and stop at the

③ Silver Center (corner of Washington Sq. E. and Washington Sq. N.)

Dash-dot-dot-dash—you've now reached the birthplace of the telegraph. Inventor Samuel Morse lived in this New York University building (he was a painting instructor) when, in 1836, he formulated the rudiments of the telegraphic alphabet, better known as Morse code. A year later, on Sept. 2, 1837, he was able to gather 1,700 feet of copper wire, which he coiled around his room, sending the world's first wire dispatches from one end to the other. Witnessing the monumental event was student Alfred Vail, son of the owner of the Speedwell Iron Works in New Jersey. Vail convinced his father to invest in the new invention and, when capital met product, a new means of communication was born.

Walk 1 block south (away from University Place), turn left on Washington Street, and walk until you get to

④ 29 Washington St. (at the corner of Green St.)

It was here on March 25, 1911, that a horrific tragedy reshaped the laws of

New York State and the history of the American labor movement. The day was a Saturday, yet 600 young women, mostly Jewish and Italian immigrants between the ages of 13 and 23, were hard at work in a garment factory on the eighth, ninth, and tenth floors of this building. They toiled in one of the most notorious sweatshops in the city, taxed by the owners for the needles they used, their clothing lockers, even the chairs they sat in.

At 5pm, the bell rang, and the girls started to get ready to leave when suddenly a fire sprang up in the southeastern corner of the eighth floor—no one has ever been able to determine the cause—and within minutes, the eighth, ninth, and tenth floors were an inferno. An inescapable inferno because seconds later the girls discovered that many of the doors had been locked from the outside (to prevent theft, the owners said later). Minutes after that, one of the fire escapes collapsed and the elevator operator fled in terror. A brave pedestrian named Joseph Zito ran into the building and was able to make five trips up through the flames, saving 25 to 30 workers on each trip. To escape the flames, girls started jumping to their deaths in front of horrified passersby. Those trapped inside suffocated from the smoke, while still others were crushed in a heap at the locked doors. In all, 146 people were killed at the Triangle Shirt Waist Factory, most within the first 10 minutes of the hour-long blaze.

After many protests and its own fire in the State House in Albany, the State Legislature responded to the tragedy by rewriting the labor code, making it the most stringent in the nation. The labor movement, struggling up until this point, gathered steam and the International Ladies Garment Workers Union (ILGWU) became a force in the industry.

All was not rosy, of course. Nine months after the fire, Max Blanck and Isaac Harris, owners of the factory, were acquitted on the charge of manslaughter in a trial many felt to be rigged. By the time of the trial, they were the proud owners of yet another sweatshop, just blocks from Washington Street, with no better working conditions for their laborers.

Walk back to Washington Square and follow the perimeter of the park south to 4th Street (aka Washington Sq. S.). Turn right and walk to Thompson Street.

⑤ Judson Church (239 Thompson St.)

The boxy, Romanesque Judson Church (1892) is another masterwork by architect Stanford White, who took his inspiration from the churches of Florence—this church's sensuous curved arches and stripes of yellow brick and terra cotta carry a hint of that ancient city. Built to commemorate the first American missionary to Burma, Adoniram Judson, the church was a center of immigrant life at the turn of the 20th century, and a center for progressive politics in the later 1950s and '60s, when the minister Howard Moody (who called himself a "Christian Atheist") was at its helm, sheltering protesters from the police and helping to overturn the short-lived ban on folk-singing in the park (for which today's Washington Square Park folk singers should be grateful).

Walk across Sullivan Street to

⑥ New York University Law School

Journalist John Reed (who was the subject of the Warren Beatty bio-pic, *Reds*) was a tenant of the famous boarding house that once stood here and wrote a poem about his neighbors, whom he called "Inglorious Miltons by the Score/And Rodins, one to every floor."

If you get the chance, take a look at the street names on this side of Washington Square Park. All were chosen in honor of Washington's Revolutionary War generals.

Keep walking to MacDougal Street, turn left onto that street, and stop beside the legendary

7 Provincetown Playhouse (133 MacDougal St.)

The more theatrical strain of Greenwich Village bohemianism found its home at this little theater, which at one time was one of the most influential playhouses in the city. That's thanks largely to Eugene O'Neill, who managed it, and whose important early works were first performed here, including *Emperor Jones, The Hairy Ape,* and *The Great God Brown.* Overturning barriers, the theater employed African Americans to play . . . African Americans, and even featured a kiss between a black man and a white woman (a radical move in 1926, and one that resulted in threats from the Ku Klux Klan). Other famous names who contributed to the theater include Edna St. Vincent Millay (her anti-war classic *Aria de Capo* debuted in 1919), John Reed, and E. E. Cummings (as a playwright). Among the famous actors who trod these boards were Eva Le Galienne; Tallulah Bankhead; Katharine Cornell; and Bette Davis, who made her stage debut here. The theater is now owned by New York University (what isn't in this neighborhood!) and used for student productions.

Stroll south, crossing West 3rd Street until you see

8 130 MacDougal St.

This perfect little brick federal town house is where Louisa May Alcott probably wrote *Little Women* (can't you just picture Professor Baer calling on the young writer here?). Alcott never had her own professor; her health damaged by her work as a nurse in Washington, D.C., during the Civil War, she never married, instead spending her limited energies on writing and lobbying for women's suffrage.

Take a Break

There are few better streets at which to grab a quick snack in the Village than MacDougal Street. For a pastry and some java, head to historic **Caffe Reggio (119 MacDougal St.; ☎ 212/475-9557; www.cafereggio.com; $),** which claims to have introduced cappuccino to America and has the huge, sculptural, copper machines to prove it. If you feel like something a bit more substantial, go Middle Eastern for fab falafel at **Mamoun's Falafel (119 MacDougal St.; www.mamounsfalafel.com; $)** or plates of creamy hummus at **Hummus Place (99 MacDougal St., near Bleecker St.; ☎ 212/533-3089; $).**

Continue downtown until you reach Minetta Lane, and take a look at

9 Minetta Tavern (113 MacDougal St.)

Formerly a speakeasy called the Black Rabbit, this was a major literary hangout of the day, serving up poetry-inspiring booze and heaping plates of spaghetti to such notables as Ezra Pound, E. E. Cummings, and Ernest Hemingway in the '20s; and Allen Ginsberg, Jack Kerouac, and Alan Corso in the '50s. Little-known fact: One of Middle America's favorite magazines, the very unbohemian *Readers Digest,* began its life in the Village, founded on this very spot. It continued to publish from the basement of the restaurant for half a dozen years before moving into proper offices.

Take a left onto Minetta Lane, and walk half its length (if you go to Sixth Ave., you've gone too far) to an unmarked, twisting street that's actually

🔟 Minetta Street

Listen carefully: A stream still runs below this street and on the rare quiet day, it's possible to hear it gurgling faintly below your feet. Though the street is now one of the most charming in the city, when the stream was at street level it was a muddy ghetto called "Little Africa" and inhabited entirely by free blacks from the 1820s through the 1910s. In 1863, when the draft riots surrounding the Civil War's first lottery for soldiers morphed into race riots, this was one of the few safe places for African Americans in the city. For 5 days, hundreds of white hooligans raged through the streets beating and lynching blacks, even burning down an orphanage for black children. It was the most violent riot of the century; 105 people were killed and many more maimed for life. But the narrow layout of Minetta Street allowed armed residents to successfully guard their homes and families from harm.

Soon after the Civil War, the area became notorious for its "black and tan" clubs, where whites and African Americans would socialize. It maintained its scandalous reputation into the Prohibition era, when nearly half the buildings on the street housed hidden speakeasies.

Follow Minetta Street around to Sixth Avenue and take a sharp left (do not cross Sixth Ave.) onto

🔟 Bleecker Street

Some things never change, including Bleecker Street. From the mid-19th-century through today, this has been a party place, lined with bars and cafes, and an integral part of the bohemian life in the Village. It's important to remember that the downside to the romanticized Village artist's life was crushing poverty. Young artists would spend hour upon hour in the cafes here not only to socialize and exchange ideas, but to stay warm (escaping often unheated tenement apartments) and to mooch food off more successful colleagues.

If you didn't get caffeinated earlier at Café Reggio, you may want to do so now, stopping at one of New York's oldest and most beloved coffee shops, the **Porto Rico Importing Company** (201 Bleecker St.). You may want to step in just for the ambrosial scent of the roasting beans.

Continue on Bleecker Street to

🔟 160 Bleecker St.

This is the flophouse in which novelist Theodore Dreiser stayed when down on his luck. Later called the Greenwich and almost as seedy, it was a crash pad for poet Allen Ginsberg in 1951.

Head down Bleecker Street to Thompson Street, take a right, and you'll arrive at

🔟 180 Thompson St.

This was the address of musician Frank Zappa in the 1960s. Lupa, a marvelous Italian restaurant owned by Mario Batalli (consider returning here for lunch or dinner) is just next door at no. 170.

Head along Thompson Street, cross Houston Street into SoHo, and walk 2 blocks more to Spring Street. Turn left on Spring Street, cross West

Broadway, and keep walking until you come to

🄮 The Manhattan Bistro (129 Spring St., btwn Wooster and Greene sts.)

Spring Street was named for the natural spring that burbled at this location. On top of that spring was a well (now in the basement of the Manhattan Bistro), where the most notorious murder of the 18th century took place. Three days before Christmas in 1799, a young milliner named Gulielma Sands told her cousins that she was to be wed that night to a fellow boarder in her house, Levi Weeks, a carpenter. She left that evening with Weeks and was never seen alive again. A week later her body was found floating in the Manhattan Well.

Weeks was accused of the crime and because he was then working on Alexander Hamilton's country estate Hamilton Grange (p. 225), he was able to convince that great man to serve as his defense lawyer (it didn't hurt that he had a wealthy uncle, either). Soon after, Hamilton's rival, Aaron Burr, owner of the well, joined the defense team, elevating it to the 1800s version of the "Dream Team." (Some speculate that Burr joined forces with Hamilton so that he could enjoy some of the publicity the trial was generating, as it was an election year.) Hamilton and Burr used the very 20th-century tactic, unusual at the time, of blaming the victim, claiming she was promiscuous and suicidal. And though half a dozen people were able to place Weeks with Sands on the night of the murder, he was acquitted. Legend has it that when the verdict was read, Sands's cousin Catharine Ring pointed at the defense team and judge, screaming: "If thee dies a natural death, I shall think there's no justice in heaven."

As we all know, Hamilton was not to die a natural death—just 4 years later his co-counsel killed him in a duel. The judge on the case, John Lansing, also met with an unusual end: He left his rooms at the City Hotel one day in 1829 and never returned. To this day, no one knows what became of him. Burr seems to be the only one to have escaped this curse, though his life after the duel was not a pleasant one. He served out his term as vice president while exiled from New York and New Jersey, suffered through financial difficulties, and was at one point made to stand trial for treason.

In a coda to the story: If you feel a chill as you read this, it could be a visit from Sands. Locals claim that she still haunts the area around the well.

Turn right onto Greene Street, walking downtown until you come to

🄯 72 Greene St.

We'll leap several decades into the future now, to the period just before the Civil War, when new materials and techniques, brought over from Britain, dramatically changed the way buildings were constructed in the U.S. Over a century earlier, in 1709, a British inventor named James Darby discovered that by adding coke (and later coal) to pig iron, he could create a new type of iron that was stronger and lighter and had more plasticity than traditional forms. Called cast iron, it caught on fairly quickly in England and started to be widely used in the U.S. in the 1840s. Soon it was all the rage, and the U.S. built more cast-iron buildings than any other nation, the biggest collection of which—approximately 250—are right where you are now, in SoHo (the acronym stands for SOuth of HOuston).

The massive cream-colored warehouse building before you (known as the King of Greene St.) is one of the best examples of the genre. It looks like stone, doesn't it? In actuality, all of the elaborate French Renaissance details, window lintels, Corinthian columns, classical pediments, and the like, are cast iron from a foundry down on the Lower East Side. Building owners would get a catalogue, very much like a Sears catalogue, which would be filled with hundreds of drawings of facades and architectural details. They would order what they liked and construct the interior of the building (using some combination of cast-iron supports and brickwork or wood). Approximately 4 months later, crates of facade would arrive, which would then be screwed onto the front of the building (the screws hidden behind ornamental details). If the owner changed his mind about the look several years down the road—and this was not uncommon— he simply ordered another facade and had it slapped up in the old one's place. The wonder of these buildings is that, while they look like the loving work of skilled artisans, they are actually the essence of pre-fabrication.

They also represented a new type of architecture, one in which the weight of the building was carried by an interior skeleton of rolled iron beams rather than being borne by the exterior and interior walls. This technique allowed for much larger windows, important in the days before electricity, and was the precursor of the one used in modern skyscrapers, where skeletons of steel support "curtain walls" of glass.

You'll see cast-iron buildings throughout SoHo. To figure out if the building you're looking at is cast iron, you can knock on it (it will have a more hollow sound than stone), look for rust spots or, best yet, attach a magnet to it.

Take a moment to wander among the other magnificent buildings on

⑯ Greene Street

Like most areas of Lower Manhattan, SoHo had many different faces over the years. Until the late 1700s it was a natural landscape of meadows and marshes, dotted by country estates (including the estate of Aaron Burr). Residential buildings, primarily for the gentry, were constructed on Broadway following the draining of the marshes and the paving of that street in 1809. By the mid-1820s, this was the most populous ward in the city, a place of booming commerce, theaters, and saloons.

Fast-forward to the 1850s: The upper classes are moving out, their homes and fancy stores replaced by these industrial buildings, warehouses, and a heckuva lot of brothels, making SoHo the city's first red-light district. Greene Street was the center of the action, with some 70 cathouses operating up and down this not-so-long street. Usually these "houses" were fronted by faux cigar stores, with little tobacco and a female salesperson at the front who would direct customers in the know to the back rooms. The brothels operated primarily in the daytime, with the peak of business taking place at lunchtime. An early guidebook called *A Directory of the Seraglios* by A. Free Loveyer was published in 1859, reviewing the goods and services at many of the houses. In a case of *"plus ça change . . . ,"* a number of current New York brothels were recently shut down, having been discovered by the police who were monitoring their online advertisements (in which prostitutes were ranked in Amazon.com–like fashion, on their skills and beauty).

Continue walking south to Broome Street. On the corner, you'll see the landmark

⑰ Gunther Building

Another cast-iron beaut', the Gunther Building was named for William H. Gunther, the fur merchant who built this warehouse in 1872. Along with unusual curved corners, which demonstrate the remarkable plasticity of cast iron, the building once had two statues made of cast iron on pedestals jutting from the second floor.

Beyond the architecture, the Gunther is a landmark for its place in the history of contemporary art. It was here, in the mid-1960s, that the very first artist/squatters took up residence in SoHo. Urban pioneers, they occupied these decrepit industrial spaces, installed heat, plumbing, kitchens, and bathrooms . . . and then thought up ways to hide these kitchens and bathrooms from fire inspectors (as the area was zoned for industrial use only). Michael T. Kaufman of the *New York Times* reported that "one artist . . . would greet a building inspector on the stairs saying, 'Wait a minute. I have a nude model posing.' Then he would go inside and, using pulleys, hoist beds above a false ceiling and camouflage the refrigerator, range, and bathtub." The artists also had to worry about safety: At that time, SoHo was known among firefighters as "Hell's hundred acres" for all the fires that occurred in these buildings, thanks to their wooden floors, and their use as storage spaces for bales of paper, rags, and the like. But low rent, huge spaces, and large windows proved irresistible, and soon artists were flocking here in droves. In 1968, the first gallery in the area opened up; a decade later, there were 60 of them.

In 1971, the artists successfully lobbied the city to create its first artists' district, making it legal for them to live in the neighborhood. The one legal hurdle they had to overcome was

receiving an "artistic certification" (a city-issued designation of "artist"—it involved bringing in a portfolio of work to show). Of course, being artists, most didn't want to wade into the city bureaucracy to pick up this official designation, and this has, unfortunately, resulted in a watering-down of the community. Most of the major galleries left a decade ago for more affordable digs, and the lofts are now as likely to be inhabited by stockbrokers as they are painters. Today, the average cost for a loft in the neighborhood is $25,000 per square foot—a big change from the '60s when artists were paying as little as $6 per square foot here.

Among the many artists who lived or still live in SoHo are Christo, Louise Nevelson, Claes Oldenburg, Robert Rauschenberg, and Frank Stella.

Face the Gunther Building, and turn left (east); walk on Broome Street until you come to Broadway. Across the street you should see the monumental

⑱ Haughwout Building

With cast-iron facades facing both Broadway and Broome Street (there's a Staples on the first floor), this is the structure that began the rage for cast-iron buildings when it was erected in 1858, the first of its kind in New York. I think it's a sensationally beautiful structure; it's been called the "Parthenon of Cast-Iron Architecture in America" and is on the National Historic Register. Designed by architect John Gaynor, the repeating arches, fluted Corinthian columns, and 92 windows on its facade are meant to call to mind the San Sorvino Library of Venice. Daniel D. Badger, owner of the largest foundry in the city, was so proud of his work on the Haughwout that he placed the building on the cover of all his catalogues.

The interior of the building, a world-famous housewares emporium, was just as swank, boasting the first passenger elevator in the world (made by Otis, it was the beginning of that company's empire), electrical lights, and a rare amenity for those days—central heating. It was here that Mary Todd Lincoln went on shopping sprees to outfit the White House, earning her a Marie Antoinette–like reputation for profligacy in the newspapers by spending hundreds of dollars of the government's money for hand-painted china while the Civil War raged.

Turn left onto Broadway and walk slightly north to

⑲ 521 and 523 Broadway

This is all that remains of the once grand St. Nicholas Hotel, which was built at a cost of $1 million in 1854 (a huge sum in those days). Sold off in pieces over the years, it once occupied the entire length of the block, giving shelter to nearly 1,500 people per night. Its ballrooms hosted the grandest fêtes of the decade. Now all you can see are these two slices, with other buildings located in between them.

During the Civil War, the St. Nicholas was requisitioned by the War Department for use as its New York headquarters, though it continued to operate as a hotel. On Nov. 25, 1864, Confederate agents attempted to create a panic—or worse—by setting fires in the heart of New York City. Checking in to the St. Nicholas and 11 other hotels, all located on Broadway, the agents went into their rooms and mixed together "Greek Fire," a combustible mixture of sulfur, naphtha, and quicklime that can cause a mighty blaze when exposed to air. One after another, beginning at 8:45pm, sometimes in multiple rooms in a hotel, flames erupted. Though the fire force was stretched thin, they managed—with the help of hotel staff and customers—to extinguish every blaze, saving the hotels, and possibly the city, from what could have been a catastrophic fire.

Continue Uptown to the

⑳ "Little Singer" Building (561 Broadway)

We end our tour with the building that could be seen as the epilogue of the cast-iron movement, as New York and other cities moved into the age of steel (which appeared on the scene in the 1890s and was stronger and more flame retardant). An avant-garde mix of steel and cast-iron elements, it's a pip, with trellises as filigreed as any you'd see in the French Quarter of New Orleans, and acres of windows. All that glass is an important innovation. Architectural critics have said that the metal-and-glass-skin of the Little Singer is a precursor to the international style of architecture—those big glass boxes—that was to flower half-a century later. Designed by Ernest Flagg, it was built for the Singer Manufacturing Company (famous for its sewing machines) in 1904, 4 years before the much larger Singer Building was completed in the Financial District (now demolished, it was the tallest building in the world for a little over a year).

9

Attention, Shoppers!

Introducing one of NYC's favorite pastimes

WHY DO THE MAJORITY OF VISITORS TO NEW YORK DESCEND ON THE CITY in fall and early winter? They come here to shop. In the run-up to Christmas, Chanukah, Kwaanza, and other big-spender holidays, avid shoppers storm the city because they know that if you can't find it in the Big Apple . . . well, it simply doesn't exist. In this chapter, I attempt to bring some order to the massive number of shopping options in the Big Apple, from the big department stores, to the flea markets, to the direct-from-the-designer sample sales (a hidden bounty for power shoppers).

THE CITY'S 10 BEST SHOPPING AREAS

Often in the Big Apple, finding what you want has less to do with picking the right store than with choosing the right area in which to shop. Similar types of stores tend to cluster together, making it quite easy for shoppers to flit from one to the next, comparing merchandise and prices. Here, beginning at the bottom of Manhattan and working my way north, is my list of the city's best shopping streets and their areas of specialty.

* **Duane Street, between Greenwich and Hudson streets** (❶ to Franklin St.). A delightful block of antiques and fine furniture stores, with such unusual options as Brazilian collectibles and "pop" furniture options. My home block of **10th Street between Broadway and University Place** has a similar confluence of antique furniture stores, the emphasis on my block being European and Art Deco pieces.

* **Canal Street, between Mott and Lafayette streets** ✪✪ (❶, ❷, ❸, ❹, ❺, ❻, Ⓝ, Ⓞ, Ⓡ to Canal St.). Best for super-cheap, knock-off accessories: purses in the style of Kate Spade, watches of all types, beaded jewelry, sunglasses, and luggage. If you're planning to buy a T-shirt to commemorate your New York vacation, buy it here for half of what you'd spend in Times Square. *Tip:* Very few stores in this area use price tags because bargaining is expected. Be prepared to walk away if a price seems too high—often the mere gesture of turning towards the door will halve the cost.

* **Broadway, between West Houston and Canal streets** ✪✪ (❶, ❷, ❸, ❹, ❺, ❻, Ⓝ, Ⓞ, Ⓡ to Canal St. or Ⓡ, Ⓦ to Prince St.). Club Kid Central. If you're between the ages of 15 and 29, and want affordable, flashy fashions similar to what you'll see on MTV, this is where to shop. See below for my description of Yellow Rat Bastard, the epicenter of this clothing scene. You'll find a similar crop of shops on **Lafayette Street, between Houston and Spring streets.**

◆ **Bleecker Street, between Sixth and Eighth avenues** ✪✪✪ (Ⓐ, Ⓔ, Ⓒ to 14th St.). Boutique heaven. If cutting-edge style is your thing and you have the pocketbook to support that appetite, the small stores along this block have all the latest fashions, with friendlier service than you'll find Uptown. There's a similar if sometimes more avant-garde scene in **Nolita, on Elizabeth, Mott, and Mulberry streets, from Broome to West Houston streets** (Ⓕ, Ⓥ to Lafayette St., or Ⓖ to Prince St.).

◆ **9th Street, between Second Avenue and Avenue A** ✪ (Ⓖ to Astor Place, Ⓛ to First Ave.). New, younger designers tend to pick this street, so you'll find a terrific assortment of "only in New York" fashions, along with shops of designers who have now become a bit more established, vintage stores, and bridal boutiques. If you have the time, wander down to St. Marks Place and 7th Street for similar stores (though not as many as you'll find on 9th St.). **Ludlow Street, between Stanton and Delancey streets** (Ⓕ, Ⓥ to Houston St.), has lately seen a blossoming of these little boutiques as well.

◆ **Fifth Avenue, between 14th and 23rd streets** (Ⓡ, Ⓦ to 23rd St. or ④, ⑤, ⑥, Ⓝ, Ⓠ, Ⓡ, Ⓛ to Union Sq.). Home furnishings and brand-name fashions. With EJ Audi on this strip, along with Restoration Hardware, Eileen Fisher, Armani, Gap, Banana Republic, and J. Crew, you have somewhat of a mall atmosphere, with a few more interesting stores mixed in.

◆ **Sixth Avenue, between 16th and 23rd streets** (❶ to 18th St. or Ⓑ, Ⓕ to 23rd St). Land of the bargain superstores, with Bed, Bath & Beyond, a huge Old Navy, and Filene's Basement leading the charge.

◆ **Fifth Avenue, between 38th and 57th streets** ✪ (Ⓝ, Ⓡ to 50th St or Ⓔ, Ⓥ to 53rd St. and Fifth Ave.). This window-shoppers' paradise is home to such grand old beauties as Saks Fifth Avenue, Tiffanys, and Bergdorf Goodman, along with a number of other luxury outlets.

◆ **Madison Avenue, 62nd through 86th streets** (Ⓖ to 66th, 79th, or 86th sts.). Overpriced baubles and garments for the ultra-rich as far as the eye can see. On Madison, you'll find the flagship branches for Ralph Lauren, Chanel, Hermès, and Prada.

◆ **47th Street, between Fifth and Sixth avenues** ✪ (Ⓑ, Ⓕ to Rockefeller Center). New York's famed Diamond District, with more than 2,600 small and large businesses located on this single block. Ninety percent of the diamonds that come into the U.S. go through New York City, many of them through this street, so you're practically guaranteed a good variety. You'll also get an extremely hard sell, and sometimes a bit of trickery, so research what you want before you come here, and make sure you're getting an untreated stone (if you're looking for the real thing). Be prepared to walk away if you're not satisfied. There are also a number of jewelry shops on Canal Street between Broadway and Houston Street, but the quality is generally better here.

◆ **Madison Avenue, between 86th and 96th streets** (④, ⑤, ⑥ to 86th St.). Veruka Salt, the spoiled rich girl in *Charlie and the Chocolate Factory*, would love this neighborhood. Store after store caters to the pampered tykes of the Upper East Side; you'll find exquisite children's togs, mostly imported, though prices can be astronomical.

THE TOP DEPARTMENT STORES

Classier than Macy's (see below) and a bit more logical in terms of layout, **Bloomingdales** ✪✪ (1000 Third Ave. btwn 59th and 60th sts.; ☎ 212/705-2000; www.bloomingdales.com; ④, ⑤, ⑥, to 59th St. or Ⓝ, Ⓡ to Lexington Ave.) is a shopping behemoth with enough excitement to keep shopaholics occupied for at least several hours. Founded in 1872 as a hoopskirt store, the vast emporium is still in the forefront of fashion with four complete floors just for garments (basement for men's; 2nd, 3rd, and 4th floors for women's). It also sells housewares, furniture, kid's clothing, luggage, kitchen tools, accessories, cosmetics, and jewelry, but its strength is the clothes. Every week Bloomies puts some department or part of a department on sale, so be sure to check out local newspapers to see what the buys are when you're here. Weekdays before lunch tend to be the least crowded time to visit, and anyone who purchases over $50 of merchandise is entitled to a free tchotchke at the Visitor's Center, so save your receipts if you have someone not too picky to whom you owe a gift.

Though it's near-heresy to say so, I count **Century 21** (22 Courtland St. btwn Broadway and Church St.; ☎ 212/227-9092; www.c21stores.com; ❶, ❷, ❸, ❹, ❺, Ⓜ to Fulton St.) as the most overrated store in the city. A four-floor discount department store right across from the World Trade Center site, it made its reputation by selling designer clothing, shoes, and housewares at steeply discounted prices. But though the clothing may say "Calvin Klein," "Mosconi," or "DKNY," I've found that in nine out of ten cases, the really inexpensive offerings look nothing like the goods you'd get from these designers at retail stores. Instead, the fabrics are the cheapest polyesters, the colors gaudy, the fit off, and even the labels themselves look different (grab a DKNY here and instead of those classy, blocky letters that are the mark of the line, the label has a cutesy script, like something taken from a schoolgirl's autograph book). I suspect this is where designers go to unload the terrible mistakes they've made, or perhaps to peddle lines of cheaper goods, created explicitly for this store and others like it. I've seen otherwise sane, well-dressed women with their arms stacked full of clothes that shouldn't be worn outside the center ring at Ringling Brothers, simply because it had a label that marked it as "a find."

That being said, I have friends who swear by the place and tell me that the key is to hit it at the right time (though they can't give advice on how to do that) and to really dig deep. I counter that you'll usually find better buys at sample sales and consignment shops. My advice to you, dear reader, would be: If you happen to be in the area, try your luck. But look at the piece itself and judge its value by that. After all, nobody actually sees the label when you're wearing the clothes, right?

Flagship of a small chain of department stores, **Lord and Taylor** ✪✪ (424 Fifth Ave. btwn 38th and 38th sts; ☎ 212/391-3344; www.lordandtaylor.com; Ⓑ, Ⓓ, Ⓕ, Ⓝ, Ⓠ, Ⓡ to 34th St.) is New York's overlooked emporium. So when you come here, you won't be battling the crowds, as you will at Bloomingdales and Macy's. Still, you experience the best of those two stores: Bloomingdales' sense of high style at Macy's discounted rates (thanks to rolling discounts; check the local papers for coupons). This is the store a number of magazine stylists I know head to when they have to populate a fashion shoot on a budget. I'm particularly wowed by the women's dress collection, which hearkens back to another era. The prices are reasonable, but the dresses are of high quality: made of natural materials, lined, and cut for a woman's (rather than a young girl's) figure. Try it, you'll like it.

With approximately one million items for sale and a huge two-building space that stretches the very long block between Broadway and Seventh Avenue, **Macy's** ⭐ (151 W. 34th St. btwn Broadway and Seventh Ave.; ☎ 212/695-4400; www.macys.com; Ⓑ, Ⓓ, Ⓕ, Ⓝ, Ⓞ, Ⓡ to 34th St.), "The World's Largest Store," is also one of NYC's top tourist attractions. It has some of the best prices of the major department stores and, in general, higher-quality goods than Century 21, though the fashions here are definitely more middle-of-the-road. Designers and manufacturers represented include fashion stars (Tommy Hilfiger, Ralph Lauren, Hugo Boss), chain-store brands (Nine West, Esprit, Coach), and well-priced no-name labels. The basement is devoted to cookware, of which there's a dazzling variety; the house brand of pots and pans (called Tools of the Trade) may be the best buy—well made and usually quite inexpensive. And the return policy here is one of the most generous in the city, so mistakes are not irrevocable. Just as with Bloomies and Lord & Taylor, be sure to look for coupons in local papers; most weeks, there's some sort of special going on. Those are the reasons you should visit. But there are also reasons you may want to pop a Valium before you attempt it. The vast scale of Macy's and the huge crowds it attracts are its Achille's heel, as there's no other place in New York quite so confounding to shop. There's never a salesperson around when you need one; on sale days the masses can be crushing; and even native New Yorkers get lost here, wandering for half an hour at a time trying to get to the right department.

One note for history buffs: Macy's escalators were the first to be installed in any store anywhere in the world and are still in use in some areas of the store (look for the wood-slatted ones).

I'm including **Pearl Paint** ⭐ (308 Canal St., on the corner of Lafayette St.; ☎ 212/431-7932; www.pearlpaint.com; Ⓡ, Ⓠ, Ⓙ, Ⓢ, Ⓖ to Canal St.) in this discussion of department stores because in the last few years it has expanded so greatly that it truly has become one of the city's top stores, and not just for art supplies. It's taken possession of three more buildings to make more room for the furniture it now sells, its home decorating center, frame shop, and craft center. In fact, the only items you probably *can't* find here are clothes (though you just may be able to make some artful ones with the available supplies). This, "The World's Largest Discount Art Store," is truly one-stop shopping for do-it-yourselfers of all stripes, and its boast is true: The prices here are terrific, often 50% lower than what you'll find in other areas of the city, or in the country, for that matter. What you might not expect to find (but will): children's art kits, chichi stationery, writing journals, lanyards, needlepoint supplies, chairs, tables, and office supplies. *One warning:* Shopping here can involve a lot of stairs, so ask one of the helpful sales staff (they're all artists) to point you towards the hidden elevator.

If you're like me, **Pearl River Mart** ⭐⭐⭐ 🈺 (477 Broadway at Broome St.; ☎ 800/878-2446 or 212/431-4770; www.pearlriver.com; Ⓐ, Ⓒ, Ⓙ, Ⓜ, Ⓝ, Ⓡ to Canal St.) will unleash yens you never knew you had. Walk into this blockwide, two-story department store dedicated to goods imported from Asia, and you'll suddenly realize how much you desperately need lacquered chopsticks, or a silk brocade Mandarin shirt, or that industrial-sized bag of rice crackers. It happens every time.

Part of the seduction is the grand size of the place; the bright colors, intricate designs and silky textures of the clothes; and the dazzling number of choices. On the first floor alone are dozens of brocade sheath dresses, Mao shirts, beaded slippers, and quilted jackets; racks of ceramic and pottery tableware as far as the eye can see; Asian foods of all kinds (just the number of different ramen soups is staggering); and candles, lamps, toys, and doodads. In the basement you'll find rice cookers, kung fu and Mary Jane shoes, bamboo shades, paper lanterns, more plates and bowls, herbs, shampoos, and more. Prices are extremely reasonable. I've found lovely silk shirts marked down to just $15, a wedding-gift-worthy hand-glazed Japanese bowl going for just $25, and fun lamps for a mere $15. And if all the shopping tires you out, simply retire to the mezzanine tearoom for a tea break—green tea, of course.

SHOPPING THE SAMPLE SALES

I have a handful of friends, native New Yorkers all, who haven't set foot in a department store or retail clothing store in at least 5 years. Instead, they do all their apparel shopping—all of it!—at the sample sales that designers hold at showrooms and warehouses across the garment district. Top names in fashion (and all of the major designers in the U.S. still have their offices in New York) sell their clothing directly to the public at discounts of up to 80% off regular prices. Jewelry, outerwear, sweaters, socks, suits, wedding gowns—you can find all these items at sample sales. And these are not damaged goods; very often it's the sample clothing made to show retailers what's on offer, discontinued lines, canceled store orders, or overstocks.

As there are literally hundreds of these showrooms in Manhattan—still the garment capital of the U.S.—there are sales every single weekday of the year (with the exception of holidays, of course). The spring and fall months have the most sample sales, though in recent years over 200 sales have been held in the months of November and December. The deals can be remarkable. My favorite buy was a pair of chocolate-brown Donna Karan slacks that I got for just $35; retail, they would have cost twice that amount, and they're the genuine article, in a soft high-quality wool that's lasted me 6 years.

One note: Though I've found things in all sorts of sizes over the years, in general these sales are better for those who wear the smaller sizes. You're going to find a lot more size 6s than size 14s, though I have seen both at sales (and sizes will also vary by designer; for example, at an Eileen Fisher sale you won't have any problems finding larger sizes, though you might at Juicy Couture).

So how do you find a sample sale? Well, if you simply stroll the not-too-picturesque area between 42nd Street and 32nd Street on Broadway or Seventh Avenue, you'll be handed half-a-dozen flyers inviting you to sales happening that day. Or you can look at the following publications for daily or weekly listings:

- *Time Out New York* (at newsstands)
- *Daily Candy* (www.dailycandy.com, sign up for free membership)
- *NY Sale* (www.nysale.com)
- *New York Magazine* (also online at www.nymetro.com)

Strategies for Sample Sales:

Avoid lunchtime shopping: Crowds of office workers shop the sales during their lunch hours. Shop early in the day to get the best merchandise.

Wear tight-fitting or terrifically baggy clothes: Because many showrooms don't provide dressing rooms, you need to wear clothing that you can try clothes on over or under. And be sure to try on the clothing, because there are no refunds on these types of sales.

Bring cash: Some sample sales do not accept credit cards.

Be prepared to hunt: Much of the merchandise may be in cardboard boxes on the ground, so be prepared to dig through clothing to get the best buys.

There are also certain venues that serve as revolving warehouses for sample sales. I've had good luck at:

- **Gabays** ★ (225 First Ave. at 13th St.; ☎ 212/254-3180; www.gabaysoutlet. com; ● to First Ave.). Much of its merchandise is Bergdorf Goodman and Henri Bendel overstocks, meaning you're going to find such luxe designers as Jil Sander, Manolo Blahnik, Ermenegildo Zenga, Prada, and Jimmy Choo here for 40% to 75% below retail. Catering to both men and women, the store features shoes, lingerie, sunglasses, and handbags along with evening-wear and daywear.

- **Prato** (28 W. 34th St., btwn Fifth and Sixth aves.; ☎ 212/629-4730; www. pratooutlets.com; ❶, ❷, ❸, ❹, ❺, ❻ to 34th St.; or 492 Seventh Ave. at 36th St.; same subways). The men's equivalent of the Find Outlet, with Ralph Lauren Polo shirts from $25, Bill Blass sweaters from $20, and suits from $89.

- **Soiffer Haskin** (www.soifferhaskin.com). An administrator of sales for different luxury-goods clients (including jewelry, clothing, and furniture), Soiffer Haskin tends to host events at the Metropolitan Pavillion at 123 W. 18th St., but there's a full list of upcoming sales on its website.

- **SSS Sample Sale** ★★ (261 W. 36th St., btwn Seventh and Eighth aves.; ☎ 212/947-8748; www.clothingline.com; ❶, ❷, ❸, ❶, ❷, ❸ to 34th St.). Mostly women's clothing. In the past I've found fine cashmere sweaters for $50, Theory slacks for $40, and chic Salt jeans for half of what they go for in the department stores.

FLEA MARKETS

Every weekend a dozen or so flea markets pop up in neighborhoods all across the city, weaving their spells on those shoppers who enjoy the thrill of the hunt as much as the purchase itself. This being the Big Apple, prices may not be as low as those at the flea market in your local town, but there are always some real values to be had, as well as some utterly unique items you may not find elsewhere. For

Tips for Flea-Market Shopping

1. **Bargain, bargain, bargain:** Always offer less than the price on the tag. That's put there as a rough estimate, and vendors expect you to haggle, so don't let them down. If a vendor won't budge, ask if he'll throw in another item to sweeten the deal; you'll be surprised at how often he will.

2. **Bring cash:** Most vendors don't accept credit cards or checks, so make sure you have enough of the "green stuff" on your person.

3. **Visit late in the day:** The golden hour for sales is the hour before the market closes, when vendors begin to dread all the packing up they're going to have to do to get home for the night. You'll find them much more willing to bargain late in the day, and many will start posting sales as the sun dips down in the west.

4. **Be careful:** Once you've bought something at a flea market, it's usually yours for life, so check the merchandise carefully before you purchase.

fleas, beyond those listed here, check the information on www.herebeold things.com.

- ◆ **The Green Flea** ✪✪ (Columbus Ave. btwn 76th and 77th sts.; Apr–Sept Sun 10am–5:45pm, Oct–Mar Sun 10am–5:15pm; **B**, **C** to 81st St. or **1** to 79th St.). The mother of all flea markets, this is where the contestants were challenged to test their merchandising skills on the first season of *The Apprentice*. It's just as huge as it looked on TV, a vast public school playground and indoor gym, every inch covered with tables and tents holding a wide variety of goods. Along with the standard antiques and collectibles vendors—primarily jewelry, small furniture, and books—more unusual items pop up, such as an entire booth dedicated to antique kimonos; another one filled with a Harlem designer's sassy shrugs and embroidered jackets; a table filled with museum-worthy, working toasters from the '20s, '30s, '40s, and '50s; and a booth of elegant, tremendously inexpensive bamboo and wood furniture from the Philippines. If you're going to do only one flea market during your stay, this Sunday market should be it.

- ◆ **The Hell's Kitchen Flea Market** (39th St., btwn Ninth and Tenth aves.; Sat–Sun 10am–sunset; **A**, **C**, **E** to 34th St.). An entire block is shut down twice a week to make room for The Hell's Kitchen market, which specializes in furniture and home goods, usually vintage. Unique here are the crystal chandelier booth that also sells a large assortment of individual crystals (for do-it-yourselfers?); the antique clothing-hooks booth; and the gramophone seller, who has a lot of old-looking brass instruments up for sale as well. Because this is such a large market, expect a good selection of clothing, jewelry, books, and small collectibles.

◆ **The Unnamed Market at the corner of Spring and Wooster** ✫ (daily 11am–6pm; ®, ◎ to Prince St.). Another 7-day market, this is a small one, but I include it for the booths right on Spring Street and to the right as you face the market. Run by a collective of young designers, they offer a cheaper outlet for the original and well-crafted clothing that these up-and-comers are making (some of which are already selling in Japan and in clothing stores at various venues in the States). Among the names you'll find at these booths (which may not sound familiar now, but I guarantee will in a couple of years) are Nancy Giallombardo, an exciting up-and-comer.

◆ **The Market** ✫ (268 Mulberry St., btwn Prince and Houston sts.; www.the marketnyc.com; Sat–Sun only 11am–7pm; ⓕ, ⓥ to Houston St.). One step up from a flea market, this weekend market in the gym of St. Patrick's Youth Center is where many of New York's most promising young designers, about 60 in all, showcase their wares. Each rents a booth for the day, and sets out whatever they have made, primarily selling one-of-a-kind articles of clothing and jewelry. When I last visited I saw elaborately embossed T-shirts, hand-embroidered raincoats, hand-blown glass necklaces, feathered shoes, and handmade leather clutches all going for far less than they would in a conventional store (and some of these designers have advanced to selling goods in stores). What I like best about shopping here, besides the fact that you are sure to find unique, inexpensive apparel is the lack of a hard sell. Instead of trying to talk customers into buying, many designers sit behind their little tables working on their next creation as you browse.

INDIVIDUAL STORES YOU'LL WANT TO VISIT

Beyond the fleas, the monolithic department stores, and random sample sales, the following stores offer consistent value and are worth special visits.

APPAREL FOR MEN & WOMEN

Basic clothing items—T-shirts, polos, underwear, sweatshirts, shorts, jogging pants—are the focus at **American Apparel** (1841 Broadway, at 61st St.; ☎ 212/772-7462; www.americanapparel.net; ①, Ⓐ, Ⓑ, Ⓒ, Ⓓ to Columbus Circle), and nearly every style comes in a rainbow of colors. The clothes are all made in the good ol' U.S. of A, with prices that are in line with the quality offered. For example, a basic T never costs more than $15, with thermal long-sleeve shirts selling for the same price.

I know fashion magazine editors who periodically pop over to **H&M** ✫✫✫ (1328 Broadway at 34th St.; ☎ 212/564-9922; www.hm.com; ⓝ, ®, Ⓑ, Ⓓ, ⓕ to 34th St.) to supplement their wardrobes with this European chain's knock-off fashions. Always reasonably priced, with an emphasis on basics (though trendier clothes are thrown in as well), these stores are getting to be well known in the so-called "Blue States," though they haven't yet hit the deep South or Southwestern areas of the U.S. In addition to the Herald Square branch, there are NYC stores in Harlem, SoHo, the Flatiron district, and Midtown on the East Side (nine branches in all).

Though its price tags aren't the lowest of the low (I have usually found discounts to be about 25% to 35% off retail), **Loehmann's** ✫✫ (101 Seventh Ave., at 17th St.; ☎ 212/352-0856; www.loehmanns.com; ① to 19th St.) offers the types of clothing you'll find at the quality department stores at rates that are the equivalent of the department stores' once-in-a-while sales (and when Loehmann's itself has a special sale, the savings can be spectacular). The "back room" features progressive designers from Europe and the United States, the men's section has a terrific selection of quality button-downs (from such names as Calvin Klein, Ralph Lauren, and Zegna), and the woman's department is just brimming with distinctive suits, evening gowns, and coats.

Curious to know what the trends in fashion will be 6 months from now? Venture to the nearest **Urban Outfitters** (162 Second Ave., at 10th St.; ☎ 212/375-1277; www.urbanoutfitters.com; ❻ to Astor Place; also 374 Ave. of the Americas at Waverly Place and 628 Broadway in SoHo), which always seems to be just ahead of the curve for street fashions, by which I mean clothing worn by trendy 20- and 30-somethings. Along with a wide variety of casual wear for both men and women, the stores have a smattering of groovy housewares as well (think throw pillows, small lamps, and rugs).

At **Uniqlo** ★ (546 Broadway between Prince and Spring Sts.; ☎ 917/237-8811; ❻ to Spring St.) T-shirts aren't just garments, they're a philosophy. A T-SHIRT IS MORE THAN JUST A T-SHIRT, say signs all over the store. 'It's an expression of who you are where you've been. And with 100's of limited edition t-shirts to choose from each year, you'll always find one that says exactly how you feel'. Which means I guess that some people feel like 'We like bagels, too', while others think 'I am what I drive' and the vast majority identify deeply with anime characters. Whether or not you buy the metaphysics, Uniqlo is a good place to get trendy, albeit disposable clothing (pants, skinny jeans, blouses, underwear designed in Japan that will last about a season), including hundreds of different patterned t's at low prices.

The ever-expanding **Steve and Barry's** ★★★ (in the Manhattan Mall, Sixth Ave. and 33rd St.; ☎ 877/762-9444; www.steveandbarrys.com; ❸, ❹, ❺, ❻, ❼, ❽, ❾ to Herald Square) chain will soon be planting its flagship store on Broadway in Noho. Until that happens, the Manhattan Mall location is perpetually jammed outlet for folks looking for a chic look at less than $10 per item. I'm far from a shopaholic, but I have to say, the clothes here are a revelation—well made, constructed from solid natural (not synthetic) fabrics and smartly cut. Designed, supposedly, by celebrities, they range over a number of styles—sporty (Venus Williams' line), teeny bopper cute (Amanda Bynes' imprint), sleek and slimming (Sarah Jessica Parker) and even surfer boy laidback (Baird Hamilton). The store will be particularly useful for plus-size men and women as a good two-thirds of the stock (when I last visited) was for size 12 and up. Kids clothes are on sale, too.

Teenagers longing for "street cred" covet the duds at **Yellow Rat Bastard** ★ (483 Broadway, btwn Broome and Grand sts.; ☎ 877/YELL-RAT; www.yellowrat bastard.com; ❶, ❷, ❸, ❹, ❺, ❻, ❼, ❽ to Canal St.). Every belly-baring, low-riding, flip-flop-flinging fashion is here, along with some of the hottest names in sneakers. The clothing is affordable even for those still relying on baby-sitting money.

CONSIGNMENT & VINTAGE CLOTHING SHOPS

A worthy excuse to trek out to Brooklyn, the 5,500-square-foot **Beacon's Closet** ★★ (88 N. 11th St., Williamsburg, Brooklyn; ☎ 718/486-0816; www.beacons closet.com; ❶ to Bedford St.) trades in both trendy and vintage clothes, brought in by the fashionistas of this hip, artsy neighborhood. Very few items cost more than $20, and the selection is huge.

The oldest resale store in the nation—it was here in 1954 that the concept of re-selling lightly used designer wear was hatched—**Encores** ✪✪✪ (1132 Madison Ave., btwn 84th and 85th sts.; ☎ 212/879-2850; www.encoreresale.com; **4**, **5**, **6** to 86th St.) is still the standard-bearer, with the best prices Manhattan. The shop has two floors, which are divided into ready-to-wear and designer clothes. This being the hoity-toity Upper East Side, Chanel has the largest rack, though you'll also find Escada, Dolce & Gabbana, Armani, Calvin Klein, and the like, most from this season or last. On my last visit I pondered a lacy Marc Jacobs cocktail dress that still had its original price tag of $2,400; it was being sold for $340. *One warning:* You can't be shy here, as there's no door on the dressing room.

Largest of the resalers—and sometimes more *is* more—**Fisch for the Hip** ✪✪ (153 W. 18th St, btwn 6th and 7th Ave.; ☎ 212/633-9053; **1** to 18th St.) is the place to go if you've been jonesing for a Hermès bag. That's its specialty, along with status jeans and such sizzling designers as Stella McCartney, Vera Wang, and Marc Jacobs. Prices can be high, but not compared with the original costs.

Housing Works Thrift Shop (306 Columbus Ave., btwn 74th and 75th sts.; ☎ 212/579-7566; www.housingworks.org/thrift; **1**, **2**, **3**, **B**, **C** to 72nd St.; other branches at 143 W. 17th St., 202 E. 77th St., and 157 E. 23rd St.) offers do-gooder shopping: Not only will you find terrific buys on all of the top designers, but part of what you spend will go to help a homeless person living with HIV or AIDS. Along with designers such as Calvin Klein, Perry Ellis, and Diane Von Furstenberg, you'll find wedding gowns and furniture as well (some of which is auctioned in advance on the website for even better savings). I've always had the best luck at the Upper West Side branch, though that could be a fluke.

Ina and Ina Men's ✪ (21 Prince St., near Elizabeth St., ☎ 212/334-9048; or 262 Mott St., near Prince, ☎ 212/334-2210; www.inanyc.com; **F**, **V** to Houston St. for both) is where the *Sex and the City* costume department resold its clothes once the series ended. Though those costumes are now gone (they sold out in 2 hr. flat) there's no other place in the city where you'll be able to achieve "Carrie's" look as affordably, replicating that character's haute but wacky sensibility. The men's store has equivalently daring clothing for men (my recent faves were a leather Calvin Klein shirt for a reasonable $130, and a green alligator jacket for $160).

Guys looking for good quality, less fashion-forward menswear head uptown to **Gentleman's Resale** (322 E. 81st St., between First and Second Aves.; ☎ 212/734-2739; **4**, **5**, **6** to 86th St.). From suits to nut-colored ties, to trench coats and tuxes, good-as-new (but not) clothing is on sale for those who take their labels seriously. I saw everything from Prada to Polo to P. Diddy (really Sean John) labels here, often at a good 60% off the original rate. The selection of oxford shirts was particularly impressive.

Not quite as cheap as Encores, **Michael's** (1041 Madison Ave., btwn 78th and 79th sts.; ☎ 212/737-7273; www.michaelsconsignment.com; **6** to 77th St.) is the only one of the six consignment stores that offers one-of-a-kind couture clothes at deep discounts, including wedding gowns.

WOMEN'S WEAR

Anthropologie ✪✪ (50 Rockefeller Center at 50th St.; ☎ 212/246-0386; www. anthropologie.com; **B**, **D**, **F**, **V** to Rockefeller Center.; for other NYC locations, see website.) is a large chain of stores that nevertheless manages to give the illusion of being a quirky neighborhood place. You'll find funky, fun clothing, geared towards trendsetters in their 20s and 30s, along with housewares, gifts, and shoes.

And speaking of shoes, if you are into serious kicks, by which I mean Blahniks, Louboutin, Prada, and other pricey footwear, there's an outlet in the Financial District which gets them all at an extreme discount ($400 pairs going for $129, and $129 sandals for $39). It's called **Anbar** (60 Reade St. off Broadway; ☎ 212/227-0253; ❶, ⓜ, ❷, ❹, ❺, ❻, Ⓡ, Ⓦ to City Hall/Brooklyn Bridge; closed Sun), and it trades in overstocks and end-of-season sales (from both manufacturers and retail outlets). So many riches are here that the salespeople wear T-shirts that say "Take the Box with You!"—it's easy to try on one shoe and then lose the other in the sea of boxes.

Wispy skirts, beaded tops, sinewy trousers, cropped cashmere sweaters, thin Ts available in every color of the rainbow—all of these goods and more, make up the hippy, chic, Caribbean-happy designs at **Calypso Outlet** ★★★ (405 Broome St., near Lafayette; ☎ 212/343-0450; www.calypso-celle.com; ❻ to Spring St.). Settle for last season's wear (and really, who will know the difference?), and you'll pay as much as 70% less than you will at this pricey chain's other stores.

Though a full-figured buddy of mine complains that the clothing at **Eileen Fisher** ★★ (314 E. 9th St., btwn First and Second aves., ☎ 212/529-5715; www.eileenfisher.com) has become more form-fitting ever since the designer herself started losing weight, this chain still remains the place to go for elegant, adult clothing in draping, richly colored fabrics that mask those extra inches. And though Fisher doesn't have a maternity line, I find her clothes to be perfect through month eight, as they often have extra give in the stomach area. There are numerous stores around the city, but the East 9th Street location serves as the city's clearinghouse for sale items.

You may not have heard of designer Meghan Kinney, but she's been a fixture in Manhattan for the past decade thanks to **Meg's** ★ (312 E. 9th St., btwn Second and First aves.; ☎ 212/260-6329; www.megshops.com; ❻ to Astor Place), and has recently opened her own shops in Los Angeles and Toronto. Taking her inspiration from Martha Graham, her designs have a fluidity to them that is quite unique. I also like her use of kicky, unusual fabrics and the fact that though the look is young, it doesn't look foolish on her middle-aged clients. Worth a visit.

Club clothes, flirty skirts and dresses, and skinny jeans, all at a reasonable price, are what keep **Pookie & Sebastian** (1322 Columbus Ave at 75th St.; ☎ 212/580-5844; www.pookieandsebastian.com; ❸, ❻ to 72nd St.) pulsing with youthful energy. This is where you go if you have a stylishly wraithlike figure and a similarly skinny wallet—very few items here break the $100 price tag, which is actually pretty good for NYC.

"Style is better than trend" is the motto at **Personal Affair** ★ (102 E. 7th St. btwn First Ave. and Ave. A; ☎ 212/420-7778; www.pa212.com; ❻ to Astor Place), and it's a fitting one for this little boutique's expertly cut, smart, frill-free, and reasonably priced clothes. All are designed by Jessica Liepelt, an American living in Germany whose clothes are featured in stores across Europe. This is currently the only outlet in the United States for her wares (there's a small annex on Lafayette St.), but I have no doubt there will be more, as these clothes look great on women of most shapes and sizes.

CHILDREN'S CLOTHES

"Can I try this on?" and "Is this one my size?" are the soundtrack when I visit **Daffy's** ✪ 🄺 (1311 Broadway at 34th St.; ☎ 212/736-4477; www.daffys.com; Ⓝ, Ⓞ, Ⓡ, Ⓦ, Ⓑ, Ⓓ, Ⓕ to Herald Sq./34th St.) with my 3- and 7-year-old daughters. They like the clothes at this off-price specialty clothing chain as much as I do (though I'm not a fan of the adult stuff). Much of it comes from European designers and those American ones with an eye for whimsy—bright, cheerful clothing that's built sturdily and priced reasonably, with jumper dresses (with shirts) coming to just $20 and pairs of shorts at $10. Daffy's is part of a small chain in the tri-state area, with six other shops scattered around Manhattan.

If your kids are like mine, there's a good percentage of their wardrobe that never makes it off the hanger. I get them a lovely new dress, or a neighbor drops by a pair of lightly used slacks, and they languish unworn while my daughter wears her favorite Mylie Cyrus T-shirt for the umpteen time, or her ratty jeans, frayed almost to the point of indecency. So I've taken to shopping for other people's barely used kids clothes at **Jane's Exchange** (191 E. 3rd St off Ave. A; ☎ 212/677-0380; Ⓕ, Ⓥ to Second Ave.), a consignment shop entirely devoted to the wardrobe of Manhattan's pampered youngsters. It goes without saying that the clothes here are quite fashionable, and most look like they've never been worn (and likely they haven't been!).

JEWELRY

I'm addicted to **Laila Rowe** ✪✪✪ (8 E. 42nd St. near Fifth Ave.; ☎ 212/949-2276; www.lailarowe.com; ④, ⑤, ⑥, Ⓛ to Grand Central Station). For $15 you can complete an outfit with a dangly, chic necklace that looks like it's coral, or shell, or some exotic kind of stone but is really, well, heavy plastic and beads in most cases. Some of the stuff looks cheap, but on others Ms. Rowe does such a good copycatting job that her wares often look like the $1,000-and-up baubles sold by such pricey modern jewelry stores as Fragments. There are also seriously cute earrings (which they'll convert to clip-ons for no extra charge), bracelets, rings, brooches, and bags, all at low prices. Along with the 42nd Street store, there are eight other branches in all parts of Manhattan.

Though jewelry is rarely cheap, **The Metropolitan Museum of Art** ✪✪✪ (Fifth Ave. btwn 82nd and 84th sts.; ④, ⑤, ⑥ to 86th St.; www.metmuseum.org) has a wide assortment of reasonably priced pieces, all knock-offs from the historic jewelry in the museum, ranging from imitation Fabergé earrings to ancient Egyptian necklaces to Byzantine crosses.

Necklaces, earrings, pins, and bracelets by New York City–based designers are the temptations at **The Shape of Lies** (127 E. 7th St., between First Ave. and Avenue A; ☎ 212/533-5290; www.ancientartisans.com; 6 to Astor Place), a tiny boutique in the East Village. They're as unique as the locals who make them, fashioned from petrified wood, hand-blown glass, baby doll parts and of course, precious metals. The name comes from the fact that the owner also makes recreations of historic jewelry for museums across the nation and abroad. When I was last there, she had some gorgeous Celtic pieces on display. Prices aren't dirt cheap, but they're reasonable for goods this unusual and well-crafted.

BOOKS, MUSIC & VIDEOS

For those still loyal to vinyl, **Academy Records** (12 W. 18th St. btwn Fifth and Sixth aves.; ☎ 212/242-3000; www.academylps.com; ❹, ❺, ❻, ⓃⒶ, ⓄⒶ, Ⓡ, Ⓦ, Ⓛ to Union Sq.) has no peer. It's the largest used-record store in the city, with music in all categories and price ranges (most standard records cost between $5 and $15, but rare LPs will have price-tags in the hundreds of dollars). True fanatics make the pilgrimage out to the "Annex" in Brooklyn (96 N. 6th St.; ☎ 718/218-8200; Ⓛ to Bedford Ave.), which houses literally thousands of records. If you don't want to travel, but can't find what you want in Manhattan, clerks will call over to Brooklyn and conduct a search on your behalf.

Both **Barnes and Noble** ★★ 🧒 (www.bn.com) and **Borders** ★★ 🧒 (www.bordersbooks.com) have dozens of bookstores throughout the city and serve not only as convenient places to purchase books, but as lecture halls, when authors known and unknown come by for book readings and signings several times a week. There are simply too many outlets to list here, but if you go to one of the above sites, you'll find the locations of the store nearest you.

Books of Wonder ★ 🧒 (18 W. 18th St., btwn Fifth and Sixth aves.; ☎ 212/989-3270; www.booksofwonder.com; ❹, ❺, ❻, Ⓝ, Ⓡ to Union Sq.) is everything a children's bookstore should be: brightly lit, cozy but not cramped, only really crowded during storytelling hours (see website for schedule), and jammed with multiple editions of all those books we loved as kids that we want to introduce to our own children. The oldest and largest children's bookstore in the city, this should also be your first stop if you're seeking out a rare edition of a kid's book, or if you want to purchase art from one of the classics. *Nice perk:* Coupons for discounts on future sales with each purchase.

If you're looking for the CD of that tuneful musical you just saw, **Colony** (1619 Broadway at the corner of 49th St.; ☎ 212/265-2050; www.colonymusic.com; Ⓡ, Ⓦ to 49th or ❶ to 50th St.), a musical theater specialist, is the store to patronize. You'll find racks upon racks of classic and contemporary theater music CDs here, plus sheet music, karaoke tracks of current musicals, and a hefty dose of pop music just to keep the kitsch and camp in line. It's open until 1am on most nights.

Every script from every play ever written (well, almost) is available at **The Drama Bookshop** ★ (250 W. 40th St., btwn Seventh and Eighth aves.; ☎ 212/944-0595; www.dramabookshop.com; ❶, ❷, ❸, Ⓝ, Ⓡ, Ⓦ, Ⓢ to Times Sq.), an off–Times Square stalwart that has served the theater community of New York for over 40 years. Other offerings run the gamut from fawning biographies to complicated treatises on stage lighting to picture books of Broadway musicals. The Bookshop has a small theater attached; even if you don't want to buy, you can attend a reading absolutely free (see website for schedule).

Whodunnit? Who wrote it? **Murder Ink** (2486 Broadway at 92nd St.; ☎ 212/362-8905; www.murderinkproductions.com; ❶, ❷, ❸ to 96th St.) will know the answer to both those questions. This murder-mystery specialist boasts the largest collection of detective novels in New York, including dozens of out-of-print and rare thrillers.

Oscar Wilde Bookstore (15 Christopher St. near Sixth Ave.; ☎ 212/255-8097; www.oscarwildebooks.com; ❶ to Christopher St.), the world's first gay bookstore, is still going strong after nearly 40 years in business. It remains the friendly, clued-in place it's always been, carrying the most up-to-the-minute gay and lesbian literature, as well as a fine selection of rare and out-of-print books.

Grungy, maddeningly disorganized, stuffy, and crowded, **The Strand** ★★★ (828 Broadway, at 12th St.; ☎ 212/473-1452; www.strandbooks.com; **4**, **5**, **6**, **N**, **Q**, **R**, **W**, **L** to Union Sq.) is nonetheless New York's premier bookstore, a place that rivals the legendary Library at Alexandria in its scope and variety. Its motto is "Eight Miles of Books," and it certainly feels like it has that many when you visit; best of all, many of these are "front list" books that are ordered directly from the publisher at a substantial discount (sometimes as much as 50%). Those looking for rare books should look no further: The Strand has the largest collection in the city, with dozens traded in each day.

I know of no better Times Square time-killer than **Virgin MegaStore** ★ (1540 Broadway btwn 45th and 46th sts.; ☎ 212/921-1020; www.virginmegamagazine. com; **1**, **2**, **3**, **S**, **N**, **R**, **Q**, **W** to Times Sq.), a buzzing, exciting, music, video, and bookstore. Six hundred listening stations for CDs from all genres are available for aural browsing, as are 100 viewing stations for previewing DVDs; and you can spend literally an hour here (between a matinee and an evening performance, perhaps?) doing just that. Prices are average, but the selection at this, the largest entertainment store in the world, is extraordinary. Another "mega store" squats on Union Square (52 E. 14th St. on the corner of Broadway; ☎ 212/598-4666; **N**, **Q**, **R**, **4**, **5**, **6**, **L** to Union Sq.).

COSMETICS & BEAUTY SUPPLIES

The oldest apothecary shop in the nation (it was founded in 1838), **Bigelow** ★★★ (414 Sixth Ave. btwn Eighth and Ninth sts.; ☎ 212/473-7324; www.bigelow chemist.com; **A**, **B**, **C**, **D**, **E**, **F**, **V** to W. 4th St.) is still an excellent place to get a prescription filled—they'll even tailor the flavor in liquid medicines if you've got a finicky patient—but in recent years it's become known for its huge range of beauty supplies, carrying some European and Japanese products that aren't available anywhere else in the U.S. Some of the products are quite unusual. There are the "foot petals," which are near-invisible inserts that claim to make even the most fashionable shoes comfortable; "frownies," an 1800s stick-'em-on cure for frown lines that claims to train the wrinkles to go in another direction as you sleep; and house skin products. Even if you don't need to buy, stop by to browse under the Victorian gas chandeliers (converted to electric but still lovely).

Founded in 1867 as an apothecary shop—its specialty back then was such magic potions as "Money Drawing Oil"—**Kiehl's** ★ (109 Third Ave., btwn 13th and 14th St.; ☎ 212/677-3171; www.kiehls.com; **4**, **5**, **6**, **N**, **R**, **Q**, **L** to Union Sq.) switched to those modern snake oils, facial creams, and cleansers in the 1960s and has been wildly popular ever since. The best things about shopping here are the historic decor (the original chandeliers are still in use) and the generous gift of numerous small samples with every purchase.

Fifth Avenue is the flagship location for **Ricky's** (509 Fifth Ave. btwn 42nd and 43rd St.; ☎ 212/949-7230; www.rickys-nyc.com; **4**, **5**, **6**, **S** to Grand Central), a punky, funky chain of cosmetics stores that goes beyond the typical drugstore selection of beauty products. Among other items, you'll find wigs, hair dyes for every shade of the rainbow, body glitters, and shampoos even your stylist's never heard of. At Halloween it's the place to shop for a costume, and year-round it's a top location for all your beauty needs—even those you wouldn't tell Mom about. It's also great for souvenirs and small gifts, as it has a number of silly toys and bath products for adults and kids. All in all, there are 18 stores located in all parts of the city.

Ray's Beauty Supply ✪✪ (721 Eighth Ave. at 45th St.; ☎ 800/253-0993; www.raybeauty.com; ❶, ❷, ❸, Ⓝ, Ⓡ to Times Sq. or Ⓐ, Ⓔ, Ⓒ to 42nd St.) is where New York's actors come to get all their makeup. The variety here is mind-blowing: 32 varieties of false eyelashes, ranging from Liza Minelli spiky to Jennifer Lopez furry; 200 different blushes; countless eye shadows and professional quality brushes; hair dryers; and other beauty gizmos, some of which you might not even know exist. The prices here are also right, often 40% to 75% less than what you'd find elsewhere (my favorite shampoo sells for $20 at the local salon, so I make the trip to Ray's where I get it for $6).

ELECTRONICS & PHOTOGRAPHY GEAR

For video and still cameras, there's only one place in the city to shop and that's **B&H** ✪✪ (420 Ninth Ave. btwn 33rd and 34th St.; ☎ 800/606-6969 or 212/444-6615; www.bhphotovideo.com; Ⓐ, Ⓔ, Ⓒ to 34th St.; closed Sat), the leader in this field for over 30 years. With an enormous selection, all of it discounted—sometimes by as much as 70%—it stands head and shoulders over every other camera store in town. B&H also barters equipment, meaning that shutterbugs can trade up their own cameras for an advanced model, or buy superb, but less expensive, used cameras. It's a darn good place for audio equipment, computers, and other electronics. The only disappointment here is the service, which can be brusque. But if you come in knowing what you're looking for you're sure to get a deal.

Founded in 1971, **J&R Music and Computer World** ✪ (15 Park Row btwn Ann and Beekman sts.; ☎ 212/238-9000; www.jr.com; ❷, ❸ to Park Place or ❹, ❺, ❻ to Brooklyn Bridge) just keeps growing, and growing, and growing. Now housed in four separate storefronts on Park Row, it offers good prices on factory-fresh DVDs, stereos, computers, palm pilots, fax machines, and other gadgets. Professionally refurbished machines are also good buys here, as they usually come with full warranties.

And I'm sending you to the **Mac Store** (767 Fifth Ave. at 58th St.; ☎ 212/336-1440; www.apple.com; Ⓝ, Ⓡ, Ⓦ to Fifth Avenue) not with the expectation that you're going to lay down a couple of thou on a new, feather-weight laptop, but just because you've gotta see this place. Set in a giant glass cube right across from the famed Plaza Hotel, it's a wonderland for tech-heads, with all the merchandise spread across massive blond wood work tables. From iPods to full computers, it's all there for you to use, and no one will frown if you just duck in to check your e-mail for free. Insomniacs and procrastinators take note: It's open 24 hours a day, 365 days a year.

FURNITURE, COOKWARE, HOUSEWARES & ANTIQUES

A museum. A temple. A sanctuary. I can't afford to buy a darn thing at **ABC Carpet & Home** ✪✪✪ (888 Broadway, btwn 19th and 20th sts.; ☎ 212/473-3000; www.abchome.com; ❹, ❺, ❻, Ⓝ, Ⓞ, Ⓡ, Ⓛ to Union Sq.), except for spiffy soaps, but I sure do love trolling the floors here, as the goods on offer are simply exquisite. You'll find children's furniture and bedding fit for a Windsor, throw pillows straight from a high-class harem, all manner of delightful Asian antique furnishings and mod furnishings of the sort Twiggy would love from the '50s and '60s and today. Floor three features the cushiest of linens. Floors four and five have antique furnishings, divided up into scruffy-chic, country-style furniture and more formal wares. And the top floor is for carpets, as is the storehouse across the street. An absolute delight (even if you don't buy, you may come away with some good ideas for furnishing your own home). A branch in the Bronx (1055 Bronx River Ave.) offers periodic sales.

High-quality cookware at serious discounts is the draw at **Broadway Panhandler** ★★★ (65 E. 8th St., right off Broadway; ☎ 866-COOKWARE; www. broadwaypanhandler.com; **N**, **R**, **W** to 8th St. or **6** to Astor Place). In business since 1976, it consistently undercuts "suggested retail pricing" on such top brands at Boedum, All Clad, and Emile Henry by a good 40% or more. On a recent visit I found a Le Creuset gratinée dish for just $40; regular retail pricing would have put it out of my range at $90. There are also such unique (and possibly gift-worthy) items as silicone glove potholders; aprons in all patterns; silicone "food loops" that you can use to truss and then cook food in; and fancy blown-glass olive oil "drizzlers."

Chefs who like to walk quietly and carry a big knife—such as Nobu Matsuhisa, Daniel Boulud, and all of the blade flingers at Benihana—buy their blades at the low-key **Korin Japanese Trading Corp** ★★ (57 Warren St., btwn Church and W. Broadway; ☎ 800/262-2172; www.korin.com; **A**, **C**, **E** to Church St., **R** to Warren St.), in the Financial District. These are samurai-strength knives, and there are dozens of them, along with affordable cotton kimonos, plateware, and other pieces of Japanalia.

If you're visiting New York and can't shop directly in North Carolina, where most furniture is manufactured and (and thus cheaper), and just have to buy an armchair, dining set, or entertainment center, **North Carolina Furniture Showrooms** (9 E. 19th St., btwn Fifth and Sixth aves.; ☎ 212/645-2524 or 800/627-3507; **4**, **5**, **6**, **N**, **O**, **R** to Union Sq.) is where you'll find the best values. The store carries Hooker, Barco Lounger, Sherril Furniture, and other top names, but because you're buying direct from the factory, you'll get these pieces at 50% off retail. The store can ship your furniture to any area of the country for an amount of money that will not undercut the savings you have on the original price.

Pippin Home (112.5 W. 17th St. off Sixth Ave.; ☎ 212/505-5159; F, L, V to 14th St.) is the sort of antique store you'd expect to find on a backcountry lane. But here it is, in the heart of Manhattan, selling quirky, handsome vintage finds at prices that would be more common in, say, Montana. I've seen framed 1930's prints for as little as $35, milkglass lampshades for $45 and darn nice 1950's-era formica table and chair sets for less than $200. Adding to the down-home ambience are the friendly staff who might exclaim, 'Gee wilikurs, you did well today' when you present your purchases at the counter (I swear, I heard it with my own ears). The store's down a small alley (hence the odd address).

Perhaps the most 'only-in-New-York' store in this chapter, **Tiny Living** (125 E. 7th St., between First Ave. and Avenue A; ☎ 212/228-2748; www.tiny-living. com; **6** to Astor Place) is a home goods store for the New Yorkers (and there are a lot of them) who cram all their worldly belongings into 400-square-foot studios.

Even if you have more space in your own home, you'll appreciate the ingenious and often downright adorable space savers on sale here. My favorites: a groovy, patterned lap desk, complete with a cup holder ($29); tiny garden elves to stick in your houseplants ($7); and an organizer for purses that you can hag in your closet ($29).

A warren of small, collectibles-crammed rooms inhabit four floors in **The Showplace** (40 W. 25th St. btwn Fifth and Sixth aves.; ☎ 212/633-6063; www. nyshowplace.com; Ⓕ, Ⓥ, Ⓑ to 23rd St.), a Flatiron-district indoor bazaar that has served as home to 74 dealers for the past 13 years. Shops run the gamut from European art ceramics, to classical antiquities from ancient Egypt and Rome, to jewelry and purses, to Japanese woodblock prints and American oil paintings. You won't find much in the way of large furniture here (except when there's an auction on the 4th floor), but you will find everything else antique or vintage. And prices here are lower than you'll find uptown or in the Village at similar stores thanks to the relatively low cost of rent on these booths. Also, the recent demise of a huge nearby flea market has forced dealers to bargain more to stay afloat as they're simply not getting the kind of foot traffic they used to. Be sure you visit the eccentric "Princess Diana Museum" at gallery 206, and ask owner Herman Morales to tell you the Byzantine tale of how he came by these relics.

GIFTS & PAPER GOODS

Kitsch heaven! Where else but **Alphabets** ★★★ (2284 Broadway, btwn 82nd and 83rd sts.; ☎ 212/579-5702; www.alphabetsnyc.com; ❶ to 79th St.; also at 115 Ave. A btwn 7th St. and St. Marks Place, and 47 Greenwich Ave. btwn Perry and Charles sts.) will you find talking Pee Wee Herman dolls, Simpson's chess sets, Curious George T-shirts, and lighters embossed with pictures of the Rat Pack? For those with more "grown-up" sensibilities, Alphabets sells luxurious French soaps, fine wood jewelry boxes, lovely linens, and much more. I dare you to leave the store without buying a gift or a card here for someone (perhaps yourself).

A far, far cry from the sex shops of the Times Square area, **Babeland** ★ (94 Rivington St. near Ludlow; ☎ 212/375-1701; www.babeland.com; Ⓕ, Ⓙ, Ⓜ, Ⓩ to Delancey St.; or 43 Mercer St., off Grand St. in SoHo) is geared towards, well, babes, with a predominantly female staff who explain every dildo, butt plug, and whip in as commonsense and expert a way as if they were selling iPods. There's a great variety of merchandise—toys, books, videos, and various "accoutrements"— with each fetish and predilection covered in a thoroughly unsleazy manner. And if you want to do your part for the environment, here's where you can purchase a solar-powered vibrator.

Who knew that there'd be a market for freeze-dried mice ($49), stuffed piranhas ($24), and pendants made from butterfly wings ($39)? Apparently the mad scientists behind **Evolution Nature Store** ★ 🄺 (120 Spring St.; ☎ 800/952-3195; www.evolutionnyc.com; Ⓡ, Ⓞ to Prince St.) did, and in 1993 they opened this mesmerizing store-cum-museum, where you can spend an engrossing hour staring at perfectly preserved skeletons (all types of animals), pristine fossils, stuffed creatures, and bugs encased in plastic. A great place to take the kids.

Know anyone who lives in a fantasy world? Either **Forbidden Planet** ★ (840 Broadway, at 13th St.; ☎ 212/475-6161; www.fpnyc.com; ❹, ❺, ❻, Ⓝ, Ⓠ, Ⓡ, Ⓛ to Union Sq.) or **Jim Hanley's Universe** (4 W. 33rd St., opposite the Empire State

Building; ☎ 212/268-7088; www.jhuniverse.com; ❽, ❿, ❻, ❽, ❽ to 34th St.) is where you should buy their gift. Both stores specialize in all of the "geek" obsessions: sci-fi, horror, Japanese anime, comic books, and fantasy games. Jim Hanley's is a comic book specialist, whereas Forbidden Planet does a brisker trade in sci-fi texts and figurines from such cult classics as *Buffy the Vampire Slayer* and *Star Wars;* gaming implements; and more such ephemera.

Silly as it may seem, I always feel my pulse quicken whenever I venture into **Kate's Paperie** ✪✪✪ (140 W. 57th St., btwn Sixth and Seventh aves.; ☎ 212/459-0700; www.katespaperie.com; ❽, ❿, ❻, ❿ to 57th St.), the largest purveyor of exotic papers in the city (the store has over 4,000 different types from 40 countries). While Kate's is not cheap, it carries smaller items—hot wax presses, tiny books, pretty collections of stationery—that are perfect for gifts, and hey, you don't need to travel elsewhere to buy the card! Four other outlets available; see website for addresses.

Pylones ✪ (right in Grand Central Station; ☎ 212/317-9822; www.pylones-usa.com; ❹, ❺, ❻ to 42nd St.) is a French company that takes everyday objects—garden tools, ashtrays, luggage tags, wall thermometers—and updates them in Crayola colors and bold patterns. So a pair of pliers ($8) now has a brilliant floral design, luggage tags are shaped like snooty pink poodles ($12), and toasters ($69) are so brightly colored and cute you half expect Ernie and Bert to show up and pop in a slice or two. Other stores in the West Village, Soho, and Upper East Side (see website).

SPECIALTY FOODS & WINES

There are wine stores with larger selections and more elbow room than **Best Cellars** ✪ (1291 Lexington Ave. at 87th St.; ☎ 212/426-4200; www.bestcellars.com; ❹, ❺, ❻ to 86th St.), but few with the unswerving focus on value that you'll find here. The owners, all longtime wine experts, have made it their mission to find great wines for around $15 or less, and they've stocked the store accordingly. With nightly tastings and an expert staff who are eager to assist even novice wine lovers, you're almost guaranteed to walk out with a great bottle for less than you'd usually pay.

Since 1925, **Di Palo** ✪✪ (200 Grand St.; ☎ 212/226-1033; ❻, ❽, ❿, ❽ to Canal St.; ❽, ❿, ❻ to Grand St.) has been fulfilling New Yorkers' needs for everything Italian: sausages, olives, cheeses—all of it the finest quality, imported directly from Italy (except for the scrumptious mozzarella and ricotta, which are made right behind the counter here). Be warned, though: Waits here can be interminable, as the place is extremely popular and the counter staff extremely chatty.

Economy Candy ✪ (108 Rivington St. at Essex St.; ☎ 800/352-4544 or 212/254-1531; www.economycandy.com; ❻ to Delancey St.), an old-fashioned neighborhood candy store, has blossomed in recent years to encompass everything sweet, a few things sour (fine vinegars), and a handful of caffeinated goods (coffees and teas). Opened in 1937, the store is still family-owned and here you'll find the finest halvah (a delicious sesame paste candy) in the city, as well as top-brand imported European chocolates—Feodora, Noir, and others—for half of what you'd pay Uptown. There are also all those great penny candies you haven't seen in years, from wax lips to Pez (in an enormous variety of dispensers) to Mallo Cups, Chocolate Babies, and Black Jack chewing gum.

A Pilgrimage to Woodbury Common

Just how good is the shopping at **Woodbury Common Premium Outlets** ✮✮✮ (498 Red Apple Court, Central Valley, NY; ☎ 845/928-4000; www.premiumoutlets.com; take I-87 to Harriman, exit 16, or see below for bus directions), a sprawling outlet mall that's an hour outside of New York City? Let me put it this way: I managed to research this entire chapter without spending a cent (though I certainly had to fight some urges). In my one day at Woodbury Common, I frittered away a hefty chunk of my advance for this book.

I couldn't help myself—with over 200 different stores, the temptation simply proved too great. Set on a large campus constructed to look like a small New England town (all two-story, white-shingled and brick buildings, with a clock tower at its center), Woodbury hosts every single American and European brand of note, from bourgeois retailers such as Gap, Samsonite, Maidenform, Sony, Levis, and OshKosh B'Gosh, to such boutique names as Prada, Escada, Frette linens, Oilily, Kate Spade, and Yves St. Laurent. Better yet, the prices at all of these stores are seriously slashed, with Adrienne Vittadini shells going for as little as $49, DKNY pants for $39, Eileen Fisher sweaters for $49, and elaborate children's flying saucers for $15 (and now you know how I spent my advance). In general, I found prices to be a good 50% below retail, sometimes more.

To get to Woodbury Commons you can drive, take the train, or ride a bus. I'd recommend the bus: It's cheaper and more direct at just $29 (with the train you'll need to also shell out for a taxi from the station; the bus takes you directly to the mall). Shortline and Gray Line buses leave from the Port Authority approximately every hour, usually about 15 minutes past the hour, and return on an hourly schedule. *A word of warning:* Do not buy the discount book from the bus company with your ticket. Those who carry AAA cards can pick them up for free at the Woodbury Common information booth (in the food court). It's also common to see them lying around the bus station at Woodbury, left there by folks who didn't use all the coupons. If you don't belong to AAA, simply go to the Woodbury Common website in advance of your trip and sign up to become a preferred customer. It's free, and you can get the coupons that way. Coupons yield savings of 10% to 15% at most stores in the complex, although occasionally you'll have to purchase over $75 or $100 worth of goods to be eligible for the discount, so crunch the numbers before purchasing the coupons.

Another Lower East Side classic, nearly 100 years old, **Gus's Pickles** ★★★ (85–87 Orchard St. near Broome St.; www.gusspickle.com; closed Sat; **F** to Delancey St.) is the store that was filmed in the romantic comedy *Crossing Delancey.* It looks like it did then, just a guy with a couple of barrels of pickles standing on the street under an awning. And the pickles have not changed in the intervening years either: They're still mouth-puckeringly tart, fizzy with garlic, snappily crisp. If you do decide to buy, a small bucketful can last for up to 1 month unrefrigerated, and 3 months in the refrigerator. Be sure to ask for a taste first: These pickles are totally unlike the bland, mass-produced ones most of us are used to, so you want to get one of appropriate strength (as I said before, they can pack a wallop).

What I like best about **Jacques Torres Chocolate** ★★ 🟢 (350 Hudson St., entrance on King St.; ☎ 212/414-2462; www.jacquestorres.com; **1** to Houston St.)—besides the fact that Jacques Torres is a dashingly handsome Frenchman who likes to cook (making him every woman's dream guy)—is its owner's willingness to blend common ingredients with splendid chocolates. He does this, for example, with two breakfast cereals—plain bran flakes and Cheerios—and the results are exquisite. You'll also want to pick up a can of his extraordinarily rich hot chocolate ($16 for an 18-oz. tin; the "Wicked" version is slightly spicy), which puts Hershey's to shame. Though the shop is a bit out of the way, it's quite fun to visit; the large, oblong room is sided by glass so that you can watch the chocolate being made, and there are even cute child-size tables and chairs for the smallest candy aficionados.

Cheese is the new wine, attracting obsessive devotees who, like oenephiles, can spend hours tasting, musing, comparing. **Murray's Cheeses** ★★★ (254 Bleecker St. btwn Sixth and Seventh aves.; ☎ 212/243-3289; www.murrayscheese.com; **1** to Christopher St.) is at the epicenter of this movement. A cavernous emporium with over 250 varieties of cheese from all over the world and multiple tasting stations, Murray's has a fanatical following (in fact, the *New York Times* once ran a story about a lawyer who takes off every Thursday just to work behind the counter there for fun). If you like cheeses, be sure to make your own pilgrimage.

The sharp, smoky smell of fresh-roasted coffee will hit you even before you enter **Porto Rico Importing Company** ★★ (201 Bleecker St., btwn MacDougal St. and Broadway; ☎ 212/477-5421; www.portorico.com; **A**, **B**, **C**, **D**, **E**, **F**, **V** to W. 4th St.), a century-old beanery. In the hands of the Albanese family all that time, it's been the tradition to only roast as many beans as will be needed for the day's sales, so the coffee you get here is extremely fresh and delicious. This is also a good place to buy fancy teas.

Veniero's ★★ (342 E. 11th St., btwn First and Second aves.; ☎ 212/674-7070; www.venierospastry.com; **L** to First Ave.) is the best Italian pastry shop in the city, with crisp yet creamy cannolis, buttery pignoli nut cookies, and cheesecakes that are solid but light, and moist but not gooey (in a word: perfect). In a nod to the times, Veniero's now sells carb-free cheesecakes and sugar-free cookies. You can come here and get a box to take home, or lounge at this 100-year-old pasticceria for an espresso and pastry.

A fine New York State wine may sound like a joke, but in the past 15 years winemaking has exploded in the Empire State. There are now 200-plus vineyards, and their surprisingly good wines are available at **Vintage** ★ (482 Broome

Flocking to the Flagships

Throughout this chapter I've tried to introduce you to the stores that are either unique to New York City; are found in few other places in the U.S.; or are somehow representative of Gotham's sense of style. But the truth is, this media capital is also where a lot of major companies park their flagship stores in the hopes of attracting attention to their brands. So even though they carry the brands you're likely to find in your local mall, they do so with such hoopla and variety that shopping in them (or just window shopping), can be a real treat. Here's a sampling of some of the Flagship Stores you may want to visit:

Abercrombie & Fitch (147 E. 57th St., near Lexington Ave.; ☎ 212/421-9000)

American Girl Place (609 Fifth Ave. at 49th St.; ☎ 877/247-5223)

Brooks Brothers (346 Madison Ave. at 44th St.; ☎ 212/682-8800)

FAO Schwartz (767 Fifth Ave. at 59th St.; ☎ 212/308-6094)

GAP (60 W. 34th St. at Herald Square; ☎ 212/760-1268)

M&M World (1600 Broadway between 48th and 49th Sts.; ☎ 212/295-3850)

NBA Store (666 Fifth Ave. at 52nd St.; ☎ 212/515-NBA1)

Nike Town (6 E. 57th St. off Fifth Ave.; ☎ 212/891-6453)

Ralph Lauren (867 Madison Ave. at 72nd St.; ☎ 212/606-2100)

Sony Style (550 Madison Ave. near 55th St.; ☎ 212/833-5336)

Tiffany & Co. (727 Fifth Ave. at 57th St.; ☎ 212/755-8000)

Tommy Hilfiger (681 Fifth Ave., between 53rd and 54th streets). Opening November of 2008.

St., at Wooster St.; ☎ 212/226-9463; www.vintagenewyork.com; ❶, ❶, ❶, ❶ or ❻ to Canal St.; also 2492 Broadway at 96th St.; ❶, ❷, ❸ to 96th St.). Designed to resemble a winery more than a wine store, Vintage boasts a large bar in the back where browsers can sample 200 wines from 60 different vineyards before purchasing.

Crowded at all hours, haphazardly organized, with gruff service, **Zabar's** ✭✭✭ (2245 Broadway, at 80th St.; ☎ 800/697-6301 or 212/782-2000; www.zabars. com; ❶ to 79th St.) is still the place to come if you want to bring home good old-fashioned deli food. The smoked fish are the finest in the city, the cheese counter boasts 600 pungent varieties, and the halvah is to die for. If you venture up to the second floor, you'll find hundreds of different kitchen gadgets, pots, pans, blenders, and the like.

TOYS

The antithesis of Toys "R" Us, **Kidding Around** ✭ 🧸 (60 W. 15th St., near Sixth Ave.; ☎ 212/645-6337; www.kiddingaroundnyc.com; ❻, ❶ to 14th St.) stays away from all of those annoying beeping, buzzing, and flashing toys. Instead the focus is on playthings that children manipulate themselves, hopefully learning something in the process. Prices are fair, and the shop has a number of unusual toys such as rubber horseshoes ($11, hey you can play in the living room), soap-making kits, and all kinds of dazzling costumes.

You should visit **The American Museum of Natural History** ☆☆☆ (Central Park West, btwn 79th and 81st sts.; www.amnh.org; **B**, **C** to 81st St.) with your kids (they'll love it), and while you're there, buy a few gifts from the museum's extensive and surprisingly reasonable shops (I recently counted almost 20 nice options for less than $3). The toys are mostly science-oriented with a wide variety of choices ranging from miners' helmets with working lights, to stuffed dinosaurs, to puzzles, microscopes, and books.

The Scholastic Store ☆☆ (545 Broadway, at the corner of Prince St.; ☎ 212/343-6166; http://shop.scholastic.com; **R**, **W** to Prince St., **6** to Spring St.) is a warehouse-sized emporium that focuses on toys that are also learning aids—science and craft kits, Leap Frog machines, stacks upon stacks of books, and more. This is also a good place to visit on a rainy day, as the store often hosts storytelling hours, shows, movies, and other events for kids.

More than just a toy store, the huge flagship **Toys "R" Us** (1514 Broadway at 44th St.; ☎ 800/TOYSRUS; www1.toysrus.com; **1**, **2**, **3**, **N**, **Q**, **R**, **S** to Times Sq.) has become one of Times Square's leading tourist attractions thanks to the three-story-high Ferris wheel at its core. As with other Toys "R" Us branches across the country, you'll find all of the major brands here—Playskool, Lego, Barbie, and others—just in greater numbers than you may find at your home branch. And if you've got an itchy kid, you can take him in, set him up in front of the electronic game station, and take a well-deserved rest for half an hour. *Warning:* It can get extremely crowded, so hold on tightly to your child's hand.

10 Nightlife in the "City That Never Sleeps"

From high culture to high jinks

IT ISN'T A BOAST BUT A PLAIN FACT: FROM OPERA TO JAZZ, FROM NIGHTCLUBS to bars, from concert recitals to ballet and modern dance, New York offers the greatest variety and sheer quantity of evening entertainment in America.

Apart from the 200-some-odd theaters presenting dramas and musicals each night (a specialized subject deserving its own treatment; see chapter 11), New York offers every sort of live, nighttime show (including operas, operettas, concerts, and recitals); as well as every kind of dance performance, from classic ballet to cutting-edge modern dance; and every variety of performance art, from exotic to weird. It has bars by the hundreds, dance clubs designed by world-famous architects, and gay and lesbian hangouts that are openly and unabashedly festive.

> *Evening is coming fast and the great city is blazing there in your vision in its terrific frontal sweep and curtain of star-flung towers, now sown with the diamond pollen of a million lights, and the sun has set behind them, and the red light of fading day is painted upon the river.*
>
> —Thomas Wolfe

It's a dizzying but important subject because most visitors enjoy New York's nightlife to the same extent they enjoy its daytime sightseeing. And in New York, unlike most other American cities, the sidewalks aren't "rolled up" when darkness descends. In New York (one of the only cities in the country that operates its public transportation throughout the night), the bright lights stay on until 4am and you owe it to yourself to take in all the after-dark excitement.

To make them easy to peruse, I've grouped the nighttime opportunities in this chapter by entertainment category.

OPERA

The big name for opera performances is, of course, the **Metropolitan Opera House** ✮✮✮ (at Lincoln Center, btwn W. 62nd and 65th sts. off Columbus Ave.; ☎ 212/362-6000; www.metoperafamily.org; ❶ to 66th St.). Everything about attending an opera here is grand—from the entrance you'll make past hanging Chagall murals to the world-class singers you'll hear (such as Renee Fleming) to the pomp and glitz of the productions themselves, many designed by such over-the-top aesthetes as Franco Zefferelli on one end of the scale and Robert Wilson on the other. The lovely little secret about the Met is that the cheap seats get the

Lincoln Center

best sounds. Sit in the theater's ground floor section and you may have trouble making out the words ($80–$375 a seat), but pay as little as $27 for a "family circle" seat, and the voices will float up to you in all their crystalline clarity. Weekday performances can be as much as 50% less expensive, depending on which tier you pick, and standing room drops prices to as little as $15 in the family circle and $20 in the orchestra (they'll even give you your own supertitles box to hold so you can follow the show). **Warning:** Don't show up late, unless you want to watch the first act on a video screen in the basement; the Met does not seat latecomers.

The Met's sister company, the **New York City Opera** ★★★ (at Lincoln Center, btwn W. 62nd and 65th sts. off Columbus Ave.; ☎ 212/362-6000; www.nyc opera.com; ❶ to 66th St.), is a house with a mission. Make that three missions, actually: to champion American singers (Beverly Sills got her start here), to perform contemporary or forgotten operas (though not exclusively), and to serve as the "People's Opera," as former Mayor Fiorella LaGuardia, a founder, put it, by keeping prices reasonable. Now this is opera, of course, so premium orchestra seats won't be cheap, but they top out at $130, which is a third of what you'll pay at the Met for similar seats. The cheapest seats start at just $16. Expect a fine opera experience with a touch, just a touch, less glitz than at the Met.

The season for high culture

With few exceptions, the great concert halls and opera stages have performances between September and June, taking off the summer months. While there are occasional free concerts in Central Park and at other venues, on the whole, lovers of the great musical classics should visit when it's colder.

Your third option is the **Amato Opera Company** ✪ (319 Bowery at 2nd St.; ☎ 212/228-8200; www.amato.org; ❻ to Bleecker St.), a mom-and-pop operation that presents postage-stamp versions of the great classics to an adoring audience of regulars. Here, the prices are right at $35 for an orchestra seat, and this being New York, the young singers getting their start here are often terrifically talented.

CLASSICAL MUSIC

More than 100 years ago, Tchaikovsky himself presided over the opening night of **Carnegie Hall** ✪✪✪ (154 W. 57th St., at Seventh Ave.; ☎ 212/247-7800; www. carnegiehall.org; ❶, ❷, ❸, ❹ to 57th St.), just one of a legion of great musicians who have graced this famous stage. Today, you'll see such stars as Dawn Upshaw, Sophie Van Otter, the Boston Symphony Orchestra (under the direction of James Levine), the Kronos Quartet, and pianist Emanuel Ax—all drawn by the unsurpassed acoustics and the honor of playing this magnificent hall (you can tour it during the daytime; call for info). Ticket prices ricochet up and down, depending on the day of the week, the act, and, of course, the theater area in which you choose to sit. For nosebleed seats (and you will be up quite high), prices start at about $26, usually going no higher than $50. Prime seating in the first tier can soar as high as $106, but you'll normally pay between $50 and $70 for a decent seat. In addition to the Isaac Stern Concert Hall (the main auditorium), Carnegie Hall maintains two smaller recital spaces.

Avery Fisher Hall ✪✪✪ (Lincoln Center, btwn W. 62nd and 65th sts. off Columbus Ave.; ☎ 212/875-1530; www.newyorkphilharmonic.org; ❶ to 66th St.) is another superb venue for classical music, the home of the New York Philharmonic, currently under the visionary direction of Lorin Maazel (he'll be succeeded by Alan Gilbert in 2009). Along with the classics, the Philharmonic commissions a number of new works each year, and lures star soloists (Midori, Itzak Perlman). A number of concerts feature pre-show talks and meet-the-artist events, and tend to be quite intimate and informative. Tickets range from $34 to $104, with matinees and balcony seats priced at the lower end of the scale. There are also kids' concerts for as little as $7 a ticket. Students are eligible for $12 "student rush" tickets, available online at **www.newyorkphilharmonic.org/student rush** up to 10 days before a concert.

Chamber music is on tap at **Alice Tully Hall** ✪✪ (Lincoln Center, btwn W. 62nd and 65th sts. off Columbus Ave.; ☎ 212/875-1530; www.chambermusic society.org; ❶ to 66th St.), home base for the esteemed Chamber Music Society of Lincoln Center. A full roster of master classes and lectures add to the performance schedule. National Public Radio listeners will be familiar with this group from their Monday night concert series, broadcast live each week.

Bargemusic ✪ (at the Fulton Ferry Landing; ☎ 718/624-2083; www.barge music.org; ❹ to High St. or ❺ to York St., both in Brooklyn) is presented on an actual barge moored near the Brooklyn Bridge. This small theater (125 seats) with a big view of the Manhattan skyline is a sheer delight, and a cheap one at that, with tickets topping out at $35, $30 for seniors, and $20 for students. Pianissimos are more piano here and fortissimos molto-loud, even when played by a solo piano or string quartet. This is one of the few truly intimate stages in the city, and the acoustics are first-rate.

DANCE

Ballet aficionados tend to swing between Lincoln Center's two resident compa-nies: **The New York City Ballet** ✪✪ (☎ 212/870-5570; www.nycballet.com) and **The American Ballet Theater** ✪✪ (☎ 212/477-3030; www.abt.org). NYCB is the more famous of the two, founded by Lincoln Kerstein and the 20th century's greatest ballet choreographer, George Balanchine. And it is for Balanchine's work that you still attend performances at the New York City Ballet; his ballets are the staple here and remain as diamond-sharp, elegant, and moving as when they were first performed, some as many as 50 years ago. Balanchine's version of *The Nutcracker* is a holiday classic and one of the most difficult tickets to get each Christmas season. ABT features more of an emphasis on story ballets—*Coppelia, Swan Lake, Sleeping Beauty*—and tends to produce more bravura stars than NYCB (where the emphasis is on ensemble work). Currently, ABT has a raft of Latino leapers who are thrilling audiences with the artistry and sheer physical prowess of their dancing.

The blockbuster modern dance shows tend to play the **Joyce Theater** ✪ (175 Eighth Ave., at 18th St.; ☎ 212/242-0800; www.joyce.org; ❹, ❸, ❺ to 15th St. or ❶ to 18th St.), and it's not hard to see why: It's simply the best space in the city to see dance—there's not a bad seat in the house. The audience sits slightly above the dancers, meaning that you won't be seeing just the feet, or just the bodies—you'll get the whole picture. In past years, this is where Pilobolus has played, as well as the Parson's Dance Company, Trisha Brown Dance Company, and Momix. (The Joyce accepts volunteer ushers, so call if you're in search of a freebie—see p. 295 on volun-teer ushering). In 2004, the Joyce was chosen to occupy the Frank Gehry–designed theater in the new buildings planned for the World Trade Center site.

Practice makes perfect

The performing arts are available at a low cost nearly 7 days a week at the **Juilliard School** ✪ (☎ 212/799-5000; www.juilliard.edu), the nation's premiere training institution for music, drama, and dance. Performances by supernaturally talented young performers, ranging from chamber music recitals and orchestral concerts to ballets and complete productions of Shakespeare, are open to the pub-lic at very reasonable prices (and often free). Because the students perform in dif-ferent venues around town, it's best to call the box office or consult the Web before attempting to attend a show.

Hipper and smaller, **Dance Theater Workshop** (219 W. 19th St., btwn Sixth and Seventh aves.; ☎ 212/691-6500; www.dtw.org; ● to 18th St.) cocoons its audiences in dance, from the performance clips that often play near the box office, to the "Meet the Artist" programs after shows, to the wine and snack gatherings at the on-site cafe usually attended by the performers after the show. You'll see top talent here, with an emphasis on "flavor-of-the-moment" emerging stars, some of whom have staying power (Bill T. Jones started here, as did David Parsons), and some of whom will ultimately succumb to the unfortunate economics of modern dance (a field in which only a handful of artists are able to make a living).

The Danspace Project (131 E. 10th St., off Second Ave.; ☎ 212/674-8112; www.danspaceproject.org; ❻ to Astor Place or ❶ to Third Ave.) is set in one of the loveliest venues in the city: the landmark St. Mark's Church, one of the oldest continuously operating churches in Manhattan and a colonial beauty. Performances are given in the wide open space that is the sanctuary, and the Project is known for the diversity of its offerings: You'll see newcomers in their 20s, mid-career artists, and even dancers and choreographers of AARP age. All present highly polished works with professional production values, though the audience pays much less to see shows here than at other venues: an average of $15.

CONCERT HALLS

Tidy categories won't do for the next three Manhattan venues, which have made a name for themselves by hosting all manner of tony performances. There's **City Center** ✭✭ (W. 55th St., btwn Fifth and Sixth aves.; ☎ 212/581-1212; www.citycenter.org; ❶, ❶, ❶, ❶ to 57th St.), which is a major dance performance space enjoying regular visits from the Paul Taylor Company, Alvin Ailey, and others; and also the producing organization behind the acclaimed **Encores** ✭✭ series—staged readings of older, often-forgotten musicals (the Broadway hit revival of *Chicago* began at Encores). Every September, the center hosts a dance festival, giving away a number of $10 seats. Farther uptown, **Merkin Concert Hall** ✭ (121 W. 67th St., off Broadway; ☎ 212/501-3303; www.kaufman-center.com; ● to 66th St.) is a friendly stop for world music groups, classic-music ensembles, and Broadway composers trying out new works (in its insider "Bound for Broadway" series). Though the lineup is eclectic, you'll nearly always find something worthwhile at the Merkin. Most diverse is **Symphony Space** ✭ (2537 Broadway at 95th St.; ☎ 212/864-5400; www.symphonyspace.org; ●, ❷, ❸ to 96th St.), which presents programs of music, film, musical theater (the excellent New Voices series of up-and-coming Broadway composers), and the spoken word. It's probably most famous for the last, as the NPR show "Selected Shorts"—short stories read aloud by big name actors—is taped here. Every Bloomsday (June 16), Symphony Space hires celebrated actors for a marathon reading of James Joyce's *Ulysses*—an all-day and all-night affair.

All three venues discount student and senior tickets, so inquire about possible savings if you fall into one of those categories. Occasionally, you'll also find City Center offerings on the board at TKTS (p. 294).

Outside of Manhattan, the finest multiuse facility is the **Brooklyn Academy of Music** ✭✭✭ (30 Lafayette Ave., Brooklyn; ☎ 718/636-4100; www.bam.org; ❷, ❸, ❹, ❺ to Atlantic Ave.), which may well be the best place in the United States for challenging, inventive, and acclaimed international productions of music, dance, performance art, and theater. It's at BAM where you'll see Germany's dance treasure Pina Bausch, the latest theater opus from Brit director Peter Brooks, or Phillip Glass's newest symphony. Along with the large BAM Opera House and the smaller BAM Harvey Theater, the organization has a dedicated movie theater for art films and a cafe space where up-and-coming talent perform. I've never been disappointed by anything I've seen here, though occasionally I've had difficulty getting a seat. It may be the most consistently exciting venue in New York, and the 45-minute-long train ride it takes to get here is well worth the effort. (For those squeamish about the subway, a BAM bus leaves an hour before the performance from in front of the Whitney Altria, on 42nd St. between Fifth and Vanderbilt aves. Bus fare $4.) *For penny pinchers:* Discounts are sometimes offered to students and seniors.

MUSEUM CRAWLS

In this "city that never sleeps," even the museums sometimes stay up late. Once or twice a week most of the great cultural centers of the city keep their doors open until 8 or 9pm and often pair the art-viewing with cocktail service. Though the practice has been going on for years, most residents don't know about these late hours, and the museums tend to get far fewer visitors at these times than during the daytime, which translates into blessedly uncrowded galleries.

For night owl museums, please see the "Museums After Dark" chart on the next page.

LIVE MUSIC CLUBS

FOR JAZZ

Since the late 1920s, when the presence of Louis Armstrong, Fletcher Henderson, Duke Ellington, and W.C. Handy transformed New York into the de facto capital of jazz, stealing that honor from Chicago, the city has been the place where jazz musicians have come to prove their mettle, learn from the greats, and hopefully land a recording contract. It's the only place in the world to have a complete concert facility devoted solely to jazz, the Frederick P. Rose Hall (better known as Jazz at Lincoln Center, see below), but there are also many smaller venues where this all-American art form is alive and kickin'. In fact, certain jazz clubs outdraw the rock-'n'-roll clubs, turning patrons away at the door night after night.

My picks for the top jazz venues are:

The Frederick P. Rose Hall ✯✯✯ **(Jazz at Lincoln Center,** in the Time Warner Center, Broadway at 60th St.; ☎ 212/721-6500; www.jazzatlincolncenter.org; ❶, Ⓐ, Ⓒ, Ⓑ, Ⓓ to Columbus Circle; performance schedule varies by the week). You've heard of food courts? This is the "Jazz court," a massive, three-theater facility with a mini-museum on-site, that has been wedged into the Uptown corner of the city's premiere mall.

Its centerpiece is the **Rose Hall,** a concert hall in the round (usually, though it can also be configured as a standard proscenium theater), with remarkable acoustics and a splendidly be-bop look created by huge boxes of light that change color throughout the night—from subtle creams to striking autumn leaf colors—forming a glowing crown around the performance space. Some seats are actually behind the musicians, giving real aficionados a chance to check out the fingering as the musicians perform. This is where Wynton Marsalis, the center's director,

Museums After Dark

Museum	Late hours	Booze?	Other comments
American Folk Art Museum (p. 150)	Fri until 7:30pm	Wine, beer, cocktails	Free admission after 5:30pm
Cooper-Hewitt National Design Museum (p. 148)	Fri until 9pm	No	Check website for exhibit listings as they change frequently
Jewish Museum (p. 162)	Thurs until 8pm	No	No
The Metropolitan Museum of Art (p. 135)	Fri–Sat, until 8:45pm	Beer, wine, cocktails	Roof garden open May–Oct. Otherwise go to balcony bar
Morgan Library & Museum (p. 143)	Fri until 9pm	Wine, cocktails	No
Museum of Arts and Design (p. 160)	Thurs until 8pm	No	No admission charged after 6pm
The Museum of Jewish Heritage (p. 154)	Wed until 8pm	No	No admission charged after 4pm
Museum of Modern Art (p. 139)	Fri until 8pm	Beer, wine, cocktails	Free admission after 5pm
Museum of the Moving Image (p. 156)	Fri until 8pm	No	Free admission after 4pm; visitors attending movie screenings will often stay until 9pm or 10pm in the theater. Museum is currently closed due to a major renovation and is expected to reopen sometime in the winter of 2009. Please check the website or call for updates.
The American Museum of Natural History (p. 137)	Fri until 8:45pm	No	Only the Rose Planetarium is open late; rest of museum closed
The Museum of Sex (p. 164)	Sat until 8pm	No	No
The Neue Gallery (p. 158)	Fri until 9pm	Beer and wine	Cabaret on-site often goes later
The Rubin Museum (p. 161)	Wed until 7pm, Fri until 10pm	Beer and wine	On-site movie theater often open later
The Whitney Museum (p. 146)	Fri until 9pm	No	Pay-what-you-wish admission after 6pm

struts his stuff in concert with the Lincoln Center Jazz orchestra. Programs here are primarily focused on swing and New Orleans–style jazz. Though the hall can be intimidating, Marsalis does his best to keep the informal jazz vibe, encouraging the audience to clap along and call out; usually by the end of the evening, they're doing just that.

The **Allen Room,** the center's second largest space, has a configuration that can be switched to accommodate a dance floor, a seven-tier amphitheater, or cocktail-table seating. Whatever the look, it's a splendidly beautiful room with a wall of glass behind the performing space, lending to the music a Central Park backdrop. **Dizzy's Club Coca Cola** is the most traditional of the theaters, a smaller cocktail and dinner jazz club (again with that transcendent view of Columbus Circle and the park), and the only one of the three facilities to operate year-round, serving as a showcase for some of the younger talents in jazz (called the "upstarts").

After Lincoln Center, **Birdland** ✫ (315 W. 44th St., btwn Eighth and Ninth aves.; ☎ 212/581-3080; www.birdlandjazz.com; daily), at 4,000 square feet is the second-grandest dedicated facility in the city for jazz. Though this is not the original Birdland where Coltrane played, it still presents top acts, with the David Berger and the Sultans of Swing (a big band specializing in the music of Duke Ellington) playing every Tuesday, and Chico O'Farrill's Afro-Cuban Jazz Big Band owning Sunday. In fact, if your idea of jazz is a small battalion of men blowing horns, this is where to come, as the large space is able to accommodate big bands that other venues (other than

> ❝ *New York seems conducted by jazz, animated by it. It is essentially a city of rhythm.* ❞
>
> —Anaïs Nin

the concert halls around town) simply can't fit. Cover charges range from $20 to $60, but seem to hold steady at $40 on weekends, $25 on weeknights; if you sit at the bar rather than at the tables, you get one drink free and escape an additional $10 food or drink minimum.

Iridium (1650 Broadway at 51st St.; ☎ 212/582-2121; www.iridiumjazzclub. com; daily; **N**, **Q**, **R** to 49th St.) tends to attract a slightly older crowd, drawn by earlier shows (the first performance of the night is at 8pm rather than 9), better-quality food than at most clubs, and a more intimate setting that allows patrons to get up close and personal with the performers. I think they probably like, as I do, the updated 1950s decor, with little shaded lamps on each table, and "hep" brown-and-maroon patterned panels on the walls. Monday night the legendary Les Paul does two sets ($45 cover); Tuesdays and Wednesdays are given over to the music of Mingus and Zappa ($30 cover); on other nights, a wide range of acts averages $30 for the cover and $10 for either food or drink.

The Village Vanguard ✫✫✫ (178 Seventh Ave., btwn Perry St. and W. 11th St.; ☎ 212/255-4037; www.villagevanguard.com; **1**, **2**, **3** to 14th St.) is now over 70 years old but still has the youngest spirit of any of the jazz clubs in town, consistently featuring the best of the new talents and cutting-edge jazz. It also looks the most like a jazz club *should* look, to my mind. You enter a red door and descend a steep staircase to a battered, triangular room, cluttered with posters and pictures of all the greats who played and recorded albums here (Mingus, Davis,

Monk, Marsalis). The club has also showcased folkies such as Pete Seeger and Harry Belafonte over the years, but today it's strictly jazz and its prices are among the most reasonable: $35 cover on weekends, which comes with drink tickets good for one of whatever you want. Weeknight shows are even cheaper (they vary in price).

The Blue Note (131 W. 3rd St., off Sullivan St.; ☎ 212/475-8592; www.bluenotejazz.com; A, C, E, B, D, F to W. 4th St.) has the most corporate feel of all the clubs (perhaps because it's now a chain, with four clubs in Japan and one in Italy). Tables are jammed together, the bar area is even more crowded, and the second floor is given over to a huge souvenir stand of such kitschy items as jazz golf balls, teddy bears, and bobble-head figurines of musicians. But it still attracts some of the best talent in the city, so it can't be overlooked; and it does have a terrific late-night series for newcomers (just an $8 cover). The Note's prices are a bit lower than those at the other clubs as well, with many shows coming in at just $25 (even on the weekends), just $15 at the bar (though I'd recommend avoiding the bar; you're too far from the music here and the atmosphere is like Grand Central Station at rush hour).

FOR CABARET

In the twilight world between jazz clubs and Broadway shows are cabaret theaters, small stages where the crooner is still king, three encores is the norm, and prices can rival those of the most expensive Broadway shows . . . with a two-drink minimum thrown in, to boot.

The classic cabarets of New York, those that attract such big names (for this small field) as Elaine Stritch, Andrea Marcovicci, Eartha Kitt, and Michael Feinstein, can be counted on one hand. They are:

- **Café Carlyle** ★★★ (35 E. 76th St. at Madison Ave.; ☎ 212/724-1600; www.thecarlyle.com; 6 to 77th St.)
- **Feinstein's at the Regency** ★★ (540 Park Ave. at 62nd St.; ☎ 212/339-4095; www.feinsteinsattheregency.com; N, R to Fifth Ave.)
- **The Algonquin** ★★ (59 W. 44th St. btwn Fifth and Sixth aves.; ☎ 212/840-6800; www.algonquinhotel.com; 1, 2, 3, S, N, Q, R, W to Times Sq.)

All three are elegant, acoustically blessed spots; which club you pick will depend on who's headlining and how plush you're feeling, as cover charges will run between $65 and $105 per person, plus a food or drink minimum.

But there's another handful of places that play host to a mix of talents, generally charging half to one-third of what the snooty three charge.

Broadway babies, in between Great White Way gigs, tend to play **Don't Tell Mama**'s (343 W. 46th St., btwn Broadway and Eighth Ave.; ☎ 212/757-0788; www.donttellmamanyc.com; R, Q, C, E to 50th St.) in the hopes of attracting agents and snaring jobs. So what you see can be a mixed bag of audition songs, confessionary patter, drag shows, and sometimes moments of unadulterated genius. Because very few of the people who play here will have names you recognize, it's a bit of a gamble; the talent in the front room tends to be a bit more polished than those who play in the back. Broadway insider Seth Rudetsky has a regular gossipy, catty show that's always worth the price of admission (which can be $12–$15, depending on the act and night).

Wrongly named, **The Duplex** ✪ (61 Christopher St., at Seventh Ave.; ☎ 212/455-5438; www.theduplex.com; ❶ to Christopher St.) is actually a triplex, with one floor devoted to piano bar shenanigans (performed by a changing cast of singers, pianists, and singing bartenders), the top floor to traditional cabaret, and the one in between called the "game room"—a lounge-type place with lots of TVs, low couches, and hot bartenders. A cover charge applies only in the cabaret room, with prices averaging between $10 and $20 (plus a 2-drink minimum), though the cover can go as high as $40 for headliners. The gayest of these options—after all, it *is* in the Village—it's a fairly low-key place with a stellar history, having witnessed the debuts of Barbara Streisand and Joanne Worley. Maybe you'll see a rising star, too.

FOR BLUES, COUNTRY & ROCK

If you're in town to see one of the megaconcerts, you probably already know to go to Radio City Music Hall (www.radiocity.com), Madison Square Garden (www.madisonsquaregarden.com), or nearby Jones Beach (www.jonesbeach.com). Listed below are the city's more intimate, interesting music venues.

Is there a more resonant place in all of Manhattan to listen to blues, jazz, or pop music than the legendary **Apollo Theater** ✪✪✪ (253 W. 125th St. btwn Adam Clayton Powell, Jr., and Frederick Douglass blvds.; ☎ 212/531-5300; www.apollotheater.com; ❹, ❺, ❻, ❼ to 125th St.)? To me, it's a thrill just to walk past the collage of all of the greats who've played here and then take a seat in this lovely, surprisingly intimate theater (it looks much bigger on TV). All sorts of celebs still play here, from Mario to Bill Cosby, but Amateur Night on Wednesday remains the headline attraction, a gladiatorial music demonstration where the winners may emerge stars and the losers are skewered with the unkindest of boos and shouted insults. To learn more about the history of the Apollo, go to p. 231.

B.B. King Blues Club and Grill (237 W. 42nd St., btwn Seventh and Eighth aves.; ☎ 212/997-4144; www.bbkingblues.com; ❶, ❷, ❸, ❹, ❺, ❻, ❼ to Times Sq.) is the "Branson" of NY's music clubs, a place where you can go and see the somewhat faded stars of rock, pop, and blues—Eddie Money, Roberta Flack, Pat Benatar—in a dignified, comfortable red-velvet curtain-type place that's large enough to accommodate all of the fans these former luminaries still have (the house seats 500). Entrance fees vary by show, as do cover charges, but my advice is to drink any cover there may be rather than eat it, as the food is lousy and expensive.

With a landmark Art Deco interior, **The Beacon Theater** ✪ (2124 Broadway, btwn 74th and 75th sts.; ☎ 212/496-7070; www.beacontheaternyc.com; ❶, ❷, ❸ to 72nd St.) has to be one of the loveliest venues in the city in which to rock out. And they really knew how to build theaters back in the 1920s: Every seat has a good view, and the acoustics are remarkable. While you won't get the molten-hot names, you will see talented stars Elvis Costello, Willie Nelson, James Blunt, and Journey. Prices vary widely by show and seat, but often start around $25.

A step down from the Beacon, in prestige and size, both the **Bowery Ballroom** (6 Delancey St.; ☎ 212/260-4700; www.boweryballroom.com; ❹, ❺ to Grand St.) and **Webster Hall** (125 E. 11th St.; ☎ 212/353-1600; ❹, ❺, ❻, ❼, ❽, ❾, ❿ to Union Sq.) play host to cutting-edge performers whose cult following is too large to just play bars anymore. If the names Vampire Weekend, Kate Nash, Chromeo, and Nada Surf mean anything to you, you'll definitely want to check these two mid-sized venues out. As for ambience, well, they're pretty gritty. The first concert I ever saw as a teen was at a previous incarnation of Webster Hall and I remember being scared to use the bathrooms; that hasn't changed!

Bob Dylan, Linda Ronstadt, Arlo Guthrie, Melissa Manchester . . . all of the big names of the '60s and '70s played **The Bitter End** (147 Bleecker St. btwn Thompson St. and LaGuardia Place; ☎ 212/673-7030; www.bitterend.com; Ⓐ, Ⓑ, Ⓒ, Ⓓ, Ⓔ, Ⓕ, Ⓥ to W. 4th St.), and the club still has the posters to prove it, so old they can't really be called "yellowing"; they're now a permanent deep woodsy brown. This is no nostalgia club, though: The Bitter End continues to act as a try-out house for new singer-songwriter types (primarily), many of whom are quite talented. I saw a terrific vibraphone and guitar duo, odd as that may sound, the last time I was here. An average cover of just $5, perfect acoustics, and abundant if somewhat cramped seating, makes for a much more pleasant music experience than at many of the other clubs in the vicinity.

Co-owned by Chris Noth, "Mr. Big" on *Sex and the City* and currently on *Law and Order: Criminal Intent*, **The Cutting Room** ✪✩ (19 W. 24th St. btwn Fifth and Sixth aves.; ☎ 212/691-1900; www.thecuttingroomnyc.com; Ⓝ, Ⓡ to 23rd St.) has a soothing retro vibe, with brass chandeliers, heavy red velvet drapes to cut down on the noise, and wise-cracking, glamorous female bartenders presiding over the long mahogany bar at the side of the front room. The lineup in the back room is just as classy, consisting usually of accomplished, mid-career, or up-and-coming rock, blues, and jazz musicians of all stripes.

A New York institution known for presenting experimental, edgy alternative rock and jazz from such iconoclasts as John Zorn and Non Phixion, **The Knitting Factory** (74 Leonard St. btwn Church St. and Broadway; ☎ 212/219-3006; www. knittingfactory.com; ❶ to Franklin) is actually three concert venues and a bar in one. The main floor houses the biggest stage and hosts the most established names, the second level is for up-and-comers, and the basement is for newbies (but usually darn talented ones). Covers vary widely, and bouncers check IDs before you enter, stamping those allowed to drink (meaning this is a club you could potentially take a teen to for the music).

You visit **Mercury Lounge** ✪ (217 E. Houston St., btwn Essex and Ludlow sts.; ☎ 212/260-4700; www.mercuryloungenyc.com; Ⓕ, Ⓥ to Second Ave.) because of the talent of its booker: If there's a band playing in and around New York City that's on the edge of hitting it big, you're going to hear them here. It's just a shame that the room they have to play in isn't more comfortable. With very few seating options and no proper bar (you have to go into the front room or ask the waitress posted in the corner for a plastic cup of $4 beer), it's not a great place to hang out. Still, if the music's your main priority, this is the place to hit.

Pianos ✪✩ (158 Ludlow St. at Stanton; ☎ 212/505-3733; www.pianosnyc. com; Ⓕ, Ⓥ to Second Ave.) is a hopping bi-level music club that really has it all. It takes its name from the former piano store that stood on this site, and it must have been a nice-looking place because the club has wide-boarded wooden floors, a pressed-tin ceiling, and an airy feel to it that's unusual for the Lower East Side. The first floor has a handsome bar up front, with serious cocktails and good vintage wines; also on this floor is a large music club. Upstairs is a spacious lounge.

For country, rockabilly, and even New Orleans–style jazz, **Rodeo Bar** ★ (375 Third Ave. at 27th St.; ☎ 212/683-6500; www.rodeobar.com; ❻ to 28th St.) gives the best imitation of a roadhouse in Manhattan, rustling up bands with names like "Jug Addicts," "Luther Wright and the Wrongs," and "The Second Fiddles" for live music shows 7 nights a week (10pm Sun–Thurs, 11pm weekends). There's never a cover charge, and they don't even seem to have a system in place to make sure you buy a drink, probably because you'll feel kinda silly hanging out in a room with peanut shells all over the floor and a converted horse trailer for a bar, without a cold one in your mitt. Patrons who pony up for a Tex-Mex meal get a seat right in front of the band, but even if you're just drinking, you can usually see the show from the bar stools in the back (it's also broadcast on TVs around the room).

FOR WORLD MUSIC

S.O.B.'s ★★★ (204 Varick St. at W. Houston; ☎ 212/243-4940; www.sobs.com; ❶ to Houston St.) may well be the single most joyous place you can visit between the hours of 8pm and 2am. A large club decorated with fake palm trees and giant parrots, it specializes in the music that you'd find in the places where, well, you'd find parrots and palm trees: India (great *bangra* or Indian pop music parties), the Dominican Republic, Trinidad, Cuba, Puerto Rico, Jamaica, and Brazil. Its "Samba Saturdays" are the longest-running party in New York, featuring throbbing music and a bravura stage show of samba dancing and *capoeira* (a dancelike Brazilian martial art). If you arrive before 8pm on Saturday and order dinner, the $20 cover is waived. Other days of the week, the cover tends to range from $10 to $20. On many nights, women get in free before a certain hour (it varies), so check the website before heading over.

FOR BURLESQUE

Good ole' striptease is making a comeback all over town, but **The Slipper Room** ★ (167 Orchard St. at the corner of Stanton St.; ☎ 212/253-7246; www.slipper room.com; ❻, ❻ to Second Ave.), is where the craze started, and it still puts on a show with plenty of, er, panache (not to mention silly gags, T&A, and sometimes even baton twirling). You'll likely see a lineup of drag comedians, monologists, and ecdysiasts of all shapes, sizes, and genders (when I was last there a zaftig brunette stripped down to pasties and a g-string while dancing with a hula-hoop; and a man dressed as Bacchus had two women suction up wine through straws from the plastic bag that covered his genitals, until—*Tah dah!*—all was revealed). The theater, actually a one-room bar, features a small stage at the back, and can get extremely crowded. Get here about an hour before the show (there are often go-go dancers at that time for entertainment) so that you can snag one of the few seats on the side of the room. Entrance is a mere $5 for the Wednesday, Friday, and Saturday burlesque shows; other nights the cover varies, depending on the acts.

FOR ALL OF THAT & EVERYTHING ELSE . . .

Seriously eclectic fare is on the bill at **Joe's Pub** ★★★ (425 Lafayette St. near Astor Place; ☎ 212/239-6200; www.joespub.com; ❻ to Astor Place), which is housed in the Public Theater, which itself is housed in the former Astor Library (first public library in the city). It's a majestic neo-Romanesque room, with a soaring ceiling, fluted columns, red velvet curtains, and plush banquettes—one of the most elegant, visually arresting clubs in the city. You never know who you're going to see perform here. The roster can range from top-Broadway stars trying out their cabaret acts, to World Music phenoms, to jazz, to poetry evenings, to Lesley "It's My Party" Gore coming out of the closet. The acts are always of a high level, the atmosphere celebratory. I recommend calling ahead for a table reservation (otherwise you'll be stuck in the back at the bar). Youngsters under the age of 18 can attend shows that start before 11pm.

COMEDY CLUBS

Here's a little secret: Because it's so insanely difficult to make a living as a comedian, most play multiple gigs at multiple clubs in the course of an evening just to make ends meet. So the funny fellow you're seeing at the 9pm show at some no-name club may be the 11pm headliner at a club with lines out the door. Therefore, if a hawker shouts out the words, "Do you like comedy?" to you in Times Square or near Astor Place (in the Village), you may want to answer, "Yes!" and snag one of the discounted passes he's handing out, even if you've never heard of the club. Just be aware that the show won't necessarily be as cheap as you first thought, as you'll have to pay a drink minimum, usually two per show, and sometimes a partial cover. Crunch the numbers before you show up at a club.

Of course, there is no guarantee you'll stumble upon one of these hawkers, so I've listed below my picks for guaranteed giggles:

STAND UP

When Jerry Seinfeld, Robin Williams, Dave Chapelle, Ray Romano, and other equally famous, New York–based comedians decide to "try out" material in front of an audience, they usually drop by the **Comedy Cellar** ✪ (117 MacDougal St. near Minetta St.; ☎ 212/254-3480; www.comedycellar.com; Ⓐ, Ⓔ, Ⓒ, Ⓑ, Ⓓ, Ⓕ to W. 4th St.), a basement room in the Village that crams in crowds 7 nights a week. On nights when these "biggies" don't make an appearance (and their sets are never advertised in advance), newer headliners—comedians with Comedy Central credits and HBO specials—take the stage. Unlike other clubs, which will create a lineup around just one of these rising stars, the Cellar always has three or more populating its hour-and-a-half shows (at 9pm and 11pm). Cover charges are $10 on weeknights and $15 on weekends.

More comedy for the cash is what's on offer for those who visit the **Comic Strip Live** ✪ (1568 Second Ave., btwn 81st and 82nd; ☎ 212/861-9386; www.comic striplive.com; ⓸, ⓹, ⓺ to 86th St.) on a weeknight. Instead of holding one set and then clearing the house for the next, the lineup starts at 8:30pm and goes on until—well, who knows when. That may be why the cover is a bit higher than the competition's: You'll pay $15 on weekdays and $20 on the weekend, plus a $20 drink minimum. But you could theoretically laugh it up here for 4 or 5 hours on that tab. Like the other clubs, the Comic Strip attracts the top performers you'll see slinging jokes on Letterman, Conan, and Leno. And on weeknights, some of the "graduates" of the place who got their start here—Chris Rock, Paul Reiser, Wanda Sykes, and others—drop in, unannounced, for a set. *Savings tip:* The Comic Strip often sells discounted tickets on the street in Times Square, so look for its reps when you're there.

Gotham Comedy Club ✰ (W. 22nd St., btwn Fifth and Sixth aves.; ☎ 212/367-9000; www.gothamcomedyclub.com; ❸, ❺ to 23rd St.) is the most civilized comedy club in town (though I won't vouch for what's going to come out of some raunchy jester's mouth). No, by civilized I mean the room which, while not large, packs fewer guests to a table, and doesn't seat anyone with their back to the stage (a problem at the Comedy Cellar). Moreover, instead of having to wait 10 or 15 minutes on the sidewalk outside the club before shows (in all kinds of weather), patrons belly up to the spacious bar in the front room before and after the shows (don't imbibe too much, though: A two-drink minimum is strictly enforced). The club often serves as an audition place for the bookers who pick acts for the Letterman show, Conan O'Brien, and others, and if you hit it on these nights the atmosphere can be electric. Cover charges range from $12 to $15.

IMPROV

In 1996, four "missionaries" of improv comedy came to New York from Chicago and founded the **Upright Citizens Brigade Theater** ✰✰ (307 W. 26th St., right off Eighth Ave; ☎ 212/366-9176; www.ucbtheater.com). Dedicated to the art of "long form improvisation," in which performers riff on one or two subjects for up to half an hour, the troupe's appreciation for the absurd, along with their smart, fearless performing style, quickly made them a hit among jaded young New Yorkers. Today, Amy Poehler, one of the Citizens, is a star of Saturday Night Live; Comedy Central created an "Upright Citizens Brigade" TV show; and the theater itself has become the hippest place in the city to laugh loud and long. Poehler still performs here, and she regularly brings to the stage other SNL stars (during the writers strike, the SNL performers did an impromptu show here, a raunchier version of what you'd see on NBC), as well as writers and staff from the *Conan O'Brien Show* and the *Daily Show with Jon Stewart.* The somewhat grungy basement theater offers shows 7 days a week, sometimes twice or three times a night, at the slacker-friendly price of $8 or less (and about 2 or 3 shows a week are free).

BARS & LOUNGES

A note before you plunge in: In the first half of this discussion, I cover bars where *generally* dancing does not occur, with dance clubs listed at the end. However, some bars do have two faces, so if you're looking for a more laid-back scene in which to drink and then, perhaps, shake your groove thing, skim through this bar section first.

LOWER EAST SIDE

Happy Ending ✰✰ (302 Broome St. btwn Eldridge and Forsythe sts.; ☎ 212/334-9676; ❸, ❻ to Grand St) is a former "massage parlor" named the XIE Health Club (the original awning is still up); you party downstairs in the white tiled rooms where the, er, "happy endings" once took place. Upstairs is an elegant, red-lit bar with a rotating abstract art display at the front. Because the bar has a number of large booths, it gets lots of groups on weekends. Tuesday is hard-core punk night, and Thursday sees a mix of gay men on the first floor and Goths in the basement.

Cocktails alfresco

For a buzz with a breeze, try one of the following outdoor hotspots (open roughly Apr–Oct):

The Garden at Ono ✪ (18 Ninth Ave., though the entrance is on Hudson St. btwn Gansevoort and W. 13th sts.; ☎ 212/660-6766; **A**, **E**, **C** to 23rd or **L** to Eighth Ave.). Call first for a "bar reservation" (yes, there is such a thing) so that you won't get stuck behind the velvet rope, and then swing by this chichi Meat-Packing District sushi-and-cocktails scene, which is a favorite of New York's trendmakers: mostly fashion designers, actors, and media-types. In the center of the space is an ancient reassembled Japanese barge; covering it is a retractable roof, making it one of the few outdoor spaces where you can party even in the rain.

  Luna Park (In Union Square Park, at around 17th St.; ☎ 212/475-8464; usually open May–Sept; **N**, **R**, **Q**, **4**, **5**, **6**, **L** to Union Sq.). Young office workers from the neighborhood and model-types from nearby agencies mingle at this friendly restaurant/bar, located right between two playgrounds (making it a good spot for parents to grab a cocktail while they watch the kids). Boppy music and solicitous service complete the scene.

  The Boat Basin Café ✪✪ (79th St. below the West Side Hwy.; ☎ 212/496-5542; www.boatbasincafe.com; mid-Apr to Oct). Follow the signs through Riverside Park and down the steps to this under-the-highway cafe, where a refreshing mix of young singles, couples with babies, and seniors, if you can believe it, all hang together to enjoy stunning river views. Though you'll have to buy a full meal to get a table, there are chairs on the slightly sloping steps leading down to the boat basin, where you can sit with a $5 Bud from the bar.

The eroticism is even more overt (if you can believe it) at **The Box** ✪ (189 Chrystie St. near Rivington St.; ☎ 212/983-9301; closed Mon; **J**, **M**, **Z** to Bowery or **F**, **V** to Second Ave.), which melds a bustling bar and an old-fashioned (tiny) music hall, complete with a show featuring topless chorus girls three times a night. According to press reports, the theater is meant to look like the famous Birdcage Saloon and Opera House in Tombstone, Ariz. and it certainly is atmospheric, with bejeweled chandeliers, private opera boxes overlooking the stage, and a dizzying pastiche of Victorian wallpapers on the walls. Don't try and eat here; not only is the food mediocre, but there's a $1,000 dollar per table entertainment charge, plus a bottle charge (2 bottles minimum at $500 each—ouch!) on many nights. Instead, stand at the back and watch the kooky show, which might range from rapping tap dancers to Thai martial arts artists to aerialists, usually with some sort of bawdy edge.

Right down the street from the Box, is another fantasy nightspot, though here you move from Burlesque to burqa (well, kinda). **The Kush Lounge** ✭ (191 Chrystie St. near Stanton; ☎ 212/677-7328; closed Sun; **B**, **D** to Grand St.), a slightly Disneyfied version of a hookah bar, is nonetheless a fun place to hang, with an Arabian nights decor, complete with metal lanterns, cushy ottomans, and pillowed nooks, for small groups. On weekends, there's belly-dancing but also a $10 cover to get in (after 10pm).

Just finding **The Back Room** ✭✭✭ (102 Norfolk near Delancey; ☎ 212/228-5098; closed Mon; **F** to Delancey St.) is a big part of the adventure. You'll head down an unmarked stairway off the street, though a dank tunnel and into a moody back alley. Knock for entry and you're likely to get in—the doormen no longer have to worry about accidentally admitting "bulls" (slang for the cops who used to close illegal bars) as they did when this spot was a notorious speakeasy in the roaring '20s. The decor recalls those days, with a roaring fireplace in the back, paisley red velvet wallpaper, and globes hiding rows of teacups (all the drinks are served in them). Tim Robbins is a co-owner, and I see his influence at the back of the drinks menu where someone writes that The Back Room is meant to remind us of a "vital point in American . . . history, when the nay saying antics of a political movement stripped us of our freedom to drink and socialize as we wish . . . Despite what social tyrants may wish, people always find a way of doing what they want to do." You go Tim! Partiers of the world, unite! You have nothing to lose but your sobriety.

SOHO

Vodka is Czar at **Pravda** ✭✭ (281 Lafayette St. btwn Houston and Prince sts.; ☎ 212/226-4944; **B**, **D**, **F**, **V** to Broadway-Lafayette), a Russian-themed basement lounge that serves 21 different brands from all parts of the potato-distilling world: Moldova, Estonia, the Czech Republic, Poland, Finland, Denmark, and, of course, Russia. You sling them back in a curved-ceiling cellar alongside Cyrillic signs posted on the walls, and surrounded by chic SoHo types lounging in armchairs and plush circular leather booths. Upstairs is a smaller bar area where things get even more USSR-era: everyone smokes up here, damn the law.

I also give a big thumbs up in this area to the **Pegu Club** ✭✭ (77 West Houston St., second floor; ☎ 212/473-7348; **B**, **D**, **F**, **V** to Broadway-Lafayette), a refreshingly adult place to start or end an evening. An elegant decor, meant to evoke the 19th-century British officer's club in Burma, for which it's named, and sophisticated cocktails keep the youngsters at bay. There's also a very fine menu of appetizers, if you're feeling peckish.

EAST VILLAGE

Latin-style romance is on tap at **Baraza** ✭ (133 Avenue C btwn 8th and 9th sts.; ☎ 212/539-0811; **L** to First Ave.), an Alphabet City standout with a bar menu heavy on the mojitos and caiparinhas, all set against a soundtrack of salsa, samba, and African beats (a different genre of music is featured each night). An entire wall is decorated with Goya labels. The only "un-Latin" element is the crowd, composed of the usual East Village hipsters, but somehow those who come here all know how to dance, and a lot of fancy footwork takes place in the small back area behind the bar.

Decibel ✪✪ (240 E. 9th St. btwn Third and Second aves.; ☎ 212/979-2733; ❻ to Astor Place) is a gritty, underground sake bar that's become a center of social life for many of the ex-pat Japanese living in New York City. In fact, most of the clientele are Japanese, the soundtrack is Japanese rock, and the bar food can be exotic (dried squid, anyone?). But all are welcome here, and if you feel a bit out of place when you enter this Tokyo transplant, you'll relax once you tuck into any of the 30-odd sakes on offer here each evening. A real experience.

If you're a man's man (which I'm obviously not), you'll like **McSorley's Old Ale House** (15 E. 7th St., btwn Bowery and Second Ave.; ☎ 212/473-9318; ❻ to Astor Place), New York's oldest continuously operating pub (est. 1854), and one that famously kept out women until a lawsuit in 1970 ended the bigotry (it was a landmark case that ultimately outlawed discrimination in all public places in the city). With sawdust on the rough wooden floor, yellowing photos and newspaper clips chronicling all of the famous people who got smashed here (Abraham Lincoln was one of them), and a jumble of relics in every nook and cranny (the handcuffs hanging from the ceiling once belonged to Houdini, the turkey bones hanging off the chandelier were hung there by soldiers having a last meal before shipping off to World War I), it's an evocative place to hang out . . . if you're smart enough to visit before 4pm in the afternoon. After that point it gets ugly—kind of like the frat parties I pretended to like in college—with out-of-towners jammed together tighter than in a rush-hour train, swilling so-so ale, and shouting over the din.

> ❝ I was sitting in mcsorley's. outside it was New York and beautifully snowing.
> Inside snug and evil. ❞
>
> —E. E. Cummings

Ignore the views of the New York cityscape from the large plate-glass windows at **Zum Schneider** (107 Avenue C at 7th St.; ☎ 212/598-1098; www.zumschneider.com; ❶ to First Ave.) and you could be in a beer hall off some gritty side street in Munich. The beers pack as much of a punch (be careful, unusual German beers such as Kolsch have a higher alcohol content than you may be used to), the bratwurst has that same snap, and if you stick around long enough—till, say, 2 or 3am—revelers here are likely to hop on top of the benches and boogie, just like they do across the pond when things get going. It's a fun, loud place with dozens of beers, a rock and hip-hop soundtrack, and a party spirit. Did you ever think you'd be going to a genuine German beer garden when you booked your NYC vacation?

GREENWICH VILLAGE

Employees Only ✪✪ (510 Hudson near Christopher St.; ☎ 212/242-3021; ❶ to Christopher St.) is the place to come if you take your cocktails seriously. A crack staff of veteran bartenders from some of the top restaurants in town man the place, squeezing their own juices daily and infusing liquors with interesting additions, such as lavender (in the gin) and herbes de Provence (in the vermouth), which they then mix into some of the most bizarre but delicious drinks in town. It's also one of the few places in the U.S. where one can try Absinthe (aka the green devil, the drink that supposedly undid van Gogh). Upping the festivity factor is a psychic who does readings for $15 a pop, and a cute garden out back for those sultry summer nights.

And **The Other Room** ✪ (143 Perry St. btwn Greenwich and Washington sts.; ☎ 212/645-9758; Sun–Mon 5pm–2am, Tues–Thurs 5pm–3am, Fri–Sat 5pm–4am; cash only; ❶ to Christopher St.) is the place to come if you take your wine and beer seriously. There's no hard stuff served, but you will find an abundance of unusual ales, beers, and wines. The bar itself is sleek and simple, with a good amount of art dotted about, and a local crowd of Villagers both gay and straight.

MEAT-PACKING DISTRICT

The gimmick at **APT** ✪✪✪ (419 W. 13th St., btwn Ninth Ave. and Washington St.; ☎ 212/414-4245; www.aptwebsite.com; ❹, ❻, ❺ to 14th St.; daily 7pm–4am) is that you're partying at someone's apartment, so the door is unmarked (look for the address). Once inside the upstairs bar, you're greeted by a painting of a mysterious occupant named "Bernard," pictures of him in his younger days in the recessed lounge, his bed (where less inhibited revelers sprawl later on in the night), and a number of cozy nooks, perfect for chatting over the not-too-loud music. Early in the evening, from 7 to 9pm, there are board games—Monopoly, dominoes, checkers—set out for Bernard's "guests." Downstairs is a happening dance club, where the crowd pulsates to the music, hemmed in by two long mahogany bars. *A word of warning:* APT sets up a velvet rope around 10pm so you have more chance of getting in earlier in the evening.

FLATIRON DISTRICT

MTV meets ESPN at **The 40/40 Club** ✪✪✪ (6 W. 25th St., btwn Broadway and Sixth Ave.; ☎ 212/989-0400; www.the4040club.com; Mon–Fri 5pm–4am, Sat–Sun 4pm–4am; ❻, ❽ to 23rd St.), a sports bar tricked out like a hip-hop mogul's crib. Which is exactly what this is—the side project of producer/artist/man-about-town Jay-Z. Inside are cushy white-leather couches (even fitted into the wide stairway btwn floors) and white-leather armchairs hanging from the ceiling. Each seating nook comes with its own LCD flatscreen TV, broadcasting the day's big game. Can you say "bling bling"? In the main space, couples dance to hip-hop; next door the screens play VH1 and the soundtrack is salsa. Apparently, the entire enterprise cost a whopping $4 million to outfit, and I have to say, just from a sociological point of view, it's a fascinating place to visit. I have felt very comfortable doing so—the place gets a happily mixed crowd of all races and, perhaps as unusual, all ages.

CHELSEA

If the paint-chipped Vespas at the front of **Bar Veloce** ✪ (176 Seventh Ave. btwn 20th and 21st sts.; ☎ 212/629-5300; www.barveloce.com; daily 5pm–3am; ❶ to 18th St.) doesn't transport you directly to Milan, the tiramisu and panini will. This narrow wine bar is more than just an alcohol joint—here you can accompany that lovely glass of wine you've ordered (30 wines from all over Italy) with freshly made, delicious Italian snack foods. These high-falutin' sandwiches cost between $4 and $7, with wines rarely going above $10 a glass. Though it's relatively cheap, there's no skimping on sophistication—the bartenders wear snazzy suits and ties, the decor is sleek blond woods and brushed steel, and the soundtrack is swinging bebop.

Glass ✪ (287 Tenth Ave. at 26th St.; ☎ 212/904-1580; daily 5pm–4am; **C**, **E** to 23rd St.) is where you retreat to lick your wounds if you don't get past the velvet ropes at any of the surrounding dance clubs. And you know what? You'll have just as much fun at Glass, a mod, hopping place, tiled like the inside of a bathroom (somehow it works), with loud house music, a disco ball, and a bamboo-filled garden out back. Just don't imbibe so much that you forget why this place has the name it does: A two-way glass mirror allows anyone on the sidewalk to see the front part of the bathroom (not the stalls). It's hilarious just to stand there and watch the primping show as tipsy club-goers tug up tube tops, adjust lipstick, and simply gaze at themselves for minutes at a time.

Drink liberally with the media at **The Half King** ✪ (505 W. 23rd St. btwn Tenth and Eleventh aves.; ☎ 212/462-4300; daily 9am–4am; **C**, **E** to 23rd), a journalists' hangout, co-owned by Sebastian Junger, author of the best-selling book *The Perfect Storm*. With the look, food, and drinks of an English pub (think foamy Guinness and shepherd's pie), it's a good place to get into a political argument (just be prepared to be outgunned). Readings and musical performances are occasionally scheduled in the large dining room on Sunday, Monday, and Tuesday.

MIDTOWN EAST & WEST

For an F. Scott Fitzgerald experience in New York, head to the **Campbell Apartment** ✪✪✪ (in Grand Central Terminal, entrance at 15 Vanderbilt Ave.; ☎ 212/953-0409; daily 3pm–1am; **4**, **5**, **6**, **S** to Grand Central), and drink the types of cocktails that Zelda over-imbibed: tall fruity drinks in oddly shaped glasses with such names as "Flapper's Delight" and "Prohibition Punch." The "apartment" was once the office of tycoon John W. Campbell, who turned this 60-foot-long room into a replica of a Florentine palazzo, inlaying the ceiling and adding an ornate balcony. Visit on a weekend, early afternoon, or late evening when the commuting hordes will have already sloshed onto Metro-North, leaving you free to enjoy this elegant space in peace (or perhaps to the swing of a jazz band if you visit on a Sat night).

Though it seems a bit morbid to name a bar for a novel about a man drinking himself to death, written by a man who drunk himself to death, **Under the Volcano** (12 E. 36th St., near Madison Ave.; ☎ 212/293-0093; **B**, **D**, **N**, **Q**, **R** to 34th St.) is quite a nice place. The only thing desperate about it is its neighborhood, which is one of the nightlife- and restaurant-free wastelands of Midtown. So much the more surprising to find this swell tequila bar (16 varieties) with its leather couches and Mexican artifacts on the walls. A top spot to unwind after battling the crowds at nearby Macy's or the Empire State Building.

One of the premiere wine bars in the city, **Morell Wine Bar and Café** (1 Rockefeller Plaza, a short stroll from Fifth Ave.; ☎ 212/262-7700; **B**, **D** to 50th St.) offers over 2,000 types of wine, many available by the glass. Although it can get crowded—it's in the heart of Rockefeller Center, after all—the scene never feels overly touristy, and the people-watching, especially from the sidewalk tables (open in good weather), can't be beat.

If you're looking for a nip of vino before or after the theater, my pick would be the sweet **Casellula Café** ✪ (401 W. 52nd St., off Ninth Ave.; ☎ 212/247-8137;

www.casellula.com; **C**, **E** to 51st St.), which combines two New York City obsessions on its menu: wine and cheese. Along with a raft of hard-to-find, boutique wines, it carves up nearly 50 artisanal cheeses per week, offering a plate at just $5 a pop or a tasting flight for $15. There are a number of gourmet, cheesy bar snacks to order from as well including quiche ($9) and a pig's ass sandwich—their terminology, not mine (it's cheddar cheese and tender meat for $12). A casually elegant place, open 'til 2am, it's a real find for this 'hood.

UPPER EAST SIDE

It takes a moment to register and then you suddenly realize why the atmosphere at **Lexington Bar and Books** (1020 Lexington Ave. at 73rd St.; ☎ 212/717-3902; www.barandbooks.cz; Sun–Wed 5pm–3am, Thurs–Sat 5pm–4am; **6** to 77th St.) is at once decidedly strange and deeply familiar: People are smoking (!) and no one is turning them in to the police. That's because Lexington Bar and Books is one of eight "cigar bars" in the city with a special license allowing cigar smoking—and cigarettes by extension. So if you've been longing for the days of a cocktail with a cig, here's the place to come, though you'll have to dress up: This is a highly patrician bar, with a crowd in their later 30s and 40s, and a dress code requiring jackets in winter and collared shirts year-round. There's also an outpost in the Village (365 Hudson St. at Horatio St.; ☎ 212/229-2642).

Every Friday and Saturday night, year-round, **The Balcony Bar at the Metropolitan Museum** ✯✯✯ (Fifth Ave., btwn 84th and 80th sts.; www.met.org; **6** to 77th St.) hosts the most sophisticated cocktail party in town, with a string quartet sawing merrily in the background and hundreds of the city's most stylish singles downing wine and gazing at ancient Asian artifacts. In the warm weather months, the party moves to the roof Sculpture Garden with its magnificent views of Central Park. There's no better place in Manhattan to watch the sunset.

UPPER WEST SIDE

Prohibition ✯ (503 Columbus Ave., btwn 84th and 85th sts.; ☎ 212/579-3100; www.prohibition.net; **1** to 86th St.) is a great neighborhood bar, with better-than-average bar food, a pool table in the back room, and live music every night of the week (usually funk or R&B). The staff is friendly, as are the patrons, and the Prohibition-era style murals and decor hit just the right note. This really fun joint attracts a crowd that ranges from people in their 20s all the way to those in their 40s and 50s.

For moguls and the models they squire, **Stone Rose** ✯✯✯ (10 Columbus Circle, 4th floor; ☎ 212/823-9769; www.mocbars.com; **A**, **B**, **C**, **D**, **1** to Columbus Circle) is a real "see and be seen" bar. Owned by a bar mogul (Randy Gerber) and his model wife (Cindy Crawford), it's an elegant 300-seater with gourmet bar food from famed chef Jean George Vongerichten. The drink prices, at $12 to $16 a pop, are on the high side of average, but they may well be worth the tab just to savor one of the loveliest views in New York (from floor-to-ceiling windows): Columbus Circle lit up, with fountains spraying and Central Park slumbering in the background.

DANCE CLUBS

Fireflies on a hot July night give off a more lasting glow than most NYC dance clubs, which burst onto the scene (and the pages of the tabloids) one week, and then disappear the next. It's nearly impossible to track them, and from the time my fingers hit my keyboard to the time you read this book, most of the "hot" ones will be icy cold (or out of business). To find out where *the* scene is when you visit, pick up any celebrity rag or *Time Out* magazine, which does a good job of tracking the parties from week to week. You could also simply wander down to the Meat-Packing District (roughly Ninth Ave. to Tenth Ave., btwn 13th and 15th sts.), or West Chelsea (27th or 28th sts. btwn Tenth and Eleventh aves.). Because of the lack of schools and churches in these neighborhoods, local zoning laws are more lenient, allowing them to serve liquor until 4am. Some keep the music going even longer; it's not unusual to see dancers limping home at 5 and 6am.

Below are clubs that have proved their staying power (for now).

MEAT-PACKING DISTRICT

Lindsay Lohan was apparently sucking face with another well-known actor the night before I last visited **Tenjune** ★ (26 Little W. 12th St near Washington St; ☎ 646/624-2410; www.tenjunenyc.com; **Ⓐ**, **Ⓔ**, **Ⓒ** to 14th St.); a week later, Timbaland chose this basement lounge as the spot for his birthday party. And it's the lure of these bold-faced names, who sit in a VIP area that everyone can see into, that drives the throngs waiting at the velvet rope *insane.* Remember the scramble to get on the last American helicopters after the fall of Saigon in 1975? The scene outside Tenjune is just as desperate and mean. Which may be why getting inside feels like winning the lottery. The revelers in this woodsy, dimly lit basement lounge are literally beaming with pride and joy, and their happiness is infectious, as is the musical mix of oldies and current Top 40 that the DJ's spin. *If* you can get into Tenjune, get ready for a real party.

Cielo ★★ (18 Little W. 12th St., off Ninth Ave; ☎ 212/645-5700; www.cielo club.com; 10pm–4am, closed Tues and Sun; **Ⓐ**, **Ⓔ**, **Ⓒ** to 14th St.) attracts a slightly older crowd of partiers in their late 20s and 30s, who prefer deep house music to commercial hip-hop and Top 40. The best nights are Monday and Wednesday when the club hosts its "Deep Space" and "Roots" parties, with well-known deejays (see the website for a lineup) and an open-door policy, so there's no hassle getting in. It's an intimate, one-room space with a funky "tubular" decor (you just gotta see it) and a sunken dance floor. There's also a garden in the back for smokers. The best part? No VIP rooms, no attitude—you just come here if you really like to dance to great music.

PM Lounge ★ (50 Gansevoort St., off Ninth Ave.; ☎ 212/255-6676; **Ⓐ**, **Ⓔ**, **Ⓒ** to 14th St.) is another of the district's smaller (450 people max) dance clubs with a distinctly Caribbean vibe (inside, the space is dominated by a large mural of Haitian men and women dancing, tall palm trees, and a characteristic island wall in the front—whitewashed and cut into small circles). The music is not reggae, calypso, Zook, or salsa, though; instead you get quick cuts between Top 40, hip-hop, and house music, thumping but not overpoweringly loud, and highly danceable. A very good time, if you can get by the off-duty firemen who serve as the bouncers.

CHELSEA

Though you have many, many choices in the vicinity of 27th street, my faves can be divided by size into massive, medium, and small. **Marquee** (289 Tenth Ave. btwn 26th and 27th sts.; ☎ 646/473-0202; www.marqueeny.com; closed Sun–Mon; **C**, **E** to 23rd St.) falls into the first category, a trendy place that's still getting those names that, yes, usually "top the marquee" (all the celebrities that grace the pages of *Us Weekly*). I can't guarantee that it will be as molten hot by the time this book is published but it should still be cranking along, disappointing legions of club-clothed 20-somethings who can't get past the hulking doormen, and damaging the hearing of those who do make it in with its brain-exploding loud music. If you want to visit a hot New York club, complete with disco ball and a huge, writhing sea of dancers (the place was designed by the famed architectural firm of Philip Johnson, but it's so dark, you can't really see the design), this is the place, though I think anybody over the age of thirty will probably feel more comfortable elsewhere.

And that elsewhere may well be **Cain** ★★★ (544 W. 27th St. near Eleventh Ave.; ☎ 212/847-8000; www.cainnyc.com; closed Sun and Mon; **C**, **E** to 23rd St.), an African-themed club with a "savannah at dusk" glow to the lighting, a zebra skin bar, and a live bongo player making the mix of world music and house music all that more infectious. Really, it's near impossible to keep from dancing here, the music and vibe are that good. The crowd ranges from Wall Street types to leggy models and their musician boyfriends, with an occasional celeb thrown into the mix to keep the crowds coming; dress sharp or you won't get past the picky door hostess.

The mighty midget on 27th street, **Bungalow 8** ★ (515 W. 27th St.; ☎ 212/629-3333; closed Sun; **C**, **E** to 23rd St.), is just one, pretty small room filled with banquettes for pricey table service parties. But it's that wee size that keeps it exclusive despite its advanced age (8 years and counting). Fake palm trees, an overarching skylight, and murals of the Beverly Hills Hotel set the sniffy tone; regular visits from the Olsen twins, Sean Penn, and other celebs keep its rep as *the* after-party hotspot fresh. *Warning:* Getting in is still *très* difficult.

LOWER EAST SIDE

As hipster as the neighborhood, **205** ★★ (205 Chrystie St at Stanton; ☎ 212/477-6688; **J**, **M**, **Z** to Bowery or **F**, **V** to Second Ave.) gets a crowd of local artists, people with creatively shaven facial hair, and fashion industry types. A silver-plated dive—literally, the grungy brick walls are covered with tinfoil (a reference to Andy Warhol's Factory)—it features a comfy, large bar room at top with loungeable couches and live music many nights. Dancing takes place in a low ceilinged basement, its plywood walls covered with personal ads from Craigslist.

GAY BARS & NIGHTCLUBS

Though the stats are shaky, most experts estimate that New York City is home to the largest gay population in North America, if not the world. All in all, there are about 70 major bars and nightclubs to suit every taste, wardrobe, and fetish, but the party only starts there. I'd recommend that you check out such publications as *HX* (www.hx.com; it's available in every gay bar for free), *The Blade* (again,

Getting Past the Velvet Ropes

There's nothing that will transport you back to the worst day of high school quicker than facing the gatekeeper at the door of a New York dance club. It's a humbling, depressing experience (especially if you don't get in), but there are ways to increase your odds of spending more time in the club than on the sidewalk.

1. **Choose your companions carefully**
   Large groups of men have little chance of getting into a club together, so if you're traveling in a pack of guys, split up until you get inside the club. Women have a better chance of getting in, as do couples.

2. **Dress the part**
   Look at the celebrity magazines and see what they're wearing when they sashay past the ropes. Usually it's an upscale casual look, but that will change season to season. Avoid suits at all costs, the same for "business casual," and if you plan to wear sneakers, make sure they're clean.

3. **Make nice**
   The "chooser" at the door has been entrusted by the owner to create a cool "mix" of people inside the club, so though you may not get in right away, you could be picked in 15 minutes, especially at a larger club, when they need more redheads, or tall women, or perhaps when the moon goes into Jupiter (I don't think even the gatekeepers have a clear idea of what they're looking for). You'll blow your chances, however, if you give the all-powerful guy at the door any argument

available in gay bars), and the more mainstream *Time Out* magazine (on newsstands) for listings of these clubs as well as the innumerable dance parties, go-go and drag shows, gay knitting circles (yes, really), and other happenings that take place every week.

Top clubs as I write this include:

GAY BARS

Therapy ★★ (348 W. 52nd St., btwn Eighth and Ninth aves.; ☎ 212/397-1700; www.therapy-nyc.com; ◉, ◉ to 50th St.) is a chic, candlelit, two-floor bar that attracts a "pretty boys in Barney's shirts" crowd of buff 20- and 30-somethings for casual cruising. You could come here and meet the love of your life, or just have a drink. It's also a hangout for Broadway dancers and actors; you'll see them after 11pm, when the shows get out.

For "bears," "cubs," and the boys who love them, **The Eagle** ★ (554 W. 28th St., btwn Tenth and Eleventh aves.; ☎ 646/473-1866; www.eaglenyc.com; ◉, ◉ to 28th St.) is the epicenter of the leather scene in New York. In fact, on my first visit (several years back), *The Sopranos* was casting for "leather types" on the second floor or attitude. Instead, wait patiently with a smile on your face, chatting with your companion, and you just might get in. Never wait more than 20 minutes at a club that can hold less than 500 (and would therefore be considered "exclusive") or half an hour at a larger place; at that point, it's pretty clear that they won't pick you.

4. **Call in advance for a reservation**
Some dance clubs, such as Tenjune (see above), have restaurants attached, and those who dine get automatic entry, later in the evening, to the dance club. You can also reserve a table at a club in advance for you and your guests, but be careful: Those who get a table are required to take "bottle service," which means you buy a bottle of liquor for you and your companions that can easily cost upwards of $400. Another ploy is to call in advance and ask for a bar reservation; it's not as surefire a method but sometimes it works (it all depends on how many advance reservations come in).

5. **Never admit to being a tourist**
Clubs are where the worst New York snobbery comes to the fore. It's sad but true: They really don't want tourists. That doesn't mean you shouldn't go; just don't attempt to get in by telling them it's your "last night before you go back to Alabama."

6. **Say you're there to meet the deejay**
This is my trickiest tip, but it actually works. Go to the club's website in advance, find out who the deejay will be that night, and say that you're meeting him or her inside.

of this cavernous, dungeonlike, two-floor club. Forgot your chaps? Not a problem—the Eagle has a tiny "leather goods" store on the first floor for all your codpiece and whipping needs. (There's also a quite civilized roof garden on the third floor, open in good weather.)

Its polar opposite, **Eastern Bloc** ★★ (505 E. 6th St., off Ave. A; ☎ 212/777-2555; ❺ to Second Ave) only flirts with brutality, of the Soviet-era type, in this case. The bathroom is filled with cartoons of buff men in perilous situations (python attacks, oh my!), the walls plastered with Cold War–style paintings of soldiers, interspersed with the mounted heads of zebras and deer, but the scene at the bar and along the wall banquettes is ultra-mellow. A good place to go if you find brooding, would-be-artists hot.

New York's first gay sports bar, **Gym** ★ (167 Eighth Ave. btwn 18th and 19th sts.; ☎ 212/337-2439; www.gymsportsbar.com; ❹, ❸, ❸ to 14th St., or ❶ to Eighth Ave.) is filled with huge TV screens that not a single guy even glanced at when I last visited (although, according to the bartender, the Yankees do get full attention when they've got a game). The crowd is casual, chatty, and friendly, like at most sports bars. There's a pool table and video games in the back, and a small patio out front.

A fabulous Art Deco space, once home to El Chico (a former flamenco cabaret whose murals still adorn the walls), **The Monster** (80 Grove St. at Sheridan Sq.; ☎ 212/924-3558; www.manhattan-monster.com; ❶ to Christopher St.) has two faces. Upstairs is a piano bar with a crowd of show-tune crazy regulars; downstairs a discotheque with go-go boys, a weekly drag show (Wed), and the most popular Latin Night (Mon) in the city. An old-fashioned classic of the gay nightlife scene.

LESBIAN BARS

Early in the evening, **The Cubby Hole** ★★ (281 W. 12th St. at the corner of 4th St.; ☎ 212/243-9041; ❶, ❷, ❸ to 14th St. or ❶ to Eighth Ave.) gets a mixed crowd of men and even straight women from the neighborhood, but by 11pm it's strictly "lipstick lesbians" and club girls rocking out to the jukebox. It's a fun scene and the decor is hilarious, with hundreds of paper animals and fish, Chinese lanterns, and plastic flying pigs dangling from the ceiling.

Dominated by a large pool table (always in use) in the center room and two bars, the no-nonsense **Henrietta Hudson** (438 Hudson St. off Morton; ☎ 212/924-3347; ❶ to Houston St.) is a favorite among Latinas and African-American women (though not exclusively). Every night has a theme, with pool tournaments on Monday and karaoke on Wednesday night; on weekends a cover charge of $10 is imposed.

A congenial bi-level bar and grill with Victorian decor and a scattering of red Christmas lights, **Ruby Fruit** (531 Hudson St., btwn Charles and W. 10th sts.; ☎ 212/929-3343; ❶, ❷, ❸ to 14th St., or ❶ to Eighth Ave.) attracts an older crowd to both its restaurant and upstairs piano bar.

A Night at the Theater

Going to a show is the quintessential New York experience

YOU CAN TRAIPSE THE ENTIRE METROPOLITAN MUSEUM OF ART, ATTEND a Yankees game, and ascend to the top of the Empire State Building, but you can't really say you've *done* New York until you spend an evening at the theater. It's an essential element in a New York City vacation, like going to the beach in Hawaii, slurping pasta in Italy, or snapping a picture with some poor sweaty guy in a mouse costume in Orlando. And though every 3 years or so some major critic issues an obituary declaring that New York theater is dead, somehow the corpse continues to rise from its glittering grave, producing Pulitzer Prize–winning plays, fine new musicals, and theatrical events of all sorts that just may, when done well, shift your perspective an iota, give you a peephole into another culture, or perhaps illuminate, for 2 fleeting hours, the human condition.

But how do you find that momentous play, that joyous musical, that thought-provoking performance-art piece? And then how do you snag an affordable ticket in a town where orchestra seats bought directly from the theater, or worse, from some commission-claiming concierge, can top $125 each? Here's what this New Yorker—and former actor—does to find a cheap seat. (Later in the chapter I'll also discuss how you can suss out which shows are worth your time and money.)

GETTING CHEAP(ER) SEATS

Let's start with a trade secret that no one in the theater industry wants you to know: Only suckers and out-of-towners pay full price for most Broadway and Off-Broadway shows. I'd say that, on average, only five or six shows *per year* get away with charging full price for their seats, and that's with eight shows a week. For the other 60-or-so productions, discounts *are the norm,* not the exception. Don't believe anyone who tells you otherwise.

Tried-and-true methods for saving on seats include:

CULLING A DISCOUNT CODE FROM THE INTERNET

Booking tickets before you arrive is the most time-effective strategy: You're able to schedule your time in advance, get early dinner reservations, and not waste any of your precious New York vacation standing in line at box offices or ticket brokers.

To do so, surf to one of the following websites, each of which is a treasure trove for valuable coupons and discount codes:

- **www.playbill.com**
- **www.theatermania.com**
- **www.broadwaybox.com**

Both **Playbill** and **Theatermania** are clubs that negotiate their own discounts with the theaters; in order to access their codes you must become a member. That's not a problem, though, as membership is free, the forms are easy, and both sites have strict privacy policies ensuring your information won't be sold. Once you gain access to these lists, you can score between 35% and 50% off the ticketed price of many, many shows—usually a full two-thirds of those playing at any one time.

Broadway Box, the other prominent player, has no membership fee, as it's actually a clearinghouse for discount codes from other sources. It, too, provides half-off coupons and codes (and occasionally discounts of 35%) for dozens of shows. It tends to have the largest selection of shows and has lately become the site I turn to first.

The one negative to using these sites is that if you book over the phone or Internet, a handling fee will be tacked onto the cost of your ticket, usually between $4 and $5, but that would also be the case if you purchased full-priced seats remotely. I've also found that you won't have quite the number of choices you would enjoy at the TKTS booth in Times Square (and at the South Street Seaport), which is why I also recommend . . .

JOINING THE DREADED LINE AT TKTS

On an unsheltered, windy island in the center of Times Square—freezing in winter, sweltering in July and August—the TKTS booth has squatted since 1973, offering discounts of 25%, 35%, and 50% off theater tickets. As I said before, it presents a greater breadth of shows than do the online discounters, but you pay for that choice with your time (during busy periods the wait in line can be up to an hour). Those who do brave the line are often rewarded with $35 seats to Off-Broadway plays and $55 seats at big Broadway musicals.

But there are ways to "game" the line, including:

- Go to the TKTS downtown at the South Street Seaport (see "What You Need to Know About TKTS," below, for the address and details). You'll rarely wait longer than 20 minutes here, and you can purchase matinee tickets the day before a show (at the Uptown booth, ticket purchases are day-of-show only). The only downside here: No day-of-matinee tickets are sold.
- Don't go early. Tickets are released from the theaters to the booths throughout the day, so you don't necessarily increase your chances of getting the show you want by going early in the day, or waiting in line before the booth opens. Instead, go when it's most convenient for you to do so.
- Go to the theater on a Tuesday night, which is the slowest night of the week. You'll encounter almost no line and will have a much bigger selection than usual. A few shows play Monday nights as well; your selection won't be big, but you probably won't have a long wait.
- Pick a play instead of a musical. In 2005, TKTS opened a window (no. 6) dedicated to the sale of plays only. The line for this window is much shorter.

What You Need to Know About TKTS

The Times Square Booth

> **Address:** 46th St. between Broadway and Seventh Avenue. Important: Do not confuse TKTS with the NY Information Center, right across the street from the booth; you'll pay full price plus commission if you purchase tickets at the latter.
>
> **Directions:** Take the ⓝ, ⓠ, ⓡ to 51st Street or the ❶, ❷, ❸ to Times Square.
>
> **Hours:** Monday through Saturday, 3 to 8pm; Sunday 3 to 8pm; additional matinee hours on Wednesday and Saturday 10am to 2pm.

The South Street Seaport Booth

> **Address:** At the corner of Front St. and John St.
>
> **Directions:** Take the ❷, ❸, ❹, ❺ to Fulton St.
>
> **Hours:** Monday through Friday 11am to 6pm; Saturday 11am to 7pm; Sunday 11am to 4pm.
>
> **Special caveat:** It sells matinee tickets the day before performance only.
>
> **Important:** Both booths accept cash and traveler's checks only (no credit cards).

OTHER TICKET OPTIONS

If you want to see a highly popular show that is *not* offering discounts, or are on a very tight budget and would prefer to see a show for free, here are a couple of additional methods that might work for you:

Rush Tickets: A number of Broadway and Off-Broadway theaters have taken to offering "rush tickets" for the first row of seats on the day of a show. The average price is $25 for these neck-benders (it's preferable to be a couple of rows back—the sightlines are better and there's less danger of being spit on by performers). The rules and methods for their sale vary by show; sometimes these seats are only available to students, while in other cases any member of the public can get them (call the theater in advance to ask). In the past, these seats were given out on a first-come, first-served basis, but recently a number of the theaters have adopted a more humane lottery method. Instead of having to sit around for hours waiting, you simply show up at 5pm or so, take a lottery number and hope you get picked (at the shows I've done it for, about 100 people showed up in hopes of winning 20 seats; not such bad odds).

Standing Room: Sold-out shows offer "standing room" tickets on the day of the show only, to about 10 people per show (depending on the size of the theater). They are sold at 10am when the box office opens, and for the really popular shows a line will form an hour earlier for these "standing spots" at the back of the house. The cost of these non-seats range from $15 to $25, again depending on the show.

Senior and student discounts: Although Broadway theaters won't care how old you are or what you do, a number of the Off-Broadway houses do sell specially priced seats (sometimes for as little as $15) to seniors and students. While some do this on the day of show only, others allow these theatergoers to purchase in advance with the correct identification. Among the theaters that usually discount in this way are The Public Theater, the New York Theater Workshop, and The Vineyard Theater. You'll also occasionally find $5 tickets to Off-Broadway shows for teenagers (and their chaperones) at a wonderful website called **High Five** (www.high5tix.org). If you're traveling with a teen, check the site before buying any tickets.

Ushering: A number of New York theaters use volunteer ushers. The shows get free labor, while you, the usher, get to see a show without paying (or really even working that hard). Here's how it works: You show up an hour before curtain dressed in black pants and a white button-down shirt; the management then teaches you the layout of the theater, and once patrons arrive, you help them find their seat and hand out playbills. As the lights dim, you scuttle into your own seat and enjoy the show. After the show, management may ask you to stick around for 15 minutes to help pick up discarded programs, but that's about it.

Theaters that use volunteer ushers include:

+ **Astor Place Theater** (434 Lafayette St.; ☎ 212/387-9415, ext 220; www.bluemen.com). The home of Blue Man Group accepts four ushers per performance; call 1 week in advance.
+ **Irish Repertory Theater** (132 W. 22nd St.; ☎ 212/255-0270, ext. 16; www.irishrepertorytheater.com). Accepts two ushers per show; call the number above on a Tuesday or Friday between 1pm and 5pm only.
+ **Lucille Lortel Theater** (121 Christopher St.; ☎ 212/924-2817; www.lortel.org). A top Off-Broadway venue, it takes three ushers per show and starts booking them 2 weeks before a show starts previews (to find out when that is, check the website).
+ **Manhattan Theater Club** (☎ 212/399-3000; www.mtc-nyc.org) Has three venues, one on Broadway and two off and offers ushering opportunities at

Getting Good Seats to Sold-Out Shows

"House seats" are the seats reserved for members of the cast and crew of Broadway shows, and they're always the best seats in the house. If no one involved with the production wants to use them for a particular performance, they will usually go on sale to the public at the box office 48 hours before that show, between 5:30 and 6pm. These seats won't be cheap, but if there's a particular show that you want to see that's sold-out, this may be your best means of snagging a seat.

Theater Basics

There are three types of theaters in New York City: Broadway, Off-Broadway, and Off-Off-Broadway. They differ in size of theater, price, and esthetic:

Broadway shows: Tend to be performed in the Times Square area (the one exception being the shows at Lincoln Center; p. 266). They cost, without a discount, between $46 for a balcony seat (as little as $26 at some plays), to $100 for an orchestra seat, all the way up to $295 for a so-called "premium" seat at certain musicals.

Off-Broadway shows: Are performed in venues all over town, with a good many now clustered in the Union Square area. Top prices for Off-Broadway musicals rarely go above $89, with plays topping out (usually) at $65. Off-Broadway theaters are much smaller than those on Broadway, pay less to cast and crew, and are thus able to present more controversial, less commercial plays and musicals. Many of the recent Pulitzer Prize drama winners began as Off-Broadway shows.

Off-Off-Broadway shows: Are staged in very small theaters, often featuring experimental works or actor's showcases. These productions also play in theaters all over town; some of the best-known venues are PS 142, The Ontological Hysterical Theater, The Performing Garage, and Here. Although you'll rarely see these shows advertised or even reviewed in the *New York Times,* they will be listed in the *Village Voice* and *Time Out* magazine.

Schedule: Broadway and most Off-Broadway shows perform eight times a week, most commonly Tuesday through Sunday, though some do play on Monday (instead of Tues or Sun). Matinee (daytime) performances are usually presented at 2pm on Wednesday and Saturday, and 3pm on Sunday. Evening performances take place 8pm Wednesday through Saturday, 7pm on Tuesday night. And if a show is geared towards children, evening performances may be even earlier.

all three. For the Biltmore Theater (Broadway), send an e-mail to volunteer@mtc-nyc.org. To usher at their City Center locales, e-mail mtchousemanager@nycitycenter.org.

- ◆ **New York Theater Workshop** (79 E. 4th St.; ☎ 212/780-9037; www.nytw.org). Five volunteer ushers per night; call 2 weeks ahead.
- ◆ **Playwrights Horizons** (416 W. 42nd St.; ☎ 212/564-1235 or e-mail usher@playwrightshorizons.org). Uses four ushers per show on its main stage; three for its smaller, studio productions. The theater starts "hiring" ushers 2 weeks before the first preview of a show, so call as soon as you know you'd like to attend a performance. Write "Add to list" in the subject line if you decide to e-mail the theater.
- ◆ **The Roundabout Theater Company** (☎ 212/719-9393; www.roundabouttheatre.org). It now has three performance spaces, two on Broadway and one

off and accepts ushers for all three: The American Airlines Theater (227 W. 42nd St.); The Studio 54 Theater (254 W. 54th St); and Laura Pels Theater (111 W. 46th St.). Usually ushers are chosen 2 weeks before the opening night of a show, but it's often possible to get an ushering gig the day or week of the show (depending on its popularity). Either speak to the box office of the following theaters, or call the number above.

♦ **Second Stage Theater** (307 W. 43rd St.; ☎ 212/787-8302; www.second stagetheater.com). Hires the most ushers (six) per show. They request that volunteers send an e-mail (to jschelifer@2st.com) 3 weeks in advance rather than calling.

♦ **The Signature Theater Company** (555 W. 42nd St.; ☎ 212/244-7529; www. signaturetheatre.org). Uses four ushers per show; starts accepting volunteers 3 weeks before a performance begins.

♦ **The Vineyard Theater** (108 E. 15th St., off Union Sq.; ☎ 212/353-0303; www. vineyardtheatre.org). Three volunteer ushers per performance; call 3 weeks ahead.

CHOOSING THE RIGHT SHOW TO SEE

I'll admit it: I'm a walker. If I accidentally pick an awful show, I leave at intermission rather than fork out extra money to the babysitter so that I can sit through something dull. It doesn't happen that often because over the years, I've formulated the following rules to help me choose which shows to see.

Skip the long-running Broadway musicals   There should be an expiration date on Broadway musicals, just as there is on milk. After about 2 years, they turn sour.

Here's why: The first cast usually leaves around the 1-year mark, and then a second cast is announced to much fanfare. When it comes to the third go-round, the big-name actors aren't willing to take over the roles, so they get lesser-known pros in the parts. These second-tier actors aren't any less talented, but because they have no clout they never get to rehearse with the director and put their own mark on the role. Instead, they are "put in" by a stage manager and are expected to re-create what the previous actor did; that can lead to wooden, dull performances. The chorus, which usually stays with the show for a few years, simply becomes bored and starts sleepwalking through their performances. I foolishly took my niece to see *Chicago* in its sixth year on Broadway, and it was utterly transformed from the vibrant, sexy show I had seen in previews to a Fosse-version of *Night of the Living Dead*.

You can find out how long a show has been on by calling the theater; asking the folks at the TKTS booth; looking at Telecharge.com (which lists when shows opened); or checking *The New Yorker* magazine, which lists "long-running" shows separately in its theater section.

Beware the "un-nominated" Broadway shows   It doesn't matter which shows win a Tony Award—that's pretty much a crapshoot. But the nominating committee, which is made up of distinguished theater professionals—actors, writers, producers, and the like—is savvy about theater and usually does a good job rewarding the most interesting shows with nominations in late May. If a new play, musical,

The Festivals of Summer

All the city's a stage come summer, with dozens of performers of all types invading the city's parks, piers, and even parking lots. Many shows are free; those that aren't are usually affordable. Here's a quick rundown of the top summer offerings:

Shakespeare in the Park: The Bard's work usually, but also classic musicals and plays with star-studded casts.

Tickets: Free, but difficult to get. Either line up at the Delacorte Theater in Central Park at the crack of dawn (tickets are given out at 1pm); or join a new online lottery at www.publictheater.org (details at the site).

Schedule: Usually June, July, and August (until about the 15th). Performances at 8pm.

Info: See website above

Summerstage: Also in Central Park, this arts fest runs the gamut from comedy nights to modern dance to world music to poetry slams attracting such top names as Vampire Weekend, Crosby, Stills and Nash, and Los Lonely Boys.

Tickets: Some shows are free, others can be quite pricey (see website for info on ordering tickets).

Schedule: June–mid-August, mostly nighttime performances, hours vary.

Info: Go to www.summerstage.org

NY International Fringe Festival: Wacky, weird, and sometimes enlightening theater, performance art, and dance mark this fun fest, the largest multi-arts festival in North America with 200-plus companies performing each year.

Tickets: Some outdoor events require no tickets; indoor performances will, but rarely top $15 a pop. Go to the website for full info.

Schedule: Two weeks in August (dates vary year to year); performances at all times of the day and night.

Info: Go to www.fringenyc.org

The River to River Festival: Rivaling the Fringe in the creativity and downright wackiness of many of the offerings, this is an all arts and more fest. Along with musical concerts of all types and works of modern dance and theater, are workshops on the construction trade, scavenger hunts, sunset singing circles, model boat expos, sailing lessons—you name it. Events held in the parks, piers, and museums of lower Manhattan, primarily.

Tickets: All events are free, but some require advance tickets (see website)

Schedule: Tuesdays through Fridays, events midday through about 10pm, most nights

Info: Go to www.rivertorivernyc.com

Met in the Parks: Grand opera and big voices in concert-style performances from the Metropolitan Opera. Performed in Central Park and other parks in the tri-state area.

Tickets: Not required, just show up early

Schedule: June performances only. 8pm kickoff, dates vary.

Info: Go to www.metoperafamily.org/metopera/season/parks.aspx

NY Philharmonic in the Parks: Orchestral concerts in all of the boroughs and New Jersey, featuring top-flight soloists and conductors.

Tickets: Not required, just show up early

Schedule: Scattered evening performances, late June to mid-July

Info: Go to www.nyphil.org

Lincoln Center Fest: An extraordinary collection of performances from around the world, from concert-poems by Laurie Anderson to Becket Evenings with Ralph Fiennes and Liam Neeson. An outdoor component is presented free during the daytime.

Tickets: Not required for outdoor festival, pricey for indoor works (see website)

Schedule: The indoor fest is in July, outdoor in August

Info: Go to www.lincolncenter.org

Bryant Park: Classic movies on a giant outdoor screen, plus other performances.

Tickets: Not required, just show up early for a seat

Schedule: Movies on Mondays at 5pm throughout the summer, yoga classes, piano concerts, and readings for children and adults, at different times throughout the summer.

Info: Go to www.bryantpark.org

or revival can't manage to get a nod (and in some years there's very little competition for nominations), take it as a sign that your theater dollars may be better spent elsewhere. Each show that gets nominations will trumpet that fact in their ads (but don't punish the Off-Broadway shows, as only Broadway shows are eligible for the Tonys). A good source for this type of information is the Telecharge.com site, which lists nominations and awards for each show.

Do some research before you buy   The Web is a treasure trove of information, including past reviews of shows. Instead of going blindly to the TKTS line (see above), surf to **www.nytimes.com** or **www.nymag.com** before you get to New York and pick a show that's garnered a fair number of good reviews. While the reviewers aren't always right (and lately, I think the *New York Times* critics have been really off in their recommendations), at least by reading up you'll have a better idea of what the shows are about.

Avoid "juke box" musicals   *Mamma Mia!* set off a frenzy of shows that simply take the catalogue of some famous pop composer and then string songs together with a silly, inorganic story. In most cases you'll hear better renditions of these songs at your local theme park—don't go!

Consider seeing an Off-Broadway show   Because of the huge financial pressures on Broadway producers, they usually (but not always) stick with tried-and-true formulas, revivals, or shows with a clear marketing hook. For anything slightly edgy or even intellectual, you often need to go to the smaller Off-Broadway theaters (see the "Theater Basics" box, above). These theaters also tend to charge substantially less for tickets, sometimes shaving $25 to $50 off the cost.

Although I can't guarantee that you'll always see a great show, the following Off-Broadway theater companies consistently produce exciting, award-winning productions. They are:

- **New York Theatre Workshop** (79 E. 4th St., btwn Second Ave. and the Bowery; ☎ 212/460-5475; www.nytw.org; ⑥ to Astor Place). The continued success of this intellectually heady and sometimes avant-garde company may just boil down to the unerring good taste of Artistic Director James Nicola. **Biggest hits include:** *Rent* (Pulitzer Prize), *Quills, Blown Sideways Through Life,* and *Mad Forest.*

- **The New Group** (410 W. 42nd St., btwn Ninth and Tenth aves.; ☎ 212/334-3380; www.thenewgroup.org; ⓐ, ⓔ, ⓒ to 42nd St.). The youngest of the Off-Broadway theater companies and the one that's had the highest number of both critical and popular successes in the past few years, the New Group specializes in both revivals of modern classics and new plays. It's known for the high caliber of the acting in its productions. **Biggest hits include:** *Hurleyburley* (with Ethan Hawke and Parker Posey), *Abigail's Party* (with Jennifer Jason Leigh), *The Fever* (with Wallace Shawn), and *Aunt Dan and Lemon* (with Lili Taylor).

- **Playwrights Horizons** (416 W. 42nd St., btwn Seventh and Eighth aves.; ☎ 212/564-1235; www.playwrightshorizons.org; ❶, ❷, ❸, ⓝ, ⓡ, ⓢ to Times Sq., ⓐ, ⓔ, ⓒ to 42nd St.). Dedicated to nurturing the art of the writer (lyricists and librettists as well as playwrights), Playwrights has always had a great eye for talent, producing the works of Stephen Sondheim, Kenneth Lonergan, Christopher Durang, A. R. Gurney, and Wendy Wasserstein. Biggest hits include: *I Am My Own Wife* (Pulitzer Prize), *Driving Miss Daisy* (Pulitzer Prize), *Sunday in the Park with George* (Pulitzer Prize), *The Heidi Chronicles* (Pulitzer Prize), and *March of the Falsettos*.

◆ **The Public Theater** (425 Lafayette St., off Astor Place; ☎ 212/564-1235; www.publictheater.org; ❻ to Astor Place). A strong emphasis on American playwrights, especially Asian-, Latin- and African-American writers, has kept this theater in the forefront of "the scene" since 1967. **Biggest hits include:** *A Chorus Line* (Pulitzer Prize), *Bring in 'Da Noise, Bring in 'Da Funk* (Pulitzer Prize), *Elaine Stritch at Liberty* (Tony Award), *Topdog/Underdog* (Pulitzer Prize), and the monologues of Anna Deveare Smith. In all, Public Theater productions have been awarded 40 Tonys (for shows that moved to Broadway) and 138 Off-Broadway or "Obie" awards.

◆ **Signature Theatre** (555 W. 42nd St.; ☎ 212/244-PLAY; www.signature theatre.org; ❹, ❺, ❻ to 42nd St.). Devotes each season to just one playwright, who gets to choose which works he or she wants represented. Because the theater picks only established playwrights to showcase, the productions are often peopled by these bigwigs' big-name actor friends, meaning that star-gazing is virtually guaranteed. But so is fresh, often compelling theater. **Biggest hits include:** *Burn This* (with Edward Norton) and *The Fifth of July* (with Robert Sean Leonard and Parker Posey).

◆ **The Vineyard Theatre** (108 E. 15th St., off Union Sq.; ☎ 212/353-0303; www.vineyardtheatre.org; ❹, ❺, ❻, ❶, ❷ to Union Sq.). The Vineyard may well be the biggest risk-taker of the major Off-Broadway theaters, presenting out-and-out performance art alongside less far-out plays and musicals. When they're good, they're great; and when their shows miss the mark, they're still usually intellectually intriguing. **Biggest hits include:** *Avenue Q* (Tony Award), *Three Tall Women* (Pulitzer Prize), and *How I Learned to Drive* (Pulitzer Prize).

◆ **Brooklyn Academy of Music** (BAM; 30 Lafayette Ave. and 651 Fulton St., both in Brooklyn; www.bam.org; ❷, ❸, ❹, ❺, ❻, ❼ to Atlantic Ave). For European performance art and dance, BAM has no peer in New York (see more on p. 270). **Biggest hits include:** Works by Pina Bausch, Ingmar Bergman, Peter Brook, and Robert Wilson.

CHILDREN'S THEATER

Broadway theaters do not allow children under the age of 5 to attend, nor do they give discounts to kids (with one exception—see below). But beyond Broadway is affordable, often mesmerizing theater that's aimed squarely at the pre-puberty crowd, with dozens of offerings each week. Two organizations in particular present a roster of consistently challenging and entertaining family shows.

New Victory Theater (209 W. 42nd St., just off Broadway; ☎ 646/223-3020; www.newvictory.org; tickets $10–$30; ❶, ❷, ❸, ❺, ❶, ❷, ❸, ❹ to Times Sq.) books shows from around the U.S. and abroad that are inventive and smart enough for the entire family to enjoy. One musical that made its debut here even moved to Broadway (now how about that for a kiddie show?). Past offerings have included quality puppet shows, acrobatic and circus troupes, "new vaudeville"

Kids' Night on Broadway

For 4 nights each winter (usually in late Jan or early Feb), the League of American Theater Producers does something unheard of—it gives away free seats to a number of Broadway shows. These freebies have a purpose: They're the Broadway community's attempt to create new theatergoers out of young people between the ages of 6 and 18. Note that each child must be accompanied by an adult who is paying full price for the tickets, and that tickets must be purchased in pairs. I took my then-6-year-old daughter to see *Fiddler on the Roof* thanks to this program, and sitting in an audience full of families, seeing a classic musical, was truly a golden affair. At the end of the show, the cast traditionally gives a short talk for the children, which only adds to the experience. For full details, go to www.kidsnightonbroadway.com or www.nycvisit.com; be sure to book your tickets several months in advance, as these nights inevitably sell out.

acts, and theater pieces (you can see a preview of their offerings on their website, thanks to streaming video).

In 2005, after years of touring the United States and presenting highly acclaimed shows at schools, theaters, and even football stadiums, **Theaterworks NYC** (121 Christopher St. btwn Bleecker and Hudson sts.; ☎ 212/279-4200; www.theatreworksusa.org; tickets $35; ❶ to Christopher St.) decided to create a home base for itself in Greenwich Village. Now, nearly every weekend of the year it presents lively, educational shows, often based on classic children's books such as *Curious George, Charlotte's Web,* and *Harold and the Purple Crayon.* Many of the authors and performers who've worked at Theaterworks have gone on to stellar Broadway careers, so this is a good place to see new talent first.

12 The Essentials of Planning

THE HIGHLIGHTS OF A VISIT TO NEW YORK—THE TOP SIGHTS AND ACTIV-ities, the hotels, restaurants, shops, and spectacles that best serve your needs—have filled the bulk of this book. But almost as important is the miscellany that doesn't fit into broader categories. Those nitty-gritty details—from trip-planning essentials to perks to tips for travelers with special interests and needs—are what you'll find in this appendix.

The good news is that New York is undeniably a visitor-friendly city and has, in its tourist office (which goes by the appropriately show-bizzy name **NYC & Company; ☎ 212/484-1200; www.nycvisit.com**), one of the best resources in the U.S. for travelers. It's a well-run, efficient organization staffed by real experts who love their jobs; and its website offers a wealth of information and discounts for the traveler. Anything that you can't find in this book—and hopefully that won't be much—you should be able to find through the tourist office.

WHEN TO VISIT?

"Anytime you like," is the short answer. New York is a 12-month, 24-hour destination, and there's always something exciting going on here.

Significantly, New York does not experience the real extremes of temperature of Minneapolis or Phoenix. Yes, we get snowstorms and 10-degree weather, but rarely for more than a day or two, with the snow usually scooped into graying piles overnight. We also have heat waves, but it's unusual for the temperature to break 100°F for more than 4 or 5 days each summer, though it will be a sticky heat when it hits and none too pleasant. In general, this type of extreme heat only hits in late July and August, whereas the most blustery and bitterly cold days fall in January and February, and occasionally December. (Of course, in this age of global warming you never know what will happen, but mild year-round temps have been the norm for a few years now and seem to have stabilized—see the chart below.)

Culture, too, is a year-round exercise. Most of the major plays, musicals, and art shows debut between September and May, so those who like to be on culture's cutting edge visit then. In the summer months NYC teems with arts events as the city transforms itself into an outdoor theater/concert hall, with dozens of free shows—from Shakespeare in the Park to Shakespeare in the Parking Lot—crowding the calendar and delighting penny-pinchers. All of the major art institutions participate in this summer free-for-all, with the Museum of Modern Art sponsoring concerts in its sculpture garden; the Metropolitan Opera bringing music to the parks; and dozens of other institutions, large and small, established and unknown, jumping on the alfresco bandwagon.

So what it all comes down to, in my mind, is cost, and here there is a *major* difference between seasons. Persons who visit in the slower months pay the right amount for their lodging, and those who come when the city is crowded—and here I'm going to sound like the clichéd New Yorker—get screwed.

So when are prices the most moderate? Deep winter, in the months of January (after the 4th) and February, it's not at all unusual to find a lovely room for as little as $109 a night. Visit in the fall, especially November and December, and that same room, in the same hotel, could cost upwards of $250 a night. Spring is also pricey, albeit slightly less so than fall, and prices drop into a middle range in summer, but really only for July and August (and not over the Fourth of July). Room rates over Christmas, New Year's, and Thanksgiving reach their pinnacles for the year. If you must visit at those times, get ready to pay a good $50 more than even the pricey fall rates.

The table below charts seasonal weather and price shifts. Look at both in tandem when planning your trip.

New York Average Temperature, Rainfall, and Hotel Prices

	Jan	Feb	Mar	Apr	May	June	July	Aug	Sept	Oct	Nov	Dec
Hi/Low Daily Temps (°F)	39/26	40/27	48/34	61/44	71/53	81/63	85/68	83/66	77/60	67/51	54/41	41/30
Hi/Low Daily Temps (°C)	4/-3	5/-3	8/1	16/6	21/11	27/17	29/18	28/19	25/16	19/10	12/5	5/-1
Days of Precipitation	11	10	11	11	11	10	11	10	8	8	9	10
Hotel Room Cost*	$125	$125	$140	$165	$179	$179	$169	$169	$220	$220	$220	$220

Excluding holiday periods, an average for a moderate double room with private bathroom (you can sometimes do better; see accommodations chapter, p. 28).

New York's Visit-Worthy Events

When planning your vacation, you may want to look at what special events or yearly festivals might be occurring during the time of your visit. I've included a very limited sampling below of what I consider to be the "visit-worthy" events. As I can make no claims to psychic abilities, I can't include all of the nifty happenings that haven't yet been announced, so this is necessarily an incomplete list. To get a complete picture, pick up a copy of *Time Out* magazine when you arrive. The "Around Town" section will leave you dizzy—usually there are upwards of 150 interesting events happening any one week. For a more selective listing, buy the current *New Yorker* magazine, which devotes the first tenth of its pages to its picks for the most intellectually stimulating or artistically important events of the week.

January

Chinese New Year: Based on the lunar calendar, Chinese New Year always falls sometime in January or February, with 2 weeks of parades, festive meals, and special performances staged throughout Chinatown. Call ☎ 212/484-1222 or go to www.nycvisit.com for full details.

Winter Restaurant Week: A misnomer, because this gourmet shindig actually lasts 2 weeks (reappearing in summer for another 2; see below), this is the time of year when cheap foodies can try out the city's best restaurants for as little as $25 at lunch, $35 at dinner for three courses at each meal. For a full discussion of this event, go to p. 81.

February

Fashion Week: Early February is when the American designers parade their new lines for the press and big department store buyers, and it's impossible to get tickets to the runway shows (they go to the likes of Gwyneth Paltrow and Madonna). I only mention Fashion Week here because the event can tie up rooms at the Midtown hotels, raising prices (better to stay Downtown or Uptown when the fashionistas are in town).

Westminster Kennel Club Dog Show: I've always found it funny that Fashion Week—that parade of "Best in Breed" women—should be followed directly by a dog show. At least at the dog show, they're upfront about the purpose of the spectacle. The winnowing from just cute to anatomically awesome takes place the second weekend of the month at Madison Square Garden. With over 2,500 pooches appearing, it's quite the scene. For information, check out www.westminster kennelclub.org.

March

St. Patrick's Day (March 17): Thanks to one of the largest Irish-American populations in the United States, St. Paddy's is an enormous event in NYC, rivaling only New Year's Eve for its displays of public inebriation. Every pub in town throws a party, and in the afternoon, all of 150,000 marchers parade down Fifth Avenue from 44th to 86th streets.

The Pier Antiques Show: Never heard of it? Then you obviously aren't into antiques and collectibles, as this is one of the largest shows in the world for folks who care about old stuff. Taking place on the Passenger Ship Terminal Piers for a weekend mid-month, the show draws literally hundreds of treasure seekers. For details, call ☎ 212/255-0020 or access www.stellashows.com.

New York International Automobile Show: Care about cars? Then you'll want to attend this massive yearly expo, which takes over the Javits Center for an entire week and jams it with Hummers, Hondas, and Hyundais (and all the new driving gadgets that go along with steering a vehicle down the road). In 2008, the show took place between March 21 and 30; find more info at ☎ 718/746-5300 or www.autoshowny.com.

April

The Easter Parade: No floats, no marching bands, just ordinary people in extraordinary hats mark Easter in one of the city's most low-key but charming celebrations. Most spend the afternoon strolling up and down in front of St. Patrick's Cathedral, and Fifth Avenue from 57th Street all the way down to 45th is closed to traffic from 11am to 4pm, with the greatest number of chapeaus in evidence around noon.

The TriBeCa Film Festival: Founded by Robert DeNiro and Jane Rosenthal in 2002, this little film festival has quickly grown into one of the most influential in the nation. You'll see films from all over the world here, from big studio pictures to tiny independent films from places such as Slovakia and Dubai. And unlike other film fests, this one is truly for all ages, with a nifty street fair on the second weekend (usually featuring a zoo and rides), as well as children's films throughout the 2-week event, which has run from the last week in April into the first week of May in the past 3 years. To learn more, visit www.tribeca filmfestival.org.

May

Fleet Week: Over a dozen naval and Coast Guard ships, along with vessels from around the world, sail into New York's welcoming harbor each year and moor here for the week preceding Memorial Day (the last Mon in May). You'll see sailors in their dress whites all over town, or you can go and visit the guys and gals on their own ships. At the docks there are usually "Best Chow" competitions, athletic matches, a parade of ships, and, of course, Memorial Day ceremonies. See http://fleetweek.navy.mil for more info.

June

Shakespeare in the Park: More than just a show, this free Shakespeare program is a yearly highlight, marrying top talent with warm, starry nights for an unforgettable theatrical experience. In recent years, Meryl Streep, Natalie Portman, Phillip Seymour Hoffman, Liev Schrieber, and Kevin Kline have trod these boards in plays by the Bard and classic American musicals. Snagging one of the free tickets is not easy, requiring a minimum 3-hour wait in line (longer if the show's a popular one). Tickets are distributed at 1pm, both on the path in Central Park in front of the theater and at the Public Theater downtown (the line's usually shorter here). Go to www.public theater.org for full information.

Central Park Summerstage: The musical equivalent of Shakespeare in the Park, though it's not free, Summerstage primarily hosts world music and alternative rock stars for afternoon and evening concerts. For a complete lineup, go to www.summer stage.org.

Summer Restaurant Week: Same as the 2-week winter fest (see above), but with better weather. For specific dates, go to www.nycvisit.com.

Museum Mile Festival: In early June, for one evening only, Fifth Avenue becomes a car free zone, bands set up on street corners, and all the museums waive their admission fees and host special events. If you ever thought museums are dull, you'll change your tune after this fest. See www.museummilefestival.org for complete information and date.

The Belmont Stakes: The final event in horse racing's grand trifecta of events (the Kentucky Derby and The Preakness are the first two). Any horse able to win all three instantly enters the record books, and his owner becomes a multi-millionaire, thanks to the breeding fees he'll be able to collect for the rest of that horse's life. Folks arrive at this jolly, crowded event in Queens before the actual race so they can view the horses and socialize. Usually the first week in June. Info: ☎ 516/488-9622 or www.belmont-stakes.info.

Gay Pride Weekend: More than just a parade (though the naughty, outrageous, rambunctious parade is still at the heart of the festivities) NY's pride weekend draws men and women from across the U.S. for a weekend of lectures, dances, and rallies. Learn more at www.nycpride.org.

Mermaid Parade: A smaller, nautically themed, daytime version of Greenwich Village's Halloween Parade, the Mermaid Parade takes place towards the end of June each year in Coney Island. Founded in 1983, the parade has the same kind of home-grown ambience and raunch as its Greenwich Village counterpart. Along with the ball that follows, featuring performances by local burlesque acts, the event is a heckuva lot of fun. Get details at www.coneyisland.com or call ☎ 718/372-5159.

July

Fourth of July: New York has less spectacular celebrations for the Fourth than, say Washington, D.C., Philadelphia, or Boston, but Macy's does put on a fab fireworks show over the East River. The rockets usually start blasting around 9pm.

Lincoln Center Festival: More than any place in the city except Central Park, Lincoln Center is abuzz with indoor and outdoor fests throughout the summer. **Midsummer Nights Swing** brings big bands to the Lincoln Center Plaza on Fridays in July and August for nights of romance and dancing; an included lesson is offered at 6pm for beginning ball-roomers. The **New York Philharmonic,** usually based at Lincoln Center, visits parks in all five boroughs for free concerts (for schedule, call ☎ 212/875-5709 or check out www.nycgovparks.org). The **Mostly Mozart Concert,** an indoor offering, brings master musicians from all over the world to play the music of the 18th-century master. And the festival that actually has the name "Lincoln Center Festival" (I'm sliding these others under its umbrella), is a multi-discipline feast of performances featuring the best of contemporary theater, music, dance, and even puppet shows. You can find out more about the lineup, prices, and dates by surfing to www.lincolncenter.org.

August
U.S. Open: For one brief, bright-tennis-whites moment each year at the end of August (and into Sept), the city becomes a center for international sport with the start of the U.S. Open, one of tennis's four Grand Slam events. For full information, go to p. 210.

September
Fashion Week: Part 2 (see earlier in this section), and because the city's already more crowded in fall, hotel rates can rise even more sharply. Try to avoid visiting this week if you can, as you're unlikely to get into any of the fashion shows but will have to contend with drastically higher prices for lodging. Go to www.mbfashion week.com/newyork for details on the dates.

Feast of San Gennaro: Coils of Italian sausages as long as cobras, carnival games, crowds, and tables full of trinkets mark New York's largest Italian fest, held over 11 days in mid-September in Little Italy. Don't make a special trip for it, but if you happen to be in town, it can be fun.

October
October 31 Halloween Parade: Men in drag, women in drag, giant coughing chickens ("avian flu"), zombies dancing to Michael Jackson's "Thriller"—all these apparitions and more made their appearance at a recent parade, and you'll see their like if you attend. This is New York's most outrageous event and the largest Halloween parade in the world. Some locals spend all year working on their costumes; if you dress up, you can march, too. For information on how to do that, and for the parade routing (which changes), call the *Village Voice* Parade hot line at ☎ 212/475-3333, ext. 14044; or go to www.halloween-nyc.com. To snag a viewing spot in Greenwich Village along the parade route, you'll need to show up at about 5pm (2 hr. before the parade starts) . . . or have a nice dinner and show up at 9pm to view the second half. The crowd will have thinned by then, and because the event usually doesn't end until close to 11pm, you'll have more than enough time to enjoy it.

November
Macy's Thanksgiving Day Parade (4th Thurs of the month): Macy's yearly extravaganza combines massive hot-air balloons of cartoon characters with floats, clowns, and performances by the casts of Broadway musicals and pop stars (usually lip-synching atop floats). It winds its way down Central Park West to Columbus Circle and then heads down Broadway to Macy's at 34th Street. In order get a good view, you'll need to snag a spot along the route no later than 8am (the parade begins at 9am). Avoid Columbus Circle and Broadway from 36th Street down to 34th Street—these are the VIP areas set aside for TV cameras and bigwigs (and no one else). The night before the parade, an impromptu party

sprouts on 77th Street as hundreds of people gather to see the balloons being inflated. For more information, call ☎ 212/484-1222 or head to www.macys. com.

Holiday Decorations: Starting the day after Thanksgiving (and often even before that), the entire city dresses up for Christmas, stringing lights, hanging tinsel, and inserting the computer chips into all of the moving figurines that have, of late, hijacked the windows of the city's large department stores. The best street to see the trimmings, by far, is Fifth Avenue, between 39th and 59th streets. Along with the spectacular windows at the big department stores—Saks Fifth Avenue, Lord & Taylor, Bergdorf Goodman, and Tiffany's—you'll also want to admire the massive fir tree at Rockefeller Center (off Fifth Ave., at 51st St., lit in late Nov; go to www.rockefellercenter.com for more details). The windows at Macy's (34th St. at Broadway) are also deservedly famous, as is the indoor winter wonderland display at the heart of which is a Santa, waiting to hear your tots' Christmas wishes (just like in *Miracle on 34th Street*). Madison Avenue, between 55th and 60th streets, is also worth a stroll, and if you have the time, drop by Bloomingdales (Lexington Ave., btwn 59th and 60th sts.) for its yearly display.

Chanukah is also a big deal in this city, with the largest Jewish population outside of Israel. On Fifth Avenue at 59th Street, a giant menorah—at 32 feet it's the largest in the world—is lit each year on the first night of Chanukah and for 7 nights thereafter. On the first and final evenings, steaming *latkes* (potato pancakes) are distributed at sunset, and live music accompanies the electric candle-lighting. The dates for Chanukah shift according to the Hebrew calendar, so it can start as early as mid-November or as late as Christmas. Call ☎ 212/736-8400 for more information.

The Radio City Music Hall Christmas Spectacular: This New York tradition now starts well before Thanksgiving, and it's still as extravagantly kitschy as ever, with laser-light shows, onstage ice-skating, horses, camels, and, of course, the fabulous Rockettes, executing their 300-plus kicks per show. Shows run approximately 7 days a week, with six daily performances (on many dates) starting at 9am and going until 10pm. For more information, call ☎ 212/247-4777 or go to www.radiocity.com.

The Nutcracker: Ballet impresario George Balanchine's masterpiece. The music is by Tchaikovsky, and half the cast is under 15, culled from New York City Ballet's famous dance school at Juilliard. Your children will love it, though it's an expensive treat. The show sells out early, so make your reservations in October if you can, when the seats first go on sale. For details, check out www.nycballet.com or call ☎ 212/870-5570.

Classical Music at the Metropolitan Museum: Several times during the holiday season, the Met stages concerts in its glorious medieval sculpture hall. The pairing of carols and art is unbeatable, making this one of the season's loveliest events. Dates and prices are listed at www.metmuseum.org.

December

The Messiah Sing-Along: Shower singers take note: Here's your chance to make your debut at Lincoln Center. Each year, usually in the last 2 weeks of December, 3,000 singers lug their own librettos to Avery Fisher Hall for a roughly 3-hour performance of Handel's *Messiah*—the audience is the chorus, backed up by a world-renowned orchestra, with rising opera stars taking the solos. Train wrecks do occur, and if you have an off-key crooner next to you (as I did when I attended), it can detract from the moment, but when all is going well, there are few experiences as soul-stirring. You can find more information at www.lincoln-center.org.

New York National Boat Show: The centenarian trade show (it turns 103 in 2008) is devoted to boats of all sorts, from yachts to pontoon boats to canoes. It starts about 2 days after Christmas and runs for the next 2 weeks, dazzling seafaring types at the Jacob Javits Convention Center with all the latest gadgets, gear, and crafts. Go to www.nyboatshow.com for info.

New Year's Eve: The "ball drop" in Times Square is just one of the celebrations for kicking off the New Year (and the least appealing one in my opinion). If you must do the Times Square thing, get there early to secure a spot in which to stand—no later than noon—and then get set for a long, chilly wait until midnight. You'll be elbow to elbow with people from all over the world—though none from New York, as the locals avoid this part of town like the plague on December 31st. They're more likely to be taking part in the **midnight run around Central Park** (☎ 212/860-4455; www.nyrrc.org); watching the fireworks over Central Park; or attending the lovely New Year's Eve Concert for Peace at St. John the Divine, a yearly highlight, featuring new works from top New York composers (www.stjohndivine.org).

ENTRY REQUIREMENTS FOR NON-AMERICAN CITIZENS

Be sure to check with the U.S. embassy or consulate for the very latest in entry requirements, as these continue to shift since 9/11. Full information can be found at the **U.S. State Department's** website, www.travel.state.gov.

VISAS

As of this writing, citizens of western and central Europe, Australia, New Zealand, Japan, and Singapore need only a valid passport and a round-trip air ticket or cruise ticket to enter the U.S. Canadian citizens can also enter without a visa; you simply need to show your passport.

Citizens of all other countries will need to obtain a tourist visa from the U.S. consulate. To get the visa, along with a passport valid to at least 6 months from the end of your scheduled U.S. visit, you'll need to complete an application and submit a 1½-inch square photo. Waits for visas have been increasing in recent years, so be sure to apply well in advance of your trip. For information about **U.S. visas,** go to **http://travel.state.gov** and click on "Visas."

PASSPORTS

To enter the United States, international visitors must have a valid passport that expires at least 6 months later than the scheduled end of your visit.

For Residents of Australia: You can pick up an application from your local post office or any branch of Passports Australia, but you must schedule an interview at the passport office to present your application materials. Call the **Australian Passport Information Service** at ☎ 131-232, or visit the government website at www.passports.gov.au.

For Residents of Canada: Passport applications are available at travel agencies throughout Canada or from the central **Passport Office,** Department of Foreign Affairs and International Trade, Ottawa, ON K1A 0G3 (☎ 800/567-6868; www.ppt.gc.ca). *Note:* Canadian children who travel must have their own passports. However, if you hold a valid Canadian passport, issued before December 11, 2001, that bears the name of your child, the passport remains valid for you and your child until it expires.

For Residents of Ireland: You can apply for a 10-year passport at the **Passport Office,** Setanta Centre, Molesworth Street, Dublin 2 (☎ 01/671-1633; www.irl gov.ie/iveagh). Those under age 18 and over 65 must apply for a 123€ 1-year passport. You can also apply at 1A South Mall, Cork (☎ **021/272-525**) or at most main post offices.

For Residents of New Zealand: You can pick up a passport application at any New Zealand Passports Office or download it from their website. Contact the **Passports Office** at ☎ 0800/225-050 in New Zealand or 04/474-8100, or log on to www.passports.govt.nz.

For Residents of the United Kingdom: To pick up an application for a standard 10-year passport (5-yr. passport for children under 16), visit your nearest passport office, major post office, or travel agency; or contact the **United Kingdom Passport Service** at ☎ 0870/521-0410. You can also search its website at www.ukpa.gov.uk.

MEDICAL REQUIREMENTS

No inoculations or vaccinations are required to enter the United States, unless you're arriving from an area that is suffering from an epidemic (cholera or yellow fever, in particular). A valid, signed prescription is required for those travelers in need of **syringe-administered medications** or medical treatment that involves **narcotics.** It is extremely important to obtain the correct documentation in these cases, as your medications could be confiscated; and if you are found to be carrying an illegal substance, you could be subject to significant penalties. Those who are **HIV-positive** may also require a special waiver in order to enter the country (as you will be asked on your visa application whether you're a carrier of any communicable diseases). The best thing to do is contact **AIDSinfo** (☎ 800/448-0440 or 301/519-6616; www.aidsinfo.nih.gov) for up-to-date information.

CUSTOMS REGULATIONS FOR INTERNATIONAL VISITORS

Strict regulations govern what can and can't be brought into the United States—and what you can take back home with you.

WHAT YOU CAN BRING INTO NEW YORK

Every visitor more than 21 years of age may bring in, free of duty, the following: (1) 1 liter of wine or hard liquor; (2) 200 cigarettes, 100 cigars (but not from Cuba), or 3 pounds of smoking tobacco; and (3) $100 worth of gifts. These exemptions are offered to travelers who spend at least 72 hours in the United

States and who have not claimed them within the preceding 6 months. It is altogether forbidden to bring into the country foodstuffs (particularly fruit, cooked meats, and canned goods) and plants (vegetables, seeds, tropical plants, and the like). Foreign tourists may carry in or out up to $10,000 in U.S. or foreign currency with no formalities; larger sums must be declared to U.S. Customs on entering or leaving, which includes filing form CM 4790. For details regarding U.S. Customs and Border Protection, consult your nearest U.S. embassy or consulate, or **U.S. Customs** (☎ 202/927-1770; www.customs.ustreas.gov).

WHAT YOU CAN TAKE HOME FROM NEW YORK

For a clear summary of **Canadian** rules, write for the booklet *I Declare,* issued by the **Canada Border Services Agency** (☎ 800/461-9999 in Canada, or 204/983-3500; www.cbsa-asfc.gc.ca).

For information, **U.K. citizens** contact **HM Customs & Excise** at ☎ 0845/010-9000 (from outside the U.K., 020/8929-0152), or the website at www.hmce.gov.uk.

A helpful brochure for **Australians,** available from Australian consulates or Customs offices, is *Know Before You Go.* For more information, call the **Australian Customs Service** at ☎ 1300/363-263, or log on to www.customs.gov.au.

Most questions regarding **New Zealand** rules are answered in a free pamphlet available at New Zealand consulates and Customs offices: *New Zealand Customs Guide for Travellers, Notice no. 4.* For more information, contact **New Zealand Customs,** The Customhouse, 17–21 Whitmore St., Box 2218, Wellington (☎ 04/473-6099 or 0800/428-786; www.customs.govt.nz).

FINDING A GOOD AIRFARE TO NEW YORK CITY

New York City is one of the busiest gateways in the nation and competition among carriers tends to keep airfares relatively reasonable. Your strategy for getting the best rates should include the following steps:

* **Look at the low-fare carriers:** Airlines such as **JetBlue, Southwest, USA3000, AirTran, and Virgin America** will sometimes have better fares than the larger airlines, but they may not be searched if you go to a site such as Expedia. So use a search tool such as **Sidestep.com, Kayak.com,** or **Momondo.com,** which search airline sites directly, adding no service charges and often finding fares that the larger travel sites miss. Only Momondo includes the prices for Southwest Airlines, which is highly proprietary about its information, but can be an excellent source of bargains. If you don't mind flying into Islip Airport (about 1½ hr. from the city), be sure to take a gander at Momondo or the **Southwest site (www.iflyswa.com)** before booking. If you're flying from Europe into the United States, scan the fares from Aer Lingus, Air Berlin, Air Canada, Air India, American Airlines, British Airways, bmi, Continental, Delta, Emirates, Eurofly, Icelandair, Lufthansa, Martinair, United, and Virgin Atlantic, as these carriers have a hearty competition going for lowest rates to the U.S., particularly from London (in fact, if you're able to hop a low-cost flight to London, it might be cheaper to fly from there, than from other gateways within the UK and Europe. I've always

Booking Hotel Rooms

There's an art to getting the best price on hotel rooms in New York City, and it's discussed in chapter 3. For tips on booking online, go to p. 35; for tips on blind bidding, go to p. 38; and for information on renting an apartment or staying in a private home, go to p. 21.

found that **Mobissimo.com**, **Momondo.com**, and **CheapFlights.co.uk** are best for searching fares that don't originate in the U.S.

◆ **Fly when others don't, and take an itinerary the biz travelers don't want.** Those who fly midweek and midday, and who stay over a Saturday night, generally pay far less than those who fly at more popular times.

◆ **Try booking through a consolidator:** Those traveling to New York from another country may wish to use a consolidator or "bucket shop" to snag a ticket. These companies buy tickets in bulk, passing along the savings to their customers. If you reside in Europe, the best way to find one that services your area is to go to the website **www.cheapflights.co.uk**, which serves as a clearinghouse for bucket shops both large and small. Many will also advertise in the Sunday papers. Be careful, though: Some charge outrageous change fees, so read the fine print before you purchase your ticket. Bucket shops will not be useful for those flying within the U.S., as they are not generally able to undercut standard pricing on domestic travel.

◆ **Don't be particular about airports:** Three major airports serve New York City—LaGuardia, JFK, and Newark—and you should fly into whichever one has the lowest fare at the time you're booking. Yes, LaGuardia has a slightly worse on-time record than the other two, and JFK and Newark are farther from the city, but none of those reasons should trump a low fare. You might even consider flying to Islip, which is Southwest's hub. It's farther from the city—90 minutes, as opposed to the 45 minutes to an hour at JFK or Newark—but if the price is right, go for it.

PACKAGE DEALS VS. BOOKING INDEPENDENTLY

To other destinations around the United States, booking a package (a travel product that bundles together airfare and hotel at one low price) can result in tremendous savings. Not so in Gotham. Because the city is booked solid nearly year-round, hotels here are less willing to play ball than their counterparts in, say, Florida. Though such entities as US Airways Vacations, American Airlines Vacations, Site59, and others sell packages to New York, they rarely undercut what you would pay if you booked on your own.

TRAVEL INSURANCE—DO YOU NEED IT?

When purchasing a big-ticket travel item—a guided tour, a cruise, a safari—it's essential to buy travel insurance. Many unforeseen circumstances can interrupt or cause you to cancel a trip, and with these types of trips, this could spell a large financial loss. But do you need it for your trip to NYC? Not necessarily. If you're purchasing the insurance to cover unforeseen medical expenses, lost luggage, or cancelled airfare, you may already be covered by your regular insurance if you're an American citizen. And hotel stays should never be insured, as hotels will usually allow you to cancel 24 hours in advance with no penalty (the only exception being if you book through a website such as Priceline that requires payment upfront for your stay).

So what might you want to insure? If you've booked an **apartment stay** and have had to put down a large deposit, that should be insured, as should **pricey airline tickets** and **any valuables you may be carrying with you** (as the airline will only pay up to $2,800 for lost luggage domestically, a lot less for foreign travel). If you're an **international visitor** coming to New York, you should probably invest in insurance that will **cover medical expenses.** Unlike most European nations, the United States does not have any form of socialized health care, meaning that hospitals and doctor visits can be extremely expensive. In non-emergency situations, both doctors and hospitals have the right to refuse care without advance payment or proof of coverage. (*Note:* We're not utter barbarians; if you're in a life-or-death situation you won't be denied health care. But as with non-emergency care, the uninsured pay dearly for any services rendered—you'll just get the bill a bit later.) American citizens usually find that your regular insurance will cover you in New York, making additional health insurance unnecessary (the exception being certain HMOs, so check first).

If you do decide to buy insurance, you càn easily parse the different policies by visiting the website **InsureMyTrip.com**, which compares the policies of all of the major companies. Or contact one of the following reputable companies directly:

- ◆ **Access America** (☎ 866/807-3982; www.accessamerica.com)
- ◆ **Travel Guard International** (☎ 800/807-3982; www.travelguard.com)
- ◆ **CSA Travel Protection** (☎ 800/873-9844; www.csatravelprotection.com)

TRAVELING FROM NEW YORK TO OTHER PARTS OF THE UNITED STATES

New York, as a major travel hub, is a convenient hopping-off point for other areas of the United States, even those located across the continent. Competition among carriers has kept fares from the Big Apple to most of the major gateways of the U.S. relatively cheap. To book airfares from New York to points west, north, and south, take a look at "Finding a Good Airfare to New York City," above.

The **USA Rail Pass** is the American equivalent to the Eurail Pass in Europe, allowing foreign visitors to travel extensively within the U.S. for one set (and fairly reasonable) rate. It's offered by **Amtrak** (www.amtrak.com) and is once again *only* for those living outside North America (Canadians and Mexicans are not eligible). On the Amtrak site you'll find listings of representative agents in countries around the globe; the passes must be purchased before entry into the United States.

Those traveling by bus will benefit from a major fare war going on between the so-called **Chinatown shuttles** and such better established companies as **Peter Pan** (www.peterpan.com) and **Greyhound** (www.greyhound.com). The Chinatown shuttles were created by Chinese Americans as a means of getting between New York City and Albany, Baltimore, Boston, Philadelphia, Washington, D.C., and Virginia Beach, and they were the first to implement rock-bottom pricing on these routes. Today, they even have super-low bus fares between NYC and

Chicago ($70 one way, $120 round-trip). The old guard got frightened, of course, and have been matching their rates of late. So to Philadelphia, the average ride on just about any bus leaving from Manhattan is just $12 one-way, $20 round-trip; for Washington, D.C. or Boston, you won't pay more than $35 round-trip. How much longer this will go on, heaven knows. Obviously the costs of Greyhound and Peter Pan are much higher as they have to pay terminal fees and have larger fleets (the Chinatown buses simply leave from street corners). So this is a classic example of "predatory pricing," an attempt by the big kahunas to drive the little guys out of business. And I have to wonder how much longer the fare war will last (so do your own price research before booking).

So which should you pick, if the prices are equivalent? I've never had problems with the Chinatown buses, but I know some who complain about the language gap with the drivers, their erratic driving, and the upkeep of the buses. Greyhound's facilities will probably be nicer, as it's made a major push in the last 2 years to upgrade its entire fleet and bus stations. That being said, sometimes their rates and Peter Pan's rates rise for last-minute bookings. So if you don't plan ahead, you may want to go with a Chinatown Shuttle. To contact those companies—and there are now nearly a dozen little bus companies operating along these routes—head for the site **GoToBus.com**. I also must recommend a new bus line, good only for travel to and from Washington, D.C. It's called DC 2 NY (www.dc2ny.com), its buses are downright cushy, and it offers all passengers free Wi-Fi and mineral water. The latter charges $22 for a one-way ticket and $40 round-trip.

HOW DO I GET TO (& FROM) THE AIRPORT? LET ME COUNT THE WAYS . . .

Unlike other major world cities, a series of shortsighted and highly political decisions have left New York with no easy, logical way to get to and from two of its three major airports (www.panynj.gov, for information on all 3 airports). Instead, travelers are left to battle gridlocked traffic in cars, taxis, and private shuttle buses. Those who choose public transportation end up jumping two or three trains or buses simply to get from Midtown Manhattan to JFK or LaGuardia. The picture has changed recently to Newark, so I'll thank the transportation gods by sharing the good news about that airport first.

GETTING TO & FROM NEWARK AIRPORT CHEAPLY

When I'm talking about good news here, I'm talking about AirTrain. That's the transit system, created half a dozen years ago, that quickly and efficiently connects each of the terminals at **Newark Liberty International Airport** (about 16 miles from Midtown Manhattan) with nearby Newark Pennsylvania Station, via a shuttle that leaves the airport every 3 minutes at most times of the day. From there, travelers can board New Jersey Transit or Amtrak to **Pennsylvania Station** (from Seventh to Eighth aves.; btwn 31st and 33rd sts.; **Ⓐ**, **Ⓔ**, **Ⓒ**, **❶**, **❷**, **❸**), a speedy 20-min. ride that costs just $15 on New Jersey Transit, much more on Amtrak ($28–$45 depending on the time of day). Those going in the opposite direction can take one of the thrice-hourly trains from New York's Penn Station to New Jersey's for exactly the same amounts of money (be sure to buy your tickets at a

Other Airport Transportation Choices

If you're overburdened with luggage, convenience may trump cost or speed. You should take either a **taxi, private car service,** or **shuttle bus.** Of the three methods, I would go with the first two rather than the latter in most cases because, although such services as **SuperShuttle** (☎ 212/258-3826; www.supershuttle.com) or **Go! Airport Shuttle** (☎ 877/544-4646 or www.goairportshuttle.com) do pick you up at your hotel or at the airport, you waste a lot of time hitting the hotels of other travelers before getting to your final destination (a particularly hair-raising prospect if you're late for a flight). Price-wise, shuttles only make sense for solo travelers; once you double the cost for a couple, taxis and private cars become cheaper (see chart for pricing).

Taxis can be hailed at any Manhattan corner, though they can be scarce all day in Harlem, and citywide between the hours of 4pm and 6pm, when the combination of rush hour and the turnover of drivers' shifts overwhelms the system. They often come out a dollar or two cheaper (see "Airport Transportation Options," below for costs) than most car services for JFK and LaGuardia, less so for Newark Airport.

Plan-ahead types go for private limousines, which guarantee that your car will be there when you need it. In general, one fare will cover up to four people. After that, the company will insist that you take a larger car, and the price may increase so substantially that taxis may make more sense (a large van that can hold up to eight people will cost about $150 to JFK; in this case, two taxis will be significantly cheaper). If you're hiring a car for airport pickup, the dispatcher will ask if you want the driver to meet you inside the terminal, at the baggage claim area. This will be significantly more costly than a curbside pickup, but you'll have the security of knowing that the driver will be there right when you pick up your bags. If you decide on curbside pickup, you have to call the dispatcher when you arrive and then may have to wait anywhere from 10 to 30 minutes for your car. Another key factor with limousines is that you must book 24 hours in advance, especially if you're planning to use a car in the morning hours. Services do sell out, so call ahead.

Dependable limousine companies include:

◆ **Tel Aviv** (☎ 800/222-9888 or 212/777-7777; www.telavivlimo.com; LaGuardia $33, JFK or Newark $48).

◆ **Carmel Limousine** (☎ 800/9-CARMEL or 212/666-6666; www.carmel limo.com; La Guardia $33, Newark $47, JFK $48).

kiosk to avoid the $5 on-train surcharge). The stations are pleasant and well-marked, the ride a quick one (in fact, it's hard to beat the speed of the AirTrain in a taxi or shuttle bus, thanks to the ugly traffic between Manhattan and the airport).

Those traveling from downtown Manhattan have the option of catching the **PATH Train** (Christopher St. and Hudson St., or along Sixth Ave. at 9th St., 23rd St., or 34th St.; or at the World Trade Center), taking it to Newark's Pennsylvania Station, and connecting there to the airport. The only real difference here is that travelers pay both at the PATH station ($1.75) and again for the AirTrain to the airport ($7.75). And while the PATH is a direct shot from the World Trade Center station to Newark's Penn Station, those traveling from the other stops will have to take the train to Journal Square and then change there for Newark Penn Station. It's still a quick and inexpensive method of getting to the airport.

I'll also mention a company called **Olympia Airport Express** (☎ 212/964-6233; www.olympiabus.com), which operates buses to and from Grand Central Station, the Port Authority, and Pennsylvania Station. It charges $15 for one-way tickets, $25 round-trip. In general, you'll get a quicker and cheaper ride with AirTrain, but if you're traveling solo or have a lot of luggage and will be staying at a hotel near one of the drop-off points, it may be worth booking.

GETTING TO & FROM JFK

Like Newark, John F. Kennedy International Airport (known better as JFK) also has an AirTrain system, but it's not nearly as quick or easy to use. In this case, riders take the subway (either the **Ⓐ** to Howard Beach or the **Ⓔ**, **Ⓙ**, or **Ⓩ** to Jamaica Station), and then scramble wildly trying to find the AirTrain (the signage is poor). With the subway fare and the AirTrain fare, this option costs $7 total. It's also possible to take the Long Island Rail Road from Pennsylvania Station to Jamaica Station, but once again, it's a difficult path to navigate and it will be pricier at $10–$12. Another dissuasion: The ride averages a stiff 90 minutes thanks to the vagaries of subway service this far out in Queens.

A better option is the **New York Airport Service** (☎ 718/875-8200; www.nyairportservice.com), a privately owned bus company that drives passengers from the Port Authority Bus Terminal (42nd St. and Eighth Ave.), a spot just above Grand Central Terminal (at Park Ave., btwn 41st and 42nd sts.), and a scattering of Midtown hotels between 27th and 59th streets, for a reasonable $15 one-way, $33 round-trip. Its buses leave every 30 minutes, 5:10am through

Surviving the airports

After you factor in travel time, do a bit of research to find out how long it will take you to get to through security lines at the airport. The government maintains a helpful website at waittime.tsa.dhs.gov that displays average and maximum waiting times at all U.S. airports, terminal by terminal, during a 4-hour time frame, based on data collected in the previous few weeks at each airport.

It's also a good idea to print out your boarding pass from home or at your hotel. You can do this up to 24 hours in advance for most domestic flights, and it makes you one of the first to check in for the flight. Not only will you be able to skip one line at the airport, but you'll be less likely to be bumped, as the last to check in is usually the first to be bumped.

Airport Transportation Options

Airports	Avg. time to airport by car from Midtown Manhattan	Avg. time to airport using AirTrain	Avg. taxi cost from Midtown to Airport	Cost for public transportation	Cost for New York Airport Service Express Bus/SuperShuttle	Avg. cost for car service	Frequency of AirTrain service
JFK	45–60 min.	70–90 min.**	$45 from airport, $44–$50 to airport* for 1–4 passengers	$7–$13***	$15/$19 per adult	$46, plus toll and tip, for up to 4 passengers	Every 2–4 minutes between 6am and 11pm; 8 minutes otherwise
LaGuardia	20–35 min.	N/A	$22–$25	$2, but no AirTrain	$10–$20 per adult	$25, plus toll and tip, for up to 4 passengers	N/A
Newark	35–65 min.	30–45 min.	$40–$60	$7–$45	$15–$20	$48, plus toll and tip	Every 2–4 minutes between 6am and 11pm; 8 minutes otherwise

* These figures are based on the flat fare that applies to trips from JFK, and an estimate of the non-regulated rates to that airport.

** The shorter trip is via the Long Island Rail Road; the longer one is via the subway.

*** Seven dollars is the combined subway and AirTrain fare, $13 is for those who take the Long Island Rail Road.

10pm. On the downside: Because it takes so long to load the buses, the company tells passengers to expect a commute of between 60 and 80 minutes from the airport to their home terminals.

GETTING TO & FROM LAGUARDIA CHEAPLY

The nearest airport to the city (about 8 miles from Manhattan), LaGuardia also has the worst panoply of options for public transportation: three turtle-slow public buses (they've been known to clock in at 100 minutes for a trip that should take 45 at most). Your time is not worth the savings you may garner. Instead, turn to the **New York Airport Service** (see above). It charges a reasonable $12 one-way, $27 round-trip—a good deal for solo travelers (though couples may simply want to bite the bullet and take a cab).

MONEY MATTERS

It's rare to go more than 4 blocks without finding an **ATM or bank machine** in Manhattan. They are ubiquitous—in banks, of course, as well as in delis and some grocery and department stores. For those changing a foreign currency, ATMs will give you a much better exchange rate than the various Currency Exchanges near Times Square and scattered in other areas of town. Do be aware, however, of shifting fees. In general you'll pay the most at non-bank ATMs (sometimes as much as

What things cost

Although New Yorkers pay far less than the citizens of Moscow, London, and Seoul (respectively ranked as the 1st, 2nd, and 3rd most expensive cities in the world in 2007) for everyday goods and services, prices here can be shocking. Here are the average costs or range of costs for some of the items and services you may need to purchase in the course of your trip.

Subway or bus ride	$2
Taxi ride (Midtown to Uptown museums)	$10
Bagel	50¢
Cup of regular coffee	$1–$2
Sandwich in a deli	$3–$5
Hot dog	$1.50
Hot pretzel	$1
Diner breakfast	$5–$7
Lunch in cheap restaurant	$5–$7
Lunch in moderate–expensive restaurant	$12–$30
Dinner in cheap restaurant	$7–$12
Dinner in moderate–expensive restaurant	$13–$50
Bottle of domestic beer in a bar	$4–$5
Bottle of imported beer in a bar	$5–$10
Cocktail in a bar	$8–$15
Bottle of water	$1–$2
Average museum entrance fee	$15
Full-price Broadway show ticket	$95–$125
Discount Broadway show ticket	$55–$75
Standing-room Broadway show ticket	$15
Movie ticket	$11
Walking tour	$15
Souvenir T-shirt	$8–$15
Tube of toothpaste	$5
Package of diapers (27 count)	$13
Contact lens solution (12 oz.)	$5

$3 per transaction), so always try to find a bank first before resorting to the little machine at the corner deli (which will be marked outside by a small hanging sign stating simply ATM). Most banks charge between $1 and $2 to non-accountholders.

Traveler's checks will elicit a confused stare from many waiters and shop clerks. With ATMs so common, hardly anyone uses these little slips of paper anymore, and there can be significant fees attached to their exchange at some banks.

I don't think they're of much use anymore. **Credit cards** are widely accepted, though certain smaller stores and restaurants don't accept American Express because of the fees it charges merchants. In general, however, Visa, MasterCard, American Express, and Discover can be used in hotels, restaurants, shops, and even subway ticket vending machines. Most restaurants will post the names of the credit cards they accept on their front door; shops, hotels, and some restaurants don't, so you'll need to ask. A $15 minimum is often attached to credit card payment, so inquire about that as well.

HEALTH & SAFETY

In 2007, the FBI ranked New York City as the safest large city in the United States. I have lived here my entire life and have been the victim of a crime only twice: In the mid-'80s my wallet was lifted out of a coat pocket on a crowded subway and in 2007, my backpack was stolen in a Starbucks. Of the friends and family I have in the city (and there are dozens), only a handful have had a firsthand experience of crime in the last 5 years, and without exception there's been no violence in the encounter.

All that being said, this is still a large city with all types of people, so it's important to be vigilant. Never carry large amounts of money on your person or a wallet in the back pocket of a backpack, where it can be easily filched. Although you don't need to resort to a money belt, you should keep your passport and any other valuable documents in your hotel's safe rather than on your person (if you're traveling with a passport, you may also want to photocopy it, so you'll have the necessary information in case it should be lost and you must have it replaced at your consulate). Women should keep their purses in sight at all times.

Along with pickpockets, scam artists remain a problem. The most common scams involve a stranger asking for the use of your ATM card, briefly they say, until they can access their funds. Don't fall for it. You will also most likely be approached by panhandlers asking for money. These unfortunate souls are not in any way dangerous, and if you want to be generous, the best thing to do is to buy them a bit of food because gifts of cash may go to feed a drug habit.

As for where in the city you can wander, with the exceptions of certain areas of Harlem, the rest of Manhattan is safe both day and night. This includes such formerly iffy neighborhoods as the Meat-Packing District, Times Square, the Lower East Side, and Alphabet City; all major nightlife areas now and teeming with partiers most nights of the week (there's safety in numbers!). You must be more careful in the outer boroughs, especially the Bronx, and some of the more far-flung areas of Brooklyn and Queens. Get full directions before you venture out of Manhattan because it's much easier to get lost in the boroughs, which do not have a grid-based street system.

As for the subway: The unexpected benefit of the terrorist threats to Manhattan has been an even safer subway system. It is now rife with undercover cops and safe to ride in Manhattan until 1am. After 1am (or if you're in one of the other boroughs, after about 10pm), you may want to take the precautions of standing in the areas marked by yellow signs stating DURING OFF HOURS STAND HERE. Make your way, at those times, to the most crowded cars, where muggings are very unlikely to occur. One other subway note: Stand well back from the edge of the platform, as you don't want to accidentally fall onto the tracks (this is not an uncommon occurrence—in 2007, two people per week fell onto the tracks, so be careful).

HEALTH CONCERNS

If you develop any kind of illness while in New York, your best bet is to talk with the desk clerk at your hotel and ask him or her to recommend a dentist or a doctor. You'll probably receive better care that way than by calling an 800-number for referrals. Doctors in New York City almost never make house calls; most only work between 10am and 6pm, but an increasing number are keeping office hours on Saturdays and evenings, to handle the overload of patients. Certain hospitals also have affiliated non-emergency, drop-in health-care centers, such as **DOCS at New York Healthcare** (55 E. 34th St., btwn Park and Madison aves.; ☎ 800/673-3627; Mon–Thurs 8am–8pm, Fri 9am–7pm, Sat 9am–3pm, and Sun 9am–2pm, holidays 9am–1pm; ❻ to 33rd St.).

If you have an acute need to see a doctor at a time of day when regular physicians aren't seeing patients, you'll have to go to a local hospital for care. Again, ask the clerk at your hotel for the nearest emergency room or, if you cannot make it there under your own steam, call ☎ **911,** which is also the number to call in the United States for emergency help from the police and fire department.

One word on prescription medications: It is crucial that you pack your prescription medications in their original containers, and bring them in your carry-on luggage. Be sure, also, to bring along copies of your prescriptions in case you run out or misplace your pills. If you need a prescription filled during your stay, the following pharmacies all have 24-hour branches:

◆ Duane Reade, 224 W. 57th St., between Seventh Ave. and Broadway; ☎ 212/541-9708; ❶, ❶, ❸, ❷, ❶, ❶, ❶, ❶ to 57th St.

◆ CVS, 540 Amsterdam Ave. at 86th St., ☎ 212/712-2821; ❶ to 86th St.

◆ CVS, 630 Lexington Ave. at 53rd St.; ☎ 212/369-8688; ❻ to 53rd St.

◆ CVS, 253 First Ave. at 14th St.; ☎ 212/254-1454; ❶ to First Ave.

PACKING

The most important item in your suitcase will be a pair of very, very comfortable shoes because your dogs are gonna be barking! This is a walking city, and what with getting from place to place and trudging through the marble halls of the Metropolitan Museum of Art or the American Museum of Natural History, a springy, supportive pair of shoes is essential (you may want to bring 2 pairs to increase your feet ease). Other than that, fill your suitcase with what pleases you most at home: Very few actual New Yorkers have the budget or time to dress like the ladies on *Sex and the City,* and unless you plan on going to the theater, the opera, or a very fancy restaurant, casual clothes should suffice. If you plan on going out clubbing, turn to p. 288 to read my advice on the specialized "club clothes" you're going to need to get past the velvet ropes.

Dressing appropriately for the weather is also key, so be sure to check the chart near the beginning of this chapter for the average temperatures at various times of the year. Those visiting in the fall and spring months (mid-Sept to mid-Nov, and mid-Mar to mid-May) are advised to bring clothes that you can layer, as a balmy afternoon can turn chilly once the sun goes down. In winter, you're going to want a woolen hat, muffler, gloves, and a heavy coat—the wind rushing between the city's buildings will often make the day feel colder than it is, especially if you're visiting the Financial District, the Statue of Liberty, or any area near water. Summer can get sultry, so be sure to pack sandals, shorts, and shirts in fabrics that breathe.

SPECIALIZED TRAVEL RESOURCES

With one of the most diverse populations in the United States, the Big Apple is welcoming to visitors of all types. But because certain visitors have special needs (and also get special perks), I want to address these groups directly with a few choice words of advice.

ADVICE FOR FAMILY TRAVELERS

Though its reputation would have you believe otherwise, New York is actually an ultra-kid-friendly destination (and I say that both as someone who grew up here and as a mother of two young daughters). Most of the "adult attractions"—the Metropolitan Museum of Art, the Museum of Modern Art, the *Intrepid,* and so forth—offer full-blown programs to make their offerings palatable to the younger set. Playgrounds dot Manhattan, the only exception being Midtown, a woefully parkless area (though Bryant Park on 42nd St., off Sixth Ave., now has a merry-go-round, if not a playground). And there are dozens of special events held around the city each week that are specifically for children. To learn about these performances and festivals, take a look at Friday's *New York Times* (the back of the "Arts" section); or pick up *Time Out* at any newsstand and scan the "For Kids" section.

When planning your own visit with kids, I recommend choosing accommodations on the Upper West Side. This will place you near Central Park, the Children's Museum, the Museum of Natural History, and dozens of child-friendly restaurants. (How can you tell that a restaurant wants your kids? Call in advance and ask about highchairs and kids' menus; those that have them are saying, "Come on in." Those that don't should be visited only by parents with exceptionally well-behaved offspring. You should also check out those restaurants that I've marked with a Kids icon in chapter 4.) Consider renting an apartment rather than staying in a hotel. It may afford you more privacy, as you may not have to share a room with the kids; and you'll have access to a kitchen so you'll save on restaurant meals (that may also save your sanity if your child is a picky eater).

Remember that children under 12 receive discounted or free admission to nearly every museum in the city and can get discounted movie tickets. If they're under 6 (or look it), they can ride the subways and buses for free. Very few hotels will charge extra for kids under 12 to share your room, and a handful (see chapter 3) extend that freebie up to the age of 18. The only place your kids will not get a discount is at Broadway shows, most of which do not admit children under the age of 5.

If you're hoping for a night or afternoon away from the kids, ask at the front desk if your hotel can provide a babysitter or has a list of reliable babysitters (better yet, ask before you book). Those staying in an apartment or a hotel without such a service should contact **The Baby Sitters' Guild** (☎ 212/682-0277; www.babysittersguild.com). The service is not cheap ($25–$30 per hr., with a 4-hr.

minimum, depending on the age of the child; siblings are an extra $5 each), but the sitters from this organization are veritable Mary Poppinses (they'll even take your kids out on the town, if you wish), and are licensed, insured, and bonded.

ADVICE FOR TRAVELERS WITH DISABILITIES

Hotels

As in many older cities, the levels of accessibility in New York can vary greatly from hotel to hotel. In the course of researching this guide, I found second-floor hotels without any elevators whatsoever, as well as other lodgings with bathrooms a step up from the bedroom floors. I've noted in my reviews in chapter 3 which lodgings are inaccessible; by and large, most of the places you'll find listed in this guide *do* provide accommodations that comply with the Americans with Disabilities Act. If you'd like to research other accommodations that are guaranteed accessible, visit the website www.access-able.com, which has a poorly organized but still useful database of accommodations in the state of New York. You can also e-mail **SATH** (Society for Accessible Travel and Hospitality; info@sath.org) with any questions on hotels, and the staff there will get back to you . . . eventually (it's understaffed) with what they know about the accessibility of the hotel in question.

Restaurants

Restaurants are more of a mixed bag when it comes to accessibility, due to space constraints. Many will be too small to admit a wheelchair; some have basement bathroom facilities, accessible only by stairs; others require diners to climb a few steps up to the entrance of the restaurant. If you're a wheelchair user or have limited mobility, I strongly recommend calling in advance to make sure the restaurant you've picked is fully accessible.

Theaters

Every Broadway theater, and most Off-Broadway theaters, now have spaces set aside for persons in wheelchairs. These are limited in number, however, so it's important to book well in advance to ensure that you get a spot at the show you wish to see. Before you book your tickets, be sure to visit the website of **Hospital Audiences** (www.hospaud.org, click on the "Access Guide"). This superb resource will tell you which theaters offer a discount for wheelchair seating (some put aside 2 spots at a lower rate), which ones have accessible toilets, how many folding armrest seats are available, which shows offer infrared hearing devices and signed performances, the locations of passenger loading zones, and much more.

Museums

In New York, the general rule is: The larger the museum, the more extensive the facilities for persons with disabilities. For example, the Metropolitan Museum of Art offers free rental of standard and extra-wide wheelchairs at all of its coat-check stands, regular sign-language and touch tours for the deaf and blind, attended elevators, and accessible bathrooms and water fountains. Go to a smaller museum, such as the American Craft Museum, and there will be fewer special services (sign language tours available only with advance reservation, unattended elevators, and so on), but on the whole, you'll find that even the smaller venues are accessible and adept at handling the needs of travelers with disabilities. Again, the best place to research the conditions and offerings at each museum is the excellent Access Guide at the Hospital Audiences website (see above).

Transportation

Perhaps the most difficult issue for travelers with mobility impairments is how to get around the city. Currently, there is only one car service, **A Ride for All** (☎ 718/706-7433), that specializes in transportation around Manhattan and from the airports for persons with wheelchairs. Its large vans can accommodate two to three wheelchairs or scooters, plus three additional riders. Costs are $90 per van (not per person) from LaGuardia, $102 from JFK and Newark, and between $35 and $45 for most rides around the city.

All New York City **buses** are wheelchair accessible—the buses "kneel" to let on passengers, and also have wheelchair lifts and special sections where a chair can be secured while the bus is in motion. Persons with disabilities pay just $1 for rides (half-price). **Subways** are more of a problem. While a handful of stations have added elevators in recent years, the vast majority of stations do not have elevators and require that a rider be able to tackle one and sometimes two flights of stairs to the subway platforms.

Taxis can also be difficult—of the 13,000 on the streets, only 29 are designed to be fully accessible. And while most will have the trunk room to accommodate a foldable wheelchair, they are sometimes less than willing to pick up people in wheelchairs or those with guide dogs, even though by law they are required to carry them. The lack of parking makes **renting a van** and driving around the city a less than ideal option, but if you feel like it would be the most convenient transportation method for you, **Wheelchair Getaways** (☎ 800/344-5005; www.wheel chair-getaways.com) rents vans with wheelchair lifts and other helpful features.

ADVICE FOR GAY & LESBIAN TRAVELERS

In truth, gay and lesbian travelers need very little special advice when it comes to New York City. With one of the largest and most politically active gay populations in the world, and dozens of gay bars and clubs (see chapter 10 for more on the city's nightlife options), you should feel welcomed and accepted in the Big Apple. After all, this is where the Broadway musical was born, right?

Traditionally, the gay community of New York has been centered around Christopher Street in the West Village, but in the last decade it's expanded to Chelsea and Hell's Kitchen. If you're a bar-hopper, these are the areas you'll want to explore, though there are gay bars in every neighborhood of Manhattan, just as there are gay people in every neighborhood. For more complete listings of bars and special events than you'll find in this tome, go into any gay bar or store and pick up a free copy of the *HX* (www.hx.com) or *Next* (www.nextnyc.com). Much of the same information is available via websites. Another good resource is *Time Out* (available on newsstands), which has a large section devoted to gay and lesbian events and festivities.

ADVICE FOR SENIORS

What seniors must remember in this pricey city is that age has it privileges and that there are many discounts available to oldsters—you just have to ask (and show a picture ID if you look particularly spry). Many of the large hotel chains offer discounts to those over 60; movie theaters and museums do as well. Seniors can also get half-price rides on the MTA's subway and city buses ($1), though in order to do so, you'll have to trek to 370 Jay St. in Brooklyn (Ⓐ, Ⓒ, Ⓕ, ❷, ❸, ❹, ❺ to Borough Hall; weekdays 9am–5pm) to prove you're over 65 and pick up a reduced-fare MetroCard (in other words, it's probably not worth your time). It's only at the theater—where seniors often make up 80% of the audience—that there are no markdowns.

Those who belong to **AARP** (601 E St. NW, Washington, DC 24009; ☎ 888/687-2277; www.aarp.org) get even more discounts, especially at hotels, so start waving around that card if you have it. Anyone over 50 can join.

In terms of meals, New York does not have the same abundance of "early-bird specials" that you'll find in cities largely populated by seniors. What it does have are heaping portions, and my father, Arthur Frommer (now over age 70), insists that with age comes a diminishment in appetite. His advice to seniors, which I pass along here, is to share food: One appetizer and one entree are what he and Roberta, his wife, have when they go out to dine, and they leave perfectly satisfied.

STAYING WIRED

In 2005, one of the candidates for the position of Public Advocate for New York City centered his campaign around the issue of Internet access. He felt that every area of the city should become a "hot zone" for Wi-Fi, from the subways to Central Park to the public libraries. He lost.

But his crusade is gathering steam nonetheless as Wi-Fi pops up in the most unexpected places (along with trees and fountains, a number of the smaller parks in the city—Bowling Green Park, City Hall Park, Union Square Park, and Bryant Park, to be precise—have sprouted hot spots). For those traveling with their own computers, it's nearly impossible to walk more than a few blocks without encountering a signal. Wi-Fi is now a given at every coffeehouse in the city; at all of the McDonald's, Kinko's, and Cosi's; at public libraries (filtered access); and in the lobbies of the more expensive hotels. You just plunk your laptop down and hook in to the network—nobody will check to see if you're staying at the hotel or have purchased a cup of java.

At most hotels around the city, Internet access in your room is charged at a standard $9.95 per day. Depending on the hotel, this will be Wi-Fi, dial-up, or a choice of either.

Laptop-less travelers will also have easy access to your e-mail by visiting any of the following locations:

- ◆ **All public libraries** (www.nypl.org; hours vary by location, but are roughly Tues–Sun 10am–5pm) offer free Internet access, though there may be a wait for a computer.
- ◆ **The Times Square Visitors Center** (1560 Broadway, btwn 46th and 47th sts.; ☎ 212/768-1560; daily 8pm–8pm) has terminals where you can send e-mail

free, courtesy of Yahoo. (Don't buy theater tickets here though; the prices are steep.)

◆ **Cyber-café** (250 W. 49th St., btwn Broadway and Eighth Ave.; www.cyber-cafe. com; Mon–Fri 8am–11pm, Sat–Sun 11am–11pm). Along with lickety-split connectivity, these cafes offer printing services, fax machines, CD/DVD burners, digital camera multi-chip readers, and more. Prices start at $6.40 per half-hour and tick off an additional $3.20 for every 15 minutes after that. Those planning to be online for a long time will save by booking by the hour.

◆ **Cyberfelds at Village Copier** (30 E. 13th St. off University Place; ☎ 212/ 647-8830; Mon–Fri 8am–midnight, Sat–Sun 10am–8pm) is a friendly cafe located above a copy shop. You'll always find an empty space among the dozen or so terminals here. There's a $2.50 minimum for 15 minutes; every additional 15 is charged at $2.50.

◆ **International Computer Café** (247 E. 57th St.; ☎ 212/872-1704; www.ny computercafe.freeservers.com; Mon–Fri 8am–11pm, Sat 10am–11pm, Sun 11am–11pm) lures patrons with fax machines, printing and copying service, low international phone rates, and Internet access ($3 for every 15 min.).

◆ **Kinko's** (multiple locations around the city; www.kinkos.com) is New York's largest chain of office service stores. Though you won't find a location in Times Square or in most areas of the Village or Harlem, everywhere else is fair game. Access costs 30¢ per minute, with an hour going for a flat $15.

RECOMMENDED BOOKS & FILMS

If you have the time and the stamina, there's no better book ever written about the history of New York than *Gotham* by Edwin G. Burroughs and Mike Wallace. A thoroughly gripping, complex, and fascinating portrait, it's literally the length of the N.Y. telephone book and therefore (unfortunately) too hefty for most time-constrained travelers to get through (and certainly too big to lug with you on your vacation). If you want to own it as a reference work at home, there's none that can match it.

Shorter histories that cover only one small section of New York's past, but are still enjoyable, thought-provoking reads include:

◆ *Great Fortune* by Daniel Okrent, the epic account of the creation of Rockefeller Center.

◆ *Low Life,* Luc Sante's rollicking tale of the crooks, prostitutes, scam artists, and other shady types who kept things interesting in Victorian Gotham.

◆ *Waterfront,* Philip Lopate's lively and insight-packed memoir/history of the waterfront of the city.

For good movies and TV series that focus on the city, the PBS television series *New York* (available at some video stores), a 12-hour epic featuring extensive interviews with the authors of *Gotham,* as well as many other historians, is superb, but once again a mammoth undertaking. Other movies that will teach you a bit about New York include Martin Scorsese's flawed *Gangs of New York,* which nonetheless provides a splendid snapshot of the underworld of New York in the 1860s;

Scorsese's *Age of Innocence,* which details upper-class life a la Edith Wharton, during the Victorian era; and his *Taxi Driver,* a searing portrayal of New York during one of the city's most troubled periods, the 1970s. Woody Allen is also, of course, a top New York portraitist; his films *Manhattan, Hannah and Her Sisters,* and *Annie Hall* have all rightly been called Valentines to the city. Other fun movies filmed in New York that will stoke you for the trip include the musical *On the Town* (the first movie musical to shoot on location), *Breakfast at Tiffany's, Rosemary's Baby, The Way We Were, Network, Saturday Night Fever, Hair, Arthur, Tootsie, Splash, After Hours, Desperately Seeking Susan, Crossing Delancey, Working Girl, When Harry Met Sally, The Fisher King, In America,* and *Maria Full of Grace.* Rent one before you come, and then look for locations as you wander 'round the city.

For TV portraits of the city (some filmed in Los Angeles or Canada, but true to the spirit of New York) you may want to tune in to: the entire *Law and Order* series, which is actually filmed in New York, as well as *NYPD Blue, CSI: New York,* and *The Equalizer.* For non-crime shows (which, with plunging crime rates, may not be as accurate as they once were), I'd recommend *Sex and the City, Seinfeld* and, for a touch of nostalgia, *Taxi* and *All in the Family.*

The ABCs of New York

Area Codes You must use the prefix "1" before you dial any number within New York City or to anywhere else in the United States or Canada. There are now two area codes for Manhattan (212 and 646) as well as two in the outer boroughs (718 and 347). Many cellphones and pagers have the area code 917. To dial outside of the United States or Canada, dial 011 before the telephone number. Calls to numbers that begin with an "800," "877," or "888" area code are toll-free.

ATMS & Currency Exchange See "Money Matters," earlier in this chapter.

Business Hours Offices are generally open on weekdays between 9am and 5pm, while banks tend to close at 3pm. A scattering of banks throughout the city are now open between the hours of 9am and 1pm on Saturday. Typically, stores open between 9am and 10am and close between 6pm and 7pm Monday through Saturday, with a number of department stores extending their hours on Thursday until 9pm. On Sunday, stores generally open at 11am and rarely stay open later than 6pm.

Drinking Laws The legal age for the purchase and consumption of any sort of alcohol is 21. Proof of age is often requested at liquor stores, bars, clubs, and restaurants, so be sure to carry photo ID with you at all times. It's illegal to carry open containers of alcohol in any public area that isn't zoned for alcohol consumption, and the police can ticket you on the spot.

Electricity The United States uses 110–120 volts AC (60 cycles), compared to the 220–240 volts AC (50 cycles) that is standard in Europe, Australia, and New Zealand. If your small appliances use 220–240 volts, be sure to buy an adaptor and voltage converter before you leave home, as these are very difficult to find in the United States.

Embassies & Consulates All embassies are located in the nation's capital, Washington, D.C. Some consulates are located in major U.S. cities, and most nations have a mission to the United Nations in New York City. If your country isn't listed below, call for directory information in Washington, D.C. (☎ 202/555-1212) or log on to **www.embassy.org/embassies.**

The embassy of **Australia** is at 1601 Massachusetts Ave. NW, Washington, DC 20036 (☎ **202/797-3000;** www. austemb.org). There are consulates in New York, Honolulu, Houston, Los Angeles, and San Francisco.

The embassy of **Canada** is at 501 Pennsylvania Ave. NW, Washington, DC 20001 (☎ **202/682-1740;** www.canadian embassy.org). Other Canadian consulates are in Buffalo (New York), Detroit, Los Angeles, New York, and Seattle.

The embassy of **Ireland** is at 2234 Massachusetts Ave. NW, Washington, DC 20008 (☎ **202/462-3939;** www.ireland emb.org). Irish consulates are in Boston, Chicago, New York, San Francisco, and other cities. See website for complete listing.

The embassy of **New Zealand** is at 37 Observatory Circle NW, Washington, DC 20008 (☎ **202/328-4800;** www.nz embassy.com). New Zealand consulates are in Los Angeles, Salt Lake City, San Francisco, and Seattle.

The embassy of the **United Kingdom** is at 3100 Massachusetts Ave. NW, Washington, DC 20008 (☎ **202/588-7800;** www.britainusa.com). Other British consulates are in Atlanta, Boston, Chicago, Cleveland, Houston, Los Angeles, New York, San Francisco, and Seattle.

Emergencies Call ☎ 911 for the police, to report a fire, or to get an ambulance. If you have a medical emergency that does not require an ambulance, you should be able to walk into the nearest hospital emergency room (see "Hospitals," below).

Holidays Banks close on the following holidays: January 1 (New Year's), the third Monday in January (Martin Luther King, Jr., Day), the third Monday in February (Presidents Day), the last Monday in May (Memorial Day), July 4 (Independence Day), the first Monday in September (Labor Day), the second Monday in October (Veterans Day), the fourth Thursday in November (Thanksgiving Day), and December 25 (Christmas Day). The handful of museums that are open on Monday tend to stay open on holidays, though almost all museums in the city close for Thanksgiving, Christmas, and New Year's (the exception on Christmas being the city's three Jewish museums).

Hospitals The following hospitals are well regarded and have emergency rooms that are open 24-hours:

Downtown: New York Downtown Hospital (170 William St. btwn Beekman and Spruce sts.; ☎ 212/312-5063); **St. Vincent's Medical Center** (153 W. 11th St. at Seventh Ave.; ☎ 212/604-7000); **Beth Israel Medical Center** (First Ave. and 16th St.; ☎ 212/420-2000).

Midtown: Bellevue Hospital Center (462 First Ave at 27th St.; ☎ 212/562-4141); **New York Medical Center** (560 First Ave. at 33rd St.; ☎ 212/263-3700); **Roosevelt Hospital** (425 W. 59th St. btwn Ninth and Tenth aves.; ☎ 212/523-6800).

Upper West Side: St Luke's Hospital Center (Amsterdam Ave. and 113th St.; ☎ 212/523-3335) and **Columbia Presbyterian Medical Center** (622 W. 168th St. btwn Broadway and Fort Washington Ave.; ☎ 212/305-3500).

Upper East Side: New York Presbyterian Hospital (525 E. 68th St. at York Ave.), **Lenox Hill Hospital** (100 E. 77th St. btwn Park and Lexington aves.; ☎ 212/434-2000), **Mount Sinai Medical Center** (Fifth Ave. at 100th St.; ☎ 212/241-6500).

Libraries Branches of the New York Public Library are scattered throughout the city and usually offer free Internet service. For a listing of branches (and their hours) go to **www.nypl.org**.

Mail At press time, domestic postage rates were 26¢ for a postcard and 41¢ for a letter. For international mail, a first-class letter or postcard of up to 1 ounce costs 90¢ (69¢ to Canada and Mexico); for more information go to **www.usps.com** and click on "Calculate Postage."

If you aren't sure what your address will be in the United States, mail can be sent to you, in your name, c/o General Delivery at New York's main post office (on Eighth Ave. btwn 32nd and 33rd sts.). (Call ☎ 800/275-8777 for information on the nearest post office.) The addressee must pick up mail in person and must produce proof of identity (driver's license, passport, and so on). Most post offices will hold your mail for up to 1 month, and are open Monday to Friday from 8am to 6pm, Saturday from 9am to 3pm.

Always include zip codes when mailing items in the U.S. If you don't know your zip code, visit www.usps.com/zip4.

Newspapers & Magazines There are four major daily newspapers in New York: The *New York Times,* the *Wall Street Journal,* the *Daily News,* and the *New York Post.* Each comes out in the morning. The *Times* is best for hard news and cultural listings, the Journal for business news, the *News* for celebrity gossip, and the *Post* is known for sports. *Time Out* **magazine** is also an excellent source for listings of concerts, performances, parties, and other special events that might be happening around town.

Pharmacies See p. 320 for a listing of 24-hour pharmacies.

Smoking Smoking is prohibited in all public indoor spaces, including offices, bars, restaurants, hotel lobbies, and most shops. In general, if you need to smoke, you'll have to go outside into the open air.

Taxes When guestimating your expenses for the trip, you should always factor in the 8.625% **sales tax** on goods and many services (including restaurant meals) and the **hotel tax** of 13.25%, plus $2 per room per night (this also applies to apartment rentals and B&B stays).

Telephone & Fax Generally, hotel surcharges on long-distance and local calls are astronomical, so you're better off using your **cellphone** or a **public pay telephone.** Many convenience groceries and packaging services sell **prepaid calling cards** in denominations up to $50; for international visitors these can be the least expensive way to call home. Many public phones at airports now accept American Express, MasterCard, and Visa credit cards. **Local calls** made from public pay phones in most locales cost either 25¢ or 35¢. Pay phones don't accept pennies, and few take anything larger than a quarter.

Most long-distance and international calls can be dialed directly from any phone. **For calls within the United States and to Canada,** dial 1 followed by the area code and the seven-digit number. **For other international calls,** dial 011 followed by the country code, the city code, and the number you are calling.

Calls to area codes **800, 888, 877,** and **866** are toll-free. However, calls to area codes **700** and **900** (chat lines, bulletin boards, "dating" services, and so on) can be very expensive—usually 95¢ to $3 or more per minute, and they sometimes have minimum charges that can run as high as $15 or more.

For **reversed-charge or collect calls,** and for person-to-person calls, dial the number 0, then the area code and number. An operator will come on the line, and you should specify whether you are calling collect, person-to-person, or both. If your operator-assisted call is international, ask for the overseas operator.

For **local directory assistance** ("information"), dial 411; for long-distance information, dial 1, then the appropriate area code and 555-1212.

Most hotels have **fax machines** available for guest use (be sure to ask about the charge to use it). Many hotel rooms are even wired for guests' fax machines. A less expensive way to send and receive faxes may be at stores such as **The UPS Store.**

Time The continental United States is divided into four time zones: Eastern Standard Time (EST), Central Standard

Time (CST), Mountain Standard Time (MST), and Pacific Standard Time (PST). New York is on Eastern Standard Time, so when it's noon in New York, it's 11am in Chicago (CST), 10am in Denver (MST) and 9am in Los Angeles (PST). Daylight saving moves the clock 1 hour ahead of standard time. (A new law extended daylight saving time in 2007; clocks now change the 2nd Sunday in March and the 1st Sunday in November.)

Tipping Tips are customary and should be factored into your budget. Waiters should receive 15% to 20% of the cost of the meal (depending on the quality of the service), bellhops get $1 per bag, chambermaids get $1 to $2 per day for straightening your room, and cab drivers should get 15% of the fare.

Toilets Any place in the city that serves coffee (most notably branches of Starbucks) will have restrooms open to the public. You will also be able to find restrooms in the lobbies of almost all Manhattan hotels, at the major bookstores in town, at major department stores, and at the New York City visitor centers (150 Broadway, btwn 46th and 47th sts.; and 810 Seventh Ave., btwn 52nd and 53rd sts.).

Index

See also Accommodations and Restaurant indexes, below.

GENERAL INDEX

334 Index

ACCOMMODATIONS

RESTAURANTS

A Guide for Every Type of Traveler

Frommer's Complete Guides
For those who value complete coverage, candid advice, and lots of choices in all price ranges.

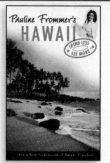

Pauline Frommer's Guides
For those who want to experience a culture, meet locals, and save money along the way.

MTV Guides
For hip, youthful travelers who want a fresh perspective on today's hottest cities and destinations.

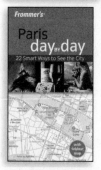

Day by Day Guides
For leisure or business travelers who want to organize their time to get the most out of a trip.

Frommer's With Kids Guides
For families traveling with children ages 2 to 14 seeking kid-friendly hotels, restaurants, and activities.

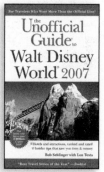

Unofficial Guides
For honeymooners, families, business travelers, and others who value no-nonsense, *Consumer Reports*–style advice.

For Dummies Travel Guides
For curious, independent travelers looking for a fun and easy way to plan a trip.

Visit Frommers.com

Now you know.

Explore over 3,500 destinations.

Frommers.com makes it easy.

Find a destination. ✓ Book a trip. ✓ Get hot travel deals.
Buy a guidebook. ✓ Enter to win vacations. ✓ Listen to podcasts. ✓ Check o
the latest travel news. ✓ Share trip photos and memories. ✓ And much mo

Frommers.com